적중100

영어 기출 문제집

중3

시사 | 박준언

Best Collection

구성과 특징

교과서의 주요 학습 내용을 중심으로 학습 영역별 특성에 맞춰 단계별로 다양한 학습 기회를 제공하여
단원별 학습능력 평가는 물론 중간 및 기말고사 시험 등에 완벽하게 대비할 수 있도록 내용을 구성

Words & Expressions

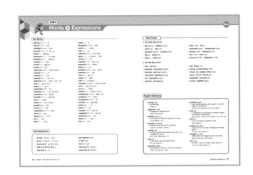

Step1 Key Words 단원별 핵심 단어 설명 및 풀이
Key Expression 단원별 핵심 숙어 및 관용어 설명
Word Power 반대 또는 비슷한 뜻 단어 배우기
English Dictionary 영어로 배우는 영어 단어

Step2 실력평가 단원별 수시평가 대비 주관식, 객관식 문제풀이

Step3 서술형 대비 학업성취도 및 수행능력평가 대비 서술형 문제풀이

Conversation

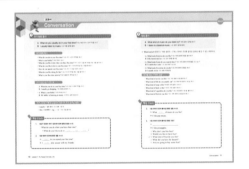

Step1 핵심 의사소통 소통에 필요한 주요 표현 방법 요약
핵심 Check 기본적인 표현 방법 및 활용능력 확인

Step2 대화문 익히기 교과서 대화문 심층 분석 및 확인

Step3 교과서 확인학습 빈칸 채우기를 통한 문장 완성 능력 확인

Step4 기본평가 시험대비 기초 학습 능력 평가

Step5 실력평가 단원별 수시평가 대비 주관식, 객관식 문제풀이

Step6 서술형 대비 학업성취도 및 수행능력평가 대비 서술형 문제풀이

Grammar

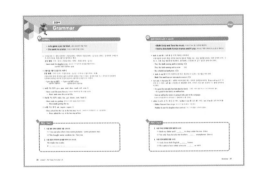

Step1 주요 문법 단원별 주요 문법 사항과 예문을 알기 쉽게 설명
핵심 Check 기본 문법사항에 대한 이해 여부 확인

Step2 기본평가 시험대비 기초 학습 능력 평가

Step3 실력평가 단원별 수시평가 대비 주관식, 객관식 문제풀이

Step4 서술형 대비 학업성취도 및 수행능력평가 대비 서술형 문제풀이

Reading

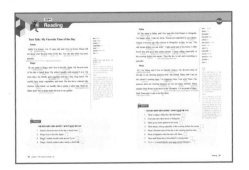

Step1 구문 분석 단원별로 제시된 문장에 대한 구문별 분석과 내용 설명
확인문제 문장에 대한 기본적인 이해와 인지능력 확인

Step2 확인학습A 빈칸 채우기를 통한 문장 완성 능력 확인

Step3 확인학습B 제시된 우리말을 영어로 완성하여 작문 능력 키우기

Step4 실력평가 단원별 수시평가 대비 주관식, 객관식 문제풀이

Step5 서술형 대비 학업성취도 및 수행능력평가 대비 서술형 문제풀이
교과서 구석구석 교과서에 나오는 기타 문장까지 완벽 학습

Composition

|영역별 핵심문제|

단어 및 어휘, 대화문, 문법, 독해 등 각 영역별 기출문제의 출제 유형을 분석하여 실전에 대비하고 연습할 수 있도록 문제를 배열

|단원별 예상문제|

기출문제를 분석한 후 새로운 시험 출제 경향을 더하여 새롭게 출제될 수 있는 문제를 포함하여 시험에 완벽하게 대비할 수 있도록 준비

|서술형 실전 및 창의사고력 문제|

학교 시험에서 점차 늘어나는 서술형 시험에 집중 대비하고 고득점을 취득하는데 만전을 기하기 위한 학습 코너

|단원별 모의고사|

영역별, 단계별 학습을 모두 마친 후 실전 연습을 위한 모의고사

교과서 파헤치기

- **단어Test1~3** 영어 단어 우리말 쓰기, 우리말을 영어 단어로 쓰기, 영영풀이에 해당하는 단어와 우리말 쓰기
- **대화문Test1~2** 대화문 빈칸 완성 및 전체 대화문 쓰기
- **본문Test1~5** 빈칸 완성, 우리말 쓰기, 문장 배열연습, 영어 작문하기 복습 등 단계별 반복 학습을 통해 교과서 지문에 대한 완벽한 습득
- **구석구석지문Test1~2** 지문 빈칸 완성 및 전문 영어로 쓰기

Contents

Lesson 5

Love for My Country

🔎 의사소통 기능

- 알고 있는지 묻기
  You know about Yun Dongju, don't you?
- 희망 · 기대 표현하기
  I'm looking forward to the visit.

🔎 언어 형식

- '과거완료' had + 과거분사
  I was hungry because I **had not eaten** breakfast.
- '목적'을 나타내는 so that 구문
  I waved at my sister **so that** she could find me.

교과서
Words & Expressions

Key Words

- **amusement park** 놀이동산
- **burial** [bériəl] 명 매장, 장례식
- **bury** [béri] 동 묻다, 매장하다
- **circle** [sə́:rkl] 명 원
- **clearly** [klíərli] 부 분명하게
- **complete** [kəmplí:t] 동 끝내다 형 완전한
- **corner** [kɔ́:rnər] 명 구석, 모퉁이
- **crown** [kraun] 명 왕관
- **deep** [di:p] 형 깊은
- **desire** [dizáiər] 명 바람, 갈망
- **direct** [dirékt] 동 감독하다. 지휘[총괄]하다
- **during** [djúəriŋ] 전 ~ 동안
- **educate** [édʒukèit] 동 교육시키다
- **entrance** [éntrəns] 명 입구
- **exhibition** [èksəbíʃən] 명 전시회
- **feed** [fi:d] 동 먹이를 주다, 먹이다
- **flag** [flæg] 명 깃발
- **foggy** [fɔ́:gi] 형 안개 낀
- **general** [dʒénərəl] 명 장군 형 일반적인
- **god** [gɑd] 명 신
- **government** [gʌ́vərmmənt] 명 정부
- **hall** [hɔ:l] 명 홀, 현관
- **Hallyu** 명 한류, 한국 문화 열풍
- **harmony** [há:rməni] 명 조화
- **independence** [ìndipéndəns] 명 독립
- **Japanese** [dʒæpəní:z] 명 일본인, 일본어 형 일본의
- **kill** [kil] 동 죽이다
- **leader** [lí:dər] 명 지도자, 리더
- **main** [mein] 형 주된, 주요한
- **mean** [mi:n] 동 의미하다

- **member** [mémbər] 명 구성원, 회원
- **mission** [míʃən] 명 임무
- **model** [mádl] 명 모형
- **movement** [mú:vmənt] 명 (정치적, 사회적) 운동
- **museum** [mju:zí:əm] 명 박물관
- **organization** [ɔ̀rgənizéiʃən] 명 조직, 기구
- **palace** [pǽlis] 명 궁전
- **patriotic** [pèitriátik] 형 애국적인
- **peace** [pi:s] 명 평화
- **poem** [póuəm] 명 시
- **president** [prézədənt] 명 대통령, 의장, 화장
- **process** [práses] 명 과정
- **protect** [prətékt] 동 보호하다
- **republic** [ripʌ́blik] 명 공화국
- **respect** [rispékt] 명 존경, 경의
- **rule** [ru:l] 명 통치, 지배
- **sacrifice** [sǽkrəfàis] 명 희생 동 희생하다
- **secret** [sí:krit] 명 비밀 형 비밀의
- **specialist** [spéʃəlist] 명 전문가
- **spread** [spred] 동 퍼지다, 퍼뜨리다
- **statue** [stǽtʃu:] 명 조각상
- **teen** [ti:n] 명 십대
- **throughout** [θru:áut] 전 ~의 도처에, ~ 내내
- **tomb** [tu:m] 명 묘, 무덤
- **treasure** [tréʒər] 명 보물
- **volunteer work** 자원봉사 활동
- **water** [wɔ́:tər] 동 (화초 등에) 물을 주다
- **war** [wɔ:r] 명 전쟁, 싸움
- **wish** [wiʃ] 명 소원, 바람
- **zip code** 우편 번호

Key Expressions

- **be in need** ~가 필요하다
- **belong to** ~에 속하다
- **carry out** ~을 수행하다
- **hear of** ~에 관해 듣다

- **look forward to**+명사/동명사 ~을 기대하다
- **look like**+명사 ~처럼 보이다
- **put on** ~을 입다
- **so that**+주어+동사 ~하기 위해서

Word Power

※ 서로 비슷한 뜻을 가진 어휘

□ **desire** : **wish** (바람, 소원)
□ **bury** : **inter** (매장하다, 묻다)
□ **protect** : **defend** (보호하다)
□ **statue** : **figure** (조각상)

□ **harmony** : **accord** (조화)
□ **rule** : **reign** (통치)
□ **specialist** : **expert** (전문가)
□ **educate** : **teach** (교육하다, 가르치다)

※ 서로 반대되는 뜻을 가진 어휘

□ **dependence** (의존) ↔ **independence** (독립)
□ **complete** (완전한) ↔ **incomplete** (불완전한)

□ **entrance** (입구) ↔ **exit** (출구)
□ **deep** (깊은) ↔ **shallow** (얕은)

English Dictionary

□ **amusement park** 놀이공원
→ a large outdoor area with fairground rides, shows, and other entertainments
박람회장 놀이기구, 쇼, 그리고 다른 오락거리가 있는 넓은 야외 공간

□ **burial** 매장, 장례식
→ the act of putting a dead body into the ground, or the ceremony connected with this
사체를 땅에 묻는 행위, 또는 이와 관련된 의식

□ **bury** 묻다
→ to place a dead body in the ground, or to put something in the ground and cover it
사체를 땅에 묻거나 어떤 것을 땅에 묻고 그것을 덮다

□ **carry out** 수행하다
→ to do or complete something, especially that you have said you would do or that you have been told
특히 당신이 하겠다고 말해 왔거나 들어 온 일을 하거나 끝내다

□ **crown** 왕관
→ a circular ornament made of gold and decorated head with jewels that is worn by a king or queen on their head
왕이나 여왕이 머리에 쓰는 금으로 만들어지고 보석으로 장식된 원형 장식물

□ **exhibition** 전시회
→ a public display of art works, pictures or other interesting things
예술 작품, 그림 또는 기타 흥미로운 것들의 공개 전시

□ **flag** 깃발
→ a piece of cloth that is usually attached at the end of a pole and represents a country or association
보통 기둥 끝에 붙어 있고 국가나 협회를 대표하는 천 조각

□ **look forward to** 기대하다
→ to feel pleased and excited about something that is going to happen
앞으로 일어날 일에 대해 기쁘고 흥분하다

□ **mission** 임무
→ any work that someone believes it is their duty to do
누군가가 자신이 할 의무라고 믿는 일

□ **organization** 조직
→ a group of people working together for a purpose of being organized
조직화될 목적으로 함께 일하는 사람들의 집단

□ **palace** 궁전
→ a large house that is the official home of a king and queen
왕과 왕비의 공식적인 주택인 큰 집

□ **poem** 시
→ a piece of writing that uses beautiful words that imply deep meanings and sounds rhythmical when you read
깊은 의미를 암시하고 읽을 때 리드미컬하게 들리는 아름다운 단어를 사용하는 한 편의 글

□ **process** 과정
→ a series of things that happen one after another for a particular result
특정한 결과를 위해 차례로 일어나는 일련의 일들

□ **republic** 공화국
→ a country governed by elected representatives
선출직 대표들에 의해 통치되는 나라

□ **sacrifice** 희생
→ giving up of something valuable for a specific purpose
특정한 목적을 위해 귀중한 어떤 것을 포기하는 것

□ **statue** 조각상
→ a sculptured figure of a person, animal, etc. in bronze, stone, wood, etc.
청동, 돌, 나무 등에 조각된 사람이나 동물 등의 형상

□ **tomb** 무덤
→ a large stone structure or underground room where someone, especially an important person, is buried
누군가, 특히 중요한 사람이 묻혀 있는 큰 돌 구조물이나 지하 공간

□ **treasure** 보물
→ what is highly valued
매우 귀중한 것

01 다음 문장의 빈칸에 들어갈 말로 가장 알맞은 것은?

> Churchill's _____ stands outside the parliament building.

① exhibition   ② entrance

③ statue   ④ poem

⑤ specialist

서답형
02 빈칸에 주어진 〈영영풀이〉에 해당하는 단어를 쓰시오.

> Nigeria gained _____ from Britain in 1960.

> ┤영영풀이├
> freedom from being governed or ruled by another country

서답형
03 다음 우리말에 맞게 빈칸에 세 단어를 쓰시오.

> 너한테 멋진 생일 선물 받기를 기대하고 있을게!

> ➡ I will _____ _____ _____ receiving a nice birthday present from you!

[04~05] 다음 설명에 해당하는 단어를 고르시오.

04
> a public display of art works, pictures or other interesting things

① flag   ② exhibition

③ comment   ④ mission

⑤ treasure

05
> a large stone structure or underground room where someone, especially an important person, is buried

① palace   ② statue

③ burial   ④ crown

⑤ tomb

06 다음 빈칸에 들어갈 말로 가장 알맞은 것끼리 짝지어진 것은?

> (A) Fire quickly _____ throughout the building.
> (B) Voting is part of your _____ duty.

	(A)	(B)
①	sacrifice	patriotic
②	water	general
③	spread	patriotic
④	feed	creative
⑤	spread	secret

서답형
07 다음 짝지어진 단어의 관계가 같도록 빈칸에 알맞은 말을 쓰시오.

> desire – wish : expert – _____

08 다음 문장의 빈칸에 들어갈 말은?

> I want to let many people know that Dokdo _____ Korea.

① puts on   ② carries on

③ consists of   ④ belongs to

⑤ turns down

01 다음 빈칸에 들어갈 말을 〈보기〉에서 찾아 쓰시오.

> ┤ 보기 ├
> kill　movement　harmony　poem

(1) Many religious leaders work hard to bring peace and _____ to the world.

(2) She was a renowned scientist and pioneer of the global environmental _____.

(3) Lack of rain could _____ the crops.

(4) Her _____ s tell us to be strong and live bravely.

02 다음 글은 빈칸에 들어갈 단어에 대한 설명이다. 알맞은 단어를 쓰시오.

> A _____ is a country where power is held by the people or the representatives that they elect.

03 다음 우리말과 같은 표현이 되도록 문장의 빈칸을 채우시오.

(1) 그녀는 병원 정문 근처에 주차 공간을 발견했다.
→ She found a parking space close to the hospital's main _____.

(2) 만델라는 대통령이 되었을 때 이미 70대였다.
→ Mandela was already in his seventies when he became _____.

(3) 영국 정부는 원조를 보내겠다고 제안했다.
→ The UK _____ has offered to send aid.

(4) 나는 여행 갔을 때 많은 일본 음식을 먹었다.
→ I ate a lot of _____ food when I went on my trip.

04 영영풀이에 해당하는 단어를 〈보기〉에서 찾아 첫 번째 빈칸에 쓰고, 두 번째 빈칸에는 우리말 뜻을 쓰시오.

> ┤ 보기 ├
> poem　organization　sacrifice　amusement park

(1) _____: a large outdoor area with fairground rides, shows, and other entertainments: _____

(2) _____: a group of people working together for a purpose of being organized: _____

(3) _____: a piece of writing that uses beautiful words that imply deep meanings and sounds rhythmical when you read: _____

(4) _____: giving up of something valuable for a specific purpose: _____

05 다음 빈칸에 공통으로 들어갈 단어를 쓰시오.

> • Some people think physical education and art classes are a _____ waste of time.
> • Sometimes he spends 20 hours to _____ just one piece of artwork.

Conversation

1 알고 있는지 묻기

You know about Yun Dongju, don't you?
너는 윤동주에 대해 알고 있지, 그렇지 않니?

■ 'You know ~, don't you?'는 알고 있는지 물어보는 표현이다.
또한 'Do you know about ~? / Did you know that ~? / Are you aware of ~? / Are you aware that ~?' 등을 이용하여 알고 있는지 물을 수 있다.

무언가에 대해 들어서 알고 있는지 물을 때는 'Did you hear about ~?'(너는 ~에 대해 들었니?)라고 말한다. 현재완료를 사용해 'Have you heard about ~?'이라고 들어 본 적이 있는지 물을 수도 있다.

■ 알고 있는지 물어보는 다양한 표현들
- **A:** You know Samgyetang, don't you? 너는 삼계탕을 알고 있지, 그렇지 않니?
  B: Yes, it's a Korean food. People eat it for their health.
  그래, 그것은 한국 음식이야. 사람들은 건강을 위해 삼계탕을 먹어.
- **A:** Have you heard that Ms. Lee is coming to our school? 이 선생님이 우리 학교에 오신다는 것 들었어?
  B: No, I haven't. 아니, 못 들었어.
- Do you know (that) ice cream is from China? 아이스크림이 중국에서 유래했다는 것을 아니?
- Have you heard about the project? 그 프로젝트에 관해 들어봤니?
- Are you aware that gold medals are made mostly of silver? 금메달이 주로 은으로 만들어진다는 것을 아니?
- Did you hear about the accident? 그 사고에 대해 들었니?

핵심 Check

1. 다음 대화의 밑줄 친 문장과 바꾸어 쓸 수 있는 것을 모두 고르시오.

   A: You know about Yun Dongju, don't you?

   B: Sure.

   ① Do you know about Yun Dongju?
   ② I'm sure I know about Yun Dongju.
   ③ Did you hear from Yun Dongju?
   ④ Have you ever heard about Yun Dongju?
   ⑤ Why don't we know about Yun Dongju?

2 희망 · 기대 표현하기

I'm looking forward to the visit.
나는 그 방문을 기대하고 있어.

■ 앞으로 하고 싶은 일에 대한 기대를 표현할 때 'I'm looking forward to ~.'나 'I look forward to ~.'의
표현을 사용한다. 여기서 to는 전치사이므로 뒤에 명사나 동명사가 와야 한다.
  - I'm looking forward to traveling to Korea.
  - I look forward to my birthday party this weekend.
  - **G:** Yubin, I hear you're taking a family trip to Thailand this winter.
    유빈아, 너 이번 겨울에 태국으로 가족 여행을 간다고 들었어.

    B: Yes. I'm looking forward to riding an elephant. 응. 코끼리를 타 보기를 기대하고 있어.
■ 'I can't wait to ~'는 원하던 일이 다가오고 있어 빨리하고 싶은 기대감을 나타내는 표현이며, 직역의
  의미대로 '~하는 것을 기다릴 수 없다' 또는 '당장 ~하고 싶다, 빨리 ~했으면 좋겠다' 정도로 해석한다.
  to 뒤에는 동사원형의 형태가 오는데, 뒤에 명사구가 올 경우에는 'I can't wait for+명사(명사구)'의 형
  태로 쓰기도 한다.
  - I can't wait for my graduation. 내 졸업이 기대된다.

기대를 나타내는 다른 표현들

- I am expecting to 동사원형 ~.
- I am longing to 동사원형 ~.
- I am eager to 동사원형 ~.
- I'm dying to 동사원형 ~.

핵심 Check

2. 다음 대화의 빈칸에 들어갈 말로 <u>어색한</u> 것은?

   A: Do you want to watch *Harry Potter* with me this weekend?
   B: Sure, I'd love to. _____

   ① I can't wait to watch it.
   ② I am longing to watch it.
   ③ I'm dying to watching it.
   ④ I'm looking forward to watching it.
   ⑤ I am eager to watch it.

Listen & Speak 1 A-1

B: Look at Suwon Hawseong. It's huge.

G: It also ❶looks strong.

B: Because ❷it was built to protect the people ❸during wars.

G: Wow. ❹Do you know who built it?

B: Yes. King Jeongjo ❺ordered Jeong Yakyong to direct the building process. ❻You know about Jeong Yakyong, don't you?

G: Yes, I've heard of him. He was a great scientist in Joseon.

B: 수원 화성을 봐. 그것은 거대해.

G: 그것은 또한 튼튼해 보여.

B: 왜냐하면 그것은 전쟁 중에 사람들을 보호하기 위해 지어졌기 때문이야.

G: 우와. 너는 누가 그것을 지었는지 아니?

B: 응. 정조가 정약용에게 건설 과정을 감독할 것을 지시했어. 너는 정약용에 대해 알고 있지, 그렇지 않니?

G: 응. 그에 대해 들어봤어. 그는 조선의 훌륭한 과학자였어.

❶ 'look+형용사'로 '~하게 보이다'라는 뜻이다.
❷ it은 'Suwon Hawseong'을 가리키고, '지어졌다'는 수동태(was built)를 사용한다.
❸ 'during'은 '~ 동안'의 의미로 '특정한 기간'과 함께 사용된다. 반면 'for'는 '숫자로 된 기간'과 함께 사용된다.
❹ 동사 'know'의 목적어 자리에 사용된 간접의문문으로 '의문사 who (주어)+동사(built)' 어순을 취한다.
❺ 'order+목적어+목적보어(to부정사)'로 '~에게 …하라고 명령[지시]하다'로 해석하는 5형식 문장이다.
❻ You know ~, don't you?는 알고 있는지 물어보는 표현이다.

Check(√) True or False

(1) Suwon Hawseong was built to protect the people during wars.　　T ☐　F ☐

(2) The girl has heard of King Jeongjo.　　T ☐　F ☐

Listen & Speak 2 A-1

G: ❶I'm planning to go to the Gansong Museum.

B: What is the Gansong Museum?

G: It's a museum ❷built by Gansong Jeon Hyeongpil.

B: I heard that he did great things for the country.

G: Yes. He bought many Korean treasures ❸that some Japanese had taken to Japan.

B: Wow. The museum ❹must be interesting.

G: Yes. ❺I'm looking forward to it!

G: 나는 간송 미술관에 갈 예정이야.

B: 간송 미술관이 뭐야?

G: 간송 전형필에 의해 지어진 미술관이야.

B: 나는 그가 나라를 위해 훌륭한 일들을 했다고 들었어.

G: 응. 그는 몇몇 일본사람들이 일본으로 가져갔었던 한국의 많은 문화재들을 샀어.

B: 우와. 그 미술관은 틀림없이 흥미로울 거야.

G: 응. 나는 그곳을 기대하고 있어!

❶ 'be planning to+동사원형'은 앞으로 할 일에 대한 계획을 나타낼 때 사용하는 표현으로 '~할 예정이다'라는 뜻이다.
❷ 명사 a museum을 수식하는 과거분사로 '지어진'의 의미다.
❸ 목적격 관계대명사절로 선행사 'many Korean treasures'를 수식하는 역할을 한다.
❹ 추측의 조동사로 '~임에 틀림없다'라는 뜻이다.
❺ 앞으로 하고 싶은 일에 대한 기대를 표현할 때 사용하는 표현으로 'to'는 전치사이기 때문에 뒤에 '명사나 동명사'를 사용한다.

Check(√) True or False

(3) The Gansong Museum was built by Jeon Hyeongpil.　　T ☐　F ☐

(4) Gansong sold Korean treasures to other countries.　　T ☐　F ☐

Listen & Speak 1 A-2

G: Brian, you know Taegeukgi, ❶don't you?

B: Sure. It's the national flag of Korea, ❷isn't it?

G: That's right. Do you know ❸what the symbols in Taegeukgi mean?

B: No, I don't. Tell me about ❹them.

G: The circle in the middle means harmony and peace.

B: What do the black lines on the four corners mean?

G: They mean four things: sky, fire, water, and earth.

❶ 부가의문문으로 상대방이 알고 있는지 물어보는 표현이다.
❷ be동사의 부가의문문이다.
❸ know의 목적어 자리에 사용된 간접의문문으로 '의문사(what)+주어(the symbols)+동사(mean)' 어순이다.
❹ 앞 문장의 'the symbols in Taegeukgi'를 나타낸다.

 Real Life Talk

Andy: Bora, what are you reading?

Bora: I'm reading *Sky, Wind, Star, and Poetry* by Yun Dongju. ❶You know about Yun Dongju, don't you?

Andy: I've heard his name, but I don't know much about him.

Bora: He wrote many beautiful poems ❷when Korea was under Japanese rule. ❸His love for the country and his desire for independence can be felt in his poems.

Andy: Really? I didn't know that. I want ❹to read his poems and learn more about him.

Bora: Great. In fact, ❺I'm planning to visit the Yun Dongju Museum soon. Do you want to come with me?

Andy: Yes, when are you going?

Bora: Next Saturday. It's near Gyeongbok Palace. Can you meet me at the palace at 2 p.m.?

Andy: Sure. Let's meet there.

Bora: Great. ❻I'm really looking forward to the visit.

❶ 'You know ~, don't you?'는 알고 있는지 물어보는 표현이다.
❷ 시간의 부사절 접속사로 '~할 때'로 해석한다.
❸ 문장의 주어는 'His love'와 'his desire'이다. 'can be felt'는 조동사가 있는 수동태로 '느껴질 수 있다'로 해석한다.
❹ want의 목적어로 'to read'와 '(to) learn'이 병렬구조로 연결되어 있다.
❺ '~할 계획이다'라는 의미로 미래의 일에 대한 계획을 말하는 표현이다.
❻ 기대를 나타내는 표현으로 'look forward to+명사/동명사'를 사용한다.

Wrap Up

B: Tomorrow ❶let's put on traditional Korean clothes, *hanbok*, and go to Insadong.

G: Good, but I want to buy gifts for my friends in Germany tomorrow.

B: In Insadong, ❷there are many gift shops.

G: Great. ❸After shopping, what should we eat for lunch?

B: Hmm. ❹You know Samgyetang, don't you?

G: No. What is it?

B: It's a traditional Korean soup. It's delicious and will ❺make you healthy.

G: Sounds good. ❻I'm looking forward to trying it.

❶ 'let's+동사원형'으로 '~하자'라고 제안을 할 때 사용한다.
❷ 'there are+복수명사'로 '~들이 있다'라는 의미다.
❸ 전치사 'After' 뒤에 동명사 'shopping'을 사용한다.
❹ 'You know ~, don't you?'는 알고 있는지 물어보는 표현이다.
❺ 'make+목적어+목적보어(형용사)' 형태로 '…을 ~하게 만들다'라는 의미이다.
❻ 'look forward to+동명사'로 '~하기를 기대하다'라는 뜻이다.

● 다음 우리말과 일치하도록 빈칸에 알맞은 말을 쓰시오.

Listen & Speak 1 A

1. B: Look _____ Suwon Hawseong. It's _____.

   G: It also _____ _____.

   B: _____ it _____ _____ to _____ the people _____ wars.

   G: Wow. Do you know _____ _____ it?

   B: Yes. King Jeongjo _____ Jeong Yakyong _____ _____ the building _____. You know about Jeong Yakyong, _____ _____ _____?

   G: Yes, I've _____ _____ him. He was a great _____ in Joseon.

2. G: Brian, you know Taegeukgi, _____ _____?

   B: Sure. It's the _____ _____ of Korea, _____ it?

   G: That's right. Do you know _____ the _____ in Taegeukgi _____?

   B: No, I don't. Tell me about them.

   G: The _____ in the middle means _____ and _____.

   B: What do the black _____ on the four _____ mean?

   G: They _____ four things: sky, fire, water, and _____.

Listen & Speak 2 A

1. G: I'm _____ _____ _____ to the Gansong Museum.

   B: What is the Gansong Museum?

   G: It's a museum _____ by Gansong Jeon Hyeongpil.

   B: I _____ that he did _____ things for the country.

   G: Yes. He bought many Korean _____ _____ some Japanese _____ _____ to Japan.

   B: Wow. The museum _____ _____ _____.

   G: Yes. I'm _____ _____ _____ it!

2. B: Soyeon, _____ _____ _____ last weekend?

   G: I went to Hyeonchungwon to do _____ _____.

   B: _____ _____ of volunteer work did you do there?

해석

1. B: 수원 화성을 봐, 그것은 거대해.
   G: 그것은 또한 튼튼해 보여.
   B: 왜냐하면 그것은 전쟁 중에 사람들을 보호하기 위해 지어졌기 때문이야.
   G: 우와. 너는 누가 그것을 지었는지 아니?
   B: 응. 정조가 정약용에게 건설 과정을 감독할 것을 지시했어. 너는 정약용에 대해 알고 있지, 그렇지 않니?
   G: 응, 그에 대해 들어봤어. 그는 조선의 훌륭한 과학자였어.

2. G: Brian, 너 태극기를 알고 있지, 그렇지 않니?
   B: 물론이지. 그것은 한국의 국기잖아, 그렇지 않니?
   G: 맞아. 너는 태극기에 있는 상징들이 무엇을 의미하는지 알고 있니?
   B: 아니, 몰라. 그것에 대해 말해 줘.
   G: 가운데 원은 조화와 평화를 의미해.
   B: 네 모서리의 검은 선들은 무엇을 의미하니?
   G: 그것은 하늘, 불, 물 그리고 땅을 의미해.

1. G: 나는 간송 미술관에 갈 예정이야.
   B: 간송 미술관이 뭐야?
   G: 간송 전형필에 의해 지어진 미술관이야.
   B: 나는 그가 나라를 위해 훌륭한 일들을 했다고 들었어.
   G: 응. 그는 몇몇 일본 사람들이 일본으로 가져갔던 한국의 많은 문화재들을 샀어.
   B: 우와. 그 미술관은 틀림없이 흥미로울 거야.
   G: 응. 나는 그곳을 기대하고 있어!

2. B: 소연아, 지난 주말에 무엇을 했니?
   G: 나는 봉사 활동을 하러 현충원에 갔어.
   B: 그곳에서 어떤 종류의 봉사 활동을 했어?

G: I _____ around the _____. I felt great _____ for the people _____ died for the country.

B: _____ great. Can I do it, too?

G: Sure. I'm _____ _____ _____ there again next Wednesday. Will you _____ me?

B: Sure. _____ _____ _____ _____ it.

Real Life Talk

Andy: Bora, what are you _____?

Bora: I'm reading *Sky, Wind, Star, and* _____ by Yun Dongju. You _____ about Yun Dongju, _____ _____?

Andy: I've _____ his name, but I don't know much about him.

Bora: He wrote many beautiful _____ _____ Korea was _____ Japanese _____. His love for the country and his _____ for _____ can _____ _____ in his _____.

Andy: Really? I didn't know that. I want _____ _____ his _____ and _____ more about him.

Bora: Great. _____ _____, I'm planning _____ _____ the Yun Dongju Museum soon. Do you want to come with me?

Andy: Yes, _____ are you going?

Bora: Next Saturday. It's _____ Gyeongbok _____. Can you meet me at the _____ at 2 p.m.?

Andy: Sure. _____ meet there.

Bora: Great. I'm really _____ _____ _____ the _____.

Wrap Up

B: Tomorrow let's _____ _____ _____ Korean clothes, *hanbok*, and go to Insadong.

G: Good, but I want to buy gifts _____ my friends in _____ tomorrow.

B: In Insadong, _____ _____ many gift shops.

G: Great. After _____, what should we eat for lunch?

B: Hmm. You _____ Samgyetang, _____ _____?

G: No. What is it?

B: It's a _____ Korean _____. It's _____ and will make you _____.

G: Sounds good. I'm looking forward _____ _____ it.

해석

G: 나는 묘 주변을 청소했어. 나는 나라를 위해 돌아가신 분들에게 깊은 경의를 느꼈어.

B: 대단하게 들린다. 나도 그것을 할 수 있을까?

G: 물론이지. 나는 다음 주 수요일에 그곳에 다시 갈 계획이야. 너도 나와 함께 갈래?

B: 물론이지. 나는 그것을 기대하고 있어.

Andy: 보라, 너 무엇을 읽고 있니?

보라: 윤동주 시인의 「하늘과 바람과 별과 시」를 읽고 있어. 너는 윤동주에 대해 알고 있지, 그렇지 않니?

Andy: 나는 그의 이름을 들어 본 적 있지만 그에 대해 잘 알지는 못해.

보라: 그는 한국이 일본의 통치하에 있을 때 아름다운 시를 많이 썼어. 나라에 대한 그의 사랑과 독립에 대한 염원이 그의 시에서 느껴질 수 있어.

Andy: 정말? 나는 그걸 몰랐어. 나는 그의 시를 읽고 그에 대해 더 많이 배우고 싶어.

보라: 아주 좋아. 사실 나는 곧 윤동주 박물관을 방문할 계획이야. 너도 나와 함께 가길 원하니?

Andy: 응, 언제 갈 거니?

보라: 다음 주 토요일에. 그곳은 경복궁 근처에 있어. 오후 2시에 궁에서 만날 수 있니?

Andy: 물론이지. 거기서 만나자.

보라: 좋아. 나는 그 방문을 정말 기대하고 있어.

B: 내일 우리 한국 전통 의상인 한복을 입고 인사동에 가자.

G: 좋아, 그런데 나 내일 독일에 있는 내 친구들을 위한 선물을 사고 싶어.

B: 인사동에 선물 가게가 많아.

G: 잘됐네. 쇼핑하고 나서 점심으로 뭘 먹을까?

B: 흠. 너는 삼계탕에 대해 알고 있지, 그렇지 않니?

G: 아니. 그게 뭐야?

B: 전통적인 한국의 국물 음식이야. 그것은 맛이 좋고 너를 건강하게 만들어 줄 거야.

G: 멋지네. 나는 그것을 먹어보는 것을 기대하고 있어.

Conversation 시험대비 기본평가

01 우리말을 영어로 옮길 때 빈칸에 알맞은 말을 쓰시오.

나는 그 방문이 정말 기대돼.

➡ I'm really _____ _____ _____ the visit.

02 다음 대화의 빈칸에 들어갈 말로 알맞은 것은?

A: _____, don't you?
B: Yes, I heard about it.

① I hope I will visit Dokdo
② You cannot know about Dokdo
③ I'm not quite sure if you know about Dokdo
④ Look at the island in the picture
⑤ You know Dokdo is windy and foggy

03 다음 대화의 빈칸에 들어갈 말로 어색한 표현은?

A: Do you remember our plan to visit the Hanok Village in July?
B: Sure. _____

① I'm looking forward to visiting there.
② I can't wait to visit there.
③ I'm dying to visiting there.
④ I'm expecting to visit there.
⑤ I am longing to visit there.

04 다음 대화의 밑줄 친 말의 의도로 알맞은 것은?

A: You know that Dokdo has two main islands and 89 small islands, don't you?
B: No, I didn't know that.

① 확신 표현하기
② 알고 있는지 묻기
③ 관심 표현하기
④ 염려 묻기
⑤ 기대 표현하기

[01~02] 다음 대화를 읽고 물음에 답하시오.

Seho: Tomorrow (a)let's put on traditional Korean clothes, *hanbok*, and go to Insadong.

Judy: Good, but I want to buy gifts for my friends in Germany tomorrow.

Seho: In Insadong, (b)there are many gift shops.

Judy: Great. (c)After shopping, what should we eat for lunch?

Seho: Hmm. You know Samgyetang, (d)don't you?

Judy: No. What is it?

Seho: It's a traditional Korean soup. It's delicious and will make you healthy.

Judy: Sounds good. I'm looking forward to (e)try it.

01 위 대화의 밑줄 친 (a)~(e) 중, 어법상 어색한 것은?

① (a) ② (b) ③ (c) ④ (d) ⑤ (e)

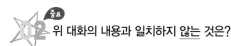 위 대화의 내용과 일치하지 <u>않는</u> 것은?

① They are talking about their plans for tomorrow.

② Judy didn't know there are many gift shops in Insadong.

③ Both Seho and Judy are going to put on *hanbok*.

④ They will eat Samgyetang for dinner.

⑤ Judy can't wait to eat Samgyetang.

03 다음 대화의 (A)~(D)를 알맞은 순서로 배열한 것은?

B: Soyeon, what did you do last weekend?

G: I went to Hyeonchungwon to do volunteer work.

(A) Sounds great. Can I do it, too?

(B) I cleaned around the tombs. I felt great respect for the people who died for the country.

(C) Sure. I'm planning to go there again next Wednesday. Will you join me?

(D) What kind of volunteer work did you do there?

B: Sure. I'm looking forward to it.

① (A)–(C)–(B)–(D) ② (B)–(A)–(C)–(D)
③ (C)–(B)–(A)–(D) ④ (D)–(B)–(A)–(C)
⑤ (D)–(C)–(A)–(B)

 다음 대화의 빈칸에 들어갈 말로 <u>어색한</u> 것은?

A: You know about An Junggeun, don't you?

B: _____

① No. I don't know much about him.

② Sure. He made a great effort for Korea's independence.

③ You can go to the An Junggeun Museum and get more information about him.

④ No. I want to learn more about him.

⑤ No, I don't. But I'm looking forward to learning more about him.

서답형
05 다음 대화의 밑줄 친 문장과 같은 의미가 되도록 주어진 단어를 이용하여 쓰시오.

A: Do you remember our plan to make Gimchi in November?

B: Sure. <u>I'm dying to make it.</u>

➡ _____

(look forward)

06 다음 두 사람의 대화가 <u>어색한</u> 것은?

① A: Do you remember our plan to visit the Hanok Village in July?
  B: Sure. I'm looking forward to visiting there.

② A: You know Seho, don't you?
  B: Yes. Isn't he the fastest boy in our school?

③ A: Do you remember our plan to learn the Korean traditional fan dance?
  B: Yes. I'm looking forward to learning it.

④ A: I'm planning to go to the Gansong Museum.
  B: I'd love to, but I'm looking forward to visiting there.

⑤ A: You know Ryu Gwansun, don't you?
  B: Of course. She was an independence activist.

[07~08] 다음 대화를 읽고 물음에 답하시오.

> B: Look at Suwon Hwaseong. It's huge.
> G: It also looks strong.
> B: Because it was built to protect the people during wars.
> G: Wow. Do you know who built it?
> B: Yes. (A)정조가 정약용에게 건설 과정을 감독할 것을 지시했어. You know about Jeong Yakyong, don't you?
> G: (B)_____ He was a great scientist in Joseon.

서답형

07 위 대화의 밑줄 친 (A)의 우리말에 맞게 주어진 어구를 이용하여 영어로 쓰시오. (단어 하나를 추가하시오.)

> ordered / direct / Jeong Yakyong / King Jeongjo / the building process

➡ _____

_____

08 위 대화의 빈칸 (B)에 들어갈 말로 알맞은 것을 <u>모두</u> 고르시오.

① I'm looking forward to seeing him.
② Yes, I've heard of him.
③ No. I can't wait to know about him.
④ No, I don't know about him.
⑤ Yes, I saw a program about him on TV.

[09~10] 다음 대화를 읽고 물음에 답하시오.

> G: Brian, (a)you know Taegeukgi, don't you?
> B: Sure. It's the national flag of Korea, (b)<u>isn't it</u>?
> G: That's right. Do you know (c)<u>what do the symbols in Taegeukgi mean</u>?
> B: No, I don't. Tell me about them.
> G: The circle in the middle (d)<u>means</u> harmony and peace.
> B: What do the black lines on the four corners (e)<u>mean</u>?
> G: They mean four things: sky, fire, water, and earth.

09 위 대화의 밑줄 친 (a)~(e) 중 어법상 <u>어색한</u> 것은?

① (a) ② (b) ③ (c) ④ (d) ⑤ (e)

10 위 대화의 내용과 일치하지 <u>않는</u> 것은?

① Brian knows what Taegeukgi is.
② The symbols in Taegeukgi have different meanings.
③ Brian wants to know about the meanings of the symbols in Taegeukgi.
④ Taegeukgi has four lines on each corner.
⑤ The black lines mean sky, fire, water and earth.

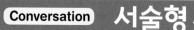

[01~02] 다음 대화를 읽고 물음에 답하시오.

Andy: Bora, what are you reading?

Bora: I'm reading *Sky, Wind, Star, and Poetry* by Yun Dongju. You know about Yun Dongju, don't you?

Andy: I've heard his name, but I don't know much about him.

Bora: He wrote many beautiful poems when Korea was under Japanese rule. His love for the country and his desire for independence can be felt in his poems.

Andy: Really? I didn't know that. I want to read his poems and learn more about him.

Bora: Great. In fact, I'm planning to visit the Yun Dongju Museum soon. Do you want to come with me?

Andy: Yes, when are you going?

Bora: Next Saturday. It's near Gyeongbok Palace. Can you meet me at the palace at 2 p.m.?

Andy: Sure. Let's meet there.

Bora: Great. (A)_____

01 위 대화를 읽고 다음 질문에 대한 답을 본문에서 찾아 쓰시오.

Q: What can be felt through Yun Dongju's poems?

➡ _____

_____

02 위 대화의 빈칸 (A)에 들어갈 말을 〈조건〉에 맞게 쓰시오.

┌ 조건 ┐
• 'look'을 이용하여 기대나 희망을 나타내는 표현을 쓸 것.
• 현재진행형을 사용하고, 'the visit'을 쓸 것.

➡ _____

03 다음 대화의 빈칸에 들어갈 말로 자연스러운 것을 〈보기〉에서 찾아 문장을 쓰시오.

G: Brian, (A)_____

B: Sure. It's the national flag of Korea, isn't it?

G: That's right. (B)_____

_____

B: No, I don't. Tell me about them.

G: The circle in the middle means harmony and peace.

B: What do the black lines on the four corners mean?

G: (C)_____

┌ 보기 ┐
• Do you know what the symbols in Taegeukgi mean?
• you know Taegeukgi, don't you?
• They mean four things: sky, fire, water, and earth.

 대화의 내용상 빈칸에 주어진 〈조건〉에 맞게 영어로 쓰시오.

┌ 조건 ┐
• 정약용에 대해 아는지 묻는 표현을 쓸 것.
• 'know'와 '부가의문문'을 사용할 것.

B: Look at Suwon Hawseong. It's huge.

G: It also looks strong.

B: Because it was built to protect the people during wars.

G: Wow. Do you know who built it?

B: Yes. King Jeongjo ordered Jeong Yakyong to direct the building process.

_____

G: Yes, I've heard of him. He was a great scientist in Joseon.

Grammar

① '과거완료' had + 과거분사

> • I thought about Kim Koo's words in My Wish that I **had read** in the exhibition hall. 나는 전시관에서 읽었던 '나의 소원'에 나오는 김구의 말에 대해 생각했다.
> • When my mom came back home, she found Judy **had watered** the plant. 나의 엄마가 집에 돌아왔을 때, 엄마는 Judy가 화분에 물을 주었던 것을 발견했다.

■ 과거완료시제는 'had + 과거분사' 형태로 표현하며, 과거의 어느 시점을 기준으로, 그 이전에 일어난 동작이나 상태를 나타낸다.

  • I lost the cellphone that he **had bought** for me. (나는 그가 사 준 핸드폰을 잃어버렸다.)

■ 과거의 특정 시점을 기준으로 그 이전에 일어난 동작의 완료, 경험, 계속, 결과를 나타낸다.

(1) 완료: '막 ~했었다'는 의미로 과거 이전에 시작된 동작이 과거의 어느 시점에 완료된 일을 나타낸다. 보통 already, yet 등의 부사와 함께 쓰인다.

  • They **had arrived** at the base camp before the snow storm began. (그들은 눈보라가 시작되기 전에 베이스 캠프에 도착했다.)

(2) 경험: '~한 적이 있었다'는 의미로 과거 이전부터 과거의 어느 시점까지의 경험을 나타낸다. 보통 never, ever, once, twice, before 등의 부사(구)와 함께 쓰인다.

  • She realized David at once, for she **had seen** him before. (그녀는 David을 즉시 알아봤는데, 전에 그를 만난 적이 있었기 때문이었다.)

(3) 결과: '(과거 이전에) ~해서, 그 결과 …했다'는 의미로 과거 이전의 동작이 과거의 어느 시점의 결과에 영향을 미치는 것을 나타낸다.

  • Her son **had gone** to the army by the time Emma was well again. (Emma가 다시 건강해질 무렵 그의 아들은 군에 입대했다.)

(4) 계속: '계속 ~하고 있었다'는 의미로 과거 이전부터 과거의 어느 시점까지 계속되는 동작이나 상태를 나타낸다. 보통 since, for 등과 함께 쓰인다.

  • Walter **had lived** there for 16 years when he was elected mayor. (Walter는 시장으로 당선되었을 때, 그곳에서 16년간을 살았다.)

■ 부정문은 'had+not+과거분사', 의문문은 'Had+주어+과거분사 ~?', 과거 어느 시점을 기준으로 전부터 진행 중인 동작을 강조할 때, 과거완료진행형 'had+been+V-ing'을 쓴다.

  • I was hungry because I **had not eaten** breakfast. (나는 아침을 먹지 않았기 때문에 배가 고팠다.)
  • **Had** James **seen** the actor before? (James가 그 배우를 전에 본 적이 있었나요?)
  • He **had been preparing** dinner when I saw him. (내가 그를 봤을 때, 그는 저녁식사를 준비하고 있던 중이었다.)

핵심 Check

1. 괄호 안에서 알맞은 단어를 고르시오.

  (1) Sally (has / had) lived in Singapore before she moved to Canada.

  (2) Judy had never eaten sushi until she (visits / visited) Japan.

② '목적', '의도'를 나타내는 so that

> • Kim Koo always carried Yun's watch in his jacket **so that** he **would** not forget Yun's sacrifice. 김구는 윤의 희생을 잊지 않기 위해서 그의 시계를 항상 재킷에 넣고 다녔다.
>
> • I waved at my sister **so that** she **could** find me. 나는 내 여동생이 나를 찾을 수 있게 그녀에게 손을 흔들었다.

■ so that은 '~하기 위해', '~하고자', '~하도록'의 의미로 '목적'이나 '의도'를 나타낸다. 일반적으로 '주절 +so that+주어+can/will(조동사)+동사원형 ~'의 구조로 쓰인다.

- Jinsu got up early **so that** he **could** catch the first train to Barcelona. (진수는 Barcelona로 가는 첫 기차를 타기 위해 일찍 일어났다.)
- Clara tried her best **so that** she **would** not disappoint her fans. (Clara는 자신의 팬들을 실망시키지 않기 위해서 최선을 다했다.)

■ so that은 다양한 표현들로 같은 의미를 나타낼 수 있다.

- She went to Mexico **so that** she **could** learn Spanish. (그녀는 스페인어를 배우러 멕시코에 갔다.)
  = She went to Mexico **in order that** she **could** learn Spanish.
  = She went to Mexico **to learn** Spanish. 〈to부정사의 부사적 용법 – 목적〉
  = She went to Mexico **so as to learn** Spanish.
  = She went to Mexico **in order to learn** Spanish.

- He worked hard **so that he wouldn't** be fired. (그는 해고되지 않으려고 열심히 일했다.)
  = He worked hard **in order that he wouldn't** be fired.
  = He worked hard **(in order) not to** be fired.
  = He worked hard **so as not to** be fired.

■ so that을 기준으로 앞과 뒤 동사의 시제를 일치시킨다.

- Sam **works** hard **so that** he **can** support his family. (Sam은 가족을 부양하기 위해 열심히 일한다.)
- Sam **worked** hard **so that** he **could** support his family.

■ so that이 '그래서'의 의미를 갖는 접속사로 쓰이기도 한다. 대개 so that 앞에 쉼표가 온다.

- Bolt ran every day, **so that** he became a great athlete. (Bolt는 매일 달렸고, 그래서 그는 훌륭한 육상선수가 되었다.)

■ so ~ that 사이에 형용사[부사]가 오면, '너무 ~해서 결국 …하다'라는 뜻이 된다.

- The girl was **so** happy **that** she cried. 그 소녀는 너무 행복해서 울었다.
- The room was **so** dark **that** I couldn't see anything. 방이 너무 어두워서 나는 아무것도 볼 수 없었다.

핵심 Check

2. 괄호 안에서 알맞은 말을 고르시오.

(1) Miranda went to London so (that / where) she could study fashion.

(2) Please turn the volume down (for that / so that) my daughter can sleep.

Grammar 시험대비 기본평가

01 다음 빈칸에 들어갈 말로 알맞은 것은?

> He came back to Sudan in 2001 as he _____.

① promise   ② promises   ③ has promised
④ to promise   ⑤ had promised

02 다음 각 문장의 빈칸에 공통으로 들어갈 말로 알맞은 것은? (대 · 소문자 구분 없음.)

> • Andrew saved much money _____ as to travel around the world.
> • Turn the volume up _____ that we can dance to the music.
> • These are _____ tough that we can't tear them.

① enough   ② too   ③ so
④ such   ⑤ quite

03 다음 밑줄 친 부분 중 어법상 옳은 것을 고르시오.

① Paul has gone to Tokyo before his wife came back.
② I ate the tuna can that I had bought a month before.
③ I had found her purse that she had left in my office.
④ They had lived here for two years until now.
⑤ When had Betty married Chris?

04 다음 두 문장의 의미가 같도록 빈칸에 알맞은 말을 쓰시오.

(1) Mina saved much money to buy the car.
  ➡ Mina saved much money so _____ she _____ buy the car.

(2) Because it was very hot, Julie turned the air conditioner on.
  ➡ It was _____ _____ _____ Julie turned the air conditioner on.

(3) Mike will walk fast in order to get there on time.
  ➡ Mike will walk fast so _____ _____ _____ get there on time.

(4) Judy can't solve the problem because it is very hard.
  ➡ The problem is _____ _____ _____ Judy _____ solve it.

 01 밑줄 친 부분이 어법상 어색한 것은?

① The suspect had already left the room when the police arrived.
② John had broken his arm, so he couldn't play tennis last weekend.
③ Susan asked her friend how to repair the machine which has broken down.
④ I had met him many times before then.
⑤ Amy lost the key that her aunt had given to her.

[02~03] 다음 우리말을 어법상 알맞게 영작한 것을 고르시오.

02

> 김구는 그의 희생을 잊지 않기 위해서 그의 시계를 항상 가지고 다녔다.

① Kim Koo always carried his watch so that he won't forget his sacrifice.
② Kim Koo carried his watch so always that he could not forget his sacrifice.
③ Kim Koo carried his watch always so what he should not forget his sacrifice.
④ Kim Koo always carried his watch so that he would not forget his sacrifice.
⑤ Kim Koo often carried his watch so he would not forget his sacrifice always.

03

> 더위를 잊으려고 우리는 얼음을 먹었다.

① We ate the ice not to forget the heat.
② We ate the ice so that we can forget the heat.
③ We ate the ice in order that forget the heat.
④ We ate the ice so cold that we would forget the heat.
⑤ We ate the ice so that we would forget the heat.

[04~05] 다음 밑줄 친 부분 중 어법상 옳은 것을 고르시오.

04 ① Yujin is hungry because she had not eaten anything so far.
② The crow lived in the jungle before it had moved to the city.
③ Their bodies had been in Japan, but Kim Koo brought them to Korea.
④ Mom required that Jane had finished the dishes.
⑤ For the past five years, I had read your books about the origin of space.

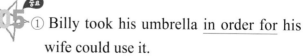
05 ① Billy took his umbrella in order for his wife could use it.
② Justin got up early so that he not being late for the contest.
③ The dolphins were so joy that they could jump above the water.
④ Martha has been saving money for 6 months so to buy a new software.
⑤ Lucy exercised regularly in order that she could reduce stress.

06 다음 두 문장의 의미가 같도록 바꿔 쓸 때 적절하지 <u>않은</u> 것은?

① Kate stood up so that her business partner could find her.
= Kate stood up in order for her business partner to find her.

② Ahn left for America so that he would get a better education.
= Ahn left for America so as to get a better education.

③ Bob made cakes so that he would feel happy.
= Bob made cakes to feel happy.

④ Elizabeth exercises regularly in order for her mom not to get worried.
= Elizabeth exercises regularly so that her mom would not get worried.

⑤ Ted left the meeting quite early not to see his rivals.
= Ted left the meeting quite early, so he could not see his rivals.

07 다음 중 밑줄 친 부분의 쓰임이 〈보기〉와 같은 것은?

┌ 보기 ┤
I <u>had</u> already <u>solved</u> the quiz when the teacher called my name.
└

① Kim Koo <u>had</u> not <u>arrived</u> at the airport when the planes landed.

② Sophia <u>had known</u> him for 10 years when she first found him attractive.

③ The Smiths <u>had lived</u> in Seoul for ten years before they moved to Incheon.

④ Grace <u>had</u> never <u>been</u> ill until last year after the accident.

⑤ Koby <u>had played</u> basketball in America for thirty years since then.

08 다음 문장에서 어법상 <u>어색한</u> 단어 한 개를 찾아서 고치시오.

My cousin has been sick in bed for a week when I visited him.

➡ _____

09 다음 중 주어진 문장과 의미가 <u>다른</u> 것은?

The soldiers trained hard so that they would defeat Japan.

① The soldiers trained hard in order that they would defeat Japan.

② The soldiers trained hard to defeat Japan.

③ The soldiers trained hard so as to defeat Japan.

④ The soldiers trained so hard that they defeated Japan.

⑤ The soldiers trained hard in order to defeat Japan.

10 다음 문장의 밑줄 친 so that의 쓰임이 흐름상 <u>어색한</u> 것은?

① The actor wore sunglasses <u>so that</u> he could hide his face.

② Brian's sisters made some dishes <u>so that</u> they could eat together.

③ Yuna practiced hard <u>so that</u> she could win the piano competition.

④ The boy band performed on the street <u>so that</u> many people could recognize them.

⑤ Irene failed the exam <u>so that</u> she had studied harder than before.

[11~12] 다음 중 어법상 옳은 문장은?

11
① April has never eaten the spice until she visited Vietnam.
② Mom can't see the flower now as my sister had picked it.
③ The students have been sitting for half an hour before the class started.
④ When I met her, Sumin had already completed the assignment.
⑤ My sister found the book that I had been given to her.

12
① My history club went to Hyochang Park so as to visit the Kim Koo Museum.
② Betty practices yoga regularly so as to be stay healthy.
③ John spent most of life in order to that he could be a novelist.
④ I study English so that in order to read many books written in English.
⑤ Mina learned French so that she can watch French movies without subtitles.

13 다음 〈보기〉와 같이 두 문장이 같은 의미가 되도록 주어진 단어를 활용하여 다시 쓰시오.

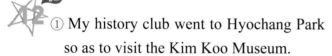

┌─ 보기 ┐
I exercise so as to keep in shape. (that, so)
→ I exercise so that I can keep in shape.
└────────┘

(1) Father Lee Taeseok returned to Sudan to help poor people there. (that, in, could, order)

➡ _____

_____

(2) Amy practices every day to join our sports club. (that, so, can)

➡ _____

_____

(3) Clara left for Paris to study fashion. (that, in, could, order)

➡ _____

_____

(4) Thames ran fast in order not to be late for the meeting. (that, would, so)

➡ _____

_____

14 다음 그림을 보고 자연스러운 문장이 되도록 괄호 안에 주어진 어구를 바르게 배열하여 빈칸을 완성하시오.

(1)

➡ Junsu _____

_____. (the pimples, they, that, disappear, squeezed out, would, so)

(2)

➡ Sudong studied hard _____

_____. (that, in order, a, get, he, college scholarship, could, full)

01 다음 우리말과 일치하도록 괄호 안에 주어진 어구를 바르게 배열하여 문장을 완성하시오.

(1) 간송은 몇몇 일본인들이 일본으로 가져갔었던 한국의 많은 문화재들을 샀다.

➡ Gansong _____

_____.

(Japan, taken, bought, to, that, many, Japanese, Korean treasures, had, some).

(2) 이순신은 사람들을 보호할 수 있게 거북선을 만들었다.

➡ Yi Sunsin _____

_____. (the Turtle Ship, could, the people, that, he, protect, made, so).

(3) 그 도둑은 아무도 들을 수 없도록 천천히 걸었다.

➡ The thief _____

_____. (hear, slowly, one, so, walked, could, him, no, that).

02 다음 그림은 학생들이 문화 유산을 조사하고 만든 미니북과 활동 감상문이다. 빈칸에 들어갈 알맞은 말을 괄호 안의 단어와 완료시제를 활용하여 쓰시오.

Before we made this cultural heritage mini book, we _____ (search) for information about the golden crowns of Silla, Bulguksa, *samullori*, and the Nanjungilgi. After we _____ (make) the book, we learned a lesson that it is important to keep our cultural treasures.

03 다음 문장에서 어법상 <u>어색한</u> 것을 바르게 고쳐 다시 쓰시오.

(1) Could you remind me of the time so order that I won't be late for the party?

➡ _____

_____

_____

(2) Whenever Jane was ill, her mom used to make her a bowl of porridge in order of her to get well.

➡ _____

(3) They are saving money so which they can buy a big house.

➡ _____

_____

(4) Remember my number in order for you can contact me.

➡ _____

_____

_____

(5) The foreigners from Italy went to Gyeongju so that they can see Bulguksa.

➡ _____

_____

(6) Many people joined the New Korean Society so order to support the Independence movement.

➡ _____

04 괄호 안에 주어진 어구와 글자 수 및 조건을 활용하여, 다음 우리말을 영작하시오.

(1) 우리가 팥빙수를 만들 수 있기 위해서는 얼음과 설탕이 필요하다. (that, so, ice, can, patbingsu, sugar, need, 11 단어)

➡ _____

(2) 그녀가 물고기 몇 마리를 잡도록 해주기 위해서 우리는 강으로 갔다. (could, that, catch, go, so, fish, the river, some, 12 단어)

➡ _____

(3) 그 코알라들을 구조하기 위해 한 소방대원이 숲 속으로 뛰어들었다. (she, rescue, firefighter, the woods, that, so, run, could, into, the koalas, 13 단어)

➡ _____

(4) 나의 할머니는 건강을 유지하도록 매일 운동을 합니다. (can, grandma, every day, exercise, healthy, keep, order that, 12 단어)

➡ _____

05 다음 우리말을 주어진 〈조건〉에 맞게 영작하시오.

조건
1. The old man을 포함, 총 19 단어로 쓸 것.
2. 숫자도 영어로 쓸 것.
3. the official, live alone, in, for, until 등을 활용할 것.

그 공무원이 작년에 방문할 때까지 그 노인은 그 집에서 33년간 혼자 살아왔다.
→ The old man _____ .

06 다음 각 문장의 밑줄 친 부분이 과거완료시제의 용법 중 어떤 것에 해당하는지 〈보기〉에서 찾아 기호를 쓰고 우리말로 해석하시오.

보기
ⓐ 완료 ⓑ 경험 ⓒ 결과 ⓓ 계속

(1) Peter had already left for New York when I got there. ( )
➡ _____

(2) William had lived in Busan for 14 years until last year. ( )
➡ _____

(3) They had waited for the singer for almost a day before the concert started. ( )
➡ _____

(4) Maria had never seen the snow until she came to Korea this winter. ( )
➡ _____

(5) By the time I arrived at the airport, the check-in had already been completed. ( )
➡ _____

(6) When we came home, we found somebody had broken the window. ( )
➡ _____

(7) I didn't recognize the person because I had never met him before. ( )
➡ _____

(8) When the couple woke up, someone had finished making shoes. ( )
➡ _____

My Wish

Last week my history club went to Hyochang Park. We visited the Kim Koo Museum inside the park. At the entrance of the museum, we saw a white statue of Kim Koo. Kim Koo is a great national hero who spent most of his life fighting for the independence of Korea from Japanese rule. In the 1900s, he helped educate young people by building schools. In 1919, when the independence movement had spread throughout the country, he moved to Shanghai, China. There he joined the Government of the Republic of Korea and later became its president.

The exhibition hall in the museum shows a lot of things about Kim Koo's life. While looking around the hall, we stopped at a photo of the Korean Patriotic Organization's members. Kim Koo formed the secret organization in 1931 to fight against Japan. Lee Bongchang and Yun Bonggil belonged to the group. At one place in the hall, we saw two watches under a photo of Kim Koo and Yun Bonggil. In 1932, Kim Koo made a plan to kill Japanese generals in a park in Shanghai.

entrance: 입구
statue: 동상
independence: 독립
Japanese: 일본의
spread: 퍼지다
throughout: ~의 전체에 걸쳐
government: 정부
republic: 공화국
president: 대통령, 의장
exhibition: 전시
hall: 큰 방, 홀, 현관

확인문제

- 다음 문장이 본문의 내용과 일치하면 T, 일치하지 않으면 F를 쓰시오.

1 The history club went to Hyochang Park last month. ☐

2 There is the statue of Kim Koo at the entrance of the park. ☐

3 Kim Koo fought for the independence of Korea from Japanese rule. ☐

4 Yun Bonggil was one of the members of the Korean Patriotic Organization. ☐

As the leader of the Korean Patriotic Organization, he directed Yun to
자격을 나타내는 전치사(~로서)

carry out the mission.
direct+목적어+toV: 목적어가 V할 것을 지시하다

When Yun left for the mission, he told Kim, "Sir, you are wearing a
상해에 있는 한 공원에서 일본 장군들을 암살하는 것

very old watch. Mine is new, but I won't need it anymore. Please take
= My watch

my watch, and let me have yours." Kim Koo always carried Yun's
사역동사+목적어+동사원형(목적어가 V하게 시키다)

watch in his jacket so that he would not forget Yun's sacrifice.
~하기 위해서(목적을 나타내는 구문)

After completing the tour of the museum, we moved to the tombs
동명사(전치사 After의 목적어)

of the three heroes, Lee Bongchang, Yun Bonggil, and Baek Jeonggi.
the three heroes와 동격

Their bodies had been in Japan, but after Korea's independence Kim
김구가 그들의 시신을 가지고 온 것은 과거이며 그 전부터 일본에 있었으므로 과거완료

Koo brought them to Hyochang Park. By doing so, he showed his
일본에 있던 시신들을 한국으로 모셔온 것

deep love and respect for the sacrifice of the three heroes.

As I left Hyochang Park, I thought about Kim Koo's words in

My Wish that I had read in the exhibition hall. It was written in
목적격 관계대명사   My Wish

Baekbeomilji.

If God asks me what my wish is, I would say clearly, "It is Korea's
조건의 부사절을 이끄는 접속사(~라면)

Independence." If he asks me what my second wish is, I would say,
간접의문문(의문사+주어+동사)

"It is the independence of my country." If he asks me what my third
wish is, I would say loudly, "It is the complete independence of my
country." That is my answer.

direct: 지시하다
carry out: 수행하다
patriotic: 애국적인
organization: 조직
member: 구성원, 회원
general: 장군
leader: 지도자
mission: 임무
belong to: ~에 속하다
sacrifice: 희생; 희생하다
tomb: 무덤
god: 하느님, 신
wish: 소원, 소망
clearly: 분명하게, 확실히

확인문제

● 다음 문장이 본문의 내용과 일치하면 T, 일치하지 않으면 F를 쓰시오.

1　Kim Koo wanted Yun to give his watch to him. ☐

2　Yun thought he wouldn't need his watch anymore. ☐

3　Kim Koo brought the bodies of the three heroes to Hyochang Park before Korea's

　independence. ☐

4　The writer read Kim Koo's words in a newspaper. ☐

5　Kim Koo's one and only wish was the complete independence of the country. ☐

● 우리말을 참고하여 빈칸에 알맞은 말을 쓰시오.

My Wish

1 Last week _____ _____ _____ went to Hyochang Park.

2 We _____ the Kim Koo Museum _____ _____ _____ .

3 _____ the _____ of the museum, we saw a white statue of Kim Koo.

4 Kim Koo is _____ _____ _____ _____ who _____ most of his life fighting for the independence of Korea _____ Japanese rule.

5 In the 1900s, he _____ _____ young people _____ _____ schools.

6 _____ 1919, _____ _____ _____ had spread throughout the country, he _____ _____ Shanghai, China.

7 There he _____ the Government of the Republic of Korea and later _____ _____ _____ .

8 _____ _____ _____ in the museum _____ a lot of things about Kim Koo's life.

9 While _____ _____ the hall, we _____ _____ a photo of the Korean _____ _____ members.

10 Kim Koo _____ the secret _____ in 1931 _____ _____ _____ Japan.

11 Lee Bongchang and Yun Bonggil _____ _____ the group.

12 _____ one place in the hall, we _____ _____ _____ under a photo of Kim Koo and Yun Bonggil.

나의 소원

1 지난주에 우리 역사 동아리는 효창 공원에 갔다.

2 우리는 공원 안에 있는 김구 기념관을 방문했다.

3 기념관 입구에서 우리는 하얀색의 김구 조각상을 보았다.

4 김구는 일본 통치로부터 대한의 독립을 위해 싸우는 데 그의 삶 대부분을 보낸 위대한 국민 영웅이다.

5 1900년대에 그는 학교를 설립함으로써 젊은이들을 교육시키는 것을 도왔다.

6 1919년에 3.1 운동이 나라 전체에 걸쳐 퍼져나갔을 때, 그는 중국 상하이로 이동했다.

7 그곳에서 그는 대한민국 임시정부에 합류했고 나중에는 그것의 대표자가 되었다.

8 기념관 안에 있는 전시관은 김구의 삶에 관한 많은 것들을 보여준다.

9 우리는 전시관을 둘러보면서 한인 애국단의 단원들 사진 앞에 섰다.

10 김구는 일본에 맞서 싸우기 위해 1931년에 비밀 조직을 형성했다.

11 이봉창과 윤봉길이 그 집단에 속해 있었다.

12 전시관의 한 곳에서, 우리는 김구와 윤봉길의 사진 아래에 있는 시계 두 개를 보았다.

13 _____ 1932, Kim Koo _____ _____ _____ _____ kill Japanese generals in a park in Shanghai.

14 As the leader of the Korean _____ _____, he _____ Yun _____ _____ out the mission.

15 When Yun _____ _____ the mission, he told Kim, "Sir, you are _____ _____ _____ _____ _____. _____ is new, but I won't need _____ anymore. Please _____ my watch, and _____ me _____ yours."

16 Kim Koo _____ _____ Yun's watch in his jacket _____ _____ he would not _____ Yun's _____.

17 After _____ the tour of the museum, we _____ _____ the _____ of the three heroes, Lee Bongchang, Yun Bonggil, and Baek Jeonggi.

18 Their bodies _____ _____ in Japan, but after Korea's _____ Kim Koo brought _____ to Hyochang Park.

19 _____ _____ _____, he showed his deep love and respect _____ _____ _____ of the three heroes.

20 _____ I _____ Hyochang Park, I thought about Kim Koo's _____ in My Wish _____ I _____ in the exhibition hall.

21 _____ was _____ _____ *Baekbeomilji*.

22 If God asks me _____ _____ _____ _____, I would say clearly, "It is _____ _____."

23 If he asks me _____ _____ _____ _____ is, I would say, "It is the _____ of my country."

24 If he _____ _____ _____ _____ _____ _____, I would say loudly, "It is the _____ _____ of my country." That is my answer.

13 1932년에 김구는 상해에 있는 한 공원에서 일본 장군들을 암살하기 위한 계획을 세웠다.

14 한인 애국단의 지도자로서 그는 윤봉길이 임무를 수행하도록 지시했다.

15 윤봉길이 임무를 위해 떠날 때, 그는 김구에게 말했다. "선생님, 당신은 매우 낡은 시계를 차고 계시는군요. 제 것은 새것이나, 저는 그것이 더 이상 필요하지 않을 것입니다. 부디 제 시계를 가져가시고, 제가 선생님 것을 가지도록 해주십시오."

16 김구는 윤봉길의 희생을 잊지 않기 위해서 윤봉길의 시계를 항상 상의에 넣고 다녔다.

17 기념관 관람을 마치고, 우리는 이봉창, 윤봉길, 그리고 백정기 의사들이 묻힌 삼의사의 묘로 이동했다.

18 그들의 시신은 일본에 있다가 독립이 되고 나서 김구가 그들의 시신을 효창 공원으로 가져왔다.

19 그는 그렇게 함으로써 삼의사들의 희생에 대한 그의 깊은 사랑과 경의를 보여 주었다.

20 내가 효창 공원을 떠날 때, 나는 전시관에서 읽었던 「나의 소원」에 있는 김구의 말을 생각했다.

21 그것은 「백범일지」에 쓰여 있었다.

22 만약 신이 나의 소원이 무엇이냐고 묻는다면, "그것은 대한 독립이오."라고 명확하게 말할 것이다.

23 만약에 그가 나의 두 번째 소원이 무엇이냐고 묻는다면, 나는 "그것은 내 나라의 독립이오."라고 말할 것이다.

24 만약 그가 나의 세 번째 소원이 무엇이냐고 묻는다면, "그것은 내 나라의 완전한 독립이오."라고 큰 소리로 말할 것이다. 그것이 나의 대답이다.

● 우리말을 참고하여 본문을 영작하시오.

1 지난주에 우리 역사 동아리는 효창 공원에 갔다.
➡ _____

2 우리는 공원 안에 있는 김구 기념관을 방문했다.
➡ _____

3 기념관 입구에서 우리는 하얀색의 김구 조각상을 보았다.
➡ _____

4 김구는 일본 통치로부터 대한의 독립을 위해 싸우는 데 그의 삶 대부분을 보낸 위대한 국민 영웅이다.
➡ _____
_____

5 1900년대에 그는 학교를 설립함으로써 젊은이들을 교육시키는 것을 도왔다.
➡ _____

6 1919년에 3.1 운동이 나라 전체에 걸쳐 퍼져나갔을 때, 그는 중국 상하이로 이동했다.
➡ _____
_____

7 그곳에서 그는 대한민국 임시정부에 합류했고 나중에는 그것의 대표자가 되었다.
➡ _____

8 기념관 안에 있는 전시관은 김구의 삶에 관한 많은 것들을 보여 준다.
➡ _____

9 우리는 전시관을 둘러보면서 한인 애국단의 단원들 사진 앞에 섰다.
➡ _____

10 김구는 일본에 맞서 싸우기 위해 1931년에 비밀 조직을 형성했다.
➡ _____

11 이봉창과 윤봉길이 그 집단에 속해 있었다.
➡ _____

12 전시관의 한 곳에서, 우리는 김구와 윤봉길의 사진 아래에 있는 시계 두 개를 보았다.
➡ _____

13 1932년에 김구는 상해에 있는 한 공원에서 일본 장군들을 암살하기 위한 계획을 세웠다.
➡ _____

14 한인 애국단의 지도자로서 그는 윤봉길이 임무를 수행하도록 지시했다.

➡ _____

15 윤봉길이 임무를 위해 떠날 때, 그는 김구에게 말했다. "선생님, 당신은 매우 낡은 시계를 차고 계시는군요. 제 것은 새것이나, 저는 그것이 더 이상 필요하지 않을 것입니다. 부디 제 시계를 가져가시고, 제가 선생님 것을 가지도록 해주십시오."

➡ _____

_____

16 김구는 윤봉길의 희생을 잊지 않기 위해서 윤봉길의 시계를 항상 상의에 넣고 다녔다.

➡ _____

17 기념관 관람을 마치고, 우리는 이봉창, 윤봉길, 그리고 백정기 의사들이 묻힌 삼의사의 묘로 이동했다.

➡ _____

_____

18 그들의 시신은 일본에 있다가 독립이 되고 나서 김구가 그들의 시신을 효창 공원으로 가져왔다.

➡ _____

19 그는 그렇게 함으로써 삼의사들의 희생에 대한 그의 깊은 사랑과 경의를 보여 주었다.

➡ _____

20 내가 효창 공원을 떠날 때, 나는 전시관에서 읽었던 「나의 소원」에 있는 김구의 말을 생각했다.

➡ _____

_____

21 그것은 「백범일지」에 쓰여 있었다.

➡ _____

22 만약 신이 나의 소원이 무엇이냐고 묻는다면, "그것은 대한 독립이오."라고 명확하게 말할 것이다.

➡ _____

23 만약에 그가 나의 두 번째 소원이 무엇이냐고 묻는다면, 나는 "그것은 내 나라의 독립이오."라고 말할 것이다.

➡ _____

24 만약 그가 나의 세 번째 소원이 무엇이냐고 묻는다면, "그것은 내 나라의 완전한 독립이오."라고 큰 소리로 말할 것이다. 그것이 나의 대답이다.

➡ _____

_____

[01~04] 다음 글을 읽고 물음에 답하시오.

Last week my history club went to Hyochang Park. We visited the Kim Koo Museum inside the park. At the entrance of the museum, we saw a white statue of Kim Koo. Kim Koo is a great national hero who spent most of his life fighting for the independence of Korea from Japanese rule. In the 1900s, he helped educate young people (A)_____ building schools. In 1919, when the independence movement had spread throughout the country, he moved to Shanghai, China. There he joined the Government of the Republic of Korea and later became its president.

01 다음 중 빈칸 (A)에 들어갈 말로 가장 적절한 것은?

① about   ② by   ③ at
④ on   ⑤ to

02 Choose the one that is CORRECT about Kim Koo.

① He used to live near Hyochang park.
② He built a museum for independence of Korea.
③ He spent most of his life fighting for Japan.
④ He built schools to educate young people.
⑤ He lived in Korea all his life.

서답형
03 Where is the statue of Kim Koo? Answer in English with eight words.

➡

서답형
04 When did Kim Koo move to Shanghai? Answer in English with six words.

➡ _____

[05~08] 다음 글을 읽고 물음에 답하시오.

The exhibition hall in the museum shows a lot of things about Kim Koo's life. While looking around the hall, we stopped at a photo of the Korean Patriotic Organization's members. Kim Koo formed the secret organization in 1931 to fight against Japan. Lee Bongchang and Yun Bonggil belonged to the group. At one place in the hall, we saw two watches under a photo of Kim Koo and Yun Bonggil. In 1932, Kim Koo made a plan to kill Japanese generals in a park in Shanghai. As the leader of the Korean Patriotic Organization, he directed Yun to carry out the mission.

When Yun left for the mission, he told Kim, "Sir, you are wearing a very old watch. Mine is new, but I won't need it anymore. Please take my watch, and let me have yours." Kim Koo always carried Yun's watch in his jacket so that he would not forget Yun's sacrifice.

05 다음 중 기념관 내 전시관에서 찾아볼 수 있는 것을 모두 고르시오.

① many books about Kim Koo's life
② a photo of the Korean Patriotic Organization's members
③ the statues of Lee Bongchang and Yun Bonggil
④ two watches which belonged to Yun Bonggil and Kim Koo
⑤ a photo of Kim Koo with his family

서답형

06 Where did Kim Koo plan to kill Japanese generals? Answer in English with twelve words.

➡ _____

_____

07 다음 중 위 글을 읽고 답할 수 있는 것은?

① Where was Kim Koo born?
② How many exhibition halls are there in the museum?
③ How many members were there in the Korean Patriotic Organization?
④ What did Kim Koo form in 1931?
⑤ When did Kim Koo and Yun Bonggil take the picture?

중요

08 다음 중 위 글의 내용을 바르게 이해한 사람은?

① Amelia: It is hard to know many things about Kim Koo at the exhibition hall.
② Brian: It is surprising that Kim Koo didn't join the Korean Patriotic Organization.
③ Claire: I'm so sorry Yun didn't leave for the mission.
④ David: Yun was the leader of the Korean Patriotic Organization.
⑤ Ethon: It's so touching that Kim Koo always carried Yun's watch.

[09~11] 다음 글을 읽고 물음에 답하시오.

(A) By doing so, he showed his deep love and respect for the sacrifice of the three heroes.
(B) Their bodies had been in Japan, but after Korea's independence Kim Koo brought them to Hyochang Park.

(C) After completing the tour of the museum, we moved to the tombs of the three heroes, Lee Bongchang, Yun Bonggil, and Baek Jeonggi.

As I left Hyochang Park, I thought about Kim Koo's words in My Wish ⓐ_____ I had read in the exhibition hall. It was written in *Baekbeomilji*.

If God asks me what my wish is, I would say clearly, "It is Korea's Independence." If he asks me what my second wish is, I would say, "It is the independence of my country." If he asks me what my third wish is, I would say loudly, "It is the complete independence of my country." That is my answer.

09 다음 중 빈칸 ⓐ에 들어갈 말로 적절한 것을 <u>모두</u> 고르시오.

① which   ② whose   ③ that
④ what   ⑤ who

중요

10 자연스러운 글이 되도록 (A)~(C)를 바르게 나열한 것은?

① (A)–(C)–(B)   ② (B)–(A)–(C)
③ (B)–(C)–(A)   ④ (C)–(A)–(B)
⑤ (C)–(B)–(A)

서답형

11 주어진 어구를 바르게 나열하여 다음 물음에 대한 답을 완성하시오.

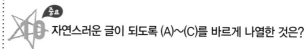

Q: What was written in *Baekbeomilji*?
A: (*Baekbeomilji* / Korea / written / of / independence / in / for / the / Kim Koo's / complete / firm wish / was)

➡ _____

_____

[12~15] 다음 글을 읽고 물음에 답하시오.

Last week my history club went to Hyochang Park. We visited the Kim Koo Museum inside the park. At the entrance of the museum, we saw a white statue of Kim Koo. Kim Koo is a great national hero who spent most of his life fighting for the independence of Korea from Japanese rule. In the 1900s, he helped educate young people by building schools. In 1919, when the independence movement had spread throughout the country, he moved to Shanghai, China. There he joined the Government of the Republic of Korea and later became its president.

서답형

12 위 글의 내용에 맞게 빈칸에 알맞은 말을 쓰시오.

The history club went to Hyochang Park in order to ＿＿＿ ＿＿＿ ＿＿＿ ＿＿＿ ＿＿＿ ＿＿＿ ＿＿＿.

13 다음 중 효창 공원에서 찾아볼 수 있는 것은?

① the school Kim Koo built for young people
② the pictures of young people taught by Kim Koo
③ a picture of independence movement
④ a large white sculpture of Kim Koo
⑤ a museum Kim Koo built

서답형

14 According to the passage, what did Kim Koo fight for? Answer in English with a full sentence.

➡ ＿＿＿＿＿＿＿＿＿＿＿＿＿＿＿

＿＿＿＿＿＿＿＿＿＿＿＿＿＿＿

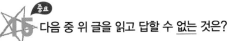

15 다음 중 위 글을 읽고 답할 수 없는 것은?

① Where is the Kim Koo Museum?
② What did the writer's history club do last week?
③ How did Kim Koo help educate young people?
④ How did the club go to the Hyochang Park?
⑤ When did the independence movement spread throughout the country?

[16~18] 다음 글을 읽고 물음에 답하시오.

The exhibition hall in the museum shows ① a lot of things about Kim Koo's life. While looking ②after the hall, we stopped ③at a photo of the Korean Patriotic Organization's members. Kim Koo ④formed the secret organization in 1931 to fight against Japan. Lee Bongchang and Yun Bonggil ⑤belonged to the group. At one place in the hall, we saw two watches under a photo of Kim Koo and Yun Bonggil.

16 다음과 같이 풀이되는 말을 위 글에서 찾아 쓰시오.

a public event at which pictures, sculptures, or other objects of interest are displayed

➡ ＿＿＿＿＿＿＿＿＿＿＿＿＿

17 밑줄 친 ①~⑤ 중 글의 흐름상 어색한 것은?

①　　　②　　　③　　　④　　　⑤

서답형

18 What were there under a photo of Kim Koo and Yun Bonggil?

➡ ＿＿＿＿＿＿＿＿＿＿＿＿＿

[19~21] 다음 글을 읽고 물음에 답하시오.

In 1932, ①Kim Koo made a plan to kill Japanese generals in a park in Shanghai. (A)As the leader of the Korean Patriotic Organization, ②he directed Yun to carry out the mission. When ③he left for the mission, Yun told Kim, "Sir, ④you are wearing a very old watch. Mine is new, but I won't need (B)it anymore. Please take my watch, and let me have yours." Kim Koo always carried Yun's watch in ⑤his jacket so that he would not forget Yun's sacrifice.

19 밑줄 친 ①~⑤ 중 가리키는 것이 다른 하나는?

①   ②   ③   ④   ⑤

20 다음 중 밑줄 친 (A)와 쓰임이 같은 것은?

① They were all dressed as clowns.
② You are as kind as your father.
③ As they were out, I left a message.
④ As you know, Susan is leaving soon.
⑤ We look up to him as a doctor.

서답형
21 밑줄 친 (B)가 의미하는 것을 두 단어의 영어로 쓰시오.

➡ _____

[22~25] 다음 글을 읽고 물음에 답하시오.

After completing the tour of the museum, we moved to the tombs of the three heroes, Lee Bongchang, Yun Bonggil, and Baek Jeonggi. ①Their bodies had been in Japan, but after Korea's ②independence Kim Koo brought them to Hyochang Park. By doing so, he showed his deep love and respect for the ③sacrifice of the three heroes.

As I left Hyochang Park, I thought about Kim Koo's words in My Wish that I had read in the exhibition hall. It was written in *Baekbeomilji*.

If God asks me what my wish is, I would say clearly, "It is Korea's Independence." If he asks me what my second wish is, I would say, "It is the independence of my country." If he asks me what my third wish is, I would say loudly, "It is the ④complement independence of my country." That is my ⑤answer.

22 밑줄 친 ①~⑤ 중 글의 흐름상 어색한 것은?

①   ②   ③   ④   ⑤

23 According to the passage, what did Kim Koo wish most?

① respect from people
② reliance on Japan
③ achieving independence of Korea
④ making Korea a rich country
⑤ making Korea dependent

24 Choose the sentence that is TRUE according to the passage.

① They have just started touring the museum.
② It is uncertain who were buried in the tombs.
③ Kim Koo brought the bodies before Korea's independence.
④ Kim Koo hardly loved the three heroes.
⑤ It was Kim Koo who brought three heroes' bodies into Korea from Japan.

서답형
25 Where are Kim Koo's words written? Answer in English with a full sentence.

➡ _____

[01~05] 다음 글을 읽고 물음에 답하시오.

Last week my history club went to Hyochang Park. We visited the Kim Koo Museum inside the park. At the entrance of the museum, we saw a white statue of Kim Koo. Kim Koo is a great national hero who spent most of his life fighting for the independence of Korea from Japanese rule. In the 1900s, he helped educate young people by building schools. In 1919, when the independence movement had spread throughout the country, he moved to Shanghai, China. (A) There he joined the Government of the Republic of Korea and later became its president.

01 밑줄 친 (A)가 가리키는 것을 위 글에서 찾아 쓰시오.

➡ _____

02 Where did the writer's history club go last week? Answer in English and use the word 'they.'

➡ _____

03 What was there at the entrance of the museum?

➡ _____

_____

04 Where was the Government of the Republic of Korea? Answer in English with a full sentence.

➡ _____

05 위 글의 내용에 맞게 빈칸에 알맞은 말을 쓰시오.

> Kim Koo(1876~1949)
> He is a great _____ who fought for _____ from Japanese rule.

[06~08] 다음 글을 읽고 물음에 답하시오.

The exhibition hall in the museum shows a lot of things about Kim Koo's life. While looking around the hall, we stopped at a photo of the Korean Patriotic Organization's members. Kim Koo formed the secret organization in 1931 to fight against Japan. Lee Bongchang and Yun Bonggil belonged to the group. At one place in the hall, we saw two watches under a photo of Kim Koo and Yun Bonggil.

06 Whose photo did the writer see?

➡ _____

_____

07 Write the reason why Kim Koo formed the secret organization in 1931. Use the phrase 'It was because' and 'try to.'

➡ _____

08 위 글의 내용에 맞게 빈칸에 알맞은 말을 쓰시오.

> A: Do you know who _____ _____ _____ _____ that Kim Koo formed?
> B: Yes, I do. Lee Bongchang and Yun Bonggil did.

[09~11] 다음 글을 읽고 물음에 답하시오.

In 1932, Kim Koo made a plan to kill Japanese generals in a park in Shanghai. As the leader of the Korean Patriotic Organization, he directed Yun to carry out the mission.

When Yun left for the mission, he told Kim, "Sir, you are wearing a very old watch. Mine is new, but I won't need it anymore. Please take my watch, and let me have yours." Kim Koo always carried Yun's watch in his jacket so that he would not forget Yun's sacrifice.

09 What was Kim Koo's plan? Answer in English with a full sentence.

➡ _____

_____

10 위 글의 내용에 맞게 빈칸에 들어갈 알맞은 말을 쓰시오.

> In 1932, Yun _____ _____ with Kim Koo before he left to carry out the mission Kim Koo directed.

11 Write the reason why Kim Koo always carried Yun's watch in his jacket. Use the phrase 'It was because.'

➡ _____

[12~15] 다음 글을 읽고 물음에 답하시오.

After completing the tour of the museum, we moved to the tombs of the three heroes, Lee Bongchang, Yun Bonggil, and Baek Jeonggi. Their bodies had been in Japan, but after Korea's independence Kim Koo brought them

to Hyochang Park. By (A)doing so, he showed his deep love and respect for the sacrifice of the three heroes.

As I left Hyochang Park, I thought about Kim Koo's words in My Wish that I had read in the exhibition hall. It was written in *Baekbeomilji*.

If God asks me what my wish is, I would say clearly, "It is Korea's Independence." If he asks me what my second wish is, I would say, "It is the independence of my country." If he asks me what my third wish is, I would say loudly, "It is the complete independence of my country." That is my answer.

12 After they completed the tour of the museum, what did they do? Answer in English with a full sentence.

➡ _____

_____

13 밑줄 친 (A)가 의미하는 것을 우리말로 쓰시오.

➡ _____

14 Where did the writer read My Wish? Answer in English with seven words.

➡ _____

15 According to the passage, what was Kim Koo's third wish? Answer in English with a full sentence.

➡ _____

_____

구석구석

Real Life Talk Step 3

My group members chose An Junggeun because we were impressed by his
<u>choose의 과거형(choose–chose–chosen)</u>   <u>~에 깊은 인상을 받았다</u>

sacrifice for the country. You can learn more about him by visiting the An
     by+Ving: V함으로써

Junggeun Museum or An Junggeun Park.

구문해설 · choose: 선택하다 · sacrifice: ~을 희생하다

해석
우리 그룹은 안중근을 선택했는데, 우리 나라를 위한 희생에 깊은 인상을 받았기 때문입니다. 여러분은 안중근 기념관이나 안중근 공원을 방문함으로써 그에 관하여 더 많은 것을 알 수 있습니다.

Enjoy Writing

Dosan An Changho

An Changho was born in 1878. When he was in his teens, he moved to Seoul

and went to school there. In 1902, he left for America so that he could get
    = in Seoul   '목적' ~하기 위해서 = in order that he could

a better education. In America, An helped improve the lives of the Korean
      = helped to improve   life의 복수형

people there and became a respected leader. After he had returned to Korea, he
<u>people there = people (who were) there</u>   <u>과거완료시제</u>

founded the New Korean Society in 1907 to fight for Korea's independence.

He also joined the Government of the Republic of Korea in Shanghai in 1919.
     타동사(전치사 불필요)

After that, he built a lot of schools to educate people until he died in 1938.
      부사적 용법(목적) = so that he could educate   접속사('~할 때까지')

구문해설 · in one's teens: 10대 시절에 · respected: 존경받는 · the New Korean Society: 신민회
· republic: 공화국

도산 안창호
안창호는 1878년에 태어났다. 그가 십 대였을 때, 그는 서울로 이사를 하고 그곳에서 학교를 다녔다. 1902년에 그는 더 나은 교육을 받기 위해서 미국으로 떠났다. 안창호는 미국에서 한국인들의 삶을 개선하는 것을 도왔고, 존경받는 지도자가 되었다. 그가 한국으로 돌아오고 나서, 그는 대한의 독립을 위해 싸우고자 1907년에 신민회를 설립했다. 그는 또한 1919년에 상해의 대한민국 임시정부에 합류했다. 그 후에, 그는 1938년에 죽을 때까지 사람들을 교육하기 위해 많은 학교들을 세웠다.

Project Step 1

A: I want to introduce Bulguksa to foreigners. You know Bulguksa, don't you?
      일반동사 긍정문의 부가의문문

B: Yes, I do. It's a temple in Gyeongju.
   = Bulguksa

C: Yes. It's one of the most beautiful temples in Korea.
     one of the 최상급+복수명사: 가장 ~한 것들 중 하나

D: It also has many treasures like the Dabotop.
     many+복수명사   전치사: ~와 같은

구문해설 · introduce: 소개하다 · foreigner: 외국인 · temple: 사원, 절 · treasure: 보물

A: 나는 외국인에게 불국사를 소개하고 싶어. 너는 불국사를 알고 있지, 그렇지 않니?

B: 응, 알고 있어. 그것은 경주에 있는 절이야.

C: 응. 그것은 한국에서 가장 아름다운 절 중 하나야.

D: 그것은 또한 다보탑과 같은 많은 문화재들을 보유하고 있어.

영역별 핵심문제

01 다음 주어진 두 단어의 관계가 같도록 빈칸에 알맞은 단어를 쓰시오.

> independence - dependence : exit - _____

02 다음 문장의 빈칸 (A)와 (B)에 들어갈 단어가 바르게 짝지어진 것은?

> • I want to work for international (A) _____ such as the UN.
> • There is no love without (B) _____.

① harmony – rule
② statue – dependence
③ specialist – desire
④ leader – member
⑤ organization – sacrifice

[03~04] 다음 영영풀이에 해당하는 것을 고르시오.

03

> a piece of cloth that is usually attached at the end of a pole and represents a country or association

① hall ② exhibition
③ flag ④ tomb
⑤ god

04

> a series of things that happen one after another for a particular result

① process ② republic
③ wish ④ president
⑤ poem

05 다음 빈칸에 주어진 철자를 이용하여 한 단어를 쓰시오.

> The museum is staging an e_____ of Picasso's works.

06 다음 밑줄 친 부분의 뜻이 잘못된 것은?

① The main part of the building is crowded with people. (주요한)
② Koreans celebrate Independence Day on August 15th. (독립)
③ The government made a new policy. (정부)
④ He had no desire to discuss the matter further. (안건)
⑤ The queen wears a crown only on certain official events. (왕관)

07 다음 대화의 빈칸에 들어갈 말을 주어진 어구를 알맞은 순서로 배열하여 완성하시오.

> G: I'm planning to go to the Gansong Museum.
> B: What is the Gansong Museum?
> G: It's a museum built by Gansong Jeon Hyeongpil.
> B: I heard that he did great things for the country.
> G: Yes. _____
> _____
> B: Wow. The museum must be interesting.
> G: Yes. I'm looking forward to it!

> some Japanese / many Korean treasures / he / had taken / bought / that / to Japan

08 그림을 보고 다음 대화의 빈칸을 완성하시오.

G: I'm making a model of the Turtle Ship. _____ _____ about it, _____ you?

B: Yes, I know about it.

[09~11] 다음 대화를 읽고 물음에 답하시오.

Andy: Bora, what are you reading?

Bora: I'm reading *Sky, Wind, Star, and Poetry* by Yun Dongju. You know about Yun Dongju, don't you?

Andy: I've heard his name, but I don't know much about him. (①)

Bora: He wrote many beautiful poems when Korea was under Japanese rule. His love for the country and his desire for independence can be felt in his poems.

Andy: (②) I want to read his poems and learn more about him.

Bora: Great. (③) In fact, I'm planning to visit the Yun Dongju Museum soon. Do you want to come with me?

Andy: Yes, when are you going?

Bora: Next Saturday. It's near Gyeongbok Palace. (④) Can you meet me at the palace at 2 p.m.?

Andy: Sure. Let's meet there. (⑤)

Bora: Great. I'm really looking forward to the visit.

09 위 대화의 (①)~(⑤) 중 주어진 문장이 들어갈 위치로 알맞은 것은?

Really? I didn't know that.

① ② ③ ④ ⑤

10 위 대화를 읽고 다음 물음에 영어로 답하시오.

Q: What are they planning to do next Saturday?

➡ _____

11 위 대화의 내용과 일치하지 않는 것은?

① Bora is reading a poem by Yun Dongju.

② Andy doesn't know much about Yun Dongju.

③ Bora suggested to Andy that he should read many poems by Yun Dongju.

④ Bora may have felt Yun Dongju's love for the country and his desire for independence.

⑤ Andy is looking forward to visiting the Yun Dongju Museum.

Grammar

[12~13] 다음 중 어법상 어색한 문장을 고르시오.

12 ① Would you share your recipe so that we can make a good dish like yours?

② Sam learned the computer science so as to develop much better devices.

③ Prepare rice and water so that you can make Juk, the Korean porridge.

④ Tim got up early so as not to miss the bus.

⑤ Isabelle practiced hard so that for her to get a scholarship.

13
① All my family were really full because we had had lunch.

② Betty had read comic books before she went to bed.

③ Yesterday, my wife lost the necklace that my son had bought for her two days before.

④ When the singer arrived at the show, the opening part had just began.

⑤ Susan wasn't able to recognize him, because she had never seen him before.

14 다음 두 문장의 의미가 같도록 바꿔 쓸 때 적절하지 <u>않은</u> 것은?

① Jenny cleaned the house so that the guests could feel comfortable.

= Jenny cleaned the house for the guests to feel comfortable.

② Robert makes pancakes in order that his five kids can eat.

= Robert makes pancakes so that his five kids can eat.

③ The young college students held the thief tight so that he could not run away.

= The young college students held the thief tight in order not for him to run away.

④ Nancy practiced her movement really hard in order to pass the audition.

= Nancy practiced her movement really hard so that she might pass the audition.

⑤ Daeho went to Tokyo so that he could learn Japanese.

= Daeho went to Tokyo in order to learn Japanese.

15 다음 그림을 보고 괄호 안의 단어를 배열하여 빈칸을 알맞게 채우시오.

(1)

➡ The students are practicing hard _____ _____ _____ _____ _____ a good performance. (show, so, can, they, that)

(2)

➡ Many tourists gathered at the Louvre Museum _____ _____ _____ _____ _____ _____. (the *Mona Lisa*, they, that, so, could, see)

16 다음 괄호 안에서 어법상 알맞은 것을 고르시오.

(1) An Junggeun was sentenced to death after he (had killed / has killed) Ito Hirobumi.

(2) Some of the K-pop fans around the world said that they (have been / had been) learning Korean to understand the lyrics of the songs clearly.

(3) Yesterday I learned that Kim Koo (had made / made) a plan to kill Japanese generals in Shanghai in 1932.

(4) The queen (has gone / had gone) to London before the prince got injured at the car accident.

(5) Sven dropped the carrot that Olaf (had pulled / has pulled) out of the field in the snow.

17 다음 그림을 참고하여 〈보기〉에 주어진 어구를 우리말과 일치하도록 어법상 알맞은 형태로 바꿔 배열하시오. (모든 단어를 한 번 이상 사용할 것.)

┌─ 보기 ─┐

the rabbit, the ant, the grasshopper, she, he, regretted, reminded, play, sleep, in, that, the middle of, the summer, the race

(1) 토끼는 경주 도중에 잤던 것을 후회했다.
(2) 개미는 베짱이가 여름에 놀았던 것을 일깨워줬다.

(1)

➡ _____

_____

(2)

➡ _____

_____

Reading

[18~20] 다음 글을 읽고 물음에 답하시오.

Last week my history club went to Hyochang Park. ① At the entrance of the museum, we saw a white statue of Kim Koo. ② Kim Koo is a great national hero who spent most of his life fighting for the independence of Korea from Japanese rule. ③ In the 1900s, he helped educate young people by building schools. ④ In 1919,

when the independence movement had spread throughout the country, he moved to Shanghai, China. ⑤ There he joined the Government of the Republic of Korea and later became its president.

18 ①~⑤ 중 주어진 문장이 들어가기에 가장 적절한 곳은?

> We visited the Kim Koo Museum inside the park.

①   ②   ③   ④   ⑤

19 Write the reason why Kim Koo built schools. Use the phrase 'in order to.'

➡ _____

_____

20 다음 중 위 글의 내용과 일치하는 것은?

① The history club went to Hyochang Park a couple of weeks ago.
② The statue of Kim Koo is at the entrance of the park.
③ Kim Koo spent most of his life educating young people.
④ The independence movement spread throughout the country until 1900s.
⑤ Kim Koo joined the Government of the Republic Korea in China.

[21~24] 다음 글을 읽고 물음에 답하시오.

An Changho was born in 1878. When he was in his teens, he moved to Seoul and went to school there. In 1902, he left for America ①so that he could get a better education. In America,

An helped ②improve the lives of the Korean people there and became a ③respecting leader. After he ④had returned to Korea, he founded the New Korean Society in 1907 to fight for Korea's independence. He also joined the Government of the Republic of Korea in Shanghai in 1919. After that, he built a lot of schools ⑤to educate people until he died in 1938.

21 ①~⑤ 중 문맥상 바르지 <u>않은</u> 것은?

①   ②   ③   ④   ⑤

22 다음 중 위 글의 내용과 일치하지 <u>않는</u> 곳을 찾아 바르게 고쳐 쓰시오.

> An Changho was born in Korea and left for America in his twenties. After spending some time in America, he returned to Korea and found the New Korean Society in 1907 in order to fight for Korea's independence.

➡ _____

23 다음 중 위 글을 읽고 답할 수 <u>없는</u> 것은?

① When was An Changho born?
② When did An Changho leave for America?
③ What did An Chanho do in America?
④ How many schools did An Changho build?
⑤ What did An Changho do until he died?

[24~26] 다음 글을 읽고 물음에 답하시오.

The exhibition hall in the museum shows (A) a lot of things about Kim Koo's life. While looking around the hall, we stopped at a photo of the Korean Patriotic Organization's members. Kim Koo formed the secret organization in 1931 to fight against Japan. Lee Bongchang and Yun Bonggil belonged to the group. At one place in the hall, we saw two watches under a photo of Kim Koo and Yun Bonggil. In 1932, Kim Koo made a plan to kill Japanese generals in a park in Shanghai. As the leader of the Korean Patriotic Organization, he directed Yun to carry out the mission.

24 다음 중 밑줄 친 (A)를 대신하여 쓰일 수 <u>없는</u> 것은?

① lots of   ② many
③ a number of   ④ the number of
⑤ plenty of

25 According to the passage, when did Kim Koo form the Korean Patriotic Organization?

➡ _____
_____

26 According to the passage, choose the sentence that is TRUE.

① The Korean Patriotic Organization was a public organization.
② Kim Koo formed an organization to fight for Japan.
③ Lee Bongchang was the only member of the Korean Patriotic Organization.
④ Kim Koo planned to kill Japanese generals in a park in Korea.
⑤ Kim Koo directed Yun Bonggil to kill Japanese generals.

01 다음 짝지어진 단어의 관계가 같도록 빈칸에 알맞은 말을
쓰시오.

> complete – incomplete : deep – _____

02 다음 영영풀이에 해당하는 단어는?

> a circular ornament made of gold and
> decorated with jewels that is worn by a
> king or queen on their head

① device   ② clown

③ crown   ④ couch

⑤ hall

[03~04] 다음 대화를 읽고 물음에 답하시오.

B: Soyeon, what did you do last weekend?

G: I went to Hyeonchungwon to do volunteer
work.

B: What kind of volunteer work did you do
there?

G: I cleaned around the tombs. (A)나는 나라를
위해 돌아가신 분들에게 대단한 경의를 느꼈어.

B: Sounds great. Can I do it, too?

G: Sure. I'm planning to go there again next
Wednesday. Will you join me?

B: Sure. I'm looking forward to it.

03 위 대화의 밑줄 친 (A)의 우리말에 맞게 주어진 어구를 알맞
은 순서로 배열하시오.

> I / for the country / who / felt / for the
> people / died / great respect

➡ _____

_____

04 위 대화의 내용과 일치하지 <u>않는</u> 것은?

① Soyeon did volunteer work in the
museum.

② Soyeon felt respect while doing
volunteer work.

③ Soyeon cleaned around the tombs.

④ Soyeon is planning to go there again
next Wednesday.

⑤ Both Soyeon and the boy will go to
Hyeonchungwon together.

[05~06] 다음 대화를 읽고 물음에 답하시오.

G: Brian, you know Taegeukgi, don't you?

B: Sure. It's the national flag of Korea, isn't it?

G: That's right. (A)_____

B: No, I don't. Tell me about them.

G: The circle in the middle means (B) _____
and peace.

B: What do the black lines on the four corners
mean?

G: They mean four things: sky, fire, water, and
earth.

05 위 대화의 빈칸 (A)에 들어갈 말로 알맞은 것은?

① What do you know about Taegeukgi?

② Can you draw Taegeukgi?

③ Do you know the origin of Taegeukgi?

④ Do you know what the symbols in
Taegeukgi mean?

⑤ Do you know who made Taegeukgi?

06 위 대화의 빈칸 (B)에 들어갈 단어를 〈영영풀이〉를 참고하여 쓰시오.

<영영풀이>

a situation in which people are peaceful and agree with each other, or when things seem right or suitable together

➡ _____

[07~08] 다음 대화를 읽고 물음에 답하시오.

Andy: Bora, what are you reading?

Bora: I'm reading *Sky, Wind, Star, and Poetry* by Yun Dongju. (A)너는 윤동주에 대해 알고 있지, 그렇지 않니?

Andy: I've heard his name, but I don't know much about him.

Bora: He wrote many beautiful poems when Korea was under Japanese rule. His love for the country and his desire for independence (B)can feel in his poems.

Andy: Really? I didn't know that. I want to read his poems and learn more about him.

Bora: Great. In fact, I'm planning to visit the Yun Dongju Museum soon. Do you want to come with me?

Andy: Yes, when are you going?

Bora: Next Saturday. It's near Gyeongbok Palace. Can you meet me at the palace at 2 p.m.?

Andy: Sure. Let's meet there.

Bora: Great. I'm really looking forward to the visit.

07 위 대화의 밑줄 친 (A)에 맞게 주어진 단어를 활용하여 영작하시오.

about, Yun Dongju

➡ _____

08 위 대화의 밑줄 친 (B)를 알맞은 형태로 고친 것은?

① can feel
② can to be felt
③ can felt
④ can be feeling
⑤ can be felt

09 대화의 밑줄 친 (A)를 문법적으로 맞게 고쳐 쓰시오.

G: I'm planning to go to the Gansong Museum.

B: What is the Gansong Museum?

G: (A)It's a museum was built by Gansong Jeon Hyeongpil.

B: I heard that he did great things for the country.

G: Yes. He bought many Korean treasures that some Japanese had taken to Japan.

B: Wow. The museum must be interesting.

G: Yes. I'm looking forward to it!

➡ _____
_____
_____

10 다음 각 빈칸에 공통으로 들어갈 단어 중 나머지 넷과 성격이 **다른** 하나는?

① Please turn the light on _____ that we can find the way out.

② Eddy hurried _____ that he wouldn't miss the plane Susan was in.

③ The police officer talked louder _____ that the old lady could understand.

④ Will and Ben woke up early _____ that they could see their daddy off.

⑤ Jacob was _____ busy that he couldn't join our party.

11 다음 〈보기〉의 문장과 같은 뜻이 되도록 각 괄호 안의 주어진 조건에 맞게 빈칸을 채우시오. (출제율 95%)

┌─ 보기 ─┐
Paula had to read the textbook many times so that she would not forget the contents.
└─────┘

(1) Paula had to read the textbook many times _____ the contents.
(to부정사의 부사적 용법 활용, 3 단어)

(2) Paula had to read the textbook many times _____ the contents.
(so as 활용, 5 단어)

(3) Paula had to read the textbook many times _____ she would not forget the contents. (in 활용, 3 단어)

12 다음 중 어법상 올바른 문장을 모두 고르면? (출제율 100%)

① The grass looked greener than before because it had rained last week.

② Sandy heard that the manager has overworked the day before.

③ Yuna's husband was surprised that she has been elected as a chairwoman.

④ The first period began when I had arrived at the court.

⑤ Jonathan returned the book which he had borrowed from the library.

13 다음 문장의 빈칸 (a)~(d)에 들어갈 말을 〈보기〉에서 골라 순서대로 나열한 것은? (출제율 95%)

┌──────────────┐
• Vicky plays classical music to her son every day (a)_____.
• Kate has been practicing 500 shots a day for the past 4 years (b)_____.
• Taylor returned all of the overdue books to the library (c)_____.
• Clara stopped eating junk food (d) _____.
└──────────────┘

┌─ 보기 ─┐
(A) so that he wouldn't be fined
(B) so that she could become healthier
(C) so that he can be a great musician
(D) so that she can win the gold medal
└─────┘

① (A)-(B)-(C)-(D)　② (A)-(C)-(D)-(B)
③ (B)-(D)-(A)-(C)　④ (C)-(D)-(A)-(B)
⑤ (C)-(A)-(B)-(D)

[14~16] 다음 글을 읽고 물음에 답하시오.

Last week my history club went to Hyochang Park. We visited the Kim Koo Museum inside the park. At the entrance of the museum, we saw a white statue of Kim Koo. Kim Koo is a great national hero ①who spent most of his life ②fight for the independence of Korea from Japanese rule. In the 1900s, he helped ③educate young people by building schools. In 1919, when the independence movement ④had spread throughout the country, he moved to Shanghai, China. There he ⑤joined the Government of the Republic of Korea and later became its president.

14 ①~⑤ 중 어법상 바르지 않은 것은? (출제율 95%)

①　　②　　③　　④　　⑤

15 주어진 단어를 활용하여 다음 물음에 답하시오. 필요하다면 어휘를 변형하시오. (출제율 90%)

┌──────────────┐
Q: What did Kim Koo do in the 1900s?
(build / to / help)
└──────────────┘

➡ _____

16 다음 중 위 글을 읽고 답할 수 있는 것은?

① Where is Hyochang Park?
② How did they get to Hyochang Park?
③ What is there inside Hyochang Park?
④ Who made the statue of Kim Koo?
⑤ How did Kim Koo build schools?

[17~19] 다음 글을 읽고 물음에 답하시오.

An Changho was born in 1878. ① When he was in his teens, he moved to Seoul and went to school there. ② In America, An helped improve the lives of the Korean people there and became a respected leader. ③ After he had returned to Korea, he founded the New Korean Society in 1907 to fight for Korea's independence. ④ He also joined the Government of the Republic of Korea in Shanghai in 1919. ⑤ After that, he built a lot of schools to educate people until he died in 1938.

17 ①~⑤ 중 주어진 문장이 들어가기에 가장 적절한 곳은?

In 1902, he left for America so that he could get a better education.

①   ②   ③   ④   ⑤

18 According to the passage, what did An Changho do until he died in 1938? Answer in English with a full sentence.

➡ _____

_____

19 다음 중 위 글의 내용과 일치하지 <u>않는</u> 것은?

① An Changho was born in the late 1800s.
② An Changho went to school in Seoul.
③ People in America respected An Changho.
④ An Changho didn't return to Korea again.
⑤ It was An Changho who founded the New Korean Society in 1907.

[20~21] 다음 글을 읽고 물음에 답하시오.

At one place in the hall, we saw two watches under a photo of Kim Koo and Yun Bonggil. In 1932, Kim Koo made a plan (A)<u>to kill</u> Japanese generals in a park in Shanghai. As the leader of the Korean Patriotic Organization, he directed Yun to carry out (B) <u>the mission</u>.

20 다음 중 밑줄 친 (A)와 쓰임이 같은 것은?

① We went into the building <u>to meet</u> them.
② Is there any chance <u>to see</u> you again?
③ It was impossible <u>to get</u> there on time.
④ <u>To make</u> it delicious, I added some sugar.
⑤ He must be generous <u>to give</u> you his watch.

21 밑줄 친 (B)가 의미하는 것을 위 글에서 찾아 우리말로 쓰시오.

➡ _____

01 다음 대화를 읽고 '수원 화성'에 대한 요약문을 완성하시오.

> B: Look at Suwon Hawseong. It's huge.
> G: It also looks strong.
> B: Because it was built to protect the people during wars.
> G: Wow. Do you know who built it?
> B: Yes. King Jeongjo ordered Jeong Yakyong to direct the building process. You know about Jeong Yakyong, don't you?
> G: Yes, I've heard of him. He was a great scientist in Joseon.

➡ Suwon Hwaseong _____ the people during wars. Jeong Yakyong _____ its _____.

02 다음 그림을 보고, 내용에 맞게 〈보기〉에서 알맞은 단어를 하나씩 선택하여 ⓐ~ⓕ의 빈칸에 어법상 알맞은 형태로 써 넣으시오. (A)의 빈칸에는 〈보기〉에 없는 단어 두 개를 이용하여, 내용과 어법에 맞게 써 넣으시오.

> ┤ 보기 ├
> like   allow   complete   burn
> use   disappoint

> The principal ⓐ_____ us ⓑ_____ the cooking studio in our school when the exam was over. Half an hour ago, before Annie and I ⓒ_____ the chocolate pie, it ⓓ_____ up. I was so ⓔ_____. I just wanted to give David

> delicious food (A)_____ he could ⓕ _____ me.

03 다음 중에서 틀린 문장을 찾아 기호를 쓰고, 바르게 고쳐 문장을 다시 쓰시오.

① The secretary said she had already finished her work before noon.
② The young politician was tired because he had played soccer the day before.
③ Shane refused to go to the theater as he had already watched the movie.
④ I had found out that she lost her bag.
⑤ The repairman said that someone had broken the toilet cover.

➡ _____

04 다음 우리말로 제시한 세 문장을 영작할 때, 〈보기〉의 어구를 사용하여 빈칸에 알맞게 써 넣으시오. (중복 사용 불가)

> ┤ 보기 ├
> could / my uncle / in order to / had / it / so that / warm / bought / show / my body / which

(1) 나는 내 몸을 덥힐 수 있도록 뜨거운 커피를 주문했다.
  ➡ I ordered hot coffee _____ _____.

(2) 우리집 반려동물 토토가 삼촌이 나를 위해 사줬던 스커트를 물어뜯었다.
  ➡ My pet Toto bit off the skirt _____ _____ for me.

(3) 세호는 어머니에게 보여드리기 위해서 춤 동작들을 연습했다.
  ➡ Seho practiced the dance movements _____ them to his mom.

An Changho was born in 1878. When he was in his teens, he moved to Seoul and went to school there. (A)In 1902, he left for America so that he could get a better education. In America, An helped improve the lives of the Korean people there and became a respected leader. After he had returned to Korea, he founded the New Korean Society in 1907 to fight for Korea's independence. He also joined the Government of the Republic of Korea in Shanghai in 1919. After that, he built a lot of schools to educate people until he died in 1938.

05 빈칸에 알맞은 말을 써서 밑줄 친 (A)와 같은 의미의 문장을 완성하시오.

> = In 1902, he left for America _____
> _____ _____ get a better
> education.
> = In 1902, he left for America _____
> get a better education.

06 Write the reason why An Changho founded the New Korean Society in 1907. Answer in English with eight words.

➡ _____

_____

07 What did An Changho do in America? Answer in Korean.

➡ _____

After completing the tour of the museum, we moved to the tombs of the three heroes, Lee Bongchang, Yun Bonggil, and Baek Jeonggi. Their bodies had been in Japan, but after Korea's independence Kim Koo brought them to Hyochang Park. By doing so, he showed his deep love and respect for the sacrifice of the three heroes.

As I left Hyochang Park, I thought about Kim Koo's words in My Wish that I had read in the exhibition hall. (A)It was written in *Baekbeomilji*.

If God asks me what my wish is, I would say clearly, "It is Korea's Independence." If he asks me what my second wish is, I would say, "It is the independence of my country." If he asks me what my third wish is, I would say loudly, "It is the complete independence of my country." That is my answer.

08 밑줄 친 (A)가 가리키는 것을 위 글에서 찾아 쓰시오.

➡ _____

09 Where are the tombs of the three heroes now? Answer in English with five words.

➡ _____

10 위 글의 내용에 맞도록 주어진 단어 중에서 골라 빈칸에 알맞게 쓰시오.

> (inspire / desire / love / crisis)

> Kim Koo's words in My Wish make us feel his _____ for the independence of Korea and his _____ for the country.

01 다음은 독도에 관한 사실이다. 이 사실을 아는지 묻는 표현을 〈보기〉처럼 쓰시오.

- Dokdo has two main islands and 89 small islands.
- Dokdo is windy and foggy.
- There is a rock on Dokdo that looks like Korea.

┤ 보기 ├

A: You know that Dokdo has two main islands and 89 small islands, don't you?
B: Yes, I heard about it.

02 다음 그림과 각 그림에 주어진 단어들을 활용하여, so that을 사용한 문장을 어법에 맞게 자유롭게 영작하시오.

(passing, rescue, shout, cry, (birds, look, watch, observe,
boat, ship, yell, help)   telescope, tool)

(1) _____
(2) _____

03 김좌진 장군에 대한 대화문을 참고하여 다음 글을 완성하시오.

Q: When was he born?
A: He was born in 1889.
Q: Who was he?
A: He was a Korean general who fought against Japanese rule.
Q: What did he do to defeat Japan?
A: He gathered and trained soldiers.
Q: How did his efforts turn out to be?
A: His efforts paid off at Cheongsanri, where his soldiers earned one of their greatest victories against Japan.

Kim Jwajin was born in Hong Seong _____. He was a Korean general _____. When Korea was under Japanese rule, he _____ _____ to defeat Japan. His efforts paid off at Cheongsanri, _____ _____.

단원별 모의고사

01 다음 단어에 대한 영어 설명이 <u>어색한</u> 것은?

① desire: a strong wish or feeling

② treasure: what is highly valued

③ look forward to: to feel pleased and excited about something that is going to happen

④ mission: any work that someone believes it is their duty to do

⑤ state: a sculptured figure of a person, animal, etc. in bronze, stone, wood, etc.

02 다음 짝지어진 단어의 관계가 같도록 빈칸에 알맞은 말을 쓰시오.

> educate – teach : reign – _____

03 다음 영영풀이에 해당하는 단어를 고르시오.

> to place a dead body in the ground, to put something in the ground and cover it

① bury   ② spread   ③ kill

④ mean   ⑤ direct

04 다음 중 짝지어진 대화가 <u>어색한</u> 것은?

① A: Do you remember our plan to go to the War Memorial?

  B: Sure. I'm looking forward to going there.

② A: What kind of volunteer work did you do there?

  B: I cleaned around the tombs.

③ A: I'm planning to go to the Gansong Museum.

  B: What is the Gansong Museum?

④ A: Have you ever heard about An Junggeun?

  B: No, I haven't. He was an independence activist.

⑤ A: I'm planning to visit the Hangeul Museum next week. Do you want to join me?

  B: I'd love to. I'm looking forward to visiting there.

[05~06] 다음 대화를 읽고 물음에 답하시오.

B: Tomorrow let's put on traditional Korean clothes, hanbok, and go to Insadong.

G: Good, but I want to buy gifts for my friends in Germany tomorrow.

B: In Insadong, there are many gift shops.

G: Great. After shopping, what should we eat for lunch?

B: Hmm. (A)_____

G: No. What is it?

B: It's a traditional Korean soup. It's delicious and will make you healthy.

G: Sounds good. (B)<u>I'm looking forward to trying it.</u>

05 위 대화의 빈칸 (A)에 들어갈 말로 알맞지 <u>않은</u> 것은? (2개)

① Have you ever heard about Samgyetang?

② Do you know how to cook Samgyetang?

③ You know Samgyetang, don't you?

④ Why don't you eat Samgyetang?

⑤ Did you hear about Samgyetang?

06 위 대화의 밑줄 친 (B)와 같은 의미가 되도록 'die'를 이용하여 기대의 표현을 쓰시오.

➡ _____

[07~08] 다음 대화를 읽고 물음에 답하시오.

Andy: Bora, what are you reading?

Bora: I'm reading *Sky, Wind, Star, and Poetry* by Yun Dongju. (a)<u>You know about Yun Dongju, don't you?</u>

Andy: I've heard his name, but I don't know much about him.

Bora: He wrote many beautiful poems (b)<u>when Korea was under Japanese rule.</u> His love for the country and his desire for independence can be felt in his poems.

Andy: Really? I didn't know (c)<u>that</u>. I want to read his poems and learn more about him.

Bora: Great. In fact, (d)<u>I'm planning to visit the Yun Dongju Museum soon.</u> Do you want to come with me?

Andy: Yes, when are you going?

Bora: Next Saturday. It's near Gyeongbok Palace. Can you meet me at the palace at 2 p.m.?

Andy: Sure. Let's meet there.

Bora: Great. (e)<u>I'm really looking forward to the visit.</u>

07 위 대화의 밑줄 친 (a)~(e)에 대한 설명 중 잘못된 것은?

① (a): 상대방이 알고 있는지 물어보는 표현이다.

② (b): '한국이 일본의 통치하에 있을 때'의 뜻으로 'when'은 부사절 접속사다.

③ (c): 지시대명사로 앞 문장의 '나라에 대한 그의 사랑과 독립에 대한 염원이 그의 시에서 느껴진다'는 문장을 대신한다.

④ (d): 미래의 계획을 말하는 표현으로 'be going to+동사원형' 구문을 이용하여 바꿔 쓸 수 있다.

⑤ (e): 앞으로 하고 싶은 일에 대한 기대를 표현하는 것으로 'to' 다음에는 명사나 동사원형이 와야 한다.

08 위 대화를 읽고 답할 수 없는 질문은?

① What is Bora reading?

② Who wrote the poem *Sky, Wind, Star, and Poetry*?

③ What can be felt through Yun Dongju's poems?

④ How many poems does Bora want to read?

⑤ What are they planning to do next Saturday?

09 다음 대화의 빈칸 (A)와 (B)에 공통으로 들어갈 말로 알맞은 것은?

G: I'm planning to go to the Gansong Museum.

B: What is the Gansong Museum?

G: It's a museum built by Gansong Jeon Hyeongpil.

B: I heard (A)_____ he did great things for the country.

G: Yes. He bought many Korean treasures (B)_____ some Japanese had taken to Japan.

B: Wow. The museum must be interesting.

G: Yes. I'm looking forward to it!

① that   ② what

③ which   ④ who

⑤ when

10 다음 대화의 (A)와 (B)가 가리키는 것을 제시된 단어 수에 맞게 찾아 쓰시오.

G: Brian, you know Taegeukgi, don't you?

B: Sure. It's the national flag of Korea, isn't it?

G: That's right. Do you know what the symbols in Taegeukgi mean?

B: No, I don't. Tell me about (A)them.

G: The circle in the middle means harmony and peace.

B: What do the black lines on the four corners mean?

G: (B)They mean four things: sky, fire, water, and earth.

➡ (A) _____ (4 단어)

(B) _____ (3 단어)

[11~12] 다음 대화를 읽고 물음에 답하시오.

(A)

B: Look at Suwon Hawseong. It's huge.

G: It also looks strong.

B: Because it (1)_____ to protect the people during wars.

G: Wow. Do you know who (2)_____ it?

B: Yes. King Jeongjo ordered Jeong Yakyong to direct the building process. (a) _____ Jeong Yakyong, don't you?

G: Yes, I've heard of him. He was a great scientist in Joseon.

(B)

G: I'm planning to go to the Gansong Museum.

B: What is the Gansong Museum?

G: It's a museum (3)_____ by Gansong Jeon Hyeongpil.

B: I heard that he did great things for the country.

G: Yes. He bought many Korean treasures that some Japanese had taken to Japan.

B: Wow. The museum must be interesting.

G: Yes. (b)_____ to it!

11 위 대화의 빈칸 (1)~(3)에 'build'를 활용하여 알맞게 써 넣으시오.

➡ (1)_____ (2)_____ (3)_____

12 위 대화 (A)의 빈칸 (a)는 '알고 있는지 묻는 표현'을, (B)의 빈칸 (b)는 '기대, 희망'을 나타내는 표현을 각각 쓰시오.

➡ (a)_____ (b) _____

13 다음 주어진 우리말을 영작한 것으로 옳지 않은 것은?

Bradley는 부자가 되기 위해 밤낮으로 일했다.

① Bradley worked day and night so as to become rich.

② Bradley worked day and night in order that he became rich.

③ Bradley worked day and night so that he could become rich.

④ Bradley worked day and night to be rich.

⑤ Bradley worked day and night in order to be rich.

14 다음 두 문장을 한 문장으로 만들 때 빈칸에 들어갈 말로 가장 알맞은 것은?

• There was a yellow dust storm all day long.

• The cars were covered with thick dust.

→ The cars were covered with thick dust because _____.

① there is a yellow dust storm all day long

② there has come a yellow dust storm all day long

③ there has been a yellow dust storm all day long

④ there had been a yellow dust storm all day long

⑤ there had been being a yellow dust storm all day long

15 다음 중 밑줄 친 부분의 쓰임이 나머지 넷과 다른 것은?

① Smith will send you his phone number so that you can contact him anytime.

② Frank hurried to the radio station so that he wouldn't be late for the program.

③ Minju did her best so that her research team could find another galaxy.

④ Dave answered loudly, so that the teacher heard him clearly.

⑤ John turned off the radio so that his wife could focus on the book better.

16 다음 각 그림을 보고, 주어진 어구를 알맞게 배열하여 영작하되, 과거완료시제를 반드시 포함하시오. (동사는 변형 가능)

(1) Pinocchio, the goddess, say, lie, that

➡ _____

(2) Pooh, the hive, after, touch, by bees, be stung, he

➡ _____

[17~18] 다음 글을 읽고 물음에 답하시오.

Last week my history club went to Hyochang Park. We visited the Kim Koo Museum inside the park. At the entrance of the museum, we saw a white statue of Kim Koo. Kim Koo is ① a great national hero who spent most of his life ②fighting for the independence of Korea from Japanese rule. In the 1900s, he helped ③educate young people by building schools. In 1919, when the independence movement had spread throughout the country, he ④moved to Shanghai, China. There he ⑤left the Government of the Republic of Korea and later became its president.

17 위 글의 내용과 일치하지 않는 것은?

① The writer is a member of the history club.

② The Kim Koo Museum is located in Hyochang Park.

③ There was a time when Korea was ruled by Japan.

④ Kim Koo lived in Korea all his life.

⑤ The Government of the Republic of Korea was in Shanghai.

18 ①~⑤ 중 글의 흐름상 어색한 것은?

①　　　②　　　③　　　④　　　⑤

[19~22] 다음 글을 읽고 물음에 답하시오.

The exhibition hall in the museum shows a lot of things about Kim Koo's life. While looking around the hall, we stopped at a photo of the Korean Patriotic Organization's members. Kim Koo formed the secret organization in 1931 to fight against Japan.

Lee Bongchang and Yun Bonggil belonged to the group. At one place in the hall, we saw two watches under a photo of Kim Koo and Yun Bonggil. In 1932, Kim Koo made a plan to kill Japanese generals in a park in Shanghai. As the leader of the Korean Patriotic Organization, he directed Yun to (A) carry out the mission.

When Yun left for the mission, he told Kim, "(B)Sir, you are wearing a very old watch. Mine is new, but I won't need it anymore. Please take my watch, and let me have yours." Kim Koo always carried Yun's watch in his jacket so that he would not forget Yun's sacrifice.

19 Choose the sentence that is TRUE about the Korean Patriotic Organization.

① It was founded by Lee Bongchang.

② It was an open organization.

③ It was formed in 1932.

④ Its purpose was to fight against Japan.

⑤ Yun Bonggil didn't know about the organization.

20 다음 중 밑줄 친 (A)를 대신하여 쓰일 수 있는 것은?

① ignore   ② perform

③ introduce   ④ practice

⑤ threat

21 다음 중 윤봉길이 밑줄 친 (B)와 같이 말한 이유로 가장 적절한 것은?

① his interest in Kim Koo's old watch

② his firm opinion to buy a new watch

③ his strong will to devote his life to the mission

④ his deep respect fot Kim Koo

⑤ his natural spirit of helping other people

22 According to the passage, what does the exhibition hall show?

➡ _____

[23~24] 다음 글을 읽고 물음에 답하시오.

An Changho was born in 1878. When he was in his teens, he moved to Seoul and went to school there. In 1902, he left for America so that he could get a better education. In America, An helped improve the lives of the Korean people there and became a respected leader. After he had returned to Korea, he founded the New Korean Society in 1907 to fight for Korea's independence. He also joined the Government of the Republic of Korea in Shanghai in 1919. After that, he built a lot of schools to educate people until he died in 1938.

23 위 글의 내용에 맞게 주어진 문장을 바르게 나열하시오.

> ⓐ He returned to Korea.
>
> ⓑ He joined the Government of the Republic of Korea.
>
> ⓒ He went to America to get a better education.
>
> ⓓ He founded the New Korean Society.
>
> ⓔ He studied in Seoul.
>
> ⓕ He became a respected leader by helping people in America.

➡ _____

24 What did An Changho do in order to fight for Korea's independence? Answer in English with a full sentence.

➡ _____

_____

MEMO

Lesson 6

Meet the World

의사소통 기능

- 주제 소개하기
  Let's talk about food.
- 제안하기 · 권유하기
  I suggest you visit Independence Hall.

언어 형식

- '계속적 용법'의 관계대명사 which/who
  Someone uses the word kiwi, **which** has several meanings.
- '부사적 용법'의 to부정사
  If you say "kia ora" to the villagers, they will be **glad to hear** it.

Words & Expressions

Key Words

- **abroad**[əbrɔ́ːd] 부 해외에(서), 해외로
- **achieve**[ətʃíːv] 동 달성하다, 성취하다
- **activity**[æktívəti] 명 활동
- **amaze**[əméiz] 동 (대단히) 놀라게 하다
- **appreciate**[əpríːʃièit] 동 진가를 알아보다, 인정하다
- **carry**[kǽri] 동 가지고 가다
- **clearly**[klíərli] 부 명확하게
- **color**[kʌ́lər] 동 칠하다
- **common**[kámən] 형 흔한
- **confused**[kənfjúːzd] 형 (사람이) 혼란스러워 하는
- **culture**[kʌ́ltʃər] 명 문화
- **European**[jùərəpíən] 명 유럽인
- **experience**[ikspíəriəns] 동 겪다, 경험하다
- **hill**[hil] 명 언덕
- **hot spring** 온천
- **information**[ìnfərméiʃən] 명 정보
- **kiwi**[kíːwi] 명 키위, 키위새, 뉴질랜드인
- **landscape**[lǽndskeip] 명 풍경
- **main**[mein] 형 주요한, 주된
- **Maori**[máuri] 명 마오리인(뉴질랜드 원주민), 마오리어
- **match**[mætʃ] 명 경기, 시합
- **native**[néitiv] 형 (특정한 곳의) 토박이의
- **natural**[nǽtʃərəl] 형 자연의, 천연의
- **New Zealander** 뉴질랜드 사람
- **nickname**[níknèim] 명 별명

- **people**[píːpl] 명 (특정 국가 지역의) 국민[민족/종족]
- **plaid**[plæd] 명 격자무늬, 격자무늬 천
- **potluck**[pátlək] 명 각자 준비한 음식을 나눠먹는 식사
- **recommend**[rèkəménd] 동 추천하다
- **return**[ritə́ːrn] 동 돌아오다[가다]
- **rival**[ráivəl] 명 경쟁자, 경쟁 상대
- **rugby**[rʌ́gbi] 명 럭비
- **several**[sévərəl] 형 몇몇의
- **society**[səsáiəti] 명 (공동체를 이루는 일반적인) 사회
- **someday**[sʌ́mdei] 부 언젠가, 언제든, 훗날
- **station**[stéiʃən] 명 [흔히 합성어에서] 방송국
- **success**[səksés] 명 성공, 성과
- **suggest**[səgdʒést] 동 제안하다
- **surely**[ʃúərli] 부 확실히, 분명히
- **symbol**[símbəl] 명 상징, 상징물
- **throughout**[θruːáut] 전 도처에
- **traditional**[trədíʃənl] 형 전통적인
- **trail**[treil] 명 자취, 오솔길
- **twin**[twin] 형 쌍둥이의 명 쌍둥이 (중의 한 명)
- **view**[vjuː] 명 (특히 아름다운 시골) 경관, 전망
- **village**[vílidʒ] 명 마을, 부락, 촌락
- **waterfall**[wɔ́tərfɔl] 명 폭포
- **wedding**[wédiŋ] 명 결혼(식)
- **wildly**[wáildli] 부 걷잡을 수 없이, 극도로

Key Expressions

- **a couple of** 두서너 개의, 몇 개의
- **all year round** 일 년 내내
- **be covered with** ~으로 덮이다
- **be famous for** ~로 유명하다
- **be glad to** ~하게 되어 기쁘다
- **be known as** ~로 알려져 있다
- **come to one's mind** 생각이 나다, 생각이 떠오르다
- **filled with** ~로 가득 찬

- **long before** 훨씬 이전에
- **look forward to** ~을 기대하다
- **look like** ~처럼 보이다
- **prepare for** ~을 준비하다
- **take a bike tour** 자전거 여행을 하다
- **take a photo of** ~의 사진을 찍다
- **try on** (옷을) 입어보다
- **with the help of** ~의 도움을 받아서

Word Power

※ 서로 비슷한 뜻을 가진 어휘
- □ **abroad** 해외에(서), 해외로 – **overseas** 해외에
- □ **achieve** 달성하다 – **accomplish** 성취하다
- □ **amaze** 놀라게 하다 – **astonish** 놀라게 하다
- □ **clearly** 명확하게 – **certainly** 확실하게
- □ **landscape** 풍경 – **scenery** 경치

- □ **main** 주요한, 주된 – **major** 주된
- □ **rival** 경쟁자, 경쟁 상대 – **competitor** 경쟁자
- □ **suggest** 제안하다 – **propose** 제안하다
- □ **surely** 확실히 – **clearly** 명확하게
- □ **wildly** 걷잡을 수 없이 – **madly** 격렬하게

※ 서로 반대되는 뜻을 가진 어휘
- □ **common** 흔한 ↔ **uncommon** 흔치 않은
- □ **natural** 자연의, 천연의 ↔ **artificial** 인위적인

- □ **confused** 혼란스러워 하는 ↔ **calm** 침착한, 냉정한
- □ **success** 성공, 성과 ↔ **failure** 실패

※ 형용사 – 명사
- □ **confused** 혼란스러워 하는 – **confusion** 혼란
- □ **natural** 자연의, 천연의 – **nature** 자연
- □ **successful** 성공적인 – **success** 성공, 성과

- □ **symbolic** 상징적인 – **symbol** 상징, 상징물
- □ **traditional** 전통적인 – **tradition** 전통

※ 동사 – 명사
- □ **achieve** 성취하다 – **achievement** 성취
- □ **act** 행동하다 – **activity** 활동
- □ **appreciate** 진가를 알아보다 – **appreciation** 평가

- □ **inform** 알려주다 – **information** 정보
- □ **recommend** 추천하다 – **recommendation** 추천
- □ **succeed** 성공하다 – **success** 성공, 성과

English Dictionary

- □ **abroad** 해외에(서), 해외로
  → in or to a foreign country
  외국에 있거나 외국으로 가는

- □ **achieve** 달성하다, 성취하다
  → to successfully complete something or get a good result
  성공적으로 일을 완수하거나 좋은 결과를 얻다

- □ **common** 흔한
  → happening often and to many people or in many places
  많은 사람에게 또는 많은 장소에서 자주 일어나는

- □ **kiwi** 키위새
  → a New Zealand bird that cannot fly
  날 수 없는 뉴질랜드의 새

- □ **Maori** 마오리인
  → someone who belongs to the race of people that first lived in New Zealand
  뉴질랜드에 처음 살았던 종족에 속하는 사람

- □ **plaid** 격자무늬
  → a pattern of crossed of lines and squares
  십자 모양의 선과 사각형으로 된 무늬

- □ **potluck** 각자 준비한 음식을 나눠먹는 식사
  → a meal in which everyone who is invited brings something to eat
  초대받은 모든 사람들이 먹을 무언가를 가지고 오는 식사

- □ **rugby** 럭비
  → an outdoor game played by two teams with an oval(= egg-shaped) ball
  타원형의 공을 가지고 두 팀이 하는 야외 경기

- □ **symbol** 상징, 상징물
  → a picture or shape that has a particular meaning or represents a particular organization or idea
  의미를 가지거나 조직, 사상을 나타내는 그림이나 모양

- □ **trail** 오솔길
  → a rough path across countryside or through a forest
  시골을 가로지르거나 숲을 지나가는 거친 길

01 다음 문장의 빈칸에 공통으로 들어갈 말로 알맞은 것은?

- This cloth is made from _____ fibers.
- Mt. Bugak impresses visitors with both its stunning _____ beauty and cultural assets.

① exhibition ② entrance
③ natural   ④ poem
⑤ specialist

02 〈영영풀이〉를 읽고 빈칸에 알맞은 단어를 쓰시오.

Wearing safety gear, including helmets and _____ pads, is also advised.

┌─영영풀이─
the joint where your leg bends
└

[03~04] 다음 설명에 해당하는 단어를 고르시오.

03

in or to a foreign country

① aboard   ② broad
③ station   ④ abroad
⑤ board

04

happening often and to many people or in many places

① main   ② common
③ sure   ④ confused
⑤ traditional

05 다음 우리말에 맞게 빈칸에 세 단어를 쓰시오.

푸른 잔디로 뒤덮였던 서울 광장이 붉은색 테니스 코트로 변했다.

➡ Seoul Plaza, which used to _____ _____ _____ green lawn, has turned into a tennis court in red.

06 다음 빈칸에 들어갈 말이 바르게 짝지어진 것은?

(A) She _____ the four judges and got a YES from all of them.
(B) They _____ music composed by Johann Bach, George Handel, and Antonio Vivaldi.

	(A)	(B)
①	amazed	recommend
②	amazed	color
③	achieved	experience
④	achieved	recommend
⑤	returned	suggest

07 다음 짝지어진 단어의 관계가 같도록 빈칸에 알맞은 말을 쓰시오.

landscape – scenery : propose – _____

08 다음 빈칸에 들어갈 가장 알맞은 말은?

I will _____ receiving a nice birthday present from you!

① look like   ② carry on
③ be famous for ④ belong to
⑤ look forward to

01 다음 빈칸에 들어갈 말을 〈보기〉에서 찾아 쓰시오. (필요하면 어형을 변화시키고, 동사는 현재형으로 쓸 것)

┌─ 보기 ┤
| landscape   fill   suggest   appreciate |

(1) He hopes to make the world a better place _____ with healthy people.

(2) Professor Achor _____ that you see the good, positive things in your life.

(3) The event teaches children to _____ all types of art.

(4) New Zealand is a country well-known for its breathtaking _____ and abundant wildlife.

02 다음 문장의 빈칸에 들어갈 알맞은 단어를 쓰시오.

| The Niagara Falls are the most popular _____ s in North America. |

03 다음 우리말과 같은 표현이 되도록 문장의 빈칸을 채우시오.

(1) 이제, 서울 도처에 추위를 피할 수 있는 도피처들이 생겨나고 있다.
➡ Now, some refuges from the cold are popping up _____ Seoul.

(2) 주의 깊은 설명을 들은 후에도, 우리는 여전히 혼란스럽다.
➡ Even after some careful explanation, we are still left _____.

(3) 그 경기는 독일의 골로 거칠게 시작되었다.
➡ The match started _____ with a goal from Germany.

(4) 그들은 온천에서 목욕을 하면서 눈을 감고 있습니다.
➡ They are closing their eyes while bathing in a _____.

04 다음 영영풀이에 해당하는 단어를 〈보기〉에서 찾아 첫 번째 빈칸에 쓰고, 두 번째 빈칸에는 우리말 뜻을 쓰시오.

┌─ 보기 ┤
| rival   length   north   wedding |

(1) _____ : the measurement of something from one end to the other end: _____

(2) _____ : the direction on your left when you are looking at the sunrise: _____

(3) _____ : a person who is competing for the same object or goal as another: _____

(4) _____ : a marriage ceremony and any celebrations such as a meal or a party that follow it: _____

05 빈칸에 'tradition'을 이용하여 알맞은 형태를 쓰시오.

| • Korea is a beautiful country with a wonderful culture and unique _____ s.
• It's the _____ way to "fight the heat with heat." |

Conversation

1 주제 소개하기

> • **Let's talk about food.** 음식에 관해 이야기해 봅시다.

■ 'Let's talk about ~.(~에 대하여 이야기해 봅시다.)'는 주제를 소개하는 표현이다. 이야기하고 싶은 주제를 소개할 때는 'I'd like to talk about ~.(~에 대하여 이야기하고 싶어요.)'라고 할 수도 있지만 'would like to' 대신에 'will', 'want to' 등을 사용하여 'Today, I will talk about ~.', 'I want to talk about ~.'라고 할 수도 있다.

■ 원하는 무엇인가를 하려고 할 때 'I'd like to ~.'라고 한다. 지금부터 상대에게 새로운 주제를 소개하려고 할 때는 '~에 대하여 말씀드리겠습니다.'라는 의미로 'I'd like to talk about ~.', 'I'd like to say something about ~.', 'I'd like to tell you ~.'라고 한다. 그 외에 주제를 소개하는 다른 표현으로 'I'm going to talk about ~.', 'Let me tell you about ~.', 'May I tell you about ~?', 'I'd like to introduce ~.' 등이 있다.

■ 상대에게 격식을 차려서 주제를 소개할 때는 'I'd like to give a presentation about ~.' 또는 'I'd like to give you an introduction about ~.'라고 할 수도 있다. '~에 대해서 말하자면 ~'이라는 뜻으로 'Speaking of ~, 주어+동사 ~.', 'Talking of ~, 주어+동사 ~.'와 같은 표현을 사용하기도 한다.

주제 소개하기

• Let's talk about ~.	~에 대하여 이야기해 봅시다.
• I'd like to say something about ~.	~에 대하여 이야기하고 싶어요.
• I'd like to talk about ~.	~에 대하여 말씀드리겠습니다.
• I'd like to tell you ~.	~에 대하여 말씀드리겠습니다.
• I want to talk about ~.	~에 대하여 말씀드리고 싶습니다.

핵심 Check

1. 밑줄 친 우리말과 일치하도록 주어진 단어를 포함하여 영작하시오.

> G: Brian, <u>세계 음식 축제를 위해서 우리가 무엇을 준비할지 이야기해 봅시다.</u> (let's, prepare, the World Food Festival, talk)
>
> B: I will make a meat pie. It is famous in Australia. How about you, Sera?
>
> G: I want to make a popular English dish, fish and chips.
>
> B: Fish and chips? What does it look like?
>
> G: It's fried fish with hot potato chips.
>
> B: That sounds interesting. Let's prepare them.

➡ _____

2 제안하기 · 권유하기

• **I suggest (that) we learn yoga.** 나는 요가를 배우자고 제안합니다.

- 'I suggest we ~.'는 상대방에게 무언가를 같이 하자고 제안하거나 권유할 때 쓰는 표현이다. 동사 'suggest(제안하다)' 다음에는 명사절을 이끄는 접속사 'that'이 생략되고 'that'절에서는 조동사 'should' 를 쓰는데, 이를 생략하고 동사원형을 사용하여 'I suggest (that)+주어+(should)+동사원형 ~.'의 구문 으로 나타낸다.
- 'suggest'를 이용한 표현은 'suggest+that (should)절' 이외에도 'suggest+-ing', 'suggest+wh-절', 'suggest+wh- to do' 등으로 나타내기도 한다. 한편 'suggest'가 '암시하다, 시사하다, 말하다' 등의 의미 로 제안의 의미가 아닌 경우에는 that절에 should를 사용하지 않는다.
- 제안이나 권유를 나타내는 유사한 표현으로 'Let's ~.(~하자.)', 'had better(~하는 편이 낫다)', 'Why don't you/we ~?(~하는 것이 어때?)', 'May I suggest that ~?(~하는 것이 어떠세요?)' 등이 있다. 'How about'과 'What about'은 'How about 명사/~ing?(~는 는 어때?)', 'What about 명사/~ing?(~하는 것이 어때?)'의 형태로 쓰며 상대에게 제안이나 권유하는 의미와 함께 상대의 의견을 물어보는 의미로도 사용한다.

제안이나 권유하기

- I suggest (that) 주어+(should)+동사원형 ~. (~하자고 제안한다.)
- You had better+동사원형 ~. (~하는 편이 낫다.)
- (I think) You should/ought to+동사원형 ~. (~해야 한다고 생각해.)
- Why don't you/we ~? (~하는 것이 어때?)
- Would you like (me) to ~? (~하기를 원하세요?)

제안이나 권유에 답하기

〈긍정〉 (That) Sounds good. / No problem.
〈부정〉 I'm afraid I can't (learn yoga). / Thank you, but I don't want to (learn yoga).

핵심 Check

2. 다음 빈칸에 주어진 단어를 적절한 형태로 쓰시오.

> **B:** Wow, we finally arrived in Hong Kong, Mom.
>
> **W:** I'm looking forward to our visit. What should we do today, Mike?
>
> **B:** I suggest we _____ (visit) Victoria Peak.

Listen & Speak 1 A-1

B: ❶Let's talk about traditional clothing from other countries.

G: Hmm... Do you know ❷what a kilt is?

B: No, I don't. What is it?

G: It is traditional clothing from Scotland. ❸It looks like a knee-length skirt and has a plaid pattern.

B: A skirt of knee length with a plaid pattern?

G: Yes. It is unique because it is a skirt for men.

B: ❹That sounds interesting. I want to try one on.

B: 다른 나라의 전통 의상에 대해 이야기해 보자.

G: 흠… 너는 킬트가 뭔지 아니?

B: 아니, 몰라. 그게 뭐야?

G: 킬트는 스코틀랜드의 전통 의상이야. 그건 무릎길이의 치마 같이 생겼고, 체크무늬가 있어.

B: 무릎길이의 체크무늬 치마라고?

G: 응. 킬트는 남자를 위한 치마이기 때문에 특이해.

B: 흥미롭게 들린다. 나는 킬트를 입어보고 싶어.

❶ 'Let's talk about ∼.(∼에 대하여 이야기해 봅시다.)'는 주제를 소개하는 표현이다.
❷ 동사 'know'의 목적어로 '의문사(what)+주어(a kilt)+동사(is)' 어순의 간접의문문이다.
❸ 'look like+명사'는 '∼처럼 보이다'라는 뜻이고, and 뒤의 has는 단수동사 'looks'와 병렬 관계이다.
❹ 'sound+형용사' 형태로 '∼하게 들리다'로 해석한다.

Check(√) True or False

(1) They are talking about a kilt.

T ☐ F ☐

(2) A kilt is a skirt for women.

T ☐ F ☐

 Listen & Speak 2 A-1

B: Wow, we finally arrived in Hong Kong, Mom.

W: ❶I'm looking forward to our visit. What should we do today, Mike?

B: ❷I suggest we visit Victoria Peak.

W: Victoria Peak?

B: It is the highest mountain in Hong Kong and is in a lot of movies. We can enjoy the fantastic view.

W: That sounds good. Let's go.

B: 와, 엄마, 우리가 마침내 홍콩에 도착했어요.

W: 우리가 방문할 곳들이 기대된다. 오늘 우리는 무엇을 해야 하니, Mike?

B: 저는 우리가 빅토리아 피크에 가는 것을 제안해요.

W: 빅토리아 피크?

B: 빅토리아 피크는 홍콩에서 가장 높은 산이고, 영화에도 많이 나왔어요. 우리는 환상적인 경관을 즐길 수 있어요.

W: 그거 좋겠구나. 가 보자.

❶ 'look forward to+명사/동명사'는 '∼을 기대하고 있다'라는 의미이다.
❷ 'I suggest we ∼.'는 상대방에게 무언가를 같이 하자고 제안하거나 권유할 때 쓰는 표현이다. 동사 'suggest(제안하다)' 다음에는 명사절을 이끄는 접속사 'that'이 생략되고 'that'절에서는 조동사 'should'를 쓰는데, 이를 생략하고 동사원형을 사용하여 'I suggest (that)+주어+(should)+동사원형 ∼.'의 구문으로 나타낸다.

Check(√) True or False

(3) Mike and his mother are traveling to Hong Kong.

T ☐ F ☐

(4) Victoria Peak is the highest mountain in Hong Kong.

T ☐ F ☐

Listen & Speak 1 A-2

G: Brian, let's talk about ❶what we will prepare for the World Food Festival.

B: I will make a meat pie. It is famous in Australia. How about you, Sera?

G: ❷I want to make a popular English dish, fish and chips.

B: Fish and chips? ❸What does it look like?

G: It's fried fish with hot potato chips.

B: That sounds interesting. Let's prepare them.

❶ 전치사 'about'의 목적어로 '의문사+주어+동사' 어순의 간접의문문이다.
❷ 'want'는 to부정사를 목적어로 취하고, 'English dish'와 'fish and chips'는 동격 관계이다.
❸ '어떻게 생겼니?'의 의미로 '사물의 모습'이나 '사람의 외모'를 물어볼 때 사용하는 표현이다.

Listen & Speak 2 A-2

G: My American friend invited me to a potluck dinner next Friday.

B: You know, you should take food ❶to share at the dinner.

G: What would you recommend ❷that I take?

B: ❸I suggest you take some Korean food. How about Gimbap, Suji?

G: Yes. It's not spicy and it's easy ❹to carry.

B: I think it'll be good for dinner.

❶ to부정사의 형용사적 용법으로 명사 'food'를 수식한다.
❷ 'that I take'는 동사 'recommend'의 목적어로 사용되었고, 'take' 앞에는 'should'가 생략되어 있다. What은 의문대명사로 take의 목적어이다.
❸ 'suggest' 뒤에 접속사 'that'이 생략되어 있고 'that'절의 해석이 '~해야 한다'일 때 '주어+should+동사원형'을 사용한다. 이때 'should'는 생략 가능하다.
❹ 형용사 'easy'를 수식하는 '부사적 용법'으로 '~하기에'로 해석한다.

Real Life Talk

Seho: Good morning.
Jessie, Andy: Hi, Seho.
Seho: I will visit my uncle in Philadelphia this winter. Can you tell me about the city?

Jessie: Sure. I was there a few years ago. First, ❶let's talk about food.

Seho: Okay. What food is Philadelphia famous for?

Jessie: ❷The most famous food in Philadelphia is the cheese steak sandwich. It is a big sandwich ❸filled with beef and melted cheese.

Seho: Good suggestion. I will try it. Are there any places ❹that are popular with tourists?

Andy: ❺I suggest you visit Independence Hall. It is very important in American history.

Seho: Wonderful. Thank you for the information.

Andy: My pleasure.

❶ 주제를 소개하는 표현이다. 이야기하고 싶은 주제를 소개할 때는 'I'd like to talk about ~.(~에 대하여 이야기하고 싶어요.)'라고 할 수도 있지만 'would like to' 대신에 'will', 'want to' 등을 사용하여 'Today, I will talk about ~.', 'I want to talk about ~.'라고 할 수도 있다.
❷ 'famous'의 최상급 형태로 'the most'를 사용한다.
❸ 'filled with beef and melted cheese.'는 명사 'a big sandwich'를 수식하는 과거분사 구문이다. 'sandwich'와 'filled' 사이에는 '주격 관계대명사 (which+)be동사(is)'가 생략되어 있다.
❹ 주격 관계대명사절로 선행사 'places'를 수식한다. 선행사가 복수명사인 'places'이기 때문에 주격 관계대명사 뒤의 동사는 복수동사 'are'를 사용한다.
❺ 'suggest' 뒤에 접속사 'that'이 생략되어 있고 'visit' 앞에는 조동사 'should'가 생략되어 있다.

Wrap Up

M: Welcome to Australia. The capital of Australia is Canberra. People speak English. Meat pie is a popular dish in Australia. Every year, ❶lots of tourists visit the Sydney Opera House and the beautiful beaches in Melbourne.

❶ 'lots of'는 'a lot of', 'plenty of'와 같은 의미로 '많은'의 뜻이다.

● 다음 우리말과 일치하도록 빈칸에 알맞은 말을 쓰시오.

Listen & Speak 1 A

1. B: _____ _____ about traditional clothing from _____ countries.

   G: Hmm... Do you know _____ _____ _____ _____ ?

   B: No, I don't. What is it?

   G: It is _____ _____ from Scotland. It _____ _____ a _____ skirt and has a _____ _____ .

   B: A skirt of knee length _____ a plaid pattern?

   G: Yes. It is _____ _____ it is a skirt for men.

   B: That sounds _____ . I want _____ _____ one _____ .

2. G: Brian, let's talk _____ what we will _____ for the World Food Festival.

   B: I will make a meat pie. It is _____ in Australia. How about you, Sera?

   G: I want to make a _____ English _____ , fish and chips.

   B: Fish and chips? _____ does it _____ _____ ?

   G: It's _____ fish _____ hot potato chips.

   B: That sounds _____ . _____ _____ them.

Listen & Speak 2 A

1. B: Wow, we finally _____ _____ Hong Kong, Mom.

   W: I'm _____ _____ _____ our visit. What should we do today, Mike?

   B: I _____ we _____ Victoria Peak.

   W: Victoria Peak?

   B: It is _____ _____ mountain in Hong Kong and is _____ _____ _____ movies. We can enjoy the _____ _____ .

   W: That _____ good. Lct's go.

해석

1. B: 다른 나라의 전통 의상에 대해 이야기해 보자.
   G: 흠… 너는 킬트가 뭔지 아니?
   B: 아니, 몰라. 그게 뭐야?
   G: 킬트는 스코틀랜드의 전통 의상이야. 그건 무릎길이의 치마같이 생겼고, 체크무늬가 있어.
   B: 무릎길이의 체크무늬 치마라고?
   G: 응. 킬트는 남자를 위한 치마이기 때문에 특이해.
   B: 흥미롭게 들린다. 나는 킬트를 입어보고 싶어.

2. G: Brian, 우리 세계 음식 축제에 무엇을 준비할 것인지 이야기해 보자.
   B: 나는 미트 파이를 만들 거야. 그건 호주에서 유명해. 너는 어때, 세라야?
   G: 나는 영국의 유명한 요리인 피시앤칩스를 만들고 싶어.
   B: 피시앤칩스? 그건 어떻게 생겼어?
   G: 그건 뜨거운 감자튀김이 곁들여진 튀긴 생선이야.
   B: 그거 흥미롭다. 우리 함께 그것들을 준비하자.

1. B: 와, 엄마, 우리가 마침내 홍콩에 도착했어요.
   W: 우리가 방문할 곳들이 기대된다. 오늘 우리는 무엇을 해야 하니, Mike?
   B: 저는 우리가 빅토리아 피크에 가는 것을 제안해요.
   W: 빅토리아 피크?
   B: 빅토리아 피크는 홍콩에서 가장 높은 산이고, 영화에도 많이 나왔어요. 우리는 환상적인 경관을 즐길 수 있어요.
   W: 그거 좋겠구나. 가 보자.

2. **G:** My American friend _____ me to a _____ dinner next Friday.

B: You _____, you should take food to _____ at the dinner.

G: What would you _____ _____ I take?

B: I _____ you _____ some Korean food. _____ about Gimbap, Suji?

G: Yes. It's not _____ and it's easy _____ _____.

B: I think it'll be good _____ dinner.

Real Life Talk

Seho: Good morning.

Jessie, Andy: Hi, Seho.

Seho: I will visit my uncle in Philadelphia this winter. _____ _____ _____ _____ _____ the city?

Jessie: Sure. I was there _____ _____ _____ _____. _____, _____ talk about food.

Seho: Okay. _____ _____ is Philadelphia _____?

Jessie: _____ _____ _____ food in Philadelphia is the cheese steak sandwich. It is a big sandwich _____ _____ beef and _____ cheese.

Seho: Good _____. I will try it. Are there any places _____ _____ _____ with tourists?

Andy: I _____ you visit _____ Hall. It is very important in American _____.

Seho: Wonderful. Thank you for the _____.

Andy: My _____.

Wrap Up

M: _____ to Australia. The _____ of Australia is Canberra. People speak English. Meat pie is a _____ _____ in Australia. Every year, _____ _____ tourists visit the Sydney Opera House and the beautiful _____ in Melbourne.

해석

2. G: 나의 미국인 친구가 다음 주 금요일에 있을 포틀럭 저녁 식사에 나를 초대했어.
   B: 네가 알다시피, 너는 저녁 식사에 함께 나눠 먹을 음식을 가지고 가야 해.
   G: 무엇을 가져갈지 추천해 줄래?
   B: 나는 네가 한국 음식을 가져가는 것을 추천해. 수지야, 김밥 어때?
   G: 그래. 김밥은 맵지도 않고, 들고 가기도 쉽겠다.
   B: 내 생각에는 김밥이 저녁 식사에 좋을 것 같아.

세호: 안녕.
Jessie, Andy: 안녕, 세호야.
세호: 나 이번 겨울에 필라델피아에 계신 삼촌을 뵈러 가. 너희들 나한테 그 도시에 대해 알려줄 수 있니?
Jessie: 물론이지. 난 몇 년 전에 거기에 갔었어. 먼저 음식에 대해 이야기해 보자.
세호: 좋아. 필라델피아는 어떤 음식이 유명해?
Jessie: 필라델피아에서 가장 유명한 음식은 치즈 스테이크 샌드위치야. 소고기와 녹인 치즈로 채워진 큰 샌드위치지.
세호: 멋진 제안이다. 먹어 볼게. 여행자들에게 인기 있는 장소가 있니?
Andy: 나는 네가 독립 기념관에 방문하는 것을 제안해. 그곳은 미국 역사에서 아주 중요해.
세호: 멋지겠다. 정보 고마워.
Andy: 천만에.

M: 호주에 온 것을 환영한다. 호주의 수도는 캔버라다. 사람들은 영어로 말한다. 고기 파이는 호주에서 인기 있는 음식이다. 매년 많은 관광객들이 시드니 오페라 하우스와 멜버른의 아름다운 해변을 방문한다.

01 우리말에 맞도록 문장의 빈칸에 알맞은 말을 쓰시오.

> 나는 네가 독립 기념관에 방문하는 것을 제안해.
>
> ➡ I _____ you _____ Independence Hall.

02 다음 대화의 빈칸에 들어갈 말로 알맞은 것은?

> A: _____
>
> B: I went to Jejudo with my family.

① I suggest we learn more about Jejudo.
② I'd like to talk about my experiences.
③ I'm not quite sure if you know about Jejudo.
④ Let's talk about travel experiences.
⑤ I'd like to tell you what this island is.

03 다음 대화의 빈칸에 들어갈 말로 <u>어색한</u> 것은?

> A: What can we do if we visit India?
>
> B: _____
>
> A: That's a good idea.

① I suggest we visit the Taj Mahal.
② I suggest we visit there.
③ I suggest we eat different kinds of curry.
④ I suggest we try on some traditional clothing.
⑤ I suggest we learn yoga.

04 다음 대화의 밑줄 친 부분의 의도로 알맞은 것은?

> A: <u>Let's talk about school life in Canada.</u>
>
> B: Students start a new school year in September.

① 권유하기   ② 알고 있는지 묻기
③ 관심 표현하기   ④ 의도 묻기
⑤ 주제 소개하기

[01~02] 다음 대화를 읽고 물음에 답하시오.

Seho: Good morning.

Jessie, Andy: Hi, Seho.

Seho: I will visit my uncle in Philadelphia this winter. (A)_____

Jessie: Sure. I was there a few years ago. First, let's talk about food.

Seho: Okay. What food is Philadelphia famous for?

Jessie: The most famous food in Philadelphia is the cheese steak sandwich. It is a big sandwich filled with beef and melted cheese.

Seho: Good suggestion. I will try it. Are there any places that are popular with tourists?

Andy: I suggest you visit Independence Hall. It is very important in American history.

Seho: Wonderful. Thank you for the information.

Andy: My pleasure.

01 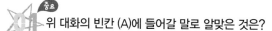 위 대화의 빈칸 (A)에 들어갈 말로 알맞은 것은?

① Are you going to visit there, too?

② Let's talk about food in the UK.

③ What should we do in Philadelphia?

④ What would you recommend that I take?

⑤ Can you tell me about the city?

02 위 대화의 내용과 일치하지 <u>않는</u> 것은?

① Seho will visit his uncle in Philadelphia.

② The cheese steak sandwich is the most famous food in Philadelphia.

③ They are talking about Philadelphia.

④ Independence Hall is Andy's favorite place.

⑤ Seho will probably eat the cheese steak sandwich in Philadelphia.

03 다음 대화의 (A)~(D)를 알맞은 순서로 배열한 것은?

G: My American friend invited me to a potluck dinner next Friday.

(A) I suggest you take some Korean food. How about Gimbap, Suji?

(B) What would you recommend that I take?

(C) You know, you should take food to share at the dinner.

(D) Yes. It's not spicy and it's easy to carry.

B: I think it'll be good for dinner.

① (A)–(C)–(B)–(D)   ② (B)–(A)–(D)–(C)

③ (C)–(B)–(A)–(D)   ④ (C)–(D)–(A)–(B)

⑤ (D)–(C)–(A)–(B)

04 다음 대화의 빈칸에 들어갈 말로 알맞은 것은?

A: _____

B: Students go to school at the age of five.

① I'm looking forward to going to school next week.

② Let's talk about school life in the UK.

③ I'd like to say something about students.

④ What time do students in the UK go to school?

⑤ I suggest that we go to school wearing a school uniform.

[05~06] 다음 대화를 읽고 물음에 답하시오.

> B: Let's talk about traditional clothing from other countries.
>
> G: Hmm... Do you know (a)what a kilt is?
>
> B: No, I don't. What is it?
>
> G: It is traditional clothing from Scotland. It looks like a knee-length skirt and (b)have a plaid pattern.
>
> B: A skirt of knee length (c)with a plaid pattern?
>
> G: Yes. It is unique (d)because it is a skirt for men.
>
> B: That sounds interesting. I want to (e)try one on.

서답형

05 위 대화를 읽고 다음 물음에 영어로 답하시오.

> Q: Why is a kilt unique?

➡ Because _____.

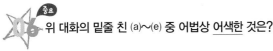

중요

06 위 대화의 밑줄 친 (a)~(e) 중 어법상 어색한 것은?

① (a) ② (b) ③ (c) ④ (d) ⑤ (e)

[07~08] 다음 대화를 읽고 물음에 답하시오.

> B: Wow, we finally arrived in Hong Kong, Mom.
>
> W: I'm looking forward to our visit. What should we do today, Mike?
>
> B: I suggest we visit Victoria Peak.
>
> W: Victoria Peak?
>
> B: (A)빅토리아 피크는 홍콩에서 가장 높은 산이고, 영화에 많이 나왔어요. We can enjoy the fantastic view.
>
> W: That sounds good. Let's go.

서답형

07 위 대화의 밑줄 친 (A)의 우리말에 맞게 주어진 단어를 알맞은 순서로 배열하여 쓰시오. (단어 하나를 추가하고, 필요시 변형하시오.)

> high / in / in Hong Kong / and / is / a lot of / mountain / movies

➡ It is _____

_____.

서답형

08 What will Mike and his mother do? Fill in the blanks with suitable words.

➡ They will _____ and _____ of Hong Kong.

중요

09 다음 짝지어진 대화 중 어색한 것은?

① A: Let's talk about the pose we will make for our picture.
  B: I think it will be good to show our teamwork in the pose.

② A: Let's talk about school life in Korea.
  B: Okay. What do you want to say about it?

③ A: The window is not clean.
  B: I suggest we should clean the window every Thursday.

④ A: Let's talk about which country we are going to look into.
  B: I'd love to, but I'm looking forward to visiting there.

⑤ A: What do you know about Australia?
  B: It is a big island on the southern part of the world.

[01~02] 다음 대화를 읽고 물음에 답하시오.

Seho: Good morning.

Jessie, Andy: Hi, Seho.

Seho: I will visit my uncle in Philadelphia this winter. Can you tell me about the city?

Jessie: Sure. I was there a few years ago. First, let's talk about food.

Seho: Okay. What food is Philadelphia famous for?

Jessie: The most famous food in Philadelphia is the cheese steak sandwich. It is a big sandwich filled with beef and melted cheese.

Seho: Good suggestion. I will try it. Are there any places that are popular with tourists?

Andy: (A)I suggest you visit Independence Hall. It is very important in American history.

Seho: Wonderful. Thank you for the information.

Andy: My pleasure.

01 What place is popular with tourists in Philadelphia? Answer in English with a full sentence.

➡ _____

02 위 대화의 밑줄 친 (A)를 관계대명사의 계속적 용법을 이용하여 한 문장으로 바꾸어 쓰시오.

➡ _____
_____

03 다음 대화의 빈칸 (A)에 들어갈 말을 〈조건〉에 맞게 쓰시오.

G: My American friend invited me to a potluck dinner next Friday.

B: You know, you should take food to share at the dinner.

G: What would you recommend that I take?

B: (A)_____ How about Gimbap, Suji?

G: Yes. It's not spicy and it's easy to carry.

B: I think it'll be good for dinner.

┤ 조건 ├
- 제안하는 표현을 사용할 것.
- 'suggest', 'some Korean food'를 사용할 것. (7 words)

➡ _____

04 밑줄 친 (A)의 우리말에 맞게 주어진 단어를 활용하여 영어로 쓰시오.

B: (A)다른 나라의 전통 의상에 대해 이야기해 보자. (let's / about / from / clothing)

G: Hmm... Do you know what a kilt is?

B: No, I don't. What is it?

G: It is traditional clothing from Scotland. It looks like a knee length skirt and has a plaid pattern.

B: A skirt of knee-length with a plaid pattern?

G: Yes. It is unique because it is a skirt for men.

B: That sounds interesting. I want to try one on.

➡ _____

Grammar

1 '계속적 용법'의 관계대명사 which / who

> • Someone uses the word kiwi, **which** has several meanings.
> 어떤 사람은 키위라는 단어를 사용하는데, 그것은 여러 가지 의미가 있다.
> • My uncle Roger, **who** was in the movie *Best Friends*, is a famous actor.
> 나의 삼촌 Roger는 영화 '절친한 친구'에 나왔고, 유명한 배우이다.

■ 계속적 용법은 형태상으로 콤마(,)를 쓰며, '선행사의 범위'가 비교적 자유롭다.

- Mike helped me with my work, **which** was too hard. (Mike는 내 일을 도와줬는데, 그 일은 너무 힘들었다.) − 선행사가 my work
- Mike helped me with my work, **which** helped me save some time. (Mike가 내 일을 도와줬는데, 그것은 내가 시간을 좀 절약하도록 도움이 되었다.) − 선행사가 앞 문장
- My baby puppy tried to feed herself, **which** I was proud of.
  = My baby puppy tried to feed herself, **and** I was proud of **that**. (나의 아기 강아지는 스스로 먹으려고 노력했는데, 나는 그것을 자랑스럽게 여겼다.) → 선행사는 앞 문장 전체(강아지가 스스로 노력한 일)이며, '접속사 and와 대명사 it/that'으로 받을 수 있다.

■ 계속적 용법의 관계대명사는 '접속사+대명사'로 전환 가능하다. (and, but, for, though 등)

- Sam bought a laptop, **which** was broken.
  = Sam bought a laptop, <u>**but it**</u> was broken. (Sam은 노트북 한 대를 구매했지만, 그것은 고장났다.)
- cf. Sam bought a laptop **which** was broken. (제한적: Sam은 고장 난 노트북 한 대를 구매했다.)
- Mom has been collecting a lot of used coins, **some of which** are rare and precious.
  = Mom has been collecting a lot of used coins, **and some of them** are rare and precious. (엄마는 많은 중고 동전들을 수집해 오고 계신데, 그 중에 어떤 것들은 진귀하다.)

■ that, what은 계속적 용법으로 쓸 수 없고, '전치사+관계대명사'는 관계부사로 바꿀 수 있다.

- Christine saw the house, **and** Van Gogh once lived **in it**. (Christine은 그 집을 봤는데, Van Gogh가 한 때 거기에서 살았다.)
  = Christine saw the house, **which** Van Gogh once lived **in**.
  = Christine saw the house, **in which** Van Gogh once lived.
  = Christine saw the house, **where** Van Gogh once lived.
  = Christine saw the house, **and** Van Gogh once lived **there**.

핵심 Check

1. 괄호 안에서 알맞은 단어를 고르시오.

   (1) Sumi studied hard, (that / which) helped her pass the test.
   (2) The teachers praised only Robert, (which / who) made his classmates jealous.
   (3) My family had lunch in a restaurant, (which / that) we liked very much.

② '부사적 용법'의 to부정사

- If you say "kia ora" to the villagers, they will be glad **to hear** it.
  네가 만약 마을 사람들에게 "kia ora"라고 말한다면, 그들은 그것을 듣고 기뻐할 것이다.

- Jane was pleased **to meet** her old friends. Jane은 오랜 친구들을 만나 기뻤다.

■ to부정사가 문장에서 주어, 목적어, 보어 등의 역할을 하면 명사적 용법, 명사를 수식하거나 be동사 뒤에서 보어 역할을 하면 형용사적 용법이다. 그 외의 to부정사는 부사적 용법으로 이해하면 된다.

- **To meet** her old friend is not possible. 그녀의 옛 친구를 만나는 것: 주어(명사적 용법)
- It is not possible for Jane **to meet** her old friend. 진주어(명사적 용법)
- Jane wants **to meet** her old friend. 목적어(명사적 용법)
- Jane's hope is **to meet** her old friend. 보어(명사적 용법)
- Jane told me a plan **to meet** her old friend. 명사 수식(형용사적 용법)
- Jane is **to meet** her old friend this evening. 보어(형용사적 용법)
- Jane wants to know **how to meet** her old friend. 의문사+to부정사(명사적 용법)

■ to부정사의 부사적 용법은 보통 해석에 따라 분류한다.

- 목적: Jane came **to meet** her old friend. (Jane은 그녀의 오랜 친구를 만나러 왔다.)
- 결과: Jane grew up **to meet** her old friend. (Jane은 자라서 그녀의 옛 친구를 만나게 되었다.)
- 원인, 이유: Jane was pleased **to meet** her old friend. (Jane은 그녀의 오랜 친구를 만나게 되어 기뻤다.)
- 판단의 근거: Jane must be pleased **to meet** her old friend. (Jane은 그녀의 오랜 친구를 만나서 기쁜 것임에 틀림없다.)
- 조건: Jane will be pleased **to meet** her old friend. (Jane이 그녀의 오랜 친구를 만난다면 기뻐할 것이다.)
- 형용사 수식: Jane's old friend is hard **to meet**. (Jane의 옛 친구는 만나기 어렵다.)
  cf. It is hard **to meet** Jane's old friend. (진주어, 명사적 용법)
- 부사 수식: Jane is not healthy enough **to meet** her old friend. (Jane은 옛 친구를 만날 수 있을 만큼 충분히 건강하지 않다.)

■ 숙어처럼 자주 쓰이는 to부정사의 부사적 용법 표현들

- be able to V: ~할 수 있다
- be willing to V: 기꺼이 ~하다
- be sure to V: 확실히 ~하다
- be eager to V: 몹시 ~하고 싶다
- be ready to V: ~할 준비가 되어 있다
- be reluctant to V: ~하기를 꺼리다
- be likely to V: ~할 것 같다
- be about to V: ~하려는 참이다

핵심 Check

2. 다음 우리말과 같은 뜻이 되도록 주어진 어구를 알맞게 배열하시오.

> 그는 파티에 초대되지 않아 슬펐다. (sad, to the party, be, not, was, he, invited, to)

➡ _____

Grammar 시험대비 기본평가

01 다음 문장을 바꿔 쓸 때 빈칸에 들어갈 말로 어법상 가장 적절한 것은?

> Mom bought Jane those books, and they influenced her so much.
> ➡ Mom bought Jane those books, _____ influenced her so much.

① who   ② whom   ③ which
④ that   ⑤ what

02 다음 중 밑줄 친 부분이 어법상 다른 하나는?

① Someone from Tokyo came here to see Robert.
② Tommy learned magic to make his wife pleased.
③ Sarah was happy to see the author of the book tonight.
④ My uncle must be a genius to solve the problem.
⑤ Jason wanted to see Ms. Smith yesterday.

03 다음 밑줄 친 부분을 바꿔 쓸 때 가장 알맞은 것은?

> Elizabeth likes the boy, who has recently changed his hair style.

① and it   ② for she   ③ him but
④ and he   ⑤ with him

04 다음 중 〈보기〉의 밑줄 친 부분과 같은 용법으로 쓰인 것을 고르시오.

> ┌─ 보기 ─
> Minsu was glad to learn the culture of the Maori.

① Andrew woke up early not to be late for school.
② Bonita went to the clinic to meet the doctor.
③ Harley planned to visit New Zealand for filming his movie.
④ Lucy can't be a fool to solve such a difficult problem.
⑤ Chris got nervous to think of meeting her father.

01 다음 중 어법상 어색한 것을 모두 골라 기호를 쓰고 알맞게 고치시오.

ⓐ A lot of kiwi fruit is grown in New Zealand, which is known as the land of kiwi.

ⓑ Many students like the lecture of the professor Potter, that will never be boring.

ⓒ My aunt Mary, which was in the movie *Killers*, is a famous actress.

ⓓ Anne bought a parrot, which speak French.

ⓔ Everyone wants to know the way which Alice got employed by Google.

ⓕ That is the house, where Schubert lived in.

➡ _____

_____

_____

02 다음 중 밑줄 친 to부정사의 용법이 나머지 넷과 다른 것은?

① We spoke Maori <u>to please</u> the villagers.

② <u>To say</u> that he agreed with them, the Maori chief nodded.

③ Yesterday I planned <u>to invite</u> Maori friends to our base camp.

④ The Maori girl cannot be a fool <u>to say</u> so.

⑤ My family went to New Zealand <u>to visit</u> the Maori village.

03 다음 우리말에 맞게 주어진 단어를 빈칸에 알맞게 배열하시오.

마오리인들은, 그들에 대해 당신이 이미 들은 적이 있겠지만, 전쟁 춤으로 하카를 추기 시작했다.

➡ The Maori people, _____

_____, started doing the haka as a war dance.(have, about, who, heard, you, already)

04 다음 문장의 빈칸 (A)~(C)에 들어갈 말로 가장 적절한 것은?

• New Zealand is known for its natural beauty, __(A)__ has allowed a lot of famous movies to be made there.

• Sam's grandparents live in Wellington, __(B)__ is the capital of New Zealand.

• Don't become confused when someone uses the word kiwi, __(C)__ may want to mean some other things.

	(A)	(B)	(C)
①	which	who	which
②	who	who	who
③	that	who	which
④	that	which	who
⑤	which	which	who

05 다음 중 어법상 옳은 문장은?

① It is raining, that makes me stay all day long.

② The CEO announced that she would resign, who was shocking.

③ There is a closet by the door, of which is made of wood.

④ The books, which I borrowed from the library, were so touching.

⑤ Michael is a famous actor, who often come to eat Korean food.

[06~07] 다음 우리말을 영어로 바르게 옮긴 것은?

06
> 민주는 그 잔인한 장면을 보지 않기 위해 고개를 돌렸다.

① Minju didn't turn her head to see the cruel scene.

② Minju was turned her head to not see the cruel scene.

③ Minju turned her head to see not the cruel scene.

④ Minju turned her head to not see the cruel scene.

⑤ Minju turned her head not to see the cruel scene.

07
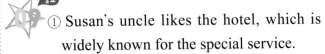
> 마을 사람들은 "키아 오라"라는 인사말을 들으면, 기뻐할 것이다.

① The villagers were glad to hear the word "kia ora."

② The villagers will be heard to say the word "kia ora."

③ The villagers do feel glad to hear the word "kia ora."

④ The villagers will be glad to hear the word "kia ora."

⑤ The villagers will be glad to be heard the word "kia ora."

[08~09] 다음 중 어법상 <u>어색한</u> 문장은?

08
① I had my car fixed by my uncle, who saved me a lot of money.

② My students helped the blind cross the street, who had trouble walking fast.

③ The audience gave the singer a big hand, which was impressive.

④ There was an airplane crash yesterday, which killed 93 people on board.

⑤ Sumi doesn't know where her phone is, which was on my table an hour ago.

09
① Susan's uncle likes the hotel, which is widely known for the special service.

② Bell invented the telephone, which made the people around the world comfortable to communicate.

③ The producer called the show's host, who didn't answer immediately.

④ I met my husband at the basketball court in 2019, which corona pandemic broke out.

⑤ The famous actor is going to move to Jeju island, where his first movie was filmed.

10 다음 그림을 보고 아래의 대화가 자연스럽게 이뤄지도록 주어진 단어를 모두 활용하여 문장을 완성하시오. (주어진 단어들 중 1 단어만 변형할 것.)

> Mom: Do you know why Mina goes to the park every day?
>
> Miju: _____
>
> (feed, she, to, the cats, there, go)

11

Haka dancers shout and move their bodies wildly to threaten their enemy.

① Please, don't forget to take an umbrella with you today!
② Robert woke up to find himself in a strange room.
③ New Zealanders felt happy to be called as kiwi.
④ Hojung went to Italy to study classical music.
⑤ It is not easy for me to master swimming as I don't have much time.

12

The enemy must be scared to watch the haka moves of the Maori warriors.

① Bob went to Egypt to see the Sphinx.
② Sunny grew up to be a famous singer.
③ Everyone was delighted to talk with the author of the popular books.
④ I think you are smart to solve the problem so easily and quickly.
⑤ We needed something to cover the baby cats.

[13~14] 다음 문장의 밑줄 친 부분과 쓰임이 다른 하나를 고르시오.

13

I searched the Internet to learn more about the kiwi birds.

① Susan stopped to watch who was following her.
② What does David do to be a robot engineer?

③ My sister went to the library to borrow a book.
④ Minsu was proud to meet his old friend who won the prize.
⑤ Plants need sunlight and water to live healthy.

14

The Maori people do the haka to scare the rival teams.

① There are a lot of beautiful places to visit in New Zealand.
② Jenny went to the playground to play badminton with her father.
③ Japanese businessmen came to my village to buy some furniture.
④ Kate met the researchers from UK to discuss the international cooperation.
⑤ My younger brother sang the songs to please the guests.

15 다음 중 어법상 올바른 문장의 개수는?

ⓐ The students helped the old man to cross the street, which was a rare thing nowadays.
ⓑ Mary purchased a scarf, who was very soft to touch.
ⓒ Susan met the lady living next door, and who had the washing machine fixed.
ⓓ Mike advised his sister to clean her desk, who was messy with books and pens.
ⓔ Hojun got hurt in the ankle, which was the reason he was late for the meeting.

① 1개   ② 2개   ③ 3개   ④ 4개   ⑤ 5개

01 다음 주어진 단어와 to부정사의 부사적 용법을 이용하여 우리 말에 맞게 영작하시오.

(1) 마오리인들은 적에게 겁을 주기 위해서 춤을 춘다. (scare, the Maori people, enemy)

➡ _____

(2) 돌고래들은 숨을 쉬기 위해 수면으로 올라온다. (come up, breathe, the surface)

➡ _____

(3) 그녀가 그 말을 믿다니 지혜롭지 않은 것임에 틀림없다. (the word, unwise, must)

➡ _____

(4) 뉴질랜드 원주민들이 그 말을 들으면, 기뻐할 것이다. (the native people, glad, hear)

➡ _____

(5) 지호의 방은 청소하기가 쉽지 않다. (easy, clean, not)

➡ _____

(6) 심청은 아버지를 다시 만나게 되어 기뻤다. (Simcheong, see, again, pleased, her father)

➡ _____

02 다음 문장을 관계대명사의 계속적 용법을 이용하여 한 문장으로 만드시오.

(1) • George Washington is widely known for the episode of his honesty.
• But it was not true.

➡ _____

(2) • Sumin fell in love with Brian.
• Brian met her only twice.

➡ _____
_____

(3) • The Maori people were so good at haka dancing.
• It made the visitors also dance with excitement.

➡ _____
_____

(4) • I added some more hot sauce into the food.
• It made my mom upset.

➡ _____
_____

03 다음 두 문장을 각각의 조건에 맞게, to부정사의 부사적 용법을 이용하여 한 문장으로 만드시오.

(1) • Jack walked to school.
• He had to save some money. (8 단어로)

➡ _____

(2) • Caroline exercises hard every day.
• She wants to lose weight. (8 단어로)

➡ _____

(3) • Potter was surprised.
• He watched the news. (7 단어로)

➡ _____

(4) • Angela woke up.
• She found herself alone in the dark. (10 단어로)

➡ _____

(5) • I am sure that Sam is happy.
• Sam meets her old friend. (조동사 must 를 반드시 사용, 9 단어로)

➡ _____

04 다음 그림을 보고, 우리말에 맞게 괄호 안의 단어를 활용하여 영작하시오.

지수의 부모님이 점심 시간에 급식 자원봉사를 해주셨는데, 그것이 그녀를 자랑스럽게 느끼도록 만들었다.
(Jisoo, her, to serve, feel, the meal, proud, make, volunteer, which 등을 사용할 것, 동사는 변형 가능, 총 14 단어)

➡ _____

_____

05 다음 주어진 문장을 to부정사의 부사적 용법을 사용하여 바꾸시오.

(1) My grandma exercises every day in order that she can keep healthy.

➡ _____

(2) She was pleased because she received thank-you notes from her neighbors.

➡ _____

(3) Sandra went to the river so that she could catch some fish.

➡ _____

(4) The stone was so heavy that I could not lift it.

➡ _____

(5) You need ice and sugar so that you can make Bingsu.

➡ _____

(6) It was impossible for Peter to solve the problem in an hour.

➡ _____

_____

(7) A lot of firefighters ran into the woods so that they could rescue the koalas.

➡ _____

_____

06 다음 각 문장에서 어법상 어색한 부분을 한 곳씩 찾아 모두 고치시오.

(1) My parents ordered my sister to meet the rich old man, that made her so depressed.

➡ _____

(2) The math teacher punished Tom for not paying attention, who made him feel sad.

➡ _____

(3) Amy made her first goal in soccer, who was very important to her.

➡ _____

07 다음 우리말을 조건에 맞게 영작하여 빈칸을 채우시오.

어제, 우리는 kiwi라는 단어를 배웠는데, 그 단어는 여러 가지 의미를 갖고 있다.
(the word kiwi, several, learn 사용, Yesterday를 포함, 10 단어로 영작할 것)

➡ Yesterday, _____

_____ .

Hello! New Zealand

New Zealand is a place of natural beauty. It has many beautiful lakes and waterfalls. New Zealand has two main islands, the South Island and the North Island. In the South Island, there are mountains that are covered with snow all year round. You will be amazed by the fantastic views.

In the North Island, there are many hot springs, lakes, and areas with green grass. Because of its natural beauty, many famous movies have been made in New Zealand. If you visit New Zealand, you will surely appreciate its nature.

When you hear the word kiwi, what comes to your mind? Maybe a fruit, but, in New Zealand the word kiwi has a couple of meanings. First, kiwi is the name of a delicious, green fruit. A lot of kiwi fruit is grown there, so New Zealand is known as the land of kiwi fruit.
Kiwi is also the name of one of New Zealand's native birds. The kiwi is special to New Zealanders because it is the symbol of the nation. Also, kiwi is a nickname for people from New Zealand. Today, New Zealanders are sometimes called Kiwis throughout the world.

---

natural: 자연의, 천연의
waterfall: 폭포
main: 주요한, 주된
amaze: (대단히) 놀라게 하다
view: 경관, 전망
be covered with: ~으로 덮이다
all year round: 일 년 내내
surely: 확실히, 분명히
appreciate: 진가를 알아보다, 인정하다
kiwi: 키위, 키위새, 뉴질랜드인
hot spring: 온천
a couple of: 두 서너 개의, 몇 개의
symbol: 상징, 상징물
throughout: 도처에
several: 몇몇의

 확인문제

● 다음 문장이 본문의 내용과 일치하면 T, 일치하지 <u>않으면</u> F를 쓰시오.

1 We can enjoy the natural beauty when we visit New Zealand. ☐

2 There are many areas with green grass in the South Island. ☐

3 Kiwi is the only bird which is native to New Zealand. ☐

4 People know New Zealand as the land of kiwi fruit. ☐

Now, you know that kiwi is the name of a fruit, a bird, and also a
명사절 접속사(know의 목적어를 이끎)
people. Next time, don't become confused when someone uses the
부정관사와 함께 쓰일 때는 '국민, 민족'이라는 의미   혼란을 느끼는 것이므로 과거분사
word kiwi, which has several meanings.
관계대명사의 계속적 용법(앞 문장이나 단어에 대한 부연 설명)

Now, let's talk about the Maori. They are the native people of New
Zealand. They went to live on the islands long before Europeans
The Maori 지칭   시간을 나타내는 접속사
arrived. The Maori culture is an important part of today's New Zealand
society. The Maori language is taught at some schools and there are
언어는 가르쳐 지는 것이므로 수동태
Maori language radio and TV stations. There are Maori villages in
many parts of the country. You can visit Maori villages and experience
가능을 나타내는 조동사   visit에 병렬 연결
Maori culture. If you say "kia ora" to the villagers, they will be glad to
조건의 부사절에서 현재시제로 미래를 대신함
hear it. It means "hi" in English.
to부정사의 부사적 용법 중 감정의 원인

Have you ever watched the haka? The haka may look scary because
경험을 묻는 현재완료   감각동사의 보어로 형용사
haka dancers shout and move their bodies wildly. The Maori people,
who you've already heard about, started doing the haka as a war
관계대명사의 계속적 용법   = to do   자격이나 기능을 나타내는 전치사(~으로)
dance. Today, however, New Zealanders do the haka at sport matches,
weddings, or other important events. For example, New Zealand's
national rugby team members do the haka before every match. It is
every+단수 명사
famous all over the world. If you see the haka, you will probably agree
that the rival team must be scared.
확실한 추측을 나타낼 때 쓰는 조동사(~임에 틀림없다)
Like the kiwi bird, the haka is a national symbol.
전치사(~처럼)

Maori: 마오리인
European: 유럽인
society: 사회
station: 방송국
village: 마을, 부락, 촌락
experience: 겪다, 경험하다
long before: 훨씬 이전에

확인문제

● 다음 문장이 본문의 내용과 일치하면 T, 일치하지 않으면 F를 쓰시오.

1 The word kiwi has three meanings in New Zealand. ☐

2 European people brought the Maori people to New Zealand. ☐

3 The Maori culture is considered to be important in New Zealand. ☐

4 It is possible to experience the Maori culture in their villages. ☐

5 People move their bodies wildly when they do the haka. ☐

6 Today, New Zealanders do the haka only at sport matches. ☐

● 우리말을 참고하여 빈칸에 알맞은 말을 쓰시오.

Hello! New Zealand

1 New Zealand is _____ _____ _____ _____ _____.
It has many beautiful _____ and _____.

2 New Zealand has _____ _____ _____, the South Island
and the North Island.

3 In the South Island, there _____ _____ that _____
_____ _____ snow all year round.

4 You will _____ _____ _____ the fantastic views.

5 In the North Island, there are _____ _____ _____, lakes,
and areas _____ green grass.

6 _____ _____ its natural beauty, many famous movies
_____ _____ _____ in New Zealand.

7 If you visit New Zealand, you _____ _____ _____ its
nature.

8 When you _____ the word kiwi, what _____ _____ your
mind?

9 Maybe a fruit, but, in New Zealand the word kiwi has _____
_____ _____ _____.

10 First, kiwi is _____ _____ of a _____, green fruit.

11 A lot of kiwi fruit _____ _____ there, so New Zealand
_____ _____ _____ the land of kiwi fruit.

12 Kiwi is also the name of _____ of _____ _____
_____ _____.

13 The kiwi is _____ _____ New Zealanders _____ it is
the _____ of the nation.

14 Also, kiwi is _____ _____ _____ people _____ New
Zealand.

15 Today, New Zealanders _____ _____ _____ Kiwis
throughout the world.

16 Now, you know _____ kiwi is _____ _____ _____ a
fruit, a bird, and also a people.

안녕! 뉴질랜드

1 뉴질랜드는 자연의 아름다움이 가득한 곳이다. 뉴질랜드는 아름다운 호수와 폭포들이 많다.

2 뉴질랜드에는 남섬과 북섬, 두 개의 본섬이 있다.

3 남섬에는 일 년 내내 눈으로 덮인 산들이 있다.

4 당신은 굉장히 멋진 경관에 놀랄 것이다.

5 북섬에는 많은 온천과 호수, 초원 지역이 있다.

6 뉴질랜드 자연의 아름다움 때문에 많은 유명한 영화들이 뉴질랜드에서 촬영되었다.

7 뉴질랜드를 방문하면, 분명히 그 자연의 진가를 인정할 것이다.

8 키위라는 단어를 들을 때, 무엇이 떠오르는가?

9 아마도 과일이 떠오르겠지만, 뉴질랜드에서 키위는 몇 가지 뜻이 있다.

10 먼저, 키위는 맛있는 초록색 과일의 이름이다.

11 많은 키위가 그곳에서 자라기 때문에 뉴질랜드는 키위의 나라로 알려져 있다.

12 키위는 뉴질랜드 토종 새의 이름이기도 하다.

13 키위 새는 국가의 상징이기 때문에, 뉴질랜드 사람들에게 특별하다.

14 또한, 키위는 뉴질랜드 출신의 사람들을 부르는 별명이기도 하다.

15 오늘날 뉴질랜드인들은 전 세계적으로 키위라고 불리기도 한다.

16 이제, 당신은 키위가 과일과 새, 그리고 국민의 명칭이라는 것을 알았다.

17 Next time, don't become _____ when someone _____ the word kiwi, _____ _____ several meanings.

18 Now, _____ _____ about the Maori. _____ are _____ _____ _____ of New Zealand.

19 They went to _____ _____ the islands _____ _____ Europeans _____.

20 The Maori culture is _____ _____ _____ of _____ New Zealand society.

21 The Maori language _____ _____ at some schools and _____ _____ Maori language radio and TV stations.

22 There are Maori villages _____ _____ _____ _____ the country.

23 You can _____ Maori _____ and _____ Maori _____.

24 If you _____ "kia ora" _____ the villagers, they _____ _____ _____ _____ _____ _____ it. It _____ "hi" in English.

25 _____ you ever _____ the haka?

26 The haka may _____ _____ _____ haka dancers _____ and _____ their bodies _____.

27 The Maori people, _____ you've already _____ _____, started _____ the haka _____ a war dance.

28 Today, _____, New Zealanders _____ the haka _____ _____ _____, weddings, or other important events.

29 _____ _____, New Zealand's _____ _____ _____ do the haka _____ every match.

30 It is _____ _____ _____ the world.

31 If you see the haka, you _____ probably _____ _____ the rival team _____ _____ _____.

32 _____ the kiwi bird, the haka is _____ _____ _____.

---

17 다음에는 누군가가 키위라는 단어를 사용할 때 혼동하지 마라. 그 단어는 여러 뜻을 가지고 있기 때문이다.

18 이제, 마오리족에 대해 이야기해 보자. 마오리족은 뉴질랜드의 원주민이다.

19 그들은 유럽인들이 도착하기 오래 전에 이 섬에 와서 살았다.

20 마오리족의 문화는 오늘날 뉴질랜드 사회의 중요한 부분이다.

21 몇몇 학교에서 마오리어를 가르치고 있으며, 마오리어의 라디오와 TV 방송국이 있다.

22 나라의 여러 곳에 마오리 마을이 있다.

23 당신은 마오리 마을을 방문해 마오리 문화를 경험할 수 있다.

24 당신이 마을 사람들에게 "kia ora"라고 말한다면 그들은 그것을 듣고 좋아할 것이다. 그것은 영어로 "안녕"이라는 뜻이다.

25 하카를 본 적이 있는가?

26 하카 춤을 추는 사람들이 소리 지르고, 그들의 몸을 사납게 움직이기 때문에 하카는 무서워 보일 수도 있다.

27 당신이 이미 그들에 대해 들은 적이 있겠지만, 마오리인들은 전쟁 춤으로 하카를 추기 시작했다.

28 하지만, 오늘날 뉴질랜드 사람들은 하카를 운동 경기, 결혼식 또는 다른 중요한 행사가 있을 때 한다.

29 예를 들어, 뉴질랜드의 럭비 국가 대표 팀 선수들은 모든 경기 전에 하카를 춘다.

30 그것은 전 세계적으로 유명하다.

31 당신이 하카를 본다면, 상대 팀이 틀림없이 겁을 먹을 것이라는 것에 아마 동의할 것이다.

32 키위와 마찬가지로 하카는 나라의 상징이다.

● 우리말을 참고하여 본문을 영작하시오.

1 뉴질랜드는 자연의 아름다움이 가득한 곳이다. 뉴질랜드는 아름다운 호수와 폭포들이 많다.

➡ _____

2 뉴질랜드에는 남섬과 북섬, 두 개의 본섬이 있다.

➡ _____

3 남섬에는 일 년 내내 눈으로 덮인 산들이 있다.

➡ _____

4 당신은 굉장히 멋진 경관에 놀랄 것이다.

➡ _____

5 북섬에는 많은 온천과 호수, 초원 지역이 있다.

➡ _____

6 뉴질랜드 자연의 아름다움 때문에 많은 유명한 영화들이 뉴질랜드에서 촬영되었다.

➡ _____

7 뉴질랜드를 방문하면, 분명히 그 자연의 진가를 인정할 것이다.

➡ _____

8 키위라는 단어를 들을 때, 무엇이 떠오르는가?

➡ _____

9 아마도 과일이 떠오르겠지만, 뉴질랜드에서 키위는 몇 가지 뜻이 있다.

➡ _____

10 먼저, 키위는 맛있는 초록색 과일의 이름이다.

➡ _____

11 많은 키위가 그곳에서 자라기 때문에 뉴질랜드는 키위의 나라로 알려져 있다.

➡ _____

12 키위는 뉴질랜드 토종 새의 이름이기도 하다.

➡ _____

13 키위 새는 국가의 상징이기 때문에, 뉴질랜드 사람들에게 특별하다.

➡ _____

14 또한, 키위는 뉴질랜드 출신의 사람들을 부르는 별명이기도 하다.

➡ _____

15 오늘날 뉴질랜드인들은 전 세계적으로 키위라고 불리기도 한다.

➡ _____

16 이제, 당신은 키위가 과일과 새, 그리고 국민의 명칭이라는 것을 알았다.

➡ _____

17 다음에는 누군가가 키위라는 단어를 사용할 때 혼동하지 마라. 그 단어는 여러 뜻을 가지고 있기 때문이다.

➡ _____

18 이제, 마오리족에 대해 이야기해 보자. 마오리족은 뉴질랜드의 원주민이다.

➡ _____

19 그들은 유럽인들이 도착하기 오래 전에 이 섬에 와서 살았다.

➡ _____

20 마오리족의 문화는 오늘날 뉴질랜드 사회의 중요한 부분이다.

➡ _____

21 몇몇 학교에서 마오리어를 가르치고 있으며, 마오리어의 라디오와 TV 방송국이 있다.

➡ _____

_____

22 나라의 여러 곳에 마오리 마을이 있다.

➡ _____

23 당신은 마오리 마을을 방문해 마오리 문화를 경험할 수 있다.

➡ _____

24 당신이 마을 사람들에게 "kia ora"라고 말한다면 그들은 그것을 듣고 좋아할 것이다. 그것은 영어로 "안녕"이라는 뜻이다.

➡ _____

25 하카를 본 적이 있는가?

➡ _____

26 하카 춤을 추는 사람들이 소리 지르고, 그들의 몸을 사납게 움직이기 때문에 하카는 무서워 보일 수도 있다.

➡ _____

27 당신이 이미 그들에 대해 들은 적이 있겠지만, 마오리인들은 전쟁 춤으로 하카를 추기 시작했다.

➡ _____

28 하지만, 오늘날 뉴질랜드 사람들은 하카를 운동 경기, 결혼식 또는 다른 중요한 행사가 있을 때 한다.

➡ _____

29 예를 들어, 뉴질랜드의 럭비 국가 대표 팀 선수들은 모든 경기 전에 하카를 춘다.

➡ _____

30 그것은 전 세계적으로 유명하다.

➡ _____

31 당신이 하카를 본다면, 상대 팀이 틀림없이 겁을 먹을 것이라는 것에 아마 동의할 것이다.

➡ _____

32 키위와 마찬가지로 하카는 나라의 상징이다.

➡ _____

[01~03] 다음 글을 읽고 물음에 답하시오.

New Zealand is a place of ⓐ_____. It has many beautiful lakes and waterfalls. New Zealand has two main islands, the South Island and the North Island. In the South Island, there are mountains that are covered with snow ⓑall year round. You will be amazed by the fantastic views.

In the North Island, there are many hot springs, lakes, and areas with green grass. Because of its ⓒ_____, many famous movies have been made in New Zealand. If you visit New Zealand, you will surely appreciate its nature.

01 다음 중 빈칸 ⓐ와 ⓒ에 공통으로 들어갈 말로 가장 적절한 것은?

① beautiful minds of people

② the famous tradition

③ lots of water

④ natural beauty

⑤ natural life style

02 다음 중 밑줄 친 ⓑ의 의미로 가장 적절한 것은?

① from time to time

② all of a sudden

③ throughout the year

④ once in a while

⑤ here and there

서답형

03 What is New Zealand made up with? Answer in English.

➡ _____

_____

[04~06] 다음 글을 읽고 물음에 답하시오.

When you hear the word kiwi, what comes to your mind? Maybe a fruit, but, in New Zealand the word kiwi has a couple of meanings. First, kiwi is the name of a delicious, green fruit. A lot of kiwi fruit is grown there, so New Zealand is known as the land of kiwi fruit.

Kiwi is also the name of one of New Zealand's native birds. The kiwi is special to New Zealanders because it is the symbol of the nation. Also, kiwi is a nickname for people from New Zealand. Today, New Zealanders are sometimes called Kiwis throughout the world. Now, you know that kiwi is the name of a fruit, a bird, and also a people. Next time, don't become confused when someone uses the word kiwi, which has several meanings.

서답형

04 Write the reason why the kiwi is special to New Zealanders. Use the phrase 'It's because.'

➡ _____

05 다음 중 위 글의 내용과 일치하는 것은?

① The word kiwi has one meaning in New Zealand.

② It is hard to find kiwi fruit grown in New Zealand.

③ A kiwi bird is one of foreign birds in New Zealand.

④ Kiwis is a word to refer to people who came from New Zealand.

⑤ New Zealanders don't have any special nickname.

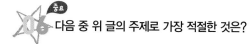

06 다음 중 위 글의 주제로 가장 적절한 것은?

① the world's largest producer of kiwi

② various meanings the word kiwi has in New Zealand

③ the most popular fruit in the world

④ the reason lots of kiwi fruit is grown in New Zealand

⑤ many words to refer to kiwi in New Zealand

07 다음 글을 읽고 답할 수 있는 것은?

> Now, let's talk about the Maori. They are the native people of New Zealand. They went to live on the islands long before Europeans arrived. The Maori culture is an important part of today's New Zealand society. The Maori language is taught at some schools and there are Maori language radio and TV stations. There are Maori villages in many parts of the country. You can visit Maori villages and experience Maori culture. If you say "kia ora" to the villagers, they will be glad to hear it. It means "hi" in English.

① What is the population of New Zealand?

② When did the Maori start to live in New Zealand?

③ When did Europeans arrive in New Zealand?

④ Where is the Maori language taught?

⑤ Why did the Maori settle in New Zealand?

[08~11] 다음 글을 읽고 물음에 답하시오.

> Have you ever watched the haka? The haka may look scary because haka dancers shout and move their bodies wildly. The Maori

people, who you've already heard about, started doing the haka as a war dance. Today, (A)_____, New Zealanders do the haka at sport matches, weddings, or other important events. For example, New Zealand's national rugby team members do the haka before every match. It is famous all over the world. If you see the haka, you will probably agree that (B)상대 팀이 틀림없이 겁을 먹을 것이다. Like the kiwi bird, the haka is a national symbol.

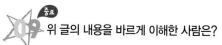

08 다음 중 빈칸 (A)에 들어갈 말로 가장 적절한 것은?

① for example   ② that is

③ however   ④ what's worse

⑤ unfortunately

09 위 글의 내용을 바르게 이해한 사람은?

① Jane: The haka danced by the Maori must be really relaxing.

② Paul: It is interesting that the Maori did the haka during weddings.

③ Carl: I'm so sorry that the haka isn't danced anymore.

④ David: The haka is known to only New Zealanders.

⑤ Zach: I want to see the Maori move their bodies wildly when doing the haka.

서답형

10 When do New Zealand's national rugby team members do the haka? Answer in English with seven words.

➡ _____

서답형

11 주어진 단어를 활용하여 밑줄 친 우리말 (B)를 영어로 쓰시오.

> (rival, must)

➡ _____

[12~15] 다음 글을 읽고 물음에 답하시오.

Have you ever ①watched the haka? The haka may look ②scary because haka dancers (A)_____. The Maori people, who you've already heard ③about, started doing the haka as a war dance. Today, however, New Zealanders do the haka at sport matches, weddings, or other important events. For example, New Zealand's national rugby team members do the haka before every ④matches. It is famous all over the world. If you see the haka, you will probably agree that the rival team must be ⑤scared. Like the kiwi bird, the haka is a national symbol.

12 다음 중 빈칸 (A)에 들어갈 말로 가장 적절한 것은?

① move their bodies like swans

② make some funny faces on purpose

③ shout and move their bodies wildly

④ make loud noises to wake people up

⑤ shout but dance with joy

13 다음 중 위 글의 내용과 일치하는 것은?

① The Maori learned how to do the haka from New Zealanders.

② The Maori don't know what the haka is.

③ The haka is the only national symbol.

④ People don't want to do the haka at all.

⑤ The haka still makes people scared.

서답형
14 At what events do New Zealanders do the haka today? Answer in English.

➡ _____

_____

15 밑줄 친 ①~⑤ 중 어법상 어색한 것은?

①   ②   ③   ④   ⑤

[16~18] 다음 글을 읽고 물음에 답하시오.

When you hear the word kiwi, what comes to your mind? Maybe a fruit, but, in New Zealand the word kiwi has a couple of meanings. ① First, kiwi is the name of a delicious, green fruit. A lot of kiwi fruit is grown there, so New Zealand is known as the land of kiwi fruit. ② Kiwi is also the name of one of New Zealand's native birds. ③ The kiwi is special to New Zealanders because it is the symbol of the nation. ④ Today, New Zealanders are sometimes called Kiwis throughout the world. Now, you know that kiwi is the name of a fruit, a bird, and also a people. ⑤ Next time, don't become (A)_____ when someone uses the word kiwi, which has several meanings.

16 빈칸 (A)에 들어갈 말로 가장 적절한 것은?

① amazed   ② confused   ③ upset

④ nervous   ⑤ bored

17 다음 중 주어진 문장이 들어가기에 가장 적절한 곳은?

Also, kiwi is a nickname for people from New Zealand.

①   ②   ③   ④   ⑤

서답형
18 Write the reason why New Zealand is known as the land of kiwi fruit. Use the phrase 'It's because.'

➡ _____

_____

[19~21] 다음 글을 읽고 물음에 답하시오.

Now, let's talk about the Maori.

(A) You can visit Maori villages and experience Maori culture. If you say "kia ora" to the villagers, they will be glad ⓐto hear it. It means "hi" in English.

(B) The Maori language is taught at some schools and there are Maori language radio and TV stations. There are Maori villages in many parts of the country.

(C) They are the native people of New Zealand. They went to live on the islands long before Europeans arrived. The Maori culture is an important part of today's New Zealand society.

19 자연스러운 글이 되도록 (A)~(C)를 바르게 나열한 것은?

① (A)–(C)–(B) ② (B)–(A)–(C)
③ (B)–(C)–(A) ④ (C)–(A)–(B)
⑤ (C)–(B)–(A)

20 What can we do when we visit Maori villages? Answer in English with five words.

➡ _____

21 다음 중 밑줄 친 ⓐ와 쓰임이 같은 것은?

① He must be generous to lend you money.
② It was my job to take care of the employees.
③ Do you have paper to write on?
④ She was upset to see him using her computer without asking.
⑤ They tried hard to get the first prize.

[22~24] 다음 글을 읽고 물음에 답하시오.

New Zealand is a place of natural beauty. It has many beautiful lakes and waterfalls. New Zealand has two main islands, the South Island and the North Island. In the South Island, there are mountains (A)that are covered with snow all year round. You will be amazed by the fantastic views.

In the North Island, there are many hot springs, lakes, and areas with green grass. Because of its natural beauty, many famous movies have been made in New Zealand. If you visit New Zealand, you will surely appreciate its nature.

22 다음과 같이 풀이되는 말을 위 글에서 찾아 쓰시오.

to like something because you recognize its good qualitie.

➡ _____

23 다음 중 밑줄 친 (A)를 대신하여 쓸 수 있는 것은?

① who ② whom ③ which
④ whose ⑤ what

24 다음 중 위 글의 내용과 일치하는 것은?

① New Zealand is famous for its cities.
② The view of the South Island is similar to that of the North Island.
③ The writer is sure that the fantastic view of New Zealand will make people amazed.
④ It is hard to find mountains covered with snow in New Zealand.
⑤ We can find many lakes and waterfalls in many countries except New Zealand.

[01~04] 다음 글을 읽고 물음에 답하시오.

New Zealand is a place of natural beauty. It has many beautiful lakes and waterfalls. New Zealand has two main islands, the South Island and the North Island. In the South Island, there are mountains that are covered with snow all year round. You will be amazed by the fantastic views.

In the North Island, there are many hot springs, lakes, and areas with green grass. Because of its natural beauty, many famous movies have been made in New Zealand. (A)If you will visit New Zealand, you will surely appreciate its nature.

01 What are there in the South Island of New Zealand? Answer in English.

➡ _____

_____

02 If you want to enjoy hot springs in New Zealand, where should you go? Answer in English.

➡ _____

03 밑줄 친 (A)를 어법에 맞게 바르게 고쳐 쓰시오.

➡ _____

_____

04 According to the passage, what is New Zealand famous for? Answer in English.

➡ _____

[05~08] 다음 글을 읽고 물음에 답하시오.

When you hear the word kiwi, what comes to your mind? Maybe a fruit, but, in New Zealand the word kiwi has a couple of meanings. First, kiwi is the name of a delicious, green fruit. A lot of kiwi fruit is grown there, so New Zealand is known as the land of kiwi fruit.

Kiwi is also the name of one of New Zealand's native birds. The kiwi is special to New Zealanders because it is the symbol of the nation. Also, kiwi is a nickname for people from New Zealand. Today, New Zealanders are sometimes called Kiwis throughout the world. Now, you know that kiwi is the name of (A)_____. Next time, don't become confused when someone uses the word kiwi,   (B)   has several meanings.

05 빈칸 (A)에 들어갈 말을 위 글을 읽고 바르게 유추하여 쓰시오.

➡ _____

06 빈칸 (B)에 들어갈 알맞은 말을 쓰시오.

➡ _____

07 Where is a lot of kiwi fruit grown? Answer in English with a full sentence.

➡ _____

08 위 글의 내용에 맞게 빈칸에 알맞은 말을 쓰시오. 한 칸에 하나의 단어만 쓰시오.

Unless you understand _____ _____ _____ _____, you will become confused.

[09~12] 다음 글을 읽고 물음에 답하시오.

Now, let's talk about the Maori. They are the native people of New Zealand. They went to live on the islands long before Europeans arrived. The Maori culture is an important part of today's New Zealand society. The Maori language is taught at some schools and there are Maori language radio and TV stations. There are Maori villages in many parts of the country. You can visit Maori villages and experience Maori culture. If you say "kia ora" to the villagers, they will be glad to hear it. It means "hi" in English.

09 Before Europeans arrived in New Zealand, who went to live on there?

➡ _____

_____

10 What can we find in many parts of New Zealand? Answer in English.

➡ _____

_____

11 If you want to say "hi" to the villagers in the Maori language, what should you say?

➡ _____

12 다음 중 위 글의 내용과 일치하지 <u>않는</u> 것을 두 군데 찾아 바르게 고쳐 쓰시오.

The Maori people are the native people of Canada. Their food is an important part of today's New Zealand society.

➡ _____

_____

[13~16] 다음 글을 읽고 물음에 답하시오.

(A)하카를 본 적이 있는가? The haka may look scary because haka dancers shout and move their bodies wildly. The Maori people, who you've already heard about, started doing the haka as a war dance. Today, however, New Zealanders do the haka at sport matches, weddings, or other important events. For example, New Zealand's national rugby team members do the haka before every match. It is famous all over the world. If you see the haka, you will probably agree that the rival team must be scared. Like the kiwi bird, the haka is a national symbol.

13 주어진 단어를 활용하여 밑줄 친 우리말 (A)를 영어로 쓰시오. (6 words)

(watch)

➡ _____

14 Write the reason why the haka may look scary. Use the phrase 'it's because.'

➡ _____

_____

15 According to the passage, what are we likely to see the rugby players do before their match? Answer in English and use the word 'them.'

➡ _____

_____

16 위 글의 내용에 맞게 빈칸에 알맞은 말을 쓰시오.

_____ as well as _____ is a national symbol.

Before You Read

Rugby is a popular sport in New Zealand.
넓은 장소에 쓰는 전치사

New Zealand is in the southern part of the world.
방향을 나타내는 말 앞에 정관사 the

The Maori people are the native people of New Zealand and have their
원주민   동사 are와 병렬 연결

culture.

구문해설 ・popular: 인기 있는 ・southern: 남쪽의 ・native: 토박이의, ~ 태생인 ・culture: 문화

해석

럭비는 뉴질랜드에서 인기 있는 운동이다.
뉴질랜드는 남반구에 있다.
마오리족은 뉴질랜드의 원주민들이고, 그들의 문화가 있다.

Enjoy Writing

We Invite You

Do you know about New Zealand? It has two main islands and 600 smaller

islands. Its capital is Wellington. The kiwi, which is a bird native to New
소유격 It's(×)   관계대명사 계속적 용법(주어)

Zealand, is one of the symbols of the country. If you come to New Zealand,
one of+복수 명사   조건의 부사절(현재시제)

you should visit a Maori village, which shows the native culture of New
관계대명사의 계속적 용법

Zealand. We suggest you try a traditional dish of the Maori people. They cook
suggest(제안)+that+주어+should+원형동사: should 생략 가능

meat and vegetables in the ground with heated rocks. It is great. Many people
수동의 의미(과거분사)

visit New Zealand to enjoy the beautiful nature. We are happy to invite you to
to부정사의 부사적 용법(목적)   to부정사의 부사적 용법(감정의 원인)

this beautiful country.

구문해설 ・capital: 수도 ・native to: ~ 태생의, 원산지의 ・traditional dish: 전통 요리 ・heated rock: 가열된 돌

우리는 당신을 초대합니다
당신은 뉴질랜드에 대해 아는가? 그곳은 두 개의 본섬과 600개의 작은 섬들로 되어 있다. 그곳의 수도는 웰링턴이다. 키위는 뉴질랜드 태생의 새인데, 그 나라의 상징 중 하나이다. 뉴질랜드에 온다면 마오리 마을을 반드시 방문해야 하는데, 왜냐하면 그 마을이 뉴질랜드 원주민들의 문화를 보여 주기 때문이다. 우리는 당신이 마오리족의 전통 요리를 먹어 보는 것을 제안한다. 그들은 열을 가한 돌로 땅 속에서 고기와 채소를 요리한다. 그것은 훌륭하다. 많은 사람들은 아름다운 자연을 즐기기 위해 뉴질랜드를 방문한다. 우리는 당신을 이 아름다운 나라에 초대하게 되어 기쁘다.

Project Step 1

A: Let's talk about which country we are going to look into.
전치사 about의 목적어 역할로 '의문사(which country)+주어(we)+동사(are going~)' 형태의 간접의문문이다.

B: Which country do you prefer, Australia or the UK?
'Which+명사+do you prefer, A or B?' 형태의 선택의문문이다.

C: I suggest we search for information on the UK.
'suggest (that)+주어+(should)+동사원형'으로 '~할 것을 제안한다'라는 의미이다.

   There is a lot of information to work with.
information을 수식하는 형용사 용법이다.

D: Okay.

구문해설 ・look into: ~을 조사하다 ・prefer: 선호하다 ・suggest: 제안하다 ・search for: ~을 조사하다
・information: 정보

A: 어느 나라를 조사할 것인지 이야기해 보자.
B: 호주와 영국 중에서 어느 나라를 선호하니?
C: 나는 영국에 관한 정보를 찾아볼 것을 제안해. 우리가 작업해야 할 많은 정보들이 있잖아.
D: 그래.

Words & Expressions

01 다음 주어진 두 단어의 관계가 같도록 빈칸에 알맞은 단어를 쓰시오. (주어진 철자로 시작할 것)

> abroad – overseas : accomplish – a _____

02 다음 문장의 빈칸 (A)와 (B)에 들어갈 단어가 바르게 짝지어진 것은?

> • The Chinese consider a panda as a (A)_____ of bravery.
> • The Maori people are the (B)_____ people of New Zealand.

① harmony – several
② statue – dependent
③ sign – desirable
④ symbol – native
⑤ organization – traditional

[03~04] 다음 영영풀이에 해당하는 것을 고르시오.

03

> a pattern of crossed lines and squares

① hall
② confusion
③ flag
④ trail
⑤ plaid

04

> a meal in which everyone who is invited brings something to eat

① potluck
② dinner
③ lunch
④ breakfast
⑤ snack

05 다음 우리말에 맞게 주어진 문장의 빈칸을 네 단어로 채우시오.

> 유명인들의 도움으로 그러한 정치인들은 대중에 더 쉽게 다가갈 수 있다.
> ➡ _____ celebrities such politicians can easily approach the public.

06 다음 중 밑줄 친 부분의 뜻이 잘못된 것은?

① Of course, you have to commit to your goal until you achieve it! (달성하다)
② She is not only my best friend but also a strong rival! (경쟁자)
③ I recommend this dictionary to you. (빌려주다)
④ He has made cameo appearances in several Indian movies, too. (몇몇의)
⑤ The main reason is that the food here is so delicious! (주요한)

Conversation

07 다음 대화의 빈칸에 들어갈 말로 알맞은 것은?

> A: _____
> What do you think about it?
> B: I think Group 1's picture is very nice.

① Let's talk about the pose we will make for our picture.
② Let's talk about places in the UK.
③ I saw Group 1 in the National Museum.
④ Let's talk about the picture of Group 1.
⑤ How much do you know about the picture?

08 다음 그림을 보고, 대화의 빈칸에 주어진 단어를 이용하여 제안하는 표현을 쓰시오.

> A: Let's talk about activities we can enjoy in the UK. What should we do in the UK?
> B: _____
> (suggest, watch, soccer game) (7 words)

[09~11] 다음 대화를 읽고 물음에 답하시오.

Seho: Good morning.

Jessie, Andy: Hi, Seho.

Seho: I will visit my uncle in Philadelphia this winter. Can you tell me about the city?

Jessie: Sure. (①) I was there a few years ago. First, let's talk about food.

Seho: Okay. (②) What food is Philadelphia famous for?

Jessie: The most famous food in Philadelphia is the cheese steak sandwich. (③) It is a big sandwich filled with beef and melted cheese.

Seho: (④) Are there any places that are popular with tourists?

Andy: I suggest you visit Independence Hall. It is very important in American history. (⑤)

Seho: Wonderful. Thank you for the information.

Andy: My pleasure..

09 위 대화의 (①)~(⑤) 중 주어진 문장이 들어갈 위치로 알맞은 것은?

> Good suggestion. I will try it.

①   ②   ③   ④   ⑤

10 What is a cheese steak sandwich like?

➡ _____

_____

11 위 대화를 읽고 답할 수 없는 질문은?

① When will Seho visit his uncle in Philadelphia?

② What food is Philadelphia famous for?

③ What is Independence Hall for?

④ What place is popular with tourists in Philadelphia?

⑤ Why does Andy suggest to Seho that he visit Independence Hall?

> Grammar

12 다음 중 어법상 올바른 문장을 모두 고르면?

① Taylor recently attended Mr. Robert's lecture, that was boring.

② James visited a traditional market in Mokpo, which sell fresh seafood.

③ Mom read the letter from Daddy before he died, which made all of us cry.

④ Dave is proud of the works of his brother, who are helpful for the blind.

⑤ I respect Father Lee, who devoted his whole life to helping poor people in Southern Africa.

13 다음 중 문장의 의미가 나머지 넷과 다른 것은?

① My older sister gets up early not to be late for work.

② My older sister gets up early so that she may not be late for work.

③ My older sister gets up early in order not to be late for work.

④ My older sister gets up early but she isn't late for work.

⑤ My older sister gets up early so as not to be late for work.

[14~15] 다음 중 밑줄 친 부분의 쓰임이 주어진 문장과 다른 것은?

14

> The kiwi birds poke the ground with its beak <u>to find</u> their food.

① The Maori people waved their hands <u>to welcome</u> the visitors from Korea.

② I went to New Zealand <u>to study</u> the species of kiwi birds.

③ My ex-girlfriend just called <u>to say</u> she missed me much.

④ Sarah doesn't like <u>to make</u> the same mistakes again.

⑤ What do your family members do <u>to keep</u> healthy?

15

> A lot of movie directors go to New Zealand <u>to film</u>.

① The Maori warriors danced <u>to scare</u> their enemy.

② Alex was disappointed <u>to receive</u> his grade report card.

③ Laura lived <u>to be</u> 103, which was surprising.

④ The people of New Zealand do their best not <u>to lose</u> the endangered species.

⑤ Sally promised not <u>to smoke</u> again in front of her kids.

16 다음 주어진 세 문장을 관계대명사의 계속적 용법과 제한적 용법을 활용하여, 〈조건〉에 맞게 한 문장으로 표현하시오.

> • The public library introduced a new system.
> • The new system would help the people to easily borrow the audio books.
> • The audio books had always been difficult to borrow.

┌─ 조건 ├─
that과 which를 반드시 사용할 것. 본문에 있는 표현만을 활용할 것. (변형불가)
└─

➡ _____

_____

_____

17 다음 중 어법상 어색한 문장은?

① We were surprised to hear the sound, which was from across the street.

② The children in my class like David's P.E. class, which are fun.

③ Everybody voted for Sarah, which was good for her future.

④ These are Jamie's books published a year ago, which I've read three times.

⑤ Andrew was talking about New Zealand, which is his home country.

18 주어진 우리말에 맞게 영작할 때 어법상 <u>어색한</u> 문장을 하나 고르시오.

> Clara가 가방을 샀는데, 내가 어제 삼촌으로부터 받은 것과 비슷하다.

① Clara bought a bag, and it is very similar to the one what I received from my uncle yesterday.

② Clara bought a bag, which is very similar to the one that I received from my uncle yesterday.

③ Clara bought a bag, which is very similar to what I received from my uncle yesterday.

④ Clara bought a bag, and it is very similar to the one which I received from my uncle yesterday.

⑤ Clara bought a bag, and it is very similar to what I received from my uncle yesterday.

19 다음 사진을 보고 우리말과 조건에 맞게 영작하여 빈칸을 채우시오.

> 뉴질랜드 축구 선수들은 상대를 겁먹게 하기 위해 하카를 춘다.
>
> (the haka, their opponents, do, scare 활용, 7단어)

➡ New Zealand soccer players _____

_____ .

[20~22] 다음 글을 읽고 물음에 답하시오.

New Zealand is a place of natural ①beauty. It has many beautiful lakes and waterfalls. New Zealand has two main islands, the South Island and the North Island. In the South Island, there ②are mountains that ③ are covered (A)_____ snow all year round. You will be amazed ④by the fantastic views.

In the North Island, there are many hot springs, lakes, and areas with green grass. ⑤Because its natural beauty, many famous movies have been made in New Zealand. If you visit New Zealand, you will surely appreciate its nature.

20 What are there in the North Island of New Zealand? Answer in English with a full sentence.

➡ _____

_____

21 다음 중 빈칸 (A)에 들어갈 말과 같은 말이 들어가는 것은?

① David was anxious _____ his test results.

② The restaurant was crowded _____ many people.

③ You must devote yourself _____ learning English.

④ Did you apply _____ the job that you wanted to get?

⑤ She is not accustomed _____ riding a bike.

22 밑줄 친 ①~⑤ 중 문맥상 바르지 <u>않은</u> 것은?

①　　　②　　　③　　　④　　　⑤

[23~25] 다음 글을 읽고 물음에 답하시오.

Have you ever watched the haka? ① The haka may look scary because haka dancers shout and move their bodies wildly. ② The Maori people, who you've already heard about, started doing the haka as a war dance. ③ For example, New Zealand's national rugby team members do the haka before every match. ④ It is famous all over the world. If you see the haka, you will probably agree that the rival team must be scared. ⑤ Like the kiwi bird, the haka is a national symbol.

23 ①~⑤ 중 주어진 문장이 들어가기에 가장 적절한 곳은?

> Today, however, New Zealanders do the haka at sport matches, weddings, or other important events.

①   ②   ③   ④   ⑤

24 본문의 단어를 활용하여 빈칸에 알맞은 말을 쓰시오.

> New Zealand's national rugby team members do the haka before every match in order to _____ the rival team.

25 다음 중 위 글을 읽고 답할 수 있는 것은?

① When was the haka invented?
② How long have the Maori people done the haka?
③ How many people do you need to do the haka?
④ Why did the kiwi bird become a national symbol?
⑤ Why does the haka look scary?

[26~29] 다음 글을 읽고 물음에 답하시오.

We Invite You

(A) They cook meat and vegetables in the ground with heated rocks. It is delicious. Many people visit New Zealand to enjoy the beautiful nature. We are happy to invite you to this beautiful country.

(B) If you come to New Zealand, you should visit a Maori village, which shows the native culture of New Zealand. We suggest you try a traditional dish of the Maori people.

(C) Do you know about New Zealand? It has two main islands and 600 smaller islands. Its capital is Wellington. The kiwi, which is a bird native to New Zealand, is one of the symbols of the country.

26 자연스러운 글이 되도록 (A)~(C)를 바르게 나열하시오.

➡ _____

27 If you want to see the native culture of New Zealand, where should you visit? Answer in English with six words.

➡ _____

28 According to the passage, why do many people visit New Zealand?

➡ _____

_____

29 다음 중 위 글의 내용과 일치하는 것은?

① The Maori people cook meat and vegetables with cold rocks.
② The food that the Maori people make is not tasty.
③ The writer recommends us not to try a traditional food of the Maori people.
④ New Zealand is made up of many islands.
⑤ The kiwi is the only national symbol of New Zealand.

출제율 95%

01 다음 짝지어진 단어의 관계가 같도록 빈칸에 알맞은 말을 쓰시오.

> confused – calm : artificial – _____

출제율 90%

02 다음 영영풀이에 해당하는 단어는?

> a rough path across countryside or through a forest

① society   ② street   ③ trail
④ station   ⑤ hall

[03~04] 다음 대화를 읽고 물음에 답하시오.

B: Wow, we finally arrived in Hong Kong, Mom.
W: (A)우리가 방문할 곳들이 기대된다. (I'm / our / looking / to / visit / forward) What should we do today, Mike?
B: I suggest we visit Victoria Peak.
W: Victoria Peak?
B: It is the highest mountain in Hong Kong and is in a lot of movies. We can enjoy the fantastic view.
W: That sounds good. Let's go.

출제율 100%

03 위 대화의 밑줄 친 (A)의 우리말에 맞게 주어진 단어를 알맞은 순서로 배열하시오.

➡ _____

출제율 95%

04 위 대화의 내용과 일치하지 않는 것은?

① Mike and his mother is in Hong Kong.
② They will first visit Victoria Peak.
③ Victoria Peak is the highest mountain in China.
④ Victoria Peak is in a lot of movies.
⑤ They will enjoy the fantastic view in Victoria Peak.

[05~06] 다음 대화를 읽고 물음에 답하시오.

B: Let's talk about (a)traditional clothing from other countries.
G: Hmm... Do you know what a kilt is?
B: No, I don't. What is it?
G: It is traditional clothing from Scotland. It looks like a knee-length (b)skirt and has a (c)plaid pattern.
B: A skirt of knee-length with a plaid pattern?
G: Yes. It is (d)common because it is a skirt for men.
B: That sounds (e)interesting. I want to try one on.

출제율 95%

05 위 대화의 밑줄 친 (a)~(e) 중 어휘의 쓰임이 어색한 것은?

① (a)   ② (b)   ③ (c)   ④ (d)   ⑤ (e)

출제율 90%

06 위 대화에서 다음 〈영영풀이〉가 설명하는 단어를 찾아 쓰시오.

> following the customs or ways of behaving that have continued in a group of people for a long time

➡ _____

[07~08] 다음 대화를 읽고 물음에 답하시오.

G: Brian, let's talk about what we will prepare for the World Food Festival.
B: I will make a meat pie. It is famous in Australia. How about you, Sera?
G: I want to make a popular English dish, fish and chips.
B: Fish and chips? (A)_____
G: It's fried fish with hot potato chips.
B: That sounds interesting. Let's prepare them.

07 위 대화의 빈칸 (A)에 들어갈 말로 알맞은 것은?

① What do you do?
② How can we make fish and chips?
③ What does it look like?
④ How much do you like it?
⑤ What kind of food do you like?

08 위 대화를 읽고 답할 수 <u>없는</u> 질문은?

① What kind of festival will Brian and Sera participate in?
② What dish is popular in England?
③ What dish is famous in Australia?
④ What does fish and chips look like?
⑤ What does a meat pie look like?

09 다음 글에서 문법적으로 틀린 부분 두 곳을 찾아 바르게 고쳐 쓰시오.

> Welcome to Australia. The capital of Australia is Canberra. People are spoken English. Meat pie is a popular dish in Australia. Every year, lots of tourists visits the Sydney Opera House and the beautiful beaches in Melbourne.

➡ _____

10 다음 중 어법상 어색한 문장은?

① My father bought me a watch, that I don't like very much.
② Ms. Johnson moved her daughter to new school, who had trouble adjusting.
③ Gloria always wore the shirt, which her aunt bought for her.
④ I got my umbrella stolen, which I had put next to James' desk.
⑤ The clients urged the clerk to bring them chairs, which were for VIP.

11 다음 각 문장의 밑줄 친 to부정사의 용법을 〈보기〉에서 기호를 골라 각각의 괄호 안에 써 넣으시오.

> ┤ 보기 ├
> ⓐ 명사적 용법
> ⓑ 형용사적 용법
> ⓒ 부사적 용법 '목적'
> ⓓ 부사적 용법 '감정의 원인, 이유'
> ⓔ 부사적 용법 '판단의 근거'
> ⓕ 부사적 용법 '결과'
> ⓖ 부사적 용법 '형용사/부사 수식'

(1) I would like to drink zero calorie soda not to gain weight. (_____)

(2) Mina practiced the drum solo 8 hours a day to make her parents proud. (_____)

(3) Hermione hurried to the station only to miss the train. (_____)

(4) They were disappointed to find out the dark side of the organization. (_____)

(5) My parents were quite relieved to know that I wasn't hurt at the accident. (_____)

(6) David must have been so upset to accept the offer. (_____)

(7) The math problem is too difficult for Robert to solve in 10 minutes. (_____)

(8) We have a lot of friends to support us. (_____)

(9) Alicia grew up to be a world wide super star in fashion industry. (_____)

(10) Ms. Baek has learned to cook Italian food to open her own restaurant. (_____)

(11) Mina can't be lonely to have such friends like you. (_____)

(12) Jake is very rich enough to buy all the houses in this city. (_____)

(13) It is impossible for Natalie to move the furniture to the next room. (_____)

출제율 95%

12 다음 중 밑줄 친 관계대명사가 가리키는 것으로 바르지 <u>않은</u> 것은?

① Karen is a doctor at the hospital, <u>which</u> is her second work place.
(➡ the hospital)

② The reporter forgot the singer's name, <u>which</u> started with the letter C.
(➡ the singer's name)

③ Mr. Brett was not afraid of sea water, <u>which</u> let him be a professional diver.
(➡ sea water)

④ Alice is a teacher at Yujin middle school, <u>which</u> is located in Incheon.
(➡ Yujin middle school)

⑤ The foreign visitors should take the subway line 2, <u>which</u> circulates Seoul.
(➡ the subway line 2)

출제율 90%

13 다음 중 밑줄 친 부분의 쓰임이 같은 것끼리 연결된 것은?

ⓐ All the employees went to the public health center <u>to check</u> their condition.

ⓑ During my visit to London, I need <u>to see</u> the tower and bridge.

ⓒ Sumi and her friends went to the street <u>to watch</u> the live performance of the band.

ⓓ The actor went outside <u>to run</u> a little.

ⓔ Yoyo practices the piano hard <u>to do</u> well on the school festival.

ⓕ I'd like <u>to play</u> basketball this afternoon.

ⓖ It's important for her <u>to keep</u> promises.

① ⓑ, ⓓ, ⓔ, ⓖ ② ⓐ, ⓒ, ⓓ, ⓔ
③ ⓐ, ⓑ, ⓔ, ⓕ ④ ⓐ, ⓒ, ⓓ, ⓖ
⑤ ⓑ, ⓔ, ⓕ, ⓖ

출제율 90%

14 다음 문장의 밑줄 친 부분과 쓰임이 같은 것은?

> If you say "kia ora" to the villagers, they will be glad <u>to hear</u> it. It means "hi" in English.

① The Maori boy grew up <u>to be</u> a world famous athlete.

② It was not easy for the Maori villagers <u>to learn</u> Korean Fan dance.

③ I'd like to go to New Zealand <u>to study</u> the animals only living there.

④ The New Zealanders were satisfied <u>to hear</u> the news of their winning.

⑤ Please don't forget <u>to visit</u> New Zealand.

[15~16] 다음 글을 읽고 물음에 답하시오.

Now, let's talk about the Maori. They are the native people of New Zealand. They went to live on the islands long before Europeans arrived. The Maori culture is (A)_____. The Maori language is taught at some schools and there are Maori language radio and TV stations. There are Maori villages in many parts of the country. You can visit Maori villages and experience Maori culture. If you say "kia ora" to the villagers, they will be glad to hear it. It means "hi" in English.

출제율 90%

15 다음 중 빈칸 (A)에 들어갈 말로 가장 적절한 것은?

① hard to find in New Zealand

② protected in an small island of New Zealand

③ paid no attention to by people in New Zealand

④ destroying an important part of New Zealand society

⑤ an important part of today's New Zealand society

16 다음 중 위 글의 내용과 일치하지 <u>않는</u> 것은? 출제율 100%

① The Maori people are native to New Zealand.

② There are some schools teaching the Maori language.

③ The Maori villages are concentrated on one place.

④ We can hear radio broadcast in the Maori language.

⑤ Before Europeans arrived in New Zealand, the Maori people had lived there.

[17~18] 다음 글을 읽고 물음에 답하시오.

New Zealand is a place of natural beauty. It has many beautiful lakes and waterfalls. New Zealand has two main islands, the South Island and the North Island. In the South Island, there are mountains that are covered with snow all year round. You will be amazed by the fantastic views.

In the North Island, there are many hot springs, lakes, and areas with green grass. Because of its natural beauty, many famous movies have been made in New Zealand. If you visit New Zealand, you will surely appreciate its nature.

17 출제율 90% Write the reason why many famous movies have been made in New Zealand. Answer in English with five words.

 _____

18 다음 중 위 글의 내용과 일치하지 <u>않는</u> 곳을 두 군데 찾아 바르게 고쳐 쓰시오. 출제율 95%

In the South Island, there are hills that are covered with snow all year round. Many hot springs, and areas with tall trees are in the North Island.

➡ _____
_____

[19~20] 다음 글을 읽고 물음에 답하시오.

Do you know about New Zealand? It has two main islands and 600 smaller islands. Its capital is Wellington. The kiwi, ①<u>which</u> is a bird native to New Zealand, ②<u>is</u> one of the symbols of the country. If you come to New Zealand, you should visit a Maori village, which ③<u>show</u> the native culture of New Zealand. We suggest you try a traditional dish of the Maori people. They cook meat and vegetables in the ground with ④<u>heated</u> rocks. It is delicious. Many people visit New Zealand ⑤<u>to enjoy</u> the beautiful nature. We are happy to invite you to this beautiful country.

19 출제율 90% 밑줄 친 ①~⑤ 중 어법상 바르지 <u>않은</u> 것은?

① ② ③ ④ ⑤

20 출제율 100% 위 글을 읽고 뉴질랜드에 관하여 답할 수 <u>없는</u> 것은?

① How many main islands does it have?

② What is its capital?

③ How many symbols does it have?

④ Why do many people visit there?

⑤ Where should you visit when you go there?

01 Read the dialogue and answer the question in English.

> G: Brian, let's talk about what we will prepare for the World Food Festival.
> B: I will make a meat pie. It is famous in Australia. How about you, Sera?
> G: I want to make a popular English dish, fish and chips.
> B: Fish and chips? What does it look like?
> G: It's fried fish with hot potato chips.
> B: That sounds interesting. Let's prepare them.

Q: What do you think Sera will prepare for the festival?

➡ _____

02 다음 대화의 밑줄 친 (A)와 같은 의미가 되도록 주어진 단어를 사용하여 바꿔 쓰시오.

> B: Wow, we finally arrived in Hong Kong, Mom.
> W: I'm looking forward to our visit. What should we do today, Mike?
> B: (A)I suggest we visit Victoria Peak. (why / we)
> W: Victoria Peak?
> B: It is the highest mountain in Hong Kong and is in a lot of movies. We can enjoy the fantastic view.
> W: That sounds good. Let's go.

➡ _____

03 다음 〈보기〉와 같이 두 문장이 같은 의미가 되도록 관계대명사나 관계부사를 활용하여 영작하시오.

> ┤ 보기 ├
> We met the Maori people and they showed us haka dance.
> → We met the Maori people, who showed us haka dance.

(1) New Zealand is known as the land of kiwi fruit, and a lot of kiwi fruit is grown there.

➡ _____
_____

(2) I won't get confused when somebody uses the word kiwi, and it has several meanings.

➡ _____
_____

(3) Janet received a letter of invitation from her friend, but she didn't read it.

➡ _____
_____

(4) All the employees in the company stop working at noon, and they go out for lunch then.

➡ _____
_____

(5) The boss praised Sean, though he didn't mean to do well this time.

➡ _____
_____

04 다음 그림을 보고 우리말과 조건에 맞게 영작하여 빈칸을 채우시오.

> 나는 베트남의 아름다운 밤 풍경 사진을 찍기 위해 카메라를 가져갔다.
> (night scenery, take pictures 활용, 8 단어)

➡ I took a camera _____ _____ of Vietnam.

[05~07] 다음 글을 읽고 물음에 답하시오.

Have you ever watched the haka? The haka may look scary because haka dancers shout and move their bodies wildly. The Maori people, who you've already heard about, started doing the haka as a war dance. Today, however, New Zealanders do the haka at sport matches, weddings, or other important events. For example, New Zealand's national rugby team members do the haka before every match. It is famous all over the world. If you see the haka, (A)상대팀이 틀림없이 겁을 먹을 것이라는 것에 아마 동의할 것이다. Like the kiwi bird, the haka is a national symbol.

05 주어진 단어를 활용하여 밑줄 친 우리말 (A)를 영어로 쓰시오.

(probably / that / team, 11단어)

➡ _____
_____

06 위 글의 내용과 맞지 <u>않는</u> 부분을 두 군데 찾아 바르게 고쳐 쓰시오.

Haka dancers sing and move their bodies wildly, so the haka may look happy. New Zealanders do the haka at many kinds of important events.

➡ _____
_____

07 As what did the Maori people start doing the haka? Answer in English.

➡ _____
_____

[08~09] 다음 글을 읽고 물음에 답하시오.

Do you know about New Zealand? It has two main islands and 600 smaller islands. Its capital is Wellington. The kiwi, (A)_____, is one of the symbols of the country. If you come to New Zealand, you should visit a Maori village, which shows the native culture of New Zealand. We suggest you try a traditional dish of the Maori people. They cook meat and vegetables in the ground with heated rocks. It is delicious. Many people visit New Zealand to enjoy the beautiful nature. We are happy to invite you to this beautiful country.

08 주어진 어구를 바르게 나열하여 빈칸 (A)에 들어갈 말을 완성 하시오.

(a bird / which / to / New Zealand / native / is)

➡ _____

09 위 글의 내용에 맞게 빈칸에 알맞은 말을 쓰시오.

New Zealand has _____ besides two main islands.

창의사고력 서술형 문제

01 주어진 그림과 문장을 참고하여 〈보기〉와 같이 주제를 소개하는 표현을 쓰시오.

- learn the Maori language
- start a new school year in September
- go to school at the age of five
- change the classroom for each subject

| 보기 |
A: Let's talk about school life in the USA.
B: Students change the classroom for each subject.

02 다음 Yujin에 대해 설명하는 글을 읽고, 관계대명사나 관계부사의 계속적 용법을 사용하여 빈칸에 알맞은 내용을 자유롭게 영작하시오.

- Yujin usually listens to the international radio channels online from various countries.
- Yujin enjoys talking to the foreigner about each other's life and culture.
- Yujin makes the club in her school to study various languages and cultures.
- Yujin wants to go to a foreign language high school, _____.

03 주어진 정보를 이용하여 아일랜드를 홍보하는 글을 완성하시오.

land: the third largest island in Europe
capital: Dublin
the symbol of the country: the color green – It stands for the green land.
the place to visit: the Cliffs of Moher – They show the beautiful nature of Ireland.
the traditional dish: bread boiled in milk with some sugar
the reason people visit Ireland: to get refreshed

We Invite You
Do you know about Ireland? It is _____. Its capital is _____.
The color green, _____, is one of the symbols of the country. If
you come to Ireland, you should visit _____
_____. We suggest you try _____ in Ireland. It is _____
_____. It is very delicious. Many people visit Ireland to _____.

단원별 모의고사

01 다음 단어에 대한 영어 설명이 <u>어색한</u> 것은?

① a couple of: approximately two or three

② appreciate: to feel thanks about something

③ chip: very thinly sliced potato snacks that is sold in a plastic bag

④ native: relating to the place where someone or something grows naturally

⑤ rival: a person who works together with others for a special purpose

02 다음 짝지어진 단어의 관계가 같도록 빈칸에 알맞은 말을 쓰시오.

achieve – achievement : act – _____

03 다음 영영풀이에 해당하는 어구를 고르시오.

to think of an idea suddenly

① be covered with

② look forward to

③ come to one's mind

④ be known as

⑤ take care of

04 다음 중 짝지어진 대화가 <u>어색한</u> 것은?

① A: What can we do if we visit India?
B: I suggest we learn yoga.

② A: Let's talk about places in the UK. Where should we visit in the UK?
B: I suggest we visit Big Ben.

③ A: Let's talk about activities we can enjoy in Canada. What should we do in Canada?
B: I suggest we go skiing.

④ A: When you hear the word kiwi, what comes to your mind?
B: I prefer kiwis to apples.

⑤ A: Some students use their cellphones during class.
B: I suggest we promise to turn off our cellphones before the class.

[05~07] 다음 대화를 읽고 물음에 답하시오.

Seho: Good morning.

Jessie, Andy: Hi, Seho.

Seho: (a)I will visit my uncle in Philadelphia this winter. Can you tell me about the city?

Jessie: Sure. I was there a few years ago. First, (A)let's talk about food.

Seho: Okay. What food is Philadelphia famous for?

Jessie: (b)The most famous food in Philadelphia is the cheese steak sandwich. (c)It is a big sandwich filled with beef and melted cheese.

Seho: Good suggestion. I will try it. (d)Are there any places that are popular with tourists?

Andy: (e)I suggest you visit Independence Hall. It is very important in American history.

Seho: Wonderful. Thank you for the information.

Andy: My pleasure.

05 위 대화의 밑줄 (A)와 같은 의미로 사용된 표현이 <u>아닌</u> 것은?

① I'd like to say something about food.

② let me tell you about food.

③ I want to talk about food.

④ may I tell you about food?

⑤ can you tell me about food?

06 위 대화의 밑줄 친 (a)~(e)에 대한 설명 중 잘못된 것은?

① (a) 이번 겨울에 필라델피아를 방문할 것이라는 미래 계획을 말하는 표현으로, 'I'm going to visit'으로 바꾸어 쓸 수 있다.

② (b) 'famous'의 최상급 형태로 'the most famous'를 사용했다.

③ (c) 'filled'는 'sandwich'가 소고기와 녹인 치즈로 채워져 있다는 의미로 현재분사 'filling'으로 고치는 것이 올바르다.

④ (d) 'that are popular with tourists'는 명사 'any places'를 수식하는 주격 관계대명사절로 'that are'는 생략 가능하다.

⑤ (e) 제안하는 표현으로 'you should visit'에서 'should'가 생략된 형태이다.

07 위 대화의 내용과 일치하지 않는 것은?

① Both Jessie and Andy know well about Philadelphia.

② Jessie has been to Philadelphia before.

③ Many people in Philadelphia like to eat the cheese steak sandwich.

④ Seho decides to eat the cheese steak sandwich.

⑤ Andy suggests Seho visit Independence Hall because it is a popular place for Americans.

08 다음 대화의 밑줄 친 우리말에 맞게 주어진 단어를 알맞은 순서로 배열하시오.

> G: My American friend invited me to a potluck dinner next Friday.
>
> B: You know, you should take food to share at the dinner.
>
> G: 무엇을 가져갈지 추천해 줄래?(that / recommend / what / you / I / would / take / ?)

> B: I suggest you take some Korean food. How about Gimbap, Suji?
>
> G: Yes. It's not spicy and it's easy to carry.
>
> B: I think it'll be good for dinner.

➡ _____

09 다음 그림의 빈칸에 주어진 어구를 이용하여 제안이나 권유하는 말을 영어로 쓰시오.

G: _____

crossing the street. (we, look right)

10 다음 대화의 빈칸 (A)에 들어갈 말로 나머지와 성격이 다른 하나는?

> B: Wow, we finally arrived in Hong Kong, Mom.
>
> W: I'm looking forward to our visit. What should we do today, Mike?
>
> B: (A)_____
>
> W: Victoria Peak?
>
> B: It is the highest mountain in Hong Kong and is in a lot of movies. We can enjoy the fantastic view.
>
> W: That sounds good. Let's go.

① I suggest we visit Victoria Peak.

② We'd better visit Victoria Peak.

③ I'd like to say something about visiting Victoria Peak.

④ I think we should visit Victoria Peak.

⑤ Why don't we visit Victoria Peak?

11 다음 내용을 읽고, 질문에 대한 답을 조건에 맞게 영작하시오.

> • Nowadays, people are afraid of the corona virus.
> • The virus causes the critical disease.
> • People hope the cure will come out soon so that they may not worry any longer.

(1) What are people afraid of and why are they afraid of it? (계속적 용법의 관계대명사를 반드시 사용할 것, 12 단어)

➡ _____

(2) What do people hope? (to부정사의 '부사적' 용법을 반드시 사용할 것, 13 단어)

➡ _____

12 다음 중 밑줄 친 부분이 나머지와 다른 용법으로 사용되었고, 어법상으로도 어색한 것을 찾으시오.

① All my school students will go to New Zealand to learn its nature and culture.
② The Maori people practice the haka dance to keep their tradition.
③ The native people of New Zealand like to call 'Kiwis' by the people of other countries.
④ The people of New Zealand do many things to protect the kiwi birds.
⑤ I was sad not to be invited to the festival at the Maori village.

13 다음 중 밑줄 친 to부정사의 용법이 '부사적 용법'으로 쓰인 것은?

① Remember to protect kiwi birds.
② There are many places to see in New Zealand.

③ I was pleased to learn several meanings of the word kiwi.
④ Many people in my country would like to visit New Zealand.
⑤ It's important to save the kiwi birds.

14 다음 그림과 우리말 설명을 보고 괄호 안에 주어진 단어를 모두 활용하여 조건에 맞게 배열하시오.

> 사다리는 이상한 믿음과 관련되어 있는데, 그것은 그 아래로 지나가는 것은 불운을 가져온다는 것이다.
> (a strange belief / linked with / passing / bad luck / ladders are / brings / under them / is that)

(1) 접속사와 대명사를 추가하여 배열하시오.

➡ _____

(2) 계속적 용법의 관계대명사를 추가하여 배열하시오.

➡ _____

[15~16] 다음 밑줄 친 부분과 어법상 쓰임이 같은 것은?

15

> • The students chose to go on a field trip to New Zealand, which is well known for its natural beauty.

① The captain announced which of the players his team would accept.

② Suji has been doing volunteer work, <u>which</u> is doing laundries for the people in need.

③ This is the hospital in <u>which</u> Janet's first daughter was born.

④ If there are only two pens for you to use in the world, <u>which</u> will you choose?

⑤ What she told me didn't bother me but the way in <u>which</u> she said made me totally upset.

16

• Tiffany hurried to the subway station not <u>to be</u> late for the meeting.

① My pet dog likes <u>to ring</u> the bell to say something to me.

② It is not always easy for me <u>to memorize</u> all the guests' names.

③ The judge looked at her watch <u>to check</u> the time.

④ Please don't forget <u>to come</u> a little earlier than we agreed.

⑤ <u>To master</u> swimming skills is too difficult for the little kids.

17 다음 그림을 보고 우리말과 조건에 맞게 영작하시오.

내가 잔디밭에서 네잎 클로버를 발견했는데, 그것이 나에게 행운을 가져올 것이다.
(good luck, would, me, bring 등을 활용, 6 단어)

➡ I found a four-leaf clover among the grass, _____.

[18~21] 다음 글을 읽고 물음에 답하시오.

When you hear the word kiwi, what comes to your mind? Maybe a fruit, but, in New Zealand the word kiwi has a couple of meanings. First, kiwi is the name of a delicious, green fruit. A lot of kiwi fruit is grown there, so New Zealand is known (A)_____ the land of kiwi fruit.

Kiwi is also the name of one of New Zealand's native birds. The kiwi is special to New Zealanders because it is the symbol of the nation. Also, kiwi is a nickname for people from New Zealand. Today, New Zealanders are sometimes called Kiwis throughout the world. Now, you know that kiwi is the name of (B)_____, (C)_____, and also (D)_____. Next time, don't become confused when someone uses the word kiwi, which has several meanings.

18 다음 중 빈칸 (A)에 들어갈 말과 같은 말이 들어가는 것은?

① Let me introduce myself _____ you.

② She is worried _____ her test results.

③ He thought of the place _____ his home.

④ The detective promised to look _____ the matter.

⑤ Some people are very difficult to deal _____.

19 빈칸 (B)~(D)에 들어갈 말을 위 글에서 찾아 쓰시오.

➡ (B)_____ (C)_____ (D)_____

20 According to the passage, what can you call people from New Zealand? Answer in English with five words.

➡ _____

21 다음 중 위 글의 내용과 일치하지 <u>않는</u> 것은?

① Kiwi has various meanings in New Zealand.

② New Zealand is known as the land of kiwi fruit.

③ Kiwi is the most popular fruit in New Zealand.

④ New Zealanders think the bird kiwi to be special.

⑤ It can be confusing to understand what kiwi means unless you know its several meanings.

[22~23] 다음 글을 읽고 물음에 답하시오.

New Zealand is a place of natural beauty. It has many beautiful lakes and waterfalls. ① In the South Island, there are mountains that are covered with snow all year round. ② You will be amazed by the fantastic views. ③
In the North Island, there are many hot springs, lakes, and areas with green grass. ④ Because of its natural beauty, many famous movies have been made in New Zealand. ⑤ If you visit New Zealand, you will surely appreciate its nature.

22 ①~⑤ 중 주어진 문장이 들어가기에 가장 적절한 곳은?

New Zealand has two main islands, the South Island and the North Island.

①   ②   ③   ④   ⑤

23 다음 중 위 글을 읽고 답할 수 <u>없는</u> 것은?

① What is New Zealand famous for?

② What are there in the North Island?

③ How many main islands does New Zealand have?

④ How many movies have been made in New Zealand?

⑤ What will we appreciate when we visit New Zealand?

[24~25] 다음 글을 읽고 물음에 답하시오.

Now, let's talk about the Maori. They are the native people of New Zealand. They went to live on the islands long before Europeans arrived. (A)The Maori culture is an important part of today's New Zealand society. The Maori language is taught at some schools and there are Maori language radio and TV stations. There are Maori villages in many parts of the country. You can visit Maori villages and experience Maori culture. If you say "kia ora" to the villagers, they will be glad to hear it. It means "hi" in English.

24 According to the passage, what does "kia ora" mean in English?

➡ _____

25 글쓴이가 밑줄 친 (A)와 같이 말한 이유로 가장 적절한 것은?

① New Zealanders don't care about the Maori people.

② People in New Zealand maintain the Maori language and culture.

③ It is easy to find people speaking only the Maori language.

④ There live only the Maori people in New Zealand.

⑤ The Maori people have built many schools in New Zealand.

MEMO

Lesson 7

How to Get Along with People

🎤 의사소통 기능

- 요청하기

  Do you mind helping me?

- 감사하기

  I really appreciate your advice.

🎤 언어 형식

- 관계부사 'how'

  June didn't like **how** Mike had acted.

- The + 비교급 ~, the + 비교급 …

  The more sincere your apology is, **the better** it will be received.

Words & Expressions

Key Words

- **accidentally** [æksədéntəli] 부 우연히, 뜻하지 않게
- **apologize** [əpálədʒàiz] 동 사과하다
- **apology** [əpálədʒi] 명 사과
- **appreciate** [əprí:ʃièit] 동 고마워하다, 감사하다
- **borrow** [bárou] 동 빌리다
- **brave** [breiv] 형 용감한
- **break** [breik] 동 (관계를) 끝내다, 끊다
- **cafeteria** [kæfətíəriə] 명 구내식당
- **case** [keis] 명 사례, 경우
- **casual** [kǽʒuəl] 형 대충하는, 건성의
- **cheerful** [tʃíərfəl] 형 발랄한, 쾌활한
- **delete** [dilí:t] 동 삭제하다
- **dislike** [disláik] 동 싫어하다
- **elementary school** 초등학교
- **emotional** [imóuʃəul] 형 감정적인
- **especially** [ispéʃəli] 부 특히, 유난히
- **feeling** [fí:liŋ] 명 느낌, 감정
- **generous** [dʒénərəs] 형 너그러운
- **helpful** [hélpfəl] 형 도움이 되는, 유용한
- **humorous** [hjú:mərəs] 형 재미있는, 유머러스한
- **hurry** [hə́:ri] 동 서두르다, 급히 가다
- **hurt** [hə:rt] 명 상처 형 기분이 상한, 상처를 입은 동 마음을 아프게 하다, 감정을 상하게 하다
- **ignore** [ignɔ́:r] 동 무시하다
- **include** [inklú:d] 동 포함하다

- **intend** [inténd] 동 의도하다
- **let** [let] 동 (~하게) 놓아두다, (~을 하도록) 허락하다
- **loud** [laud] 형 소리가 큰, 시끄러운
- **mind** [maind] 동 꺼리다, 싫어하다 명 마음
- **mistake** [mistéik] 명 실수, 잘못
- **necessary** [nésəsèri] 형 필요한
- **nervous** [nə́:rvəs] 형 긴장하는, 초조해 하는
- **prepare** [pripɛ́ər] 동 ~을 준비하다(for)
- **proper** [prápər] 형 적절한, 제대로 된
- **receive** [risí:v] 동 받다, 받아들이다
- **regret** [rigrét] 동 후회하다
- **relationship** [riléiʃənʃip] 명 관계
- **relaxed** [rilǽkst] 형 느긋한, 여유 있는
- **responsibility** [rispànsəbíləti] 명 책임
- **right** [rait] 부 바르게, 정확하게
- **seem** [si:m] 동 (~인 것처럼) 보이다, ~인 것 같다
- **serious** [síəriəs] 형 심각한, 진지한
- **sincere** [sinsíər] 형 진정한, 진심 어린
- **sincerely** [sinsíərli] 부 진심으로
- **solve** [salv] 동 해결하다
- **suggestion** [səgdʒéstʃən] 명 의견, 제안
- **thoughtful** [θɔ́:tfəl] 형 사려 깊은, 생각에 잠긴
- **tray** [trei] 명 식판, 쟁반
- **treat** [tri:t] 동 처리하다, 대우하다
- **wound** [wu:nd] 명 상처, 부상

Key Expressions

- **add up to** (결과가) ~가 되다, ~임을 보여 주다
- **after all** (설명 · 이유를 덧붙일 때) 어쨌든, (예상과는 달리) 결국에는
- **at once** 즉시
- **be busy –ing** ~하느라 바쁘다
- **bump into** ~에 부딪히다
- **care about** ~에 마음을 쓰다, ~에 관심을 가지다
- **get along with** ~와 잘 지내다
- **get into the rhythm** 리듬을 타다
- **laugh off** ~을 웃어넘기려 하다

- **make a mistake** 실수를 하다
- **pass by** 지나가다
- **pick out** 선택하다, 고르다
- **seem to+동사원형** ~처럼 보이다
- **take responsibility for** ~에 책임을 지다
- **think nothing of** ~을 아무렇지 않게 여기다
- **trip over** ~에 걸려 넘어지다
- **turn down** (소리를) 줄이다
- **with all one's heart** 진심으로

Word Power

※ 서로 비슷한 뜻을 가진 어휘

- ☐ **thoughtful** 사려 깊은 – **considerate** 배려하는
- ☐ **accidentally** 우연히 – **by chance** 우연히
- ☐ **delete** 삭제하다 – **cancel** 삭제하다, 지우다
- ☐ **dislike** 싫어하다 – **hate** 싫어[혐오]하다
- ☐ **generous** 너그러운, 후한 – **lavish** 아끼지 않는
- ☐ **helpful** 유용한, 도움이 되는 – **useful** 유용한

- ☐ **ignore** 무시하다 – **disregard** 무시하다
- ☐ **regret** 후회하다 – **repent** 후회하다
- ☐ **nervous** 긴장하는 – **anxious** 초조한
- ☐ **proper** 적절한 – **appropriate** 적절한
- ☐ **sincere** 진심어린 – **serious** 진지한, 진정인
- ☐ **prepare** 준비하다 – **arrange** 정하다, 준비하다

※ 서로 반대되는 뜻을 가진 어휘

- ☐ **emotional** 감정적인 ↔ **emotionless** 감정이 없는
- ☐ **necessary** 필요한 ↔ **unnecessary** 불필요한
- ☐ **generous** 후한, 너그러운 ↔ **stingy, mean** 인색한
- ☐ **brave** 용감한 ↔ **timid** 겁 많은, 소심한

- ☐ **receive** 받다 ↔ **give** 주다
- ☐ **right** 바르게 ↔ **wrong** 틀리게
- ☐ **cheerful** 즐거운, 쾌활한 ↔ **gloomy** 우울한

※ 형용사 – 명사

- ☐ **generous** 너그러운, 후한 – **generosity** 관대함
- ☐ **nervous** 긴장하는 – **nerve** 신경, 긴장

- ☐ **helpful** 도움이 되는 – **help** 도움
- ☐ **proper** 적절한 – **propriety** 적절, 적당함

※ 동사 – 명사

- ☐ **ignore** 무시하다 – **ignorance** 무지, 무식
- ☐ **include** 포함하다 – **inclusion** 포함

- ☐ **solve** 해결하다 – **solution** 해결책, 해법
- ☐ **intend** 의도하다 – **intention** 의도

English Dictionary

- ☐ **accidentally** 우연히
  → in a way that was not planned or intended
  계획되거나 의도되지 않은 방식으로

- ☐ **apology** 사과
  → an act of saying that you are sorry for something wrong you have done
  당신이 저지른 잘못된 일에 미안하다고 말하는 행위

- ☐ **appreciate** 감사하다
  → to be grateful for something
  무언가에 고마워하다

- ☐ **brave** 용감한
  → showing no fear of dangerous or difficult things
  위험하거나 어려운 일에 대해 어떠한 두려움도 보이지 않는

- ☐ **delete** 삭제하다
  → to remove part or all of a written or electronic text
  서면이나 전자 텍스트의 일부 또는 전부를 제거하다

- ☐ **generous** 관대한, 너그러운
  → willing to give money, help, kindness, etc., especially more than is usual or expected
  평소 또는 예상했던 것보다 더 많이 돈, 도움, 친절을 기꺼이 주는

- ☐ **ignore** 무시하다
  → to intentionally not listen or give attention to
  의도적으로 듣지 않거나 주의를 기울이지 않다

- ☐ **prepare** 준비하다
  → to make or get something or someone ready for something that will happen in the future
  어떤 일이나 사람이 미래에 일어날 일에 준비가 되도록 하다

- ☐ **relationship** 관계
  → the way in which two things are connected
  두 가지가 연결되는 방식

- ☐ **responsibility** 책임
  → something that it is your job or duty to deal with
  당신이 처리해야 할 일이나 의무인 것

- ☐ **sincere** 진정한, 진심어린
  → honest and true, and based on what you really feel and believe
  정직하고 진실하며, 당신이 정말로 느끼고 믿는 것에 근거하는

- ☐ **suggestion** 제안
  → an idea, plan, or action that is suggested or the act of suggesting it
  제안되는 아이디어, 계획 또는 행동 또는 제안하는 행위

- ☐ **thoughtful** 사려 깊은
  → always thinking of the things you can do to make people happy or comfortable
  사람들을 행복하게 하거나 편안하게 하기 위해 할 수 있는 일들을 항상 생각하는

01 중요 다음 문장의 빈칸에 공통으로 들어갈 말로 알맞은 것은?

• Those are not _____ clothes for an interview.

• Their goal is to promote _____ Korean language usage among Koreans.

① nervous　　② gloomy

③ proper　　④ generous

⑤ casual

02 서답형 빈칸에 주어진 〈영영풀이〉를 읽고 알맞은 단어를 쓰시오.

The high school principal was touched by such a _____ gesture.

┌─영영풀이─

always thinking of the things you can do to make people happy or comfortable

[03~04] 다음 설명에 해당하는 단어를 고르시오.

03

honest and true, and based on what you really feel and believe

① repair　　② proper

③ anxious　　④ cheerful

⑤ sincere

04

to make or get something or someone ready for something that will happen in the future

① repair　　② prepare

③ proper　　④ promote

⑤ solve

05 서답형 다음 우리말에 맞게 빈칸에 알맞은 말을 쓰시오.

야생 동물들은 보통 다른 종들과는 잘 어울리지 않습니다.

➡ Wild animals usually don't _____ _____ well _____ other species.

06 중요 다음 빈칸에 들어갈 말이 바르게 짝지어진 것은?

(A) Remember that anything you post on the Internet will stay there forever, even if you _____ it.

(B) If you are interested in this program, you should _____ because only 100 lucky students will be able to attend this school.

	(A)	(B)
①	store	recommend
②	store	apologize
③	post	receive
④	delete	hurry
⑤	delete	appreciate

07 다음 짝지어진 단어의 관계가 나머지와 다른 하나는?

① generous – generosity

② nervous – nerve

③ proper – propriety

④ helpful – help

⑤ intend – intention

01 다음 빈칸에 들어갈 말을 〈보기〉에서 찾아 쓰시오. (필요하면 어형을 변화시키고, 동사는 현재형으로 쓸 것.)

┌─ 보기 ┐
emotion   relax   suggest   appreciate
└─────────┘

(1) Do you have any _____ or ideas to improve education and your school?

(2) Some people believe that pets may help patients recover faster with _____ support.

(3) Stretching is a good way to stay fit and feel _____.

(4) We _____ someone's listening to us, because it shows that the person cares.

02 다음 문장의 빈칸에 공통으로 들어갈 단어를 주어진 철자로 시작하여 쓰시오.

┌──────────────────────────┐
• If you feel n_____, try standing straight with your shoulders back.
• Try to act confidently, even if you feel n_____.
• I thought I would remain calm, but when I was confronted with the TV camera, I became very n_____.
└──────────────────────────┘

03 다음 우리말과 같은 표현이 되도록 문장의 빈칸을 채우시오.

(1) 운전자들은 가끔 속도를 내고, 신호를 무시하고 달리며, 도로의 규칙들을 무시한다.
➡ Divers often speed, run lights, and _____ the rules of the road.

(2) 그는 일을 그만두기로 한 자신의 결정을 조금도 후회하지 않는다.
➡ He does not _____ his decision to quit his job one bit.

(3) 화장실을 쓰려고 줄을 서서 기다리고 있었는데, 한 아이가 우연히 내 신발에 침을 뱉었어.
➡ I waited in line to use the bathroom, and a kid _____ spat on my shoes.

(4) 거주자들은 관광객 또는 고양이들을 꺼리는 것 같지 않습니다.
➡ The residents do not seem to _____ the tourists or the cats.

04 영영풀이에 해당하는 단어를 〈보기〉에서 찾아 첫 번째 빈칸에 쓰고, 두 번째 빈칸에는 우리말 뜻을 쓰시오.

┌─ 보기 ┐
relationship   generous   responsibility
apology
└─────────┘

(1) _____: something that it is your job or duty to deal with: _____

(2) _____: an act of saying that you are sorry for something wrong you have done: _____

(3) _____: the way in which two things are connected: _____

(4) _____: willing to give money, help, kindness, etc., especially more than is usual or expected: _____

① 요청하기

Do you mind helping me? 나를 도와 줄 수 있나요?

■ 'Do you mind ~ing?'는 '당신은 ~하는 것이 괜찮으신가요?'라는 뜻으로 상대방에게 무엇인가를 조심스럽고 정중하게 요청할 때 사용하는 표현이다. mind는 동명사를 목적어로 취하기 때문에 동사 뒤에 ~ing를 붙인 형태를 사용한다. 동명사 대신 if절을 사용하여 'Do you mind if ~?'로 좀 더 정중하게 물을 수 있으며 'Would you mind ~?'로 물을 수도 있다.

■ 요청에 답하는 표현
  • 요청을 승낙할 때 mind는 '꺼리다'의 뜻이므로 부정어(not)를 써서 승낙을 표현한다.
    Of course not. / Not at all. / Surely not. / Certainly not. / No, I don't (mind).
  • 요청을 거절할 때 Sorry라고 말하면서 거절하는 이유를 덧붙여 말하며, Yes라고 답하면 '꺼린다'라는 거절의 표현이 된다.
    (I'm) Sorry, but I can't ~. / Yes, I do[would]. / Sure. / Of course.
    • **A:** Do you mind opening the door? 문을 열어 주시겠어요?
      B: Not at all (= Of course not. / No problem.) 물론입니다.
    • **A:** Do you mind turning off your cell phone? 네 휴대전화를 꺼 줄 수 있니?
      B: Of course not. 물론이야.

요청하기의 다른 표현들

- (Please) Help me.
- Can you help me(, please)?
- Could I ask you to help me?
- Is it okay if I ~?
  • 제안, 권유, 요청에 답하기
    (긍정) Yes. / Okay. / Sure. / All right. / No problem.
    (부정) (I'm) Sorry, but I can't. / I'm afraid I can't. / Thank you, but ~. / No, thank you.

핵심 Check

1. 다음 우리말과 일치하도록 빈칸에 알맞은 말은?

> **A:** Do you mind taking a picture with us? 우리랑 사진 찍을래?
> **B:** _____ Let's use my phone. 물론이야. 내 전화기를 사용하자.

① Of course.　　② Certainly.　　③ Of course not.
④ Yes, I do.　　⑤ Sure.

2 감사하기

I really appreciate your advice. 당신의 충고에 정말 감사드립니다.

■ 감사하기 표현

감사하는 표현은 아주 간단히 'Thank you.'로 할 수 있지만 좀 더 정중하게 표현할 때는 '감사하다'는 의미를 가지는 동사 appreciate를 사용하여 'I appreciate ~.'로 표현할 수 있다. 이때 appreciate 뒤에는 감사의 내용이 오면 된다.

예를 들어 너의 친절이 감사하다고 할 때는 'I appreciate your kindness.'라고 쓰면 된다. '네가 ~해주면 감사하겠다.'고 상대방에게 정중히 부탁할 때에는 'I would appreciate it if you ~.'라고 표현한다.

• **A:** I really appreciate your advice. 당신의 충고에 정말 감사드립니다.

  B: Not at all. I'm glad that I could help you. 천만에요. 당신을 도울 수 있어서 기쁩니다.

■ 감사하기 표현에 대한 응답 표현

'I appreciate ~.'에 대한 대답은 'You're welcome.', 'No problem.', 'Not at all.', '(It was) My pleasure.', 'Don't mention it.' 등을 사용하면 된다.

• **A:** I appreciate your help.

  B: You're welcome.

■ 감사하기의 다른 표현

– Thanks for your advice.

– Thanks (a lot). / Thank you (very / so) much.

핵심 Check

2. 다음 빈칸에 들어갈 말로 <u>어색한</u> 것은?

> **B:** Irene, what are you doing?
>
> **G:** Well, I've lost my favorite cap. I can't find it.
>
> **B:** Let me help you. What does it look like?
>
> **G:** It's red. My name is written in black on the side.
>
> **B:** Oh, is this yours? It was under the table.
>
> **G:** Yes, it is. Thank you, Jim. I appreciate your help.
>
> **B:** _____

① It's my pleasure.　② Don't mention it.　③ You're welcome.

④ Not at all.　⑤ You're right.

Listen & Speak 1 A-1

B: Judy, ❶do you mind turning down the volume?

G: ❷No, I don't. Is it too loud?

B: Yes, it is. I can hear it in my room.

G: I'm sorry. I'll ❸turn it down.

B: Thanks a lot.

B: Judy, 볼륨을 좀 낮춰 줄래?
G: 그래. 소리가 너무 크니?
B: 응, 소리가 커. 내 방에서도 소리가 들려.
G: 미안해. 내가 볼륨을 낮출게.
B: 정말 고마워.

❶ Do you mind ~ing?는 '당신은 ~하는 것이 괜찮으신가요?'라는 뜻으로 상대방에게 무엇인가를 조심스럽고 정중하게 요청할 때 사용하는 표현이다. mind는 동명사를 목적어로 취하기 때문에 동사 뒤에 ~ing를 붙인 동명사 형태를 사용한다.

❷ 요청을 승낙하는 표현으로, mind는 '꺼리다'의 뜻이므로 부정어(not)를 써서 승낙을 표현한다. Of course not. / Not at all. / Surely not. / Certainly not. / No, I don't (mind). 등으로 바꾸어 말할 수 있다.

❸ '동사(turn)+부사(down)' 형태의 '이어동사'로 목적어가 인칭대명사일 때는 반드시 '동사+대명사+부사' 어순을 취한다.

Check(√) True or False

(1) Judy asks the boy for a favor politely. T ☐ F ☐

(2) Judy is going to turn down the volume. T ☐ F ☐

Listen & Speak 2 A-1

G: You ❶seem to be busy, Minsu. Can I come in?

B: Sure. I'm preparing for the dance contest, but it's not easy.

G: I can help you. I was in the contest last year.

B: Really? That would be great, Amy.

G: You ❷are good at getting into the rhythm. But ❸one thing you need to do is to be more relaxed. You are too nervous.

B: Your advice is very helpful. ❹I really appreciate your advice.

G: ❺It's my pleasure.

G: 민수야, 너 바빠 보인다. 나 들어가도 되니?
B: 물론. 나 춤 경연대회를 준비하고 있는데 쉽지 않아.
G: 내가 도와줄게. 나 작년에 대회에 참가 했었거든.
B: 정말? Amy, 그거 정말 좋을 거 같아.
G: 너는 리듬을 타는 건 잘하는 편이야. 하지만 네가 해야 할 한 가지는 긴장을 더 푸는 것이야. 너는 너무 긴장을 해.
B: 네 조언이 정말 도움이 된다. 너의 조언 정말 고마워.
G: 도움이 됐다니 기뻐.

❶ 'seem+ 부정사'는 '~처럼 보인다'라는 의미로, 의견을 제시하는 표현이다. 'It seems (to me) that you are busy, Minsu.'로 바꾸어 쓸 수 있다.

❷ 'be good at'은 '~을 잘한다'라는 의미로, 전치사 'at' 다음에는 '동명사 'getting'이 와야 한다.

❸ 'you need to do'는 주어인 'one thing'을 수식하는 관계대명사절로 목적격 관계대명사 'that/which'가 생략되어 있다. 주어가 단수 명사(one thing)이므로 단수동사 'is'가 사용되었다. 'to be ~'는 보어 자리에 사용된 to부정사의 명사적 용법이다.

❹ 'I appreciate ~.'는 감사를 나타내는 표현으로 appreciate 뒤에는 감사의 내용이 오면 된다.

❺ I appreciate ~.에 대한 대답으로 You're welcome. No problem., Not at all., Don't mention it. 등으로 바꾸어 사용할 수 있다.

Check(√) True or False

(3) Minsu is preparing for the singing contest. T ☐ F ☐

(4) Amy advised Minsu to be more relaxed. T ☐ F ☐

Listen & Speak 1 A-3

B: Karen, do you mind coming to my house tomorrow at 7 a.m.?

G: That's very early.

B: I know, but I need the book ❶that you borrowed before class.

G: I see. Then ❷let's meet at seven.

B: See you then.

B: Karen, 내일 오전 7시에 우리 집에 와 줄래?

G: 그건 너무 이른데.

B: 그건 알지만, 수업 시작하기 전에 네가 빌려 갔던 책이 필요하거든.

G: 알겠어. 그럼 7시에 보자.

B: 그때 보자

❶ 목적격 관계대명사절로 선행사 'the book'을 수식한다. 이때 'that'은 생략 가능하다.
❷ '~하자'는 뜻으로 제안을 할 때 사용한다.

Check(√) True or False

(5) Karen won't go to the boy's house tomorrow at 7 a.m.　　T ☐ F ☐

(6) The boy needs the book that Karen borrowed before class.　　T ☐ F ☐

Listen & Speak 2 A-2

B: Irene, what are you doing?

G: Well, I've lost my favorite cap. I can't find it.

B: ❶Let me help you. ❷What does it look like?

G: It's red. My name ❸is written in black on the side.

B: Oh, is this yours? It was under the table.

G: Yes, it is. Thank you, Jim. I appreciate your help.

B: ❹No problem.

B: Irene, 너 뭐하고 있어?

G: 음, 내가 제일 좋아하는 모자를 잃어버렸어. 그 모자를 못 찾겠어.

B: 내가 도와줄게. 그것은 어떻게 생겼어?

G: 그건 빨간색이야. 모자 옆 부분에 내 이름이 검은색으로 쓰여 있어.

B: 오, 이거 네 것이니? 이거 탁자 아래에 있었어.

G: 응, 맞아. 고마워, Jim. 도와줘서 고마워.

B: 천만에.

❶ 'Let+목적어+목적보어(원형부정사)' 형태로 '…가 ~하도록 하게 하다'라는 뜻이다.
❷ 사람이나 사물의 외모나 모습을 물어보는 표현이다.
❸ 'be+과거분사'의 수동태로 '이름이 쓰여 있다'라는 의미이다.
❹ 감사를 표현하는 말에 대한 대답으로 '천만에.'라고 해석한다. 'You're welcome., Not at all., Don't mention it.' 등으로 바꾸어 사용할 수 있다.

Check(√) True or False

(7) Irene has found her favorite cap.　　T ☐ F ☐

(8) Irene's cap was under the table.　　T ☐ F ☐

Listen & Speak 1 A-2

G: I ❶accidentally broke my mom's favorite plate.

B: ❷That's too bad, Mina.

G: ❸Do you mind telling me how to say sorry to her?

B: No, not at all. You should apologize sincerely.

G: I see. I'll talk to her with all my heart.

❶ 'accidentally'는 '우연히'라는 뜻으로, 'by chance', 'by accident'로 바꾸어 쓸 수 있다.
❷ 상대방의 좋지 않은 일에 대한 반응으로 '안됐구나.'라는 뜻이다.
❸ 상대방에게 요청하는 표현으로 'Is it OK if I ask you to tell me how to say sorry to her?'로 바꾸어 쓸 수 있다.

Real Life Talk

Jessie: Hi, Andy. What's up?

Andy: Hi, Jessie. I'm going to buy a present for Amy. ❶You've been friends with her for a long time, haven't you?

Jessie: Yes, since first grade in elementary school.

Andy: Well, I know ❷you're really busy studying, but do you mind helping me? I am sure you could ❸help me pick out something nice.

Jessie: No problem. What's the present for? It's not her birthday.

Andy: Well, two months ago, when my leg was broken, she carried my backpack to school.

Jessie: That was nice of her.

Andy: Yes, it was. What should I get for her?

Jessie: Well, ❹how about a case for her smartphone? She broke her case recently.

Andy: Really? Thank you for your suggestion.

❶ 현재완료 형태로 부사구 'for a long time'과 호응하여 과거부터 현재까지의 상태를 나타낸다. 'haven't you?'는 부가의문문으로 평서문의 긍정문 조동사 'have'를 부정으로 바꾸어 사용한다.
❷ 'be busy+ing'는 '~하느라 바쁘다'라는 표현이다.
❸ 'help+목적어+목적보어(원형부정사)' 구문이다. 목적보어 자리에는 'to부정사'를 사용할 수도 있다.
❹ 'how about+명사/동명사 ~?'는 상대방에게 제안하는 표현으로 '~는 어때?'라는 뜻이다.

Wrap Up 1

G: ❶I am planning to go to Jejudo.

B: That's cool, Suhee. I ❷used to live there.

G: Do you mind telling me ❸what to do in Jejudo?

B: Not at all. Jejudo has many beautiful beaches. You should visit them.

G: Good. I will go swimming. What else can I do?

B: ❹Why don't you hike Halla Mountain? You can see the mountain from everywhere on the island.

G: Great. How about food?

B: If you like fish, on Jejudo raw fish is fresh and delicious.

G: I'll try everything. I appreciate your tips.

❶ 'be planning to+동사원형'은 '~할 계획이다, ~하려고 하다'라는 뜻으로 미래 계획을 말할 때 사용한다.
❷ 'used to+동사원형'은 '~하곤 했다'라는 과거의 습관을 나타내는 표현이다.
❸ '의문사+to부정사' 형태로 목적어 자리에 사용된 to부정사의 명사적 용법이다.
❹ 'Why don't you+동사원형?'은 제안할 때 사용하는 표현으로 '~하는 게 어때?'라는 의미이다.

Wrap Up 2

W: Mike does not feel very well. He ❶might have caught a cold. He needs to see a doctor, but he has a meeting with Jane in an hour. He wants to meet her tomorrow instead. What should he say to her?

❶ 'might have+과거분사'는 과거의 추측을 나타내는 표현으로 '~이었을지 몰라'라는 뜻이다.

● 다음 우리말과 일치하도록 빈칸에 알맞은 말을 쓰시오.

Listen & Speak 1 A-1

B: Judy, do you _____ _____ down the volume?

G: _____, _____ _____. Is it too _____?

B: Yes, it is. I can _____ it in my room.

G: I'm sorry. I'll _____ _____ _____.

B: _____ a lot.

Listen & Speak 1 A-2

G: I _____ broke my mom's _____ _____.

B: _____ _____ _____, Mina.

G: _____ _____ _____ _____ me _____ _____ _____ sorry to her?

B: No, _____ _____ _____. You should _____ _____.

G: I see. I'll talk to her _____ _____ _____ _____.

Listen & Speak 1 A-3

B: Karen, do you mind _____ to my house tomorrow at 7 a.m.?

G: That's very _____.

B: I know, but I need the book _____ you _____ before class.

G: I see. Then _____ meet at seven.

B: See you _____.

Listen & Speak 1 B

A: Hellen, do you mind _____ _____?

B: No, I don't. / Sorry _____ I can't.

A: Hellen, do you mind _____ _____ _____?

B: No, I don't. / Sorry but I _____.

해석

B: Judy, 볼륨을 좀 낮춰 줄래?
G: 그래. 소리가 너무 크니?
B: 응, 소리가 커. 내 방에서도 들려
G: 미안해. 내가 볼륨을 낮출게.
B: 정말 고마워.

G: 내가 실수로 엄마가 제일 좋아하는 접시를 깼어.
B: 그것 참 안됐구나, 미나야.
G: 엄마한테 미안하다고 어떻게 말해야 하는지 말해 줄래?
B: 응, 물론이지. 너는 진심으로 사과해야 해.
G: 알겠어. 엄마에게 진심으로 이야기해야겠어.

B: Karen, 내일 오전 7시에 우리 집에 와 줄래?
G 그건 너무 이른데.
B: 그건 알지만, 수업 시작하기 전에 네가 빌려 갔던 책이 필요하거든.
G: 알겠어. 그럼 7시에 보자.
B: 그때 보자

A: Hellen, 조용히 좀 해 줄래?
B: 알았어. / 미안하지만 그럴 수 없어.

A: Hellen, 쓰레기 좀 주워 줄래?
B: 알았어. / 미안하지만 그럴 수 없어.

해석

Listen & Speak 2 A-1

G: You _____ _____ be busy, Minsu. Can I come in?

B: Sure. I'm _____ for the dance _____, but it's not easy.

G: I can help you. I was in the _____ last year.

B: Really? That would be _____, Amy.

G: You _____ _____ _____ _____ into the _____. But one thing you need to do is to be more _____. You are too _____.

B: Your _____ is very _____. I really _____ your advice.

G: It's my _____.

G: 민수야, 너 바빠 보인다. 나 들어가도 되니?
B: 물론. 나 춤 경연대회를 준비하고 있는데 쉽지 않아.
G: 내가 도와줄게. 나 작년에 대회에 참가했었거든.
B: 정말? Amy, 그거 정말 좋을 거 같아.
G: 너는 리듬을 타는 건 잘하는 편이야. 하지만 네가 해야 할 한 가지는 긴장을 더 푸는 것이야. 너는 너무 긴장을 해.
B: 네 조언이 정말 도움이 된다. 너의 조언 정말 고마워.
G: 도움이 됐다니 기뻐.

Listen & Speak 2 A-2

B: Irene, what are you doing?

G: Well, I've _____ my favorite cap. I can't find it.

B: _____ _____ _____ you. _____ does it look _____?

G: It's red. My name _____ _____ in black on the side.

B: Oh, is this _____? It was under the table.

G: Yes, it is. Thank you, Jim. I _____ your help.

B: _____ _____.

B: Irene, 너 뭐 하고 있어?
G: 음, 내가 제일 좋아하는 모자를 잃어버렸어. 그 모자를 못 찾겠어.
B: 내가 도와줄게. 그것은 어떻게 생겼어?
G: 그건 빨간색이야. 모자 옆 부분에 내 이름이 검은색으로 쓰여 있어.
B: 오, 이거 네 것이니? 이거 탁자 아래에 있었어.
G: 응, 맞아. 고마워, Jim. 도와줘서 고마워.
B: 천만에.

Listen & Speak 2 B

A: _____ me _____ you the way.

B: I _____ your time.

A: _____ _____ _____ your backpack.

B: I _____ _____.

A: 제가 길을 알려 줄게요.
B: 시간 내 줘서 감사합니다.

A: 내가 너의 가방을 들어 줄게.
B: 도와 줘서 고마워.

Real Life Talk

Jessie: Hi, Andy. _____ _____?

Andy: Hi, Jessie. I'm going to buy a present for Amy. You'_____ _____ friends with her for a long time, _____ you?

Jessie: Yes, _____ first grade in _____ school.

Andy: Well, I know you're really _____ _____, but _____ _____ _____ _____ me? I am sure you could _____ _____ _____ something nice.

Jessie: 안녕, Andy. 무슨 일이니?
Andy: 안녕, Jessie. 나는 Amy한테 줄 선물을 사려고 해. 너는 그 애와 오랫동안 친구로 지냈지, 그렇지 않니?
Jessie: 응, 초등학교 1학년 때부터.
Andy: 음, 네가 공부하느라 바쁘다는 것을 알지만, 나를 좀 도와줄 수 있니? 괜찮은 것을 고르도록 네가 도와줄 수 있을 것이라고 확신해.

Jessie: No _____ . What's the present _____ ? It's not her birthday.

Andy: Well, two months ago, when my leg _____ _____ , she carried my backpack to school.

Jessie: That was nice _____ _____ .

Andy: Yes, it was. What should I get for her?

Jessie: Well, _____ _____ a case for her smartphone? She broke her case _____ .

Andy: Really? Thank you for your _____ .

Wrap Up 1

G: I _____ _____ _____ _____ to Jejudo.

B: That's _____ , Suhee. I _____ _____ _____ there.

G: _____ _____ _____ me _____ _____ _____ in Jejudo?

B: _____ _____ _____ . Jejudo has many beautiful _____ . You should visit them.

G: Good. I will go _____ . What _____ can I do?

B: Why _____ _____ hike Halla Mountain? You can see the mountain from _____ on the island.

G: Great. _____ _____ food?

B: If you like fish, on Jejudo _____ _____ is _____ and _____ .

G: I'll try everything. I _____ your _____ .

Wrap Up 2

W: Mike does not feel very _____ . He _____ _____ _____ a cold. He _____ _____ see a doctor, but he has a meeting with Jane in an hour. He wants _____ _____ her tomorrow _____ . What should he say to her?

동 해석:

Jessie: 좋아. 무엇을 위한 선물이니? 그 애의 생일은 아닌데.
Andy: 음, 두 달 전에 내 다리가 부러졌을 때, 그 애가 학교까지 내 가방을 들어줬어.
Jessie: 그 애는 정말 친절했구나.
Andy: 응, 그랬어. 그 애를 위해 무엇을 사야 할까?
Jessie: 음, 스마트폰 케이스는 어떠니? 그 애는 최근에 케이스를 깨뜨렸어.
Andy: 정말? 제안해 줘서 고마워.

G: 나는 제주도에 갈 계획이야.
B: 그거 멋지다, 수희야. 나 예전에 제주도에 살았어.
G: 내가 제주도에서 뭘 해야 하는지 말해 줄래?
B: 물론. 제주도에는 아름다운 해변들이 많아. 그 해변들을 꼭 가봐야 해.
G: 좋아. 나는 수영하러 갈 거야. 그 밖에 내가 할 수 있는 것은 무엇이니?
B: 한라산을 등반해 보는 건 어때? 섬의 모든 곳에서 그 산을 볼 수 있어.
G: 좋아. 음식은 어때?
B: 네가 생선을 좋아한다면, 제주도에서는 회가 신선하고 맛있어.
G: 나는 모든 걸 다 해 볼 거야. 조언해 줘서 고마워.

W: Mike는 몸이 좋지 않아. 그는 감기에 걸렸을지도 몰라. 그는 병원에 가야 하지만, 한 시간 후에 Jane과 회의가 있어. 그는 대신 내일 그녀를 만나기를 원해. 그는 그녀에게 뭐라고 말해야 할까?

01 우리말에 맞도록 문장의 빈칸에 알맞은 말을 쓰시오.

> Do you _____ _____ me? (나를 도와 줄 수 있나요?)

02 대화의 빈칸에 들어갈 말로 알맞은 것을 <u>모두</u> 고르시오.

> A: Let me carry your backpack.
>
> B: _____

① I appreciate your kindness.

② I appreciate your advice.

③ I'm not quite sure if you can carry my backpack.

④ I appreciate your help.

⑤ I appreciate your consideration.

03 다음 대화의 빈칸에 들어갈 말로 <u>어색한</u> 표현은?

> G: I accidentally broke my mom's favorite plate.
>
> B: That's too bad, Mina.
>
> G: Do you mind telling me how to say sorry to her?
>
> B: _____ You should apologize sincerely.
>
> G: I see. I'll talk to her with all my heart.

① No, not at all.　　　② Of course.

③ Surely not.　　　　④ Certainly not.

⑤ No, I don't.

04 다음 대화의 밑줄 친 부분의 의도로 알맞은 것은?

> A: I really <u>appreciate your advice.</u>
>
> B: Not at all. I'm glad that I could help you.

① 권유하기　　　　② 요청하기

③ 관심 표현하기　　④ 능력 말하기

⑤ 감사하기

[01~02] 다음 대화를 읽고 물음에 답하시오.

Jessie: Hi, Andy. What's up?

Andy: Hi, Jessie. I'm going to buy a present for Amy. You've been friends with her for a long time, haven't you?

Jessie: Yes, since first grade in elementary school.

Andy: Well, I know you're really busy studying, but (A)_____ I am sure you could help me pick out something nice.

Jessie: No problem. What's the present for? It's not her birthday.

Andy: Well, two months ago, when my leg was broken, she carried my backpack to school.

Jessie: That was nice of her.

Andy: Yes, it was. What should I get for her?

Jessie: Well, how about a case for her smartphone? She broke her case recently.

Andy: Really? Thank you for your suggestion.

01 위 대화의 빈칸 (A)에 들어갈 말로 알맞은 것은?

① do you mind picking up the present?

② do you mind closing the window?

③ do you mind putting the books back in the right places?

④ do you mind helping me?

⑤ do you mind studying with me?

 위 대화의 내용과 일치하지 <u>않는</u> 것은?

① Andy and Jessie have been friends since first grade in elementary school.

② Jessie is busy studying.

③ Amy carried Andy's backpack to school two months ago.

④ Andy really appreciates Amy's help.

⑤ Amy broke her smartphone case recently.

 다음 대화의 (A)~(D)를 알맞은 순서로 배열한 것은?

B: Irene, what are you doing?

(A) It's red. My name is written in black on the side.

(B) Oh, is this yours? It was under the table.

(C) Well, I've lost my favorite cap. I can't find it.

(D) Let me help you. What does it look like?

G: Yes, it is. Thank you, Jim. I appreciate your help.

B: No problem.

① (A) – (C) – (B) – (D)

② (B) – (A) – (D) – (C)

③ (C) – (B) – (A) – (D)

④ (C) – (D) – (A) – (B)

⑤ (D) – (C) – (A) – (B)

04 다음 대화의 빈칸에 들어갈 말로 알맞은 것은?

A: Sue, _____

B: Of course not. We don't have enough fresh air in the room.

① can you help me open the window?

② do you mind opening the window?

③ could I ask you to help me close the window?

④ can you open the door, please?

⑤ is it OK if I open the door?

[05~06] 다음 대화를 읽고 물음에 답하시오.

G: You (a)seem to be busy, Minsu. Can I come in?

B: Sure. I'm preparing for the dance contest, but it's not easy.

G: I can help you. I (b)was in the contest last year.

B: Really? That would be great, Amy.

G: You are good at (c)getting into the rhythm. But one thing you need to do (d)are to be more (e)relaxed. You are too nervous.

B: Your advice is very helpful. I really appreciate your advice.

G: It's my pleasure.

서답형

05 위 대화를 읽고 다음 물음에 영어로 답하시오.

Q: What is Minsu good at according to Amy? (8 단어로 답하시오.)

➡ _____

06 위 대화의 밑줄 친 (a)~(e) 중 어법상 어색한 것은?

① (a) ② (b) ③ (c) ④ (d) ⑤ (e)

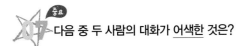

중요

17 다음 중 두 사람의 대화가 어색한 것은?

① A: Let me read the directions for you.
   B: I appreciate your time.

② A: Mike, do you mind putting the books back in the right places?
   B: No, I don't.

③ A: Do you mind closing the window?
   B: Of course. Go ahead.

④ A: Let me set the table.
   B: I appreciate your kindness.

⑤ A: Happy birthday! This is for you.
   B: Thank you for your present.

[08~09] 다음 대화를 읽고 물음에 답하시오.

B: Karen, do you mind coming to my house tomorrow at 7 a.m.?

G: That's very early.

B: I know, but (A)수업 시작하기 전에 네가 빌려갔던 책이 필요하거든.

G: I see. Then let's meet at seven.

B: See you then.

서답형

08 위 대화의 밑줄 친 (A)의 우리말에 맞게 주어진 단어를 알맞은 순서로 배열하여 쓰시오. (단어 하나를 추가하고, 필요시 변형하시오.)

I / need / class / you / book / before / the / borrowed

➡ _____
   _____

서답형

09 위 대화를 읽고 다음 물음에 괄호 안의 주어진 단어를 활용하여 영어로 답하시오.

Q: Why is Karen going to meet the boy at 7 a.m.? (have to / return / borrow)

➡ Because she _____ _____ _____
   the _____ book to the boy.

서답형

10 다음 글의 마지막 물음에 대한 답을 주어진 어구를 활용하여 영작하시오.

W: Mike does not feel very well. He might have caught a cold. He needs to see a doctor, but he has a meeting with Jane in an hour. So he wants to meet her tomorrow. What should he say to her?

(mind / put off / until tomorrow)

➡ _____

[01~02] 다음 대화를 읽고 물음에 답하시오.

Jessie: Hi, Andy. What's up?

Andy: Hi, Jessie. I'm going to buy a present for Amy. (A)You were friends with her for a long time, weren't you?

Jessie: Yes, (a)since first grade in elementary school.

Andy: Well, I know you're really busy studying, but do you mind helping me? I am sure you could help me pick out something nice.

Jessie: No problem. What's the present for? It's not her birthday.

Andy: Well, two months ago, when my leg was broken, she carried my backpack to school.

Jessie: That was nice of her.

Andy: Yes, it was. What should I get for her?

Jessie: Well, how about a case for her smartphone? She broke her case recently.

Andy: Really? Thank you for your suggestion.

01 다음 질문에 대한 답을 'Because'로 시작하여 쓰시오.

> Q: Two months ago, why did Amy carry Andy's backpack to school?

➡ _____

02 위 대화의 밑줄 친 (A)는 문법적으로 틀린 문장이다. 밑줄 친 (a) 문장을 참고하여 바르게 고치시오.

➡ _____

_____

03 다음 대화의 밑줄 친 (A)를 〈조건〉에 맞게 영어로 쓰시오.

> G: I am planning to go to Jejudo.
>
> B: That's cool, Suhee. I used to live there.
>
> G: (A)내가 제주도에서 뭘 해야 하는지 말해 줄래?
>
> B: Not at all. Jejudo has many beautiful beaches. You should visit them.
>
> G: Good. I will go swimming. What else can I do?
>
> B: Why don't you hike Halla Mountain? You can see the mountain from everywhere on the island.
>
> G: Great.

┤ 조건 ├
- 'mind'를 이용하여 요청하는 표현을 사용할 것
- '의문사+to부정사'를 사용할 것.

➡ _____

04 빈칸 (A)에 들어갈 말을 주어진 단어를 이용하여 쓰시오.

> B: Irene, what are you doing?
>
> G: Well, I've lost my favorite cap. I can't find it.
>
> B: Let me help you. (A)_____
>
> G: It's red. My name is written in black on the side.
>
> B: Oh, is this yours? It was under the table.
>
> G: Yes, it is. Thank you, Jim. I appreciate your help.
>
> B: No problem.

(what / look like)

➡ _____

Grammar

> • June didn't like **how** Mike had acted. June은 Mike의 행동 방식이 마음에 들지 않았다.
> • That is **how** I solved the difficult problem. 그것이 내가 그 어려운 문제를 풀었던 방법이다.

■ 관계부사는 접속사와 부사의 역할을 동시에 하는 것으로 선행사를 수식한다.

　• I want to know **the way**. He became the leader **in the way**.
　= I want to know **the way (how)** he became the leader. 나는 그가 리더가 된 방법을 알고 싶다. (선행사 the way와 관계부사 how는 같이 쓰지 않는다.)

■ 선행사가 장소, 시간, 이유, 방법 등의 명사일 때 전치사와 관계대명사로 표현 가능하며, 생략 등 각각의 용례도 조금씩 다르다.

　(1) 장소(where): This is **the house**. Mozart was born **in the house**.
　　→ This is **the house which[that]** Mozart was born **in**.
　　→ This is **the house in which** Mozart was born. (in that 불가)
　　→ This is **the house where** Mozart was born. 이곳이 Mozart가 태어난 집이다.
　(2) 시간(when): This is **the day**. Mozart was born **on the day**.
　　→ This is **the day which[that]** Mozart was born **on**.
　　→ This is **the day on which** Mozart was born. (on that 불가)
　　→ This is **the day when** Mozart was born. 이 날이 Mozart가 탄생한 날이다.
　(3) 이유(why): This is **the reason**. Mozart is a genius **for the reason**.
　　→ This is **the reason which[that]** Mozart is a genius **for**.
　　→ This is **the reason for which** Mozart is a genius. (for that 불가)
　　→ This is **the reason why** Mozart is a genius. 이것이 Mozart가 천재인 이유이다.
　　→ This is **why** Mozart is a genius. : the reason 또는 why 둘 중 하나 생략 가능
　(4) 방법(how): This is **the way**. Mozart composed music **in the way**.
　　→ This is **the way which[that]** Mozart composed music **in**.
　　→ This is **the way in which** Mozart composed music. (in that 불가)
　　→ This is **the way how** Mozart composed music. (✗) (the way와 how 동시 불가)
　　→ This is **the way** Mozart composed music. : the way / how 둘 중 하나만 쓴다.
　　→ This is **how** Mozart composed music. 이것이 Mozart가 음악을 작곡한 방법이다.

■ 선행사가 'the place, the time, the reason'과 같은 일반적 의미일 경우 생략 가능하다.

　• This is (the place) **where** children can play. 이곳은 아이들이 놀 수 있는 장소이다.

핵심 Check

1. 괄호 안에서 알맞은 말을 고르시오.

　(1) This manual shows (how / which) we can use the machine.
　(2) I don't know the reason (how / why) she is late.

② The+비교급 ~, the+비교급 … 구문

- **The more sincere** your apology is, **the better** it will be received. 당신의 사과가 더 진실할
수록 그것은 더 잘 받아들여질 것이다.
- **The faster** you walk, **the earlier** you will arrive. 당신이 더 빨리 걸을수록, 더 일찍 도착할 것이다.

■ 'The+비교급+주어+동사 ~, the+비교급+주어+동사 …'는 '~하면 할수록 더 …하다'의 의미로, 상응
하는 두 절의 형용사나 부사, 형용사를 포함한 명사절의 비교급 형태를 'the'와 함께 주어 앞으로 이동하
여 만든다.

(1) 형용사

- You are good at something. + You should be careful when doing it.
  → **The better** you are at something, **the more careful** you should be when doing it. 당신이 어떤
  일을 더 잘하게 될수록, 그것을 할 때 더욱 주의해야 한다.
- **The older** we get, **the wiser** we become. 우리는 나이를 먹을수록 더 지혜로워진다.

(2) 부사

- They get up early. + They will get there soon.
  → **The earlier** they get up, **the sooner** they will get there.
  그들이 더 일찍 일어날수록, 그곳에 더 빨리 도착할 것이다.
- **The higher** you go up the mountain, **the more** you can see of the lake below.
  당신이 그 산에 더 높이 올라갈수록, 아래의 호수를 더 잘 볼 수 있다.

(3) 형용사를 포함한 명사절

- People eat healthy food. + People can live a healthy life.
  → **The healthier food** people eat, **the healthier life** people can live.
  사람들이 더 건강한 음식을 먹을수록, 더욱 건강한 삶을 살 수 있다.

(4) 의미가 통할 경우, '동사' 또는 '주어+동사' 생략 가능

- **The warmer** the weather, **the lighter** the air. 날씨가 더 따뜻할수록, 공기가 더 가볍다.
- **The more, the better.** 많으면 많을수록 좋다.

■ 'The+비교급 ~, the+비교급 …' 구문은 접속사 If 또는 As를 사용해서 전환할 수 있다.

- **The earlier** you finish the report, **the better grade** you will get.
  = **If** you finish the report eariler, you will get a better grade.
  = **As** you finish the report eariler, you will get a better grade.

핵심 Check

2. 다음 우리말에 맞게 괄호 안의 어구를 바르게 배열하시오.

> 그들에게 숙제가 많을수록 학생들은 더 피곤하게 느낀다. (the students, homework,
> tired, the more, the more, feel, have, they)

➡ _____

01 다음 빈칸에 들어갈 말로 알맞은 것은?

> The greater the risk of virus is, the _____ people meet.

① often   ② most often   ③ less often

④ more oftener   ⑤ less oftener

02 다음 두 문장을 한 문장으로 연결할 때, 각각의 빈칸에 들어갈 알맞은 말을 써 넣으시오. (반드시 관계사가 포함되도록 할 것)

(1) They learned the way. The researcher found it in the way.

➡ They learned the way _____ _____ the researcher found it.

➡ They learned _____ the researcher found it.

(2) Sam visited the house. The legendary singer lived in the house.

➡ Sam visited the house _____ _____ the legendary singer lived.

➡ Sam visited the house _____ the legendary singer lived.

03 다음 밑줄 친 부분 중 어법상 옳지 <u>않은</u> 것을 고르시오.

① I don't know the reason <u>why</u> she left me.

② I want to know the way <u>how</u> he earned so much money.

③ She was interested in the restaurant <u>where</u> the cook worked.

④ This is <u>how</u> the basketball player became the MVP of the year.

⑤ Let me know the way <u>in which</u> Paula got an A on the subject.

04 다음 〈보기〉에서 필요한 단어를 골라, 어법에 알맞은 형태로 빈칸에 써 넣으시오.

> ┤ 보기 ├
>
> flexible, much, climb, high, old, hot

(1) _____ _____ the weather gets, the _____ water we drink.

(2) The _____ the mountain is, the harder it is _____ _____ .

(3) The _____ you get, the _____ _____ you become.

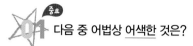
 다음 중 어법상 <u>어색한</u> 것은?

① This is the street where you can enjoy a lot of street foods.
② They wondered about the reason why Sam Smith was so mad at the officer.
③ Those are the buildings where this movie is going to be filmed.
④ I will show my students the way how I could be a teacher.
⑤ Can you remember the day when you first ate the blue berry?

[02~03] 다음 빈칸에 들어갈 말이 알맞게 짝지어진 것을 고르시오.

02

The _____ you work, the _____ money you can earn.

① much – much
② well – better
③ more – most
④ more – more
⑤ best – more

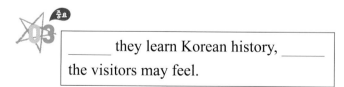

_____ they learn Korean history, _____ the visitors may feel.

① So much – as much interested
② The more well – more interested for
③ The more – the more interested
④ More as – the more interesting
⑤ The better – most interesting

[04~05] 다음 우리말을 어법상 알맞게 영작한 것을 고르시오.

04

그것이 경쟁이 치열한 연예계에서 Joseph이 성공한 이유이다.

① That is which Joseph succeeded in the world of competitive show business for.
② That is the reason which Joseph succeeded in the world of competitive show business.
③ That is the reason why Joseph succeeded in the world of competitive show business for.
④ That is why Joseph succeeded in the world of competitive show business.
⑤ That is the reason on which Joseph succeeded in the world of competitive show business.

05

그 발표가 어디에서 열리는지 그녀가 알고 있습니까?

① Does she know where will the presentation be held?
② Where does she know the place the presentation will be held?
③ Does she know the place at where the presentation will be held?
④ Does she know the place on which the presentation will be held in?
⑤ Does she know the place where the presentation will be held?

[06~07] 다음 주어진 문장의 의미가 자연스럽게 되도록 빈칸에 들어갈 말로 가장 적절한 것은?

06

> The less sincerely a close friend apologizes for his or her mistake, _____.

① the easier people feel
② the happier people get
③ the more pleased people become
④ the more easily people get hurt
⑤ the more easily people get along

07

> The more sincere your apologies are, _____.

① the more they will be necessary
② the better they will be received
③ the lighter they will be considered
④ the more casually they will be received
⑤ the more they will be ignored

[08~10] 다음 중 어법상 <u>어색한</u> 문장은?

08 ① Sumin's sister disliked the way that Sumin had treated her.
② Sumin's sister disliked how Sumin had treated her.
③ Sumin's sister disliked the way in which Sumin had treated her.
④ Sumin's sister disliked the way in how Sumin had treated her.
⑤ Sumin's sister disliked the way Sumin had treated her.

09 ① This was not the first time Jane hadn't apologized to her little sister.
② This was not the first time when Jane hadn't apologized to her little sister.
③ This was not the first time of which Jane hadn't apologized to her little sister.
④ This was not the first time that Jane hadn't apologized to her little sister.
⑤ This was not the first time for which Jane hadn't apologized to her little sister.

10 ① He wanted to know the reason Michelle didn't say anything about the problem.
② He wanted to know why Michelle didn't say anything about the problem.
③ He wanted to know the reason for which Michelle didn't say anything about the problem.
④ He wanted to know the reason which Michelle didn't say anything about the problem for.
⑤ He wanted to know why didn't Michelle say anything about the problem.

11 다음 〈보기〉의 문장과 가장 가까운 뜻을 가진 문장을 고르시오.

> ┤ 보기 ├
> Quicker apology will show that you are more thoughtful and responsible.

① As the quicker your apology is, you look more thoughtful and responsible.
② The more quicker your apology is, the most thoughtful and responsible you will look.

③ The quicker your apology is, the more thoughtful and responsible you will look.

④ The quickest your apology is, the most thoughtful and responsible you will look.

⑤ If you apology quicker, the more thoughtful and responsible you look.

서답형

[12~13] 다음 두 문장을 한 문장으로 표현할 때, 빈칸에 들어갈 알맞은 한 단어를 쓰시오.

12

- Tom wants to know the way.
- Kate recovered from the disease in the way earlier than the doctor expected.

➡ Tom wants to know _____ Kate recovered from the disease earlier than the doctor expected.

13

- The famous composer was born on the day.
- Germany was unified on that day.

➡ The famous composer was born on the day _____ Germany was unified.

서답형

[14~15] 우리말과 일치하도록 괄호 안에 주어진 어구를 바르게 배열하시오.

14

당신이 뉴스를 많이 볼수록, 세상일이 어떻게 되는지 더 잘 알게 된다.

(the news, know, watch, you, the better, you, the more) what the world is like.

➡ _____

_____ what the world is like.

15

어떤 제품들은 가격이 비싸면 비쌀수록 더 많은 사람들이 사려고 한다.

→ (some products, buy, people, the more, the more, are, them, to, expensive, want).

➡ _____

_____

[16~17] 다음 빈칸 (A), (B), (C)에 들어갈 말로 가장 적절한 것은?

16

- The way (A)_____ she persuaded her parents is not known.
- The ladies have just come out of the building (B)_____ is next to my office.
- Mom remembers the day (C)_____ I was allowed to go to the college.

	(A)	(B)	(C)
①	which	which	on which
②	in which	where	when
③	that	which	when
④	how	where	that
⑤	how	which	on which

17

- Is there anyone to tell me (A)_____ Susan answered the impossible question?
- Mike wants to know the reason (B)_____ his wife is upset about him.
- Christina will never forget the name of the cafe (C)_____ she met the man.

	(A)	(B)	(C)
①	why	why	which
②	what	which	where
③	that	for which	which
④	how	why	where
⑤	when	for which	on which

01 다음 우리말과 일치하도록 괄호 안에 주어진 어구를 바르게 배열하여 문장을 완성하시오.

(1) 당신이 실수에 대해 빨리 사과할수록, 사람들은 덜 상처받게 된다. (people, you, apologize for, hurt, the sooner, the less, get, the mistake)

➡ _____

_____

(2) 우리는 더 많이 가질수록, 더 많이 원한다. (we, we, the, the, more, more, want, have)

➡ _____

(3) 당신에게 선택사항들이 더 많을수록, 결정하는 일은 더 어려워진다. (it, you, decide, to, options, difficult, have, the more, the more, is)

➡ _____

_____

(4) 그 친구를 더 많이 알수록, 그녀를 향한 내 신뢰는 더 강해진다. (my trust, the more, the stronger, know, becomes, I, in, her, the friend)

➡ _____

_____

(5) 우리가 더 많이 줄수록, 우리는 더 많은 것을 보상으로 얻게 될 것이다. (in, we, we, the, the, more, more, return, get, give, will)

➡ _____

_____

(6) 그가 열심히 일할수록, 그의 미래는 더욱 밝을 것이다. (his future, works, the brighter, he, be, the harder, will)

➡ _____

_____

02 다음 그림을 보고 자연스러운 문장이 되도록 괄호 안에 주어진 단어를 바르게 배열하여 빈칸을 완성하시오.

(1)

➡ Ms. Kim didn't _____ _____ for the problem. (her son, the way, excuses, like, made)

(2)

➡ The animals wonder _____ _____. (his, has, the turtle, health, how, managed)

(3)

➡ That is the famous restaurant _____ _____.

(Bulgogi, people, line up, to eat, every morning, where)

03 다음 괄호 안에 주어진 단어를 이용하여 어법에 맞게 빈칸을 완성하시오.

(1) _____ _____(old) the student gets,
_____ _____(much) he looks like
his grandfather.

(2) _____ _____(many) books your
kids read, _____ _____ _____
(intelligent) they will become.

(3) _____ _____(loud) you practice,
_____ _____(well) you can speak a
foreign language.

(4) _____ _____(far) the patient walks
every day, _____ _____(healthy)
she will get.

04 다음 학급 신문의 〈내 친구를 소개합니다〉 코너에 나온 글을 읽고, 어법상 불필요해서 삭제해야 하는 단어를 <u>모두</u> 찾아 쓰시오. (2개)

My Great Friend, Miso

I'd like to introduce my friend, Miso. I have known her for ten years. She is always funny, generous, and cheerful. This is the way how she helped me. Two weeks ago, I forgot to take my lunch to school. Miso shared her lunch with me. I am lucky to have her as my friend. The more I know her, the more happier I am.

➡ (1) _____

(2) _____

05 다음 (A)와 (B) 문장을 〈조건〉에 맞게 영작하시오.

┤ 조건 ├

1. (A)와 (B)를 연결하여 (A)가 앞에 오는 한 문장으로 만들 것.
2. 표의 위에서부터 순서대로 영작할 것.
3. 가급적 '선행사+관계부사'로 영작할 것.
4. 관계부사는 생략하지 말 것. (that은 사용할 수 없음.)

(A)	(B)
The researchers found the special planet.	He made his films in the way.
The director taught us the way.	She can enjoy white snow and skiing in the season.
Her favorite season is winter.	The President of Brazil stayed at the hotel.
Please let me know the reason.	My daughter walked for herself on the day.
This is the hotel.	My professor was mad at me for the reason.
I would never forget the day.	Life can live on the planet.

(1) _____

_____

(2) _____

(3) _____

_____

(4) _____

_____

(5) _____

_____

(6) _____

_____

Reading

Three Things about a Proper Apology

Because we are human, we all make mistakes. It is not easy to get
이유를 이끄는 접속사   실수하다   가주어   진주어
along with everyone all the time. Sometimes we hurt people's feelings

without intending to. Sometimes, we do something wrong and regret
동명사(전치사의 목적어) 대부정사   –thing으로 끝나는 부정대명사는 형용사의 수식을 뒤에서 받음
it later. When that happens, what should we do? We should apologize.

Read the following case studies and learn three things about a proper

apology.

When June tripped over a backpack and fell, Mike found it funny and
5형식 동사(목적어+목적격보어)
laughed. He took a picture and uploaded it on an SNS. June saw the

picture and became angry. Mike said, with a laugh, "Sorry, June!" and
웃으면서
deleted it. After that, June felt even more hurt because of Mike's casual
비교급 강조 부사(훨씬)   ~ 때문에
apology. June didn't like how Mike had acted. Mike seemed to think it
= the way Mike had acted
was nothing serious.
–thing으로 끝나는 부정대명사는 형용사의 수식을 뒤에서 받음
What did you learn from this case? Yes. You guessed right. You

should be sincere when you apologize. Apologizing is necessary to

build good friendships. Saying you're sorry is more than just words.
to부정사의 부사적 용법 중 목적(~하기 위해서)   Saying (that) you're sorry
You need to show that you respect the other person and care about his
명사절 접속사
or her feelings. If you truly want to make things right, be sincere in
명령문 (~해라)
your apology. The more sincere your apology is, the better it will be
The 비교급 S+V, the 비교급 S+V: ~하면 할수록 더 ~한
received.
Here is another case. While Kate was hurrying across the cafeteria,
she accidentally bumped into Hojun. Some food on Hojun's tray fell
on his jacket.

---

proper: 적절한
apology: 사과
mistake: 실수, 잘못
intend: 의도하다
regret: 후회하다
delete: 삭제하다
casual: 대충하는, 건성의
seem: ~인 것 같다
sincere: 진정한, 진심 어린
receive: 받다, 받아들이다
trip over: ~에 걸려 넘어지다
care about: ~에 마음을 쓰다, ~에 관심을 가지다
cafeteria: 구내식당
accidentally: 우연히
bump into: ~에 부딪히다
tray: 쟁반, 식판

확인문제

● 다음 문장이 본문의 내용과 일치하면 T, 일치하지 않으면 F를 쓰시오.

1 Although we don't intend to hurt other people, we often do. ☐

2 June was upset despite Mike's serious apology. ☐

3 Showing that you care about people's feelings is necessary when apologizing. ☐

Kate didn't apologize. Hojun felt bad. He thought, 'Why doesn't she say something? It would be nothing if she apologized right now.'
가정법 과거(Kate가 바로 사과하지 않은 것에 대한 호준이의 아쉬움을 나타냄)

This case shows that when an apology is necessary, you should
명사절 접속사
apologize at once. A quick apology shows that you are thoughtful and take responsibility for your action. All you need to do is to say, "I'm
단수 취급
sorry." Then, the hurt friend will think nothing of it and laugh it off.
Kate가 호준이와 부딪힌 일

Finally, apologies are necessary among family members and loved
사랑하는 사람들(나에게서 사랑을 받는 사람이라는 의미)
ones, too. One day, Sunmin borrowed her sister's favorite book.
역시(긍정에 대한 동의)
Later, she lost it. Sunmin didn't apologize because she thought it was
선민이가 잃어버린 책
not important. She thought, 'We're sisters, after all.' Sunmin's sister disliked how Sunmin had treated her. How could her own sister ignore
= the way Sunmin had treated her
her feelings? This was not the first time Sunmin hadn't apologized to
예전부터 선민이가 사과하지 않았다는 의미이므로 과거완료(had p.p.)
her little sister.

People need to apologize when they do something wrong. This includes family members and the people who are close to you. People
주격 관계대명사
get hurt more easily when the hurt comes from a family member or a friend. We may think that they will let it go because they are close to
명사절 접속사   사역동사+목적어+동사원형
us. Remember, however, that small mistakes and no apology add up to
명사절 접속사
big emotional wounds. This is especially true among family members and loved ones.

Have you ever heard of the saying, "No more apologies, no more
경험을 묻는 현재완료
chances"? People make mistakes, but don't let one mistake break a
사역동사+목적어+동사원형
beautiful relationship. Do you want to apologize to someone? Try to do it now. A quick and sincere "I'm sorry" can solve many problems.

thoughtful: 사려 깊은
at once: 즉시
take responsibility for: ~에 책임을 지다
think nothing of: ~을 아무렇지 않게 여기다
laugh off: ~을 웃어넘기려 하다
borrow: 빌리다
dislike: 싫어하다
treat: 대하다, 대우하다
ignore: 무시하다
after all: 결국에는
include: 포함하다
emotional: 감정적인
wound: 상처, 부상
especially: 특히, 유난히
relationship: 관계
break: (관계를) 끝내다, 끊다
add up to: (결과가) ~가 되다

 확인문제

● 다음 문장이 본문의 내용과 일치하면 T, 일치하지 <u>않으면</u> F를 쓰시오.

1   It is good to apologize at once when an apology is necessary. ☐

2   It is not necessary to apologize family members or loved ones. ☐

3   Sunmin's sister thought her feelings were ignored by Sunmin. ☐

Reading **139**

● 우리말을 참고하여 빈칸에 알맞은 말을 쓰시오.

1 _____ we are human, we all make mistakes. _____ _____ not easy _____ _____ _____ _____ everyone all the time.

2 Sometimes we _____ people's feelings _____ _____ _____. Sometimes, we do _____ _____ and regret it later.

3 When _____ happens, what should we do? We _____ _____.

4 Read the _____ _____ studies and learn three things about _____ _____ _____.

5 When June _____ _____ a backpack and fell, Mike found _____ _____ and _____. He _____ a picture and _____ it on an SNS.

6 June _____ the picture and _____ _____. Mike said, _____ a laugh, "Sorry, June!" and _____ _____.

7 After that, June felt _____ more hurt _____ _____ Mike's casual apology.

8 June didn't like _____ _____ _____ _____. Mike _____ _____ _____ it was _____ _____.

9 What did you learn from this case? Yes. You guessed right. You _____ _____ _____ when you apologize.

10 _____ is necessary _____ build good friendships. _____ you're sorry is _____ _____ just words.

11 You need to show _____ you _____ the other person and _____ _____ his or her _____.

12 If you truly want to _____ _____, be _____ in your apology.

13 _____ _____ sincere your apology is, _____ _____ it will be _____.

14 Here is _____ case. While Kate was hurrying across the cafeteria, she _____ _____ _____ Hojun.

15 Some food _____ Hojun's tray _____ _____ his jacket. Kate didn't _____. Hojun _____ _____.

1 우리는 인간이기 때문에 모두가 실수한다. 모든 사람과 항상 잘 지내기는 쉽지 않다.

2 때때로 우리는 의도하지 않게 다른 사람의 감정을 상하게 한다. 때때로 우리는 나쁜 일을 하고 나중에 그것을 후회한다.

3 이런 일이 생기면, 우리는 무엇을 해야 할까? 우리는 사과해야 한다.

4 다음 사례 연구들을 읽고 올바른 사과를 위한 세 가지를 알아보자.

5 June이 가방에 걸려 넘어졌을 때, Mike는 그것이 재미있다고 생각하고 웃었다. 그는 사진을 찍어서 SNS에 올렸다.

6 June은 그 사진을 보고 화가 났다. Mike는 웃으면서 "미안해, June!"이라고 말하고 사진을 삭제했다.

7 그 후, June은 Mike의 가벼운 사과에 한층 더 화가 났다.

8 June은 Mike의 행동 방식이 마음에 들지 않았다. Mike는 이 일이 심각한 일이 아니라고 생각하는 것처럼 보였다.

9 이 사례로부터 무엇을 배웠는가? 맞다. 당신은 바르게 추측했다. 당신은 사과할 때에 진실해야 한다.

10 사과하는 것은 좋은 교우 관계를 만들기 위해 필요하다. 미안하다고 말하는 것은 단지 말 이상이다.

11 당신이 타인을 존중하고, 타인의 감정에 관심을 갖고 있음을 보여 주어야 한다.

12 당신이 진실로 일을 바로잡기를 원한다면, 당신의 사과는 진실해야 한다.

13 당신의 사과가 진실할수록, 그것은 더 잘 받아들여질 것이다.

14 또 다른 사례가 있다. Kate가 급식실을 가로질러 급하게 뛰어갈 때, 호준이와 실수로 부딪쳤다.

15 호준이의 급식판에 있던 음식이 그의 재킷에 떨어졌다. Kate는 사과하지 않았다. 호준이는 기분이 나빴다.

16 He thought, '_____ _____ she _____ something? It would be nothing _____ she apologized _____ _____.'

17 This case shows _____ when an apology _____ _____, you should _____ _____ _____.

18 A quick apology _____ _____ you are _____ and take _____ for your action.

19 _____ you need _____ _____ is to say, "I'm sorry." Then, the hurt friend will _____ _____ of it and _____ _____ _____.

20 Finally, apologies _____ necessary _____ family _____ and _____ _____, too.

21 One day, Sunmin _____ her sister's _____ book. Later, she _____ it.

22 Sunmin didn't _____ because she thought it was _____ _____. She thought, 'We're sisters, after all.'

23 Sunmin's sister disliked how Sunmin had treated her. How could her own sister _____ her feelings?

24 This was not the first time Sunmin _____ _____ _____ her little sister.

25 People need _____ _____ when they do _____ _____. This _____ family members and the people _____ _____ to you.

26 People _____ _____ _____ _____ when the hurt _____ _____ a family member or a friend.

27 We may think that they will _____ _____ _____ because they _____ _____ to us.

28 Remember, however, that _____ _____ and _____ _____ _____ _____ big emotional wounds.

29 This is especially true _____ family members and _____ _____.

30 Have you ever _____ _____ the saying, "_____ _____ apologies, _____ _____ _____"?

31 People _____ mistakes, but don't _____ one mistake _____ a beautiful relationship.

32 Do you want to _____ _____ someone? _____ _____ it now. A quick and sincere "I'm sorry" _____ _____ many problems.

---

16 그는 '왜 그녀는 아무 말도 하지 않지? 그녀가 즉시 사과한다면 아무 일도 아닐 텐데.' 라고 생각했다.

17 이 사례는 사과가 필요할 때는 사과를 즉시 해야 한다는 것을 보여준다.

18 신속한 사과는 당신이 사려 깊고, 당신의 행동에 책임을 진다는 것을 보여준다.

19 당신이 해야 할 행동은 "미안해."라고 말하는 것뿐이다. 그러면 상처받은 친구는 당신의 잘못을 아무렇지 않게 생각하고, 웃어넘길 것이다.

20 마지막으로 사과는 가족이나 사랑하는 사람들 사이에서도 필요하다.

21 어느 날, 선민이는 여동생이 가장 좋아하는 책을 빌렸다. 나중에 그녀는 그것을 잃어버렸다.

22 선민이는 그것이 중요하지 않다고 생각하여 사과하지 않았다. 그녀는 '우리는 어쨌든 자매니까.'라고 생각했다.

23 선민이의 여동생은 언니가 본인을 대했던 방식이 마음에 들지 않았다. 어떻게 자신의 언니가 그녀의 기분을 무시할 수 있는가?

24 선민이가 여동생에게 사과하지 않았던 것은 이번이 처음이 아니었다.

25 사람들은 잘못했을 때, 사과해야 한다. 이것은 가족이나 당신에게 가까운 사람도 포함한다.

26 사람들은 마음의 상처가 가족이나 친구에게서 올 때 더 쉽게 상처 받는다.

27 우리는 아마 그들이 가깝기 때문에 그냥 넘어갈 것이라고 생각할지 모른다.

28 하지만 작은 실수를 하고 사과하지 않는 것은 큰 감정적인 상처가 된다는 것을 기억하라.

29 이것은 가족과 사랑하는 사람들에게 특히 더 그러하다.

30 당신은 "더 이상 사과하지 않는다면 더 이상 기회가 없다."는 말을 들어본 적이 있는가?

31 사람들은 실수하지만, 그 실수가 아름다운 관계를 깨뜨리게 해서는 안 된다.

32 누군가에게 사과하고 싶은가? 지금 하려고 노력해라. 빠르고 진정한 "미안해."라는 말이 많은 문제를 해결해 줄 것이다.

● 우리말을 참고하여 본문을 영작하시오.

1 ▶ 우리는 인간이기 때문에 모두가 실수한다. 모든 사람과 항상 잘 지내기는 쉽지 않다.
➡ _____

2 ▶ 때때로 우리는 의도하지 않게 다른 사람의 감정을 상하게 한다. 때때로 우리는 나쁜 일을 하고 나중에 그것을 후회한다.
➡ _____
_____

3 ▶ 이런 일이 생기면, 우리는 무엇을 해야 할까? 우리는 사과해야 한다.
➡ _____

4 ▶ 다음 사례 연구들을 읽고 올바른 사과를 위한 세 가지를 알아보자.
➡ _____

5 ▶ June이 가방에 걸려 넘어졌을 때, Mike는 그것이 재미있다고 생각하고 웃었다. 그는 사진을 찍어서 SNS에 올렸다.
➡ _____
_____

6 ▶ June은 그 사진을 보고 화가 났다. Mike는 웃으면서 "미안해, June!"이라고 말하고 사진을 삭제했다.
➡ _____

7 ▶ 그 후, June은 Mike의 가벼운 사과에 한층 더 화가 났다.
➡ _____

8 ▶ June은 Mike의 행동 방식이 마음에 들지 않았다. Mike는 이 일이 심각한 일이 아니라고 생각하는 것처럼 보였다.
➡ _____

9 ▶ 이 사례로부터 무엇을 배웠는가? 맞다. 당신은 바르게 추측했다. 당신은 사과할 때에 진실해야 한다.
➡ _____

10 ▶ 사과하는 것은 좋은 교우 관계를 만들기 위해 필요하다. 미안하다고 말하는 것은 단지 말 이상이다.
➡ _____

11 ▶ 당신이 타인을 존중하고, 타인의 감정에 관심을 갖고 있음을 보여 주어야 한다.
➡ _____

12 ▶ 당신이 진실로 일을 바로잡기를 원한다면, 당신의 사과는 진실해야 한다.
➡ _____

13 ▶ 당신의 사과가 진실할수록, 그것은 더 잘 받아들여질 것이다.
➡ _____

14 ▶ 또 다른 사례가 있다. Kate가 급식실을 가로질러 급하게 뛰어갈 때, 호준이와 실수로 부딪쳤다.
➡ _____
_____

15 ▶ 호준이의 급식판에 있던 음식이 그의 재킷에 떨어졌다. Kate는 사과하지 않았다. 호준이는 기분이 나빴다.
➡ _____

16 그는 '왜 그녀는 아무 말도 하지 않지? 그녀가 즉시 사과한다면 아무 일도 아닐 텐데.'라고 생각했다.

➡ _____

17 이 사례는 사과가 필요할 때는 사과를 즉시 해야 한다는 것을 보여준다.

➡ _____

18 신속한 사과는 당신이 사려 깊고, 당신의 행동에 책임을 진다는 것을 보여준다.

➡ _____

19 당신이 해야 할 행동은 "미안해."라고 말하는 것뿐이다. 그러면 상처받은 친구는 당신의 잘못을 아무렇지 않게 생각하고, 웃어넘길 것이다.

➡ _____
_____

20 마지막으로 사과는 가족이나 사랑하는 사람들 사이에서도 필요하다.

➡ _____

21 어느 날, 선민이는 여동생이 가장 좋아하는 책을 빌렸다. 나중에 그녀는 그것을 잃어버렸다.

➡ _____

22 선민이는 그것이 중요하지 않다고 생각하여 사과하지 않았다. 그녀는 '우리는 어쨌든 자매니까.'라고 생각했다.

➡ _____
_____

23 선민이의 여동생은 언니가 본인을 대했던 방식이 마음에 들지 않았다. 어떻게 자신의 언니가 그녀의 기분을 무시할 수 있는가?

➡ _____

24 선민이가 여동생에게 사과하지 않았던 것은 이번이 처음이 아니었다.

➡ _____

25 사람들은 잘못했을 때, 사과해야 한다. 이것은 가족이나 당신에게 가까운 사람도 포함한다.

➡ _____
_____

26 사람들은 마음의 상처가 가족이나 친구에게서 올 때 더 쉽게 상처 받는다.

➡ _____

27 우리는 아마 그들이 가깝기 때문에 그냥 넘어갈 것이라고 생각할지 모른다.

➡ _____

28 하지만 작은 실수를 하고 사과하지 않는 것은 큰 감정적인 상처가 된다는 것을 기억하라.

➡ _____

29 이것은 가족과 사랑하는 사람들에게 특히 더 그러하다.

➡ _____

30 당신은 "더 이상 사과하지 않는다면 더 이상 기회가 없다."는 말을 들어본 적이 있는가?

➡ _____

31 사람들은 실수하지만, 그 실수가 아름다운 관계를 깨뜨리게 해서는 안 된다.

➡ _____

32 누군가에게 사과하고 싶은가? 지금 하려고 노력해라. 빠르고 진정한 "미안해."라는 말이 많은 문제를 해결해 줄 것이다.

➡ _____
_____

[01~03] 다음 글을 읽고 물음에 답하시오.

Because we are human, we all make mistakes. ① It is not easy to get along with everyone all the time. ② Sometimes we hurt people's feelings without intending to. ③ Sometimes, we do something wrong and regret it later. ④ When that happens, what should we do? ⑤ Read the following case studies and learn three things about a proper apology.

01 ①~⑤ 중 주어진 문장이 들어가기에 가장 적절한 곳은?

We should apologize.

①   ②   ③   ④   ⑤

서답형

02 다음과 같이 풀이되는 말을 위 글에서 찾아 쓰시오.

correct or most suitable

➡ _____

03 다음 중 위 글에 이어질 내용으로 가장 적절한 것은?
① when to do case studies
② how to apologize appropriately
③ why we make mistakes occasionally
④ the way you forgive your friends
⑤ some rules not to hurt your friends' feelings

[04~07] 다음 글을 읽고 물음에 답하시오.

When June tripped over a backpack and fell, Mike found it ①funny and laughed. He took a picture and uploaded it on an SNS. June saw the picture and became ②angry. Mike said, with a laugh, "Sorry, June!" and ③ deleted it. After that, June felt (A)_____ more hurt because of Mike's ④serious apology. June didn't like how Mike had acted. Mike seemed to think it was nothing ⑤serious.

What did you learn from this case? Yes. You guessed right. You should be sincere when you apologize. Apologizing is necessary to build good friendships. Saying you're sorry is more than just words. You need to show that you respect the other person and care about his or her feelings. If you truly want to make things right, be sincere in your apology. The more sincere your apology is, the better it will be received.

04 빈칸 (A)에 들어갈 말로 적절하지 <u>않은</u> 것은?
① far   ② still   ③ very
④ much   ⑤ even

05 ①~⑤ 중 글의 흐름상 어색한 것은?

①   ②   ③   ④   ⑤

06 위 글을 읽고 답할 수 있는 것은?
① What time did June fall?
② How many friends saw the picture?
③ How did friends feel about the picture?
④ What didn't June like?
⑤ Which SNS did Mike upload the picture?

서답형

07 When you apologize, how should you be? Answer in English with four words.

➡ _____

[08~10] 다음 글을 읽고 물음에 답하시오.

Here is another case. While Kate was hurrying across the cafeteria, she accidentally bumped into Hojun. Some food on Hojun's tray fell on his jacket. Kate didn't apologize. Hojun felt bad. He thought, 'Why doesn't she say something? It would be nothing if she apologized right now.'

This case shows that when an apology is necessary, you should apologize (A)_____. A quick apology shows that you are thoughtful and take responsibility for your action. All you need to do is to say, "I'm sorry." Then, the hurt friend will think nothing of it and laugh it off.

08 다음 중 빈칸 (A)에 들어갈 말로 가장 적절한 것은?

① later
② for once
③ at once
④ secretly
⑤ from time to time

09 위 글의 내용에 맞게 빈칸에 알맞은 말을 다섯 단어로 쓰시오.

> When Kate bumped into Hojun, he was holding _____. The bumping made it fall on his jacket.

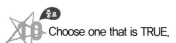

Choose one that is TRUE.

① Kate bumped into Hojun on purpose.
② Some food fell on Kate's jacket.
③ Kate wanted Hojun to apologize to her.
④ It is good to postpone apologizing.
⑤ Hojun feel bad because of Kate's attitude.

[11~12] 다음 글을 읽고 물음에 답하시오.

Finally, apologies are necessary among family members and loved ones, too.

One day, Sunmin borrowed ①her sister's favorite book. Later, ②she lost it. Sunmin didn't apologize because ③she thought (A) it was not important. She thought, 'We're sisters, after all.' Sunmin's sister disliked how Sunmin had treated her. How could her own sister ignore ④her feelings? This was not the first time Sunmin hadn't apologized to ⑤her little sister.

11 밑줄 친 (A)가 의미하는 것은?

① buying a new book
② having lost her sister's book
③ making an appointment
④ borrowing her sister's book
⑤ having apologized to her sister

12 ①~⑤ 중 지칭하는 바가 다른 하나는?

① ② ③ ④ ⑤

[13~14] 다음 글을 읽고 물음에 답하시오.

People need to apologize when they do something wrong. This includes family members and the people who are close to you. People get hurt more easily when the hurt comes from a family member or a friend. We may think that they will let it go because they are close to us. Remember, (A)_____, that small mistakes and no apology add up to big emotional wounds. This is especially true among family members and loved ones.

13 빈칸 (A)에 들어갈 말로 가장 적절한 것은?

① nevertheless ② however

③ therefore ④ as a result

⑤ for instance

서답형
14 When do people need to apologize?

➡ _____

_____

[15~17] 다음 글을 읽고 물음에 답하시오.

(A) He took a picture and uploaded it on an SNS. June saw the picture and became angry.

(B) After that, June felt even more hurt because of Mike's casual apology. June didn't like how Mike had acted. Mike seemed to think it was nothing serious.

(C) When June tripped over a backpack and fell, Mike found it funny and laughed.

(D) Mike said, with a laugh, "Sorry, June!" and deleted it.

What did you learn from this case? Yes. You guessed right. You should be sincere when you apologize. Apologizing is necessary to build good friendships. Saying you're sorry is more than just words. You need to show that you respect the other person and care about his or her feelings. If you truly want to make things right, be sincere in your apology. The more sincere your apology is, the better it will be ⓐreceived.

서답형
15 자연스러운 글이 되도록 (A)~(D)를 바르게 나열하시오.

➡ _____

중요
16 다음 중 밑줄 친 ⓐ를 대신하여 쓸 수 있는 것은?

① recalled ② accepted

③ persuaded ④ followed

⑤ regretted

17 다음 중 위 글의 내용과 일치하는 것은?

① June tripped over Mike's leg.

② Mike didn't apologize to June at all.

③ Mike took the situation seriously.

④ Apologizing is related to good friendships.

⑤ Apology shows that the other person likes you.

[18~20] 다음 글을 읽고 물음에 답하시오.

Here is another case. While Kate was hurrying across the cafeteria, she accidentally bumped into Hojun. Some food on Hojun's tray fell on his jacket. Kate didn't apologize. Hojun felt bad. He thought, 'Why doesn't she say something? It would be nothing if (A)_____.'

This case shows that when an apology is necessary, you should apologize at once. A quick apology shows that you are thoughtful and take responsibility for your action. All you need to do is to say, "I'm sorry." Then, the hurt friend will think nothing of it and laugh it (B)_____.

18 빈칸 (A)에 들어갈 말로 가장 적절한 것은?

① I forgot about it

② she apologized right now

③ she kept behaving like that

④ I asked her to say sorry to me

⑤ she thanked me for forgiving her

중요
19 빈칸 (B)에 들어갈 말과 같은 말이 들어가는 것은?

① You'd better work _____ every day.

② I was surprised to come _____ Julie.

③ The book consists ____ several chapters.

④ He kept me _____ visiting his uncle.

⑤ The moon does not give _____ any light on its own.

서답형

20 According to the passage, what should you do when an apology is necessary? Answer in English.

➡ _____

_____

[21~22] 다음 글을 읽고 물음에 답하시오.

Finally, apologies are necessary among family members and loved ones, too. One day, Sunmin borrowed her sister's favorite book. Later, she lost it. Sunmin didn't apologize because she thought it was not important. She thought, 'We're sisters, after all.' Sunmin's sister disliked (A)how Sunmin had treated her. How could her own sister ignore her feelings? This was not the first time Sunmin hadn't apologized to her little sister.

서답형

21 What happened after Sunmin borrowed her sister's favorite book? (4 words)

➡ _____

중요

22 다음 중 밑줄 친 (A)의 의미로 가장 적절한 것은?

① Sunmin had been the best sister ever.

② Sunmin had shared everything with her sister.

③ Sumin hadn't cared about her sister's feelings.

④ Sunmin's sister had borrowed everything from Sunmin.

⑤ Sunmin and her sister hadn't talked with each other for a long time.

[23~25] 다음 글을 읽고 물음에 답하시오.

People need to apologize (A)_____. This includes family members and the people who are ①close to you. People get hurt more ②easily when the hurt comes from a family member or a friend. We may think that they will let it go because they are close to us. Remember, however, that small mistakes and no apology add up to ③big emotional wounds. This is especially true among family members and loved ones.

Have you ever heard of the saying, "No more apologies, no more chances"? People make mistakes, but don't let one mistake ④break a beautiful relationship. Do you want to apologize to someone? Try to do it ⑤later. A quick and sincere "I'm sorry" can solve many problems.

서답형

23 주어진 단어를 빈칸 (A)에 바르게 쓰시오.

(do / wrong / they / something / when)

➡ _____

중요

24 What is the above passage mainly talking about?

① how to accept one's apology

② the importance of making good friends

③ why we should not hurt family members

④ the importance of apologizing

⑤ what we should do to maintain a good relationship

서답형

25 ①~⑤ 중 글의 흐름상 어색한 것을 한 군데 찾아 바르게 고쳐 쓰시오.

➡ _____

[01~03] 다음 글을 읽고 물음에 답하시오.

Because we are human, we all make mistakes. It is not easy to get along with everyone all the time. Sometimes we hurt people's feelings without intending (A)to. Sometimes, we do something wrong and regret it later. When that happens, what should we do? We should apologize. Read the following case studies and learn three things about a proper apology.

★01 밑줄 친 (A)가 의미하는 것을 위 글에서 찾아 쓰시오.

➡ _____

02 According to the passage, what is not easy to do? Answer in English with a full sentence.

➡ _____
_____

03 다음과 같이 풀이되는 말을 위 글에서 찾아 쓰시오.

> something that you say or write in order to tell someone that you are sorry that you have hurt them or caused trouble for them

➡ _____

[04~07] 다음 글을 읽고 물음에 답하시오.

When June tripped over a backpack and fell, Mike found it funny and laughed. He took a picture and uploaded it on an SNS. June saw the picture and became angry. Mike said, with a laugh, "Sorry, June!" and deleted it. After that, June felt even more hurt because of Mike's casual apology. June didn't like how Mike had acted. Mike seemed to think it was nothing serious.

What did you learn from this case? Yes. You guessed right. You should be sincere when you apologize. Apologizing is necessary to build good friendships. Saying you're sorry is more than just words. You need to show that you respect the other person and care about his or her feelings. If you truly want to make things right, be sincere in your apology. (A)당신의 사과가 진실할수록, 그것은 더 잘 받아들여질 것이다.

★04 주어진 단어를 바르게 나열하여 밑줄 친 우리말 (A)를 영어로 쓰시오. 필요하다면 어형을 바꾸시오.

> (be / is / will / receive / the better / it / the more / your / sincere / apology)

➡ _____
_____

05 What did Mike do after he took a picture of June? Answer in English.

➡ _____

06 Write the reason why June felt even more hurt after Mike deleted the picture. Use the phrase 'It's because.'

➡ _____

07 위 글의 내용에 맞게 빈칸에 알맞은 말을 쓰시오.

> According to the passage, what makes your apology sincere is to show that_____.

➡ _____
_____

Here is another case. While Kate was hurrying across the cafeteria, she accidentally bumped into Hojun. Some food on Hojun's tray fell on his jacket. Kate didn't apologize. Hojun felt bad. He thought, 'Why doesn't she say something? It would be nothing if she apologized right now.'

This case shows that when an apology is necessary, you should apologize at once. A quick apology shows that you are thoughtful and take responsibility for your action. All you need to do is to say, "I'm sorry." Then, the hurt friend will think nothing of it and laugh it off.

08 Write the reason why some food fell on Hojun's jacket. Use the word 'because.'

➡ _____

09 다음 중 위 글의 내용과 일치하지 <u>않는</u> 곳을 두 군데 찾아 바르게 고쳐 쓰시오.

> Kate bumped into Hojun by chance. Hojun was holding food on his tray and some of it fell on his jacket because of her. But she made an apology. Hojun felt good.

➡ _____

10 위 글의 내용에 맞게 빈칸에 알맞은 말을 쓰시오.

> When you want to take responsibility for your action, _____ as soon as possible.

Finally, apologies are ①necessary among family members and ②loved ones, too. One day,

Sunmin ③borrowed her sister's favorite book. Later, she lost it. Sunmin didn't apologize because she thought it was not ④important. She thought, 'We're sisters, after all.' Sunmin's sister disliked how Sunmin had treated her. How could her own sister ⑤respect her feelings? This was not the first time Sunmin hadn't apologized to her little sister.

People need to apologize when they do something wrong. (A)This includes family members and the people who are close to you. People get hurt more easily when the hurt comes from a family member or a friend. We may think that they will let it go because they are close to us. Remember, however, that small mistakes and no apology add up to big emotional wounds. This is especially true among family members and loved ones.

11 ①~⑤ 중 글의 흐름상 어색한 것을 찾아 바르게 고쳐 쓰시오.

➡ _____

12 밑줄 친 (A)가 의미하는 것을 우리말로 쓰시오.

➡ _____

13 When do people get hurt more easily? Answer in English with a full sentence.

➡ _____
_____

14 다음 빈칸에 들어갈 말을 위 글에서 찾아 쓰시오.

> No matter how _____ the person is to you, you need to apologize to them when you do _____ _____.

After You Read C

Inho went to a store to buy shoes. He was hit by a woman's bag accidentally
> to부정사의 부사적 용법 중 목적(~하기 위해서)

as she passed by. The woman said, "Sorry," and she walked away quickly.
> 때를 나타내는 접속사(~할 때)

Inho was angry because the woman did not make a sincere and proper
> 원인을 나타내는 접속사

apology. He thought that the woman should care about his feelings.
> 명사절 접속사(+완전한 절)

구문해설 • accidentally: 우연히 • pass by: 지나가다 • sincere: 진실한 • proper: 적절한

해석

인호는 신발을 사려고 가게에 갔다. 어떤 여자가 지나갈 때 그는 우연히 그 여자의 가방에 부딪혔다. 그 여자는 "미안해."라고 말하고는 빠르게 걸어갔다. 인호는 그녀가 진실되고 올바른 사과를 하지 않았다고 생각했기 때문에 화가 났다. 그는 그 여자가 그의 감정에 신경 써야 한다고 생각했다.

Enjoy Writing C

My Wonderful Friend, Jinsu

I'd like to introduce my friend, Jinsu. I have known him since elementary
> 현재완료(계속) 전치사(~ 이래로)

school. He is always humorous, brave, and cheerful. This is how he helped
> 형용사 병렬 구조 A. B. and C   관계부사(= the way (in which))

me. Last Friday I was sick and missed a math class. Jinsu showed me his class
> 4형식

notes. I am lucky to have him as my friend. The more I know him, the deeper
> to부정사(부사적 용법-원인)   The+비교급 ~, the+비교급 … 구문

our friendship becomes.

구문해설 • elementary school: 초등학교 • cheerful: 발랄한

나의 훌륭한 친구, 진수

나는 나의 친구 진수를 소개하고 싶어. 나는 그를 초등학교 때부터 알았어. 그는 항상 재미있고, 용감하고, 발랄해. 이게 그가 나를 도와주었던 방법이야. 지난 금요일 나는 아파서 수학 수업을 못 들었어. 진수가 내게 자신의 수업 노트를 보여 줬어. 나는 그를 친구로 두어서 행운이야. 내가 그를 많이 알수록 우리의 우정은 더 깊어져.

Project Step 1

A: Do you know how we write a note of apology?
> know의 목적어로 '의문사+주어+동사'의 간접의문문이다.

B: Yes. First, write about what we did.
> 전치사 'about'의 목적어로 관계대명사 'what'이 사용되었고 'what'절은 불완전한 문장이 온다.

C: Then write that we are sorry for it.
> 동사 write의 목적어로 접속사 'that'절이 사용되었다. 'that'절은 완전한 문장이 온다.

D: Do not make excuses for our actions.

A: Thank you for the tips. I really appreciate it.

구문해설 • note: 편지, 쪽지 • apology: 시과 • excuse: 변명 • tip: 조언 • appreciate: 감사하다

A: 너는 우리가 어떻게 사과 편지를 쓰는지 아니?

B: 응. 먼저, 우리가 뭘 했는지 써야 해.

C: 그리고 나서 그것에 대해 미안하다고 써야 해.

D: 우리 행동에 대해 변명을 하면 안 돼.

A: 조언해 줘서 고마워. 정말 고마워.

영역별 핵심문제

Words & Expressions

01 다음 주어진 두 단어의 관계가 같도록 빈칸에 알맞은 단어를 쓰시오.

> include – inclusion : _____ – solution

02 다음 빈칸 (A)와 (B)에 들어갈 어휘가 바르게 짝지어진 것은?

> • You (A)_____ your friends. Then you and they will get hurt.
> • Students do not have enough time to (B)_____ their clothes in the mornings.

① get into – pick up
② look into – turn down
③ put into – trip over
④ bump into – pick out
⑤ enter into – pass by

[03~04] 다음 영영풀이에 해당하는 것을 고르시오.

03

> in a way that was not planned or intended

① purposely
② especially
③ sincerely
④ friendly
⑤ accidentally

04

> to remove part or all of a written or electronic text

① delete
② suggest
③ touch
④ regret
⑤ treat

05 다음 우리말에 맞게 주어진 문장의 빈칸을 네 단어로 채우시오.

> 누군가를 진심으로 사랑할 수 있었기 때문에 그때가 제 인생에서 가장 행복했던 때 같아요.
> ➡ I think that was the best time in my life because I was able to love someone _____.

Conversation

06 Sohee와 Minsu가 영화를 보러 갔을 때 그림과 같은 상황에서 Sohee가 여자에게 요청할 말을 주어진 단어를 이용하여 완성하시오.

No, not at all.

(mind / change seats / with me)

➡ _____

07 다음 대화의 빈칸에 들어갈 말을 주어진 단어를 알맞은 순서로 배열하여 완성하시오.

> G: I accidentally broke my mom's favorite plate.
> B: That's too bad, Mina.
> G: _____
> B: No, not at all. You should apologize sincerely.
> G: I see. I'll talk to her with all my heart.

(to / you / sorry / do / mind / say / telling / me / to / her / how / ?)

➡ _____

[08~10] 다음 대화를 읽고 물음에 답하시오.

> Jessie: Hi, Andy. What's up?
>
> Andy: Hi, Jessie. I'm going to buy a present for Amy. You've been friends with her for a long time, haven't you?
>
> Jessie: Yes, since first grade in elementary school. (1)
>
> Andy: Well, I know you're really busy studying, but do you mind helping me? (2)
>
> Jessie: No problem. What's the present for? It's not her birthday. (3)
>
> Andy: Well, two months ago, when my leg was broken, she carried my backpack to school. (4)
>
> Jessie: That was nice of her.
>
> Andy: Yes, it was. What should I get for her?
>
> Jessie: Well, how about a case for her smartphone? She broke her case recently. (5)
>
> Andy: Really? Thank you for your suggestion.

08 위 대화의 (1)~(5) 중 다음 문장이 들어갈 위치로 알맞은 것은?

> I am sure you could help me pick out something nice.

① (1) ② (2) ③ (3) ④ (4) ⑤ (5)

09 다음 물음에 대한 답을 〈조건〉에 맞게 영어로 쓰시오.

> Q: What does Jessie suggest Andy buy for Amy?

> ┌ 조건 ┐
> that절을 이용하고 조동사 should는 사용하지 말 것.

➡ _____

_____

10 위 대화를 읽고 답할 수 <u>없는</u> 질문은?

① What does Andy ask to Jessie?
② Why is Andy going to buy a present for Amy?
③ Does Jessie mind helping Andy?
④ Why did Andy break his leg two months ago?
⑤ Have Jessie and Amy been friends with each other for a long time?

Grammar

11 다음 중 주어진 문장과 의미가 가장 가까운 것을 고르시오.

> As the weather gets colder, people tend to catch a cold more than before.

① The colder the weather gets, the more people catch a cold.
② Once the weather gets cold, the more cold people catch.
③ Because of the cold weather, a lot of people catch a cold.
④ The cold the weather gets, the much more people catch a cold.
⑤ When the much colder weather comes, most people catch a cold.

[12~14] 다음 중 어법상 <u>어색한</u> 문장을 고르시오.

12 ① This is how Miso helped me repair my smartphone.
② This is the way Miso helped me repair my smartphone.
③ This is the way in how Miso helped me repair my smartphone.
④ This is the way that Miso helped me repair my smartphone.
⑤ This is the way in which Miso helped me repair my smartphone.

13 ① Minsu can't forget the year when his aunt died of cancer.

② An aquarium is a glass container in which fish and other water creatures can be kept in.

③ Remember the time when you should take the medicine after every meal.

④ Can you guess the reason why James hasn't finished the work yet?

⑤ The town where the painter lived has a famous museum.

14 ① The higher we went up, the more it was difficult for us to breathe.

② The hotter the curry rice is, the harder it becomes to eat it.

③ The more you earn, the more you should save for the future.

④ The less people have, the more they want to receive.

⑤ The more promises we make, the harder it becomes to keep them.

15 다음 중 밑줄 친 부분을 생략할 수 <u>없는</u> 것은?

① I want to find out <u>the way</u> that Paul solved the difficult problem.

② Will you let me know <u>the time</u> when your uncle will arrive at the airport?

③ This Monday is <u>the day</u> when my kids first go to school.

④ She knows the way <u>in which</u> her mother supported all her kids.

⑤ Can you explain to me <u>the reason</u> why you didn't show up at the meeting?

[16~18] 다음 밑줄 친 부분 중 어법상 옳은 것을 고르시오.

16 ① This is the building <u>in which</u> my grandfather designed 30 years ago.

② The bed town <u>which</u> my neighbors are going to move is quite far from here.

③ This is the park <u>where</u> Smith picked up the ID card for the Olympic games.

④ I forgot the name of the store <u>where</u> I bought some groceries at.

⑤ The Netherlands is the country <u>where</u> is famous for growing tulips.

17 ① The longer the break time is, <u>the more relaxed the workers do.</u>

② <u>More the women eat, more</u> weight they will gain.

③ The heavier a safe is, <u>the more expensive it becomes.</u>

④ The sooner we start, <u>the more earlier we will reach the destination.</u>

⑤ The more you think, <u>the more you will be careful.</u>

18 ① He will show Jenny <u>the way how</u> the prisoner escaped from the jail.

② Does Tammy know <u>the reason why</u> her son came home late for?

③ Wendy can't forget <u>the day when</u> she first met the green fairy on.

④ That evening was <u>the moment at when</u> I fell in love with the princess.

⑤ I don't know <u>the exact time when</u> the train leaves.

Reading

[19~22] 다음 글을 읽고 물음에 답하시오.

When June tripped over a backpack and fell, Mike found it ①<u>funny</u> and laughed. He took a picture and uploaded it on an SNS. June ②<u>saw</u> the picture and became angry. Mike said, with a laugh, "Sorry, June!" and deleted it. After that, June felt even more ③<u>hurt</u> because of Mike's casual apology. June didn't like how Mike had acted. Mike seemed to think it was nothing ④ <u>casual</u>.

What did you learn from this case? Yes. You guessed right. You should be sincere when you apologize. Apologizing is ⑤<u>necessary</u> (A)<u>to build</u> good friendships. Saying you're sorry is more than just words. You need to show that you respect the other person and care about his or her feelings. If you truly want to make things right, be sincere in your apology. The more sincere your apology is, the better it will be received.

19 위 글의 밑줄 친 ①~⑤ 중 글의 흐름상 어색한 것은?

①   ②   ③   ④   ⑤

20 위 글의 밑줄 친 (A)와 쓰임이 같은 것은?

① Is there anything to watch in this room?
② It is necessary to drink lots of water.
③ Tim went there to see his brother.
④ Jake wants to meet you again.
⑤ Jane decided to make more cookies.

21 위 글의 내용을 참고하여 다섯 단어로 이루어진 조언을 쓰시오.

Jessica slipped on the floor this afternoon. I thought it was a little funny, so I laughed out loud. However, Jessica looked embarrassed and upset because of me. I think I owed her an apology. How should I apologize to her?

➡ _____

22 위 글을 읽고 답할 수 <u>없는</u> 것은?

① Why did June fall?
② What did Mike find funny?
③ Why did June feel even more hurt?
④ How did June feel when he saw the picture?
⑤ What SNS did Mike use to upload the picture?

[23~25] 다음 글을 읽고 물음에 답하시오.

Finally, apologies are necessary among family members and loved ones, too. One day, Sunmin borrowed her sister's favorite book. Later, she lost it. Sunmin didn't apologize because she thought it was not important. She thought, 'We're sisters, after all.' Sunmin's sister disliked how Sunmin had treated her. How could her own sister ignore her feelings? This was not the first time Sunmin hadn't apologized to her little sister. ① People need to apologize when they do something wrong. ② People get hurt more easily when the hurt comes from a family member or a friend. ③ We may think that they will let it go because they are close to us. ④ Remember, however, that small mistakes and no apology add up to big emotional wounds. ⑤ This is especially true among family members and loved ones.

23 ①~⑤ 중 주어진 문장이 들어가기에 가장 적절한 곳은?

> This includes family members and the people who are close to you.

①   ②   ③   ④   ⑤

24 According to the passage, what results in big emotional wounds? Answer in English with a full sentence.

➡ _____

_____

25 다음 중 위 글의 내용과 일치하는 것은?

① Sunmin lost her sister's books several times.
② Sunmin didn't apologize because she thought she did the right thing.
③ Sunmin's sister thought Sunmin didn't care about her feelings.
④ This was the first time that Sunmin didn't apologize to her sister.
⑤ It is okay not to apologize to family members when you do something wrong.

[26~28] 다음 글을 읽고 물음에 답하시오.

> I'd like to introduce my friend, Jinsu. I have known him since elementary school. He is always humorous, brave, and cheerful. This is how he helped me. Last Friday I was sick and missed a math class. Jinsu showed me his class notes. I am lucky to have him as my friend. The more I know him, the deeper our friendship becomes.

26 다음 중 위 글의 제목으로 가장 적절한 것은?

① The Hero in Our School, Jinsu
② My Wonderful Friend, Jinsu
③ The Most Popular Boy, Jinsu
④ The Smartest Boy, Jinsu
⑤ What Makes Jinsu Happy

27 What happened to the writer last Friday? Answer in English.

➡ _____

28 What is Jinsu like? Answer in English.

➡ _____

01 다음 짝지어진 단어의 관계가 같도록 빈칸에 알맞은 말을 쓰시오.

> disregard – ignore : considerate – _____

02 다음 영영풀이에 해당하는 단어는?

> showing no fear of dangerous or difficult things

① timid   ② hurt   ③ emotional

④ right   ⑤ brave

[03~04] 다음 대화를 읽고 물음에 답하시오.

Suhee: I am planning to go to Jejudo.

Minjun: That's cool, Suhee. I used to (a)living there.

Suhee: Do you mind (b)telling me what to do in Jejudo?

Minjun: Not at all. Jejudo has many beautiful beaches. You should visit them.

Suhee: Good. I will (c)go swimming. What else can I do?

Minjun: (d)Why don't you hike Halla Mountain? You can see the mountain from everywhere on the island.

Suhee: Great. How about food?

Minjun: (e)If you like fish, on Jejudo raw fish is fresh and delicious.

Suhee: I'll try everything. I appreciate your tips.

03 위 대화의 밑줄 친 (a)~(e) 중 어법상 어색한 것은?

① (a)   ② (b)   ③ (c)   ④ (d)   ⑤ (e)

04 위 대화의 내용과 일치하지 않는 것은?

① Suhee is planning to go to Jejudo.

② Minjun lived in Jejudo but he doesn't live there anymore.

③ Suhee asks Minjun to tell her what to do in Jejudo.

④ Minjun doesn't recommend climbing Halla Mountain.

⑤ Suhee is planning to do everything that Minjun recommends.

[05~06] 다음 대화를 읽고 물음에 답하시오.

G: You seem to be busy, Minsu. Can I come in?

B: Sure. I'm preparing for the dance contest, but it's not easy.

G: I can help you. I was in the contest last year.

B: Really? That would be great, Amy.

G: You are good at getting into the rhythm. But (A)네가 해야 할 한 가지는 더 긴장을 푸는 것이야.(one thing / you / more / to / need / is / be / relaxed / to do) You are too nervous.

B: Your advice is very helpful. I really appreciate your advice.

G: It's my pleasure.

05 위 대화의 밑줄 친 우리말 (A)에 맞게 주어진 단어를 알맞은 순서로 배열하시오. (one thing으로 문장을 시작하시오.)

➡ _____

06 위 대화에서 다음 〈영영풀이〉가 설명하는 단어를 찾아 쓰시오.

> to be grateful for something

➡ _____

[07~08] 다음 대화를 읽고 물음에 답하시오.

B: Irene, what are you doing?
G: Well, I've lost my favorite cap. I can't find it.
B: Let me help you. What does it look like?
G: It's red. My name is written in black on the side.
B: Oh, is this yours? It was under the table.
G: Yes, it is. Thank you, Jim. I appreciate your help.
B: (A) _____

07 출제율 95%

위 대화의 빈칸 (A)에 들어갈 말로 알맞지 <u>않은</u> 것은?

① Of course not.
② It's my pleasure.
③ No problem.
④ Don't mention it.
⑤ Not at all.

08 출제율 100%

위 대화를 읽고 답할 수 <u>없는</u> 질문은?

① What is Irene doing?
② What is written on Irene's cap?
③ Where did Jim find Irene's cap?
④ Does Jim mind helping Irene?
⑤ Why did Irene lose her cap?

09 출제율 90%

다음 글에서 문법적으로 <u>틀린</u> 부분을 찾아 바르게 고쳐 쓰시오.

W: Mike does not feel very well. He might catch a cold. He needs to see a doctor, but he has a meeting with Jane in an hour. He wants to meet her tomorrow instead. What should he say to her?

➡ _____

10 출제율 90%

다음 대화의 밑줄 친 (a)~(e) 중 어법상 어색한 것은?

Jessie: Hi, Andy. What's up?
Andy: Hi, Jessie. I'm going to buy a present for Amy. You've been friends with her for a long time, (a)<u>weren't you</u>?
Jessie: Yes, (b)<u>since</u> first grade in elementary school.
Andy: Well, I know you're really busy (c)<u>studying</u>, but do you mind helping me? I am sure you could help me (d)<u>pick out</u> something nice.
Jessie: No problem. What's the present for? It's not her birthday.
Andy: Well, two months ago, when my leg (e)<u>was broken</u>, she carried my backpack to school.
Jessie: That was nice of her.
Andy: Yes, it was. What should I get for her?
Jessie: Well, how about a case for her smartphone? She broke her case recently.
Andy: Really? Thank you for your suggestion.

① (a) ② (b) ③ (c) ④ (d) ⑤ (e)

[11~12] 다음 밑줄 친 부분의 쓰임이 〈보기〉와 <u>다른</u> 것은?

11 출제율 95%

June didn't like <u>how</u> Mike acted because of Mike's casual apology.

① That was <u>how</u> the king treated the poor people of the village.
② Show me <u>how</u> the researcher solved the problem so soon.
③ Let us see <u>how</u> you made the wild animals quiet like lambs.
④ I wonder <u>how</u> strong the bears will be in their mature state.
⑤ Everyone in this school likes <u>how</u> she laughed at what seemed so little.

12 출제율 100%

We visited the town <u>where</u> the legendary singer was born.

① This Friday is the day <u>when</u> my son will graduate from high school.

② The student saw her teacher enter the restaurant <u>where</u> she met David.

③ Steve went to the city <u>where</u> his uncle used to live.

④ Janet still misses the holiday <u>when</u> she went to Egypt and the Mediterranean Sea.

⑤ Franklin was taking a shower <u>when</u> someone rang the bell.

[13~14] 다음 주어진 우리말을 바르게 영작한 것을 고르면?

13 출제율 90%

사과를 늦게 하면 할수록 상대방과의 관계는 더 악화될 것이다.

① When you apologize the later, you are likely to be your relationship with the other the worse.

② As the later you apologize, the more your relationship with the other will be likely worse.

③ The later you apologize, the more worse the relationship with the other is to be.

④ The later you apologize, your relationship with the other will be the worse.

⑤ The later you apologize, the worse the relationship with the other will be.

14 출제율 95%

날씨가 더워지면 더워질수록, 우리는 더 많은 전기를 사용한다.

① The more hotter the weather, so much more electricity we use.

② The hotter the weather is, the more electricity we use.

③ The hotter the weather will be, the more electricity we have used.

④ The more hot the weather, we use the more electricity.

⑤ The hotter the weather is, the better electricity we will use.

[15~16] 다음 글을 읽고 물음에 답하시오.

Because we are human, we all make mistakes. It is not easy (A)<u>to get</u> along with everyone all the time. Sometimes we hurt people's feelings without intending to. Sometimes, we do something wrong and regret (B)<u>it</u> later. When that happens, what should we do? We should apologize. Read the following case studies and learn three things about a proper apology.

15 출제율 90% 밑줄 친 (A)와 쓰임이 같은 것은?

① I need someone <u>to depend</u> on.

② <u>To bake</u> cookies, you need flour.

③ The boy tried hard <u>to get</u> on the top.

④ Daisy woke up <u>to find</u> herself famous.

⑤ It was surprising <u>to see</u> her there.

16 출제율 95% 밑줄 친 (B)의 의미로 가장 적절한 것은?

① making other people happy

② doing something wrong

③ intending to hurt other people

④ getting along with friends

⑤ apologizing in the right way

[17~18] 다음 글을 읽고 물음에 답하시오.

People need to apologize when they do something wrong. This includes family members and the people who are close to you. People get hurt more easily when the hurt comes from a family member or a friend. We may think that they will let it go because they are close to us. Remember, however, that (A)_____ add up to big emotional wounds. This is especially true among family members and loved ones.

Have you ever heard of the saying, "No more apologies, no more chances"? People make mistakes, but don't let one mistake break a beautiful relationship. Do you want to apologize to someone? Try to do it now. A quick and sincere "I'm sorry" can solve many problems.

출제율 90%

17 다음 중 빈칸 (A)에 들어갈 말로 가장 적절한 것은?

① some mistakes and proper apologies
② small troubles made by close people
③ small apologies with no mistakes
④ making beautiful relationship work
⑤ small mistakes and no apology

출제율 100%

18 다음 빈칸에 들어갈 말이 바르게 짝지어진 것은?

> Unless you apologize for your mistakes _____, it can lead to _____ a beautiful relationship.

① honestly – maintaining
② immediately – breaking
③ suddenly – making
④ on purpose – breaking
⑤ easily – maintaining

[19~21] 다음 글을 읽고 물음에 답하시오.

When June tripped over a backpack and ① fell, Mike found it funny and laughed. He took a picture and uploaded ②it on an SNS. June saw the picture and ③became angry. Mike said, with a laugh, "Sorry, June!" and deleted it. After that, June felt even more hurt ④because of Mike's casual apology. June didn't like ⑤how had Mike acted. Mike seemed to think it was nothing serious.

What did you learn from this case? Yes. You guessed right. You should be sincere when you apologize. Apologizing is necessary to build good friendships. Saying you're sorry is more than just words. You need to show that you respect the other person and care about his or her feelings. If you truly want to make things right, be sincere in your apology. The more sincere your apology is, the better it will be received.

출제율 95%

19 ①~⑤ 중 어법상 어색한 것의 번호를 적고 바르게 쓰시오.

➡ _____

출제율 100%

20 Choose one that is TRUE.

① Mike thought June's situation was embarrassing.
② June was satisfied with Mike's apology.
③ Apologizing is essential in building good friendships.
④ June felt the respect and care in Mike's apology.
⑤ You need to be sincere when you make friends with someone.

출제율 90%

21 What do you need to show when we apologize to someone?

➡ _____
_____

01 다음 대화의 괄호 안의 동사를 알맞은 형태로 바꾸어 쓰시오.

> Jessie: Hi, Andy. What's up?
>
> Andy: Hi, Jessie. I'm going to buy a present for Amy. You've been friends with her for a long time, haven't you?
>
> Jessie: Yes, since first grade in elementary school.
>
> Andy: Well, I know you're really busy (A)(study), but do you mind (B)(help) me? I am sure you could help me (C)(pick) out something nice.
>
> Jessie: No problem. What's the present for? It's not her birthday.
>
> Andy: Well, two months ago, when my leg (D)(break), she carried my backpack to school.
>
> Jessie: That was nice of her.
>
> ndy: Yes, it was. What should I get for her?
>
> Jessie: Well, how about a case for her smartphone? She broke her case recently.
>
> Andy: Really? Thank you for your suggestion.

➡ (A) _____ , (B) _____
　 (C) _____ , (D) _____

02 다음 그림에서 여자의 말에 대해 집배원이 할 말을 2 단어를 추가하여 영어로 쓰시오.

> Q: What will the mail carrier say?

➡ _____ your help.

03 다음 대화의 (A)와 같은 의미가 되도록 주어진 단어를 사용하여 문장의 빈칸을 완성하시오.

> G: (A)It seems that you are busy, Minsu. Can I come in?
>
> B: Sure. I'm preparing for the dance contest, but it's not easy.

➡ _____ (seem to)

04 다음 주어진 문장의 밑줄 친 부분을 다시 쓰고자 한다. 빈칸에 알맞은 관계부사를 써 넣으시오.

(1) Can the rich woman tell the poor man the way in which she made a lot of money?

　➡ Can the rich woman tell the poor man _____ she made a lot of money?

(2) The tired medical staff at the hospital need a place in which they can take a rest.

　➡ The tired medical staff at the hospital need a place _____ they can take a rest.

(3) The book showed the reason for which the Japanese government interrupted the peace between two Koreas.

　➡ The book showed _____ the Japanese government interrupted the peace between two Koreas.

05 다음 〈보기〉에 주어진 단어 조합들을 한 번씩만 사용해서 흐름에 알맞게 빈칸을 채워 넣으시오. (필요시 변형할 것)

> ┤ 보기 ├
>
> few–happy, hard–much,
> clear–long, soon–good, old–smart

(1) The _____ you work, the _____ money you earn.

(2) The _____ the video quality is, the _____ it takes to download it.

(3) The _____ classes there are on hot summer day, the _____ the students feel.

(4) The _____ the girl grew, the _____ she became.

(5) The _____ you finish the project, the _____ position you can get in the negotiation.

06 다음 두 문장을 가능하면 선행사와 관계부사를 모두 써서 한 문장으로 쓰시오. (단, 관계부사는 반드시 사용해야 함.)

(1) • Tell me the way.
   • Mary persuaded her parents to give her the car in that way.

➡ _____

_____

(2) • No one knows the day.
   • Minju will marry the handsome guy of the idol group on the day.

➡ _____

_____

(3) • Bucheon is the city.
   • International Fantastic Film Festival will take place in Bucheon.

➡ _____

_____

[07~09] 다음 글을 읽고 물음에 답하시오.

Finally, apologies are necessary among family members and loved ones, too. One day, Sunmin borrowed her sister's favorite book. Later, she lost it. Sunmin didn't apologize because she thought it was not important. She thought, 'We're sisters, after all.' Sunmin's sister disliked how Sunmin had treated her. How could her own sister ignore her feelings? This was not the first time Sunmin hadn't apologized to her little sister.

People need to apologize when they do something wrong. This includes family members and the people who are close to you. People get hurt more easily when the hurt comes from a family member or a friend. We may think that they will let it go because they are close to us. Remember, however, that small mistakes and no apology add up to big emotional wounds. (A)This is especially true among family members and loved ones.

07 밑줄 친 (A)가 의미하는 것을 우리말로 쓰시오.

➡ _____

_____

08 위 글의 내용에 맞도록 빈칸에 알맞은 말을 <보기>에서 골라 쓰시오.

┌ 보기 ┐
close / far / necessary / hated / loved / forgiveness / hurt
└─────┘

Apologies are _____ even for family members and _____ ones. People are more likely to get _____ when the hurt comes from their _____ friends or family members.

09 Write the reason why Sunmin didn't apologize to her little sister for having lost her book. Use the phrase 'It's because.'

➡ _____

01 다음 그림을 보고 자유롭게 관계부사 how가 들어간 문장을 2개 만드시오. 단, 〈보기〉에 주어진 단어 중 하나는 반드시 포함하는 문장이어야 한다.

┌─ 보기 ───┐

find, walk, set the table, read

└──┘

(1) _____

(2) _____

(3) _____

(4) _____

02 나를 도와준 친구에 대한 질의 응답을 읽고 친구를 소개하는 글을 완성하시오.

Q: What's the name of your friend who helped you?

A: Her name is Miso.

Q: How long have you known her?

A: I have known her for ten years.

Q: What kind of a person is she?

A: She is funny, generous, and cheerful.

Q: When did she help you?

A: It was two weeks ago.

Q: Why did you need her help?

A: Because I forgot to take my lunch to school.

Q: What did she do for you?

A: She shared her lunch with me.

My Great Friend, Miso

I'd like to introduce my friend, Miso. I have known her _____. She is always _____. This is how _____. _____, _____ _____. Miso _____. I am lucky to have her as my friend. The more I know her, the happier I am.

단원별 모의고사

01 다음 단어에 대한 영어 설명이 <u>어색한</u> 것은?

① ignore: to intentionally not listen or give attention to

② appreciate: to feel thanks about something

③ suggestion: an idea, plan, or action that is suggested or the act of suggesting it

④ mistake: an action, decision, or judgment that produces an unwanted or unintentional result

⑤ borrow: to give something to someone for a short period of time, expecting it to be given back

02 다음 짝지어진 단어의 관계가 같도록 빈칸에 알맞은 말을 쓰시오.

right – wrong : generous – s_____

03 다음 영영풀이에 해당하는 어구를 고르시오.

to lose your balance after knocking your foot against something when you are walking or running, or to cause someone to do this

① turn down   ② look forward to

③ trip over   ④ give off

⑤ laugh off

04 다음 중 짝지어진 대화가 <u>어색한</u> 것은?

① A: Do you mind closing the window?
   B: No, not at all. Go ahead.

② A: I didn't bring my textbook.
   B: Let's share mine.
   A: I appreciate your kindness.

③ A: Do you know how we write a note of apology?
   B: Yes. First, we should write why we feel sorry.

④ A: Do you mind turning down the volume?
   B: Yes, I do. I'll turn it down.

⑤ A: I am planning to go to Jejudo.
   B: That's cool.

[05~06] 다음 대화를 읽고 물음에 답하시오.

G: I am planning to go to Jejudo.

B: That's cool, Suhee. I (a)used to live there.

G: (b)Do you mind telling me what to do in Jejudo?

B: (A)_____ Jejudo has many beautiful beaches. You should visit them.

G: Good. I will (c)go swimming. What else can I do?

B: (d)Why don't you hike Halla Mountain? You can see the mountain from everywhere on the island.

G: Great. How about food?

B: If you like fish, on Jejudo raw fish is fresh and delicious.

G: I'll try everything. (e)I appreciate your tips.

05 위 대화의 빈칸 (A)에 들어갈 말로 <u>어색한</u> 것은?

① Not at all.   ② No problem.

③ No, I don't.   ④ Of course not.

⑤ Yes, I do.

06 위 대화의 밑줄 친 (a)~(e)에 대한 설명 중 잘못된 것은?

① (a): '~했었다'라는 과거의 상태를 나타내는 표현이다.

② (b): 요청을 하는 표현으로 'mind'의 목적어 자리에 사용된 'telling'은 'to tell'로 바꾸어 쓸 수 있고, 'what to do'는 'what I should do'로 바꿀 수 있다.

③ (c): 'go+-ing' 형태로 '~하러 가다'라는 의미로 사용된다.

④ (d): '~하는 게 어때?'라는 의미로 제안할 때 사용하는 표현으로 'What about hiking Halla Mountain?'으로 바꾸어 쓸 수 있다.

⑤ (e): 감사하는 표현으로 'Thank you for your tips.'로 바꾸어 쓸 수 있다.

[07~08] 다음 대화를 읽고 물음에 답하시오.

Jessie: Hi, Andy. What's up?

Andy: Hi, Jessie. I'm going to buy a present for Amy. You've been friends with her for a long time, haven't you?

Jessie: Yes, since first grade in elementary school.

Andy: Well, (A)네가 공부하느라 바쁘다는 것을 알지만, 나를 좀 도와줄 수 있니?(you're / know / busy / study / really / I / but / mind / do / help / you / me) I am sure you could help me pick out something nice.

Jessie: No problem. What's the present for? It's not her birthday.

Andy: Well, two months ago, when my leg was broken, she carried my backpack to school.

Jessie: That was nice of her.

Andy: Yes, it was. What should I get for her?

Jessie: Well, how about a case for her smartphone? She broke her case recently.

Andy: Really? Thank you for your suggestion.

---

07 위 대화의 밑줄 친 (A)의 우리말에 맞게 주어진 단어를 알맞은 순서로 배열하시오. (2 단어를 반드시 변형할 것.)

➡ _____

_____

08 다음 물음에 주어진 단어를 이용하여 영어로 답하시오.

Q: What does Andy ask Jessie to do?
(ask / to help / pick out / nice / Amy)

➡ _____

_____

09 다음 대화를 읽고 답할 수 없는 질문은?

G: You seem to be busy, Minsu. Can I come in?

B: Sure. I'm preparing for the dance contest, but it's not easy.

G: I can help you. I was in the contest last year.

B: Really? That would be great, Amy.

G: You are good at getting into the rhythm. But one thing you need to do is to be more relaxed. You are too nervous.

B: Your advice is very helpful. I really appreciate your advice.

G: It's my pleasure.

① What is Minsu preparing for?

② When did Amy participate in the dance contest?

③ According to Amy, what is Minsu good at?

④ What is Minsu going to do to be relaxed?

⑤ How does Minsu respond to Amy's advice?

10 다음 대화의 흐름상 빈칸 (A)에 들어갈 말로 가장 알맞은 것은?

> G: I accidentally broke my mom's favorite plate.
> B: That's too bad, Mina.
> G: Do you mind telling me how to say sorry to her?
> B: No, not at all. You should apologize sincerely.
> G: I see. (A)_____

① I think my mom will understand me.

② I'll be more careful not to make mistakes.

③ I'll talk to my mom with all my heart.

④ I think I should often talk with my mom.

⑤ I think there is no man that doesn't make mistakes.

[11~12] 다음 중 주어진 문장과 같은 의미로 쓰인 것을 고르시오.

11

> The higher you go up the mountain, the colder it becomes.

① As you go up the mountain higher, it becomes colder.

② If you go up the mountain higher, you should feel colder.

③ Since you go up the mountain higher, the climate becomes colder.

④ Though you go up the mountain higher, it becomes colder.

⑤ While the air goes up the mountain higher, you become colder.

12

> As we grow older, our muscles and bones become less flexible.

① We get the older, the less flexible our muscles and bones become.

② Older we get, less flexible our muscles and bones become.

③ The much older we get, less flexible the muscles and bones become.

④ The older we get, the less flexible our muscles and bones become.

⑤ The older get we, the less flexible become our muscles and bones.

13 다음 각 문장의 밑줄 친 '전치사+관계대명사'를 관계부사로 바꿀 때 어법상 어색한 것은?

① Ellen will tell her instructor the reason for which she failed the test.
   → Ellen will tell her instructor the reason why she failed the test.

② This is the theater in which my parents watched the film last year.
   → This is the theater where my parents watched the film last year.

③ I will remember the moment at which I participated in the historic event.
   → I will remember the moment when I participated in the historic event.

④ That's the way in which Sean solved the difficult questions.
   → That's the way how Sean solved the difficult questions.

⑤ Egypt is the country in which a number of people live.
   → Egypt is the country where a number of people live.

14 다음 각 문장의 밑줄 친 관계부사를 관계대명사를 이용해서 전환하고자 할 때, 빈칸에 알맞은 단어를 쓰시오.

(1) Do you know the reason <u>why</u> Jenny came late for the meeting?

➡ Do you know the reason _____ _____ Jenny came late for the meeting?

(2) All the neighbors visited the restaurant <u>where</u> my mother worked.

➡ All the neighbors visited the restaurant _____ _____ my mother worked.

(3) The famous cook showed us <u>how</u> he made the delicious food.

➡ The famous cook showed us the way _____ _____ he made the delicious food.

(4) The car accident took place on the day <u>when</u> Tommy was fired from work.

➡ The car accident took place on the day _____ _____ Tommy was fired from work.

15 다음 우리말을 주어진 〈조건〉에 맞게 영작하시오.

┌─ 조건 ─┐
1. 'the 비교급 ~, the 비교급 …' 구문을 사용할 것.
2. 주어와 시제에 유의하고, 괄호 안의 단어를 활용할 것. (내용과 어법에 맞게 변형 가능함.)
3. 글자 수에 맞게 영작할 것.

(1) 비가 많이 내릴수록, 그녀는 기분이 더 우울해졌다. (depress, much, it, feel, 9 단어)

➡ _____

(2) 그녀의 사과가 더욱 진실할수록, 그가 그것을 더 잘 받아들일 것이다. (sincere, well, accept, 12 단어)

➡ _____

[16~17] 다음 글을 읽고 물음에 답하시오.

Here is another case. While Kate was hurrying across the cafeteria, she accidentally bumped into Hojun. Some food on Hojun's tray ①fell on his jacket. Kate didn't apologize. Hojun felt bad. He thought, 'Why doesn't she say something? It would be ②nothing if she apologized ③right now.'

This case shows that when an apology is necessary, you should apologize at once. A ④quick apology shows that you are ⑤thoughtless and (A)_____ responsibility for your action. All you need to do is to say, "I'm sorry." Then, the hurt friend will think nothing of it and laugh it off.

16 다음 중 빈칸 (A)에 들어갈 동사와 <u>다른</u> 것이 들어가는 것은?

① It will _____ me half an hour to get there.
② You need to _____ up your mind to do it.
③ Don't _____ advantage of your friends.
④ You can _____ off your coat. It's warm inside.
⑤ Ken, _____ your feet off your seat.

17 밑줄 친 ①~⑤ 중 글의 흐름상 어색한 것은?

① ② ③ ④ ⑤

[18~19] 다음 글을 읽고 물음에 답하시오.

People need to apologize when they do something wrong. This includes family members and the people who are close to you. People get hurt more easily when the hurt comes from a family member or a friend.

We may think that they will let it go because they are close to us. Remember, however, that small mistakes and no apology add up to big emotional wounds. This is especially true among family members and loved ones.

① Have you ever heard of the saying, "No more apologies, no more chances"? ② People make mistakes, but don't let one mistake break a beautiful relationship. ③ Do you want to apologize to someone? ④ A quick and sincere "I'm sorry" can solve many problems. ⑤

18 위 글의 ①∼⑤ 중 주어진 문장이 들어가기에 가장 적절한 곳은?

> Try to do it now.

①　　　②　　　③　　　④　　　⑤

19 위 글의 내용과 일치하지 <u>않는</u> 것은?

① It is necessary to apologize to family members when you do something wrong.
② Making mistakes with no apology leads to big emotional wounds.
③ Family members let our mistakes go even though there are no apologies.
④ You can get more chances with more apologies.
⑤ Many problems can be solved by saying quick and sincere apologies.

[20~22] 다음 글을 읽고 물음에 답하시오.

When June tripped over a backpack and fell, Mike found it funny and laughed. He took a picture and uploaded it on an SNS. June saw the picture and became angry. Mike said, with a laugh, "Sorry, June!" and deleted it. After that, June felt even more (A)[hurt / relieved] because of Mike's casual apology. June didn't like how Mike had acted. Mike seemed to think it was nothing serious.

What did you learn from this case? Yes. You guessed right. You should be sincere when you apologize. Apologizing is necessary to build good friendships. Saying you're sorry is more than just words. You need to show that you (B)[respect / ignore] the other person and care about his or her feelings. If you truly want to make things right, be sincere in your apology. The more sincere your apology is, the better it will be (C)[rejected / received].

20 What did Mike seem to think about uploading June's picture on SNS? Answer in English with a full sentence.

➡ _____

21 (A)∼(C)에서 글의 흐름상 자연스러운 것이 바르게 짝지어진 것은?

① hurt – respect – rejected
② hurt – ignore – rejected
③ hurt – respect – received
④ relieved – ignore – received
⑤ relieved – respect – received

22 위 글의 내용에 맞게 빈칸에 알맞은 말을 쓰시오.

> Mike wasn't _____ in his apology.
> That's why June felt even more hurt.

MEMO

INSIGHT
on the textbook
교과서 파헤치기

※ 다음 영어를 우리말로 쓰시오.

01	burial	22	tomb
02	respect	23	organization
03	rule	24	palace
04	sacrifice	25	treasure
05	desire	26	patriotic
06	zip code	27	foggy
07	secret	28	president
08	general	29	independence
09	government	30	direct
10	harmony	31	statue
11	educate	32	bury
12	specialist	33	republic
13	spread	34	complete
14	feed	35	exhibition
15	movement	36	belong to
16	throughout	37	put on
17	entrance	38	hear of
18	protect	39	be in need
19	reader	40	carry out
20	main	41	look like+명사
21	mission	42	so that+주어+동사
		43	look forward to+명사/동명사

※ 다음 우리말을 영어로 쓰시오.

01 묻다, 매장하다 _____

02 비밀; 비밀의 _____

03 바람, 갈망 _____

04 존경, 경의 _____

05 정부 _____

06 통치, 지배 _____

07 교육시키다 _____

08 매장, 장례식 _____

09 안개 낀 _____

10 장군 _____

11 희생; 희생하다 _____

12 시 _____

13 독립 _____

14 궁전 _____

15 주된, 주요한 _____

16 묘, 무덤 _____

17 감독하다. 지휘[총괄]하다 _____

18 보물 _____

19 먹이를 주다, 먹이다 _____

20 애국적인 _____

21 조각상 _____

22 보호하다 _____

23 퍼지다, 퍼뜨리다 _____

24 우편 번호 _____

25 입구 _____

26 끝내다; 완전한 _____

27 지도자, 리더 _____

28 조직, 기구 _____

29 전문가 _____

30 조화 _____

31 전시회 _____

32 임무 _____

33 공화국 _____

34 ~의 도처에, ~ 내내 _____

35 (정치적, 사회적) 운동 _____

36 ~을 입다 _____

37 ~에 속하다 _____

38 ~을 수행하다 _____

39 ~처럼 보이다 _____

40 ~가 필요하다 _____

41 ~에 관해 듣다 _____

42 ~하기 위해서 _____

43 ~을 기대하다 _____

※ 다음 영영풀이에 알맞은 단어를 <보기>에서 골라 쓴 후, 우리말 뜻을 쓰시오.

1 _____ : what is highly valued: _____

2 _____ : a country governed by elected representatives: _____

3 _____ : a public display of art works, pictures or other interesting things: _____

4 _____ : any work that someone believes it is their duty to do: _____

5 _____ : a large house that is the official home of a king and queen: _____

6 _____ : a group of people working together for a purpose of being organized: _____

7 _____ : to place a dead body in the ground, to put something in the ground and cover it: _____

8 _____ : a series of things that happen one after another for a particular result: _____

9 _____ : giving up of something valuable for a specific purpose: _____

10 _____ : a sculptured figure of a person animal, etc. in bronze, stone, wood, etc.: _____

11 _____ : the act of putting a dead body into the ground, or the ceremony connected with this: _____

12 _____ : a large stone structure or underground room where someone, especially an important person, is buried: _____

13 _____ : a large outdoor area with fairground rides, shows, and other entertainments: _____

14 _____ : a circular ornament made of gold and decorated with jewels that is worn by a king or queen on their head: _____

15 _____ : a piece of writing that uses beautiful words that imply deep meanings and sounds rhythmical when you read: _____

16 _____ : a piece of cloth that is usually attached at the end of a pole and represents a country or association: _____

보기			
poem	statue	republic	mission
sacrifice	crown	bury	process
flag	tomb	treasure	exhibition
burial	amusement park	palace	organization

※ 다음 우리말과 일치하도록 빈칸에 알맞은 말을 쓰시오.

Listen & Speak 1 A

1. B: _____ _____ Suwon Hawseong. It's _____.

   G: It also _____ _____.

   B: _____ it _____ _____ _____ _____ the people _____ wars.

   G: Wow. Do you know _____ _____ it?

   B: Yes. King Jeongjo _____ Jeong Yakyong _____ _____ the building _____. You know about Jeong Yakyong, _____ _____?

   G: Yes, I've _____ _____ him. He was a _____ _____ in Joseon.

2. G: Brian, you know Taegeukgi, _____ _____?

   B: Sure. It's the _____ _____ of Korea, _____ _____?

   G: That's right. Do you know _____ the _____ in Taegeukgi _____?

   B: No, I don't. _____ _____ about _____.

   G: The _____ in the middle _____ _____ and _____.

   B: What do the black _____ on the four _____ _____?

   G: They _____ four things: sky, fire, water, and _____.

Listen & Speak 2 A

1. G: I'm _____ _____ _____ to the Gansong Museum.

   B: What is the Gansong Museum?

   G: It's a _____ _____ Gansong Jeon Hyeongpil.

   B: I _____ that he did _____ _____ for the country.

   G: Yes. He _____ many Korean _____ _____ some Japanese _____ _____ to Japan.

   B: Wow. The museum _____ _____ _____.

   G: Yes. I'm _____ _____ it!

2. B: Soyeon, _____ _____ _____ last weekend?

   G: I went to Hyeonchungwon _____ _____ _____ _____.

   B: _____ _____ _____ volunteer work did you do there?

G: I _____ _____ the _____. I felt great _____ for the people _____ _____ for the country.

B: _____ great. Can I do it, _____?

G: Sure. I'm _____ _____ _____ there again next Wednesday. Will you _____ me?

B: Sure. _____ _____ _____ _____ it.

Real Life Task

Andy: Bora, what are you _____?

Bora: I'm reading *Sky, Wind, Star, and* _____ by Yun Dongju. You _____ about Yun Dongju, _____ _____?

Andy: I've _____ his name, but I don't know _____ about him.

Bora: He wrote many beautiful _____ _____ Korea was _____ Japanese _____. His love for the country and his _____ for _____ can _____ _____ _____ in his _____.

Andy: Really? I didn't know that. I want _____ _____ his _____ and _____ _____ about him.

Bora: Great. _____ _____, I'm _____ _____ _____ _____ the Yun Dongju Museum soon. Do you want to come with me?

Andy: Yes, _____ are you _____?

Bora: Next Saturday. It's _____ Gyeongbok _____. Can you meet me at the _____ _____ 2 p.m.?

Andy: Sure. _____ _____ there.

Bora: Great. I'm really _____ _____ _____ the _____.

Wrap Up

B: Tomorrow _____ _____ _____ _____ _____ Korean clothes, *hanbok*, and go to Insadong.

G: Good, but I want to buy _____ _____ my friends in _____ tomorrow.

B: In Insadong, _____ _____ many _____ _____.

G: Great. After _____, what should we eat _____ _____?

B: Hmm. You _____ Samgyetang, _____ _____?

G: No. What is it?

B: It's a _____ Korean _____. It's _____ and will _____ _____ _____.

G: Sounds good. I'm _____ _____ _____ _____ it.

G: 나는 묘 주변을 청소했어. 나는 나라를 위해 돌아가신 분들에게 깊은 경의를 느꼈어.

B: 대단하게 들린다. 나도 그것을 할 수 있을까?

G: 물론이지. 나는 다음 주 수요일에 그곳에 다시 갈 계획이야. 너도 나와 함께 갈래?

B: 물론이지. 나는 그것을 기대하고 있어.

Andy: 보라, 너 무엇을 읽고 있니?

보라: 윤동주 시인의 「하늘과 바람과 별과 시」를 읽고 있어. 너는 윤동주에 대해 알고 있지, 그렇지 않니?

Andy: 나는 그의 이름을 들어 본 적 있지만 그에 대해 잘 알지는 못해.

보라: 그는 한국이 일본의 통치하에 있을 때 아름다운 시를 많이 썼어. 나라에 대한 그의 사랑과 독립에 대한 염원이 그의 시에서 느껴질 수 있어.

Andy: 정말? 나는 그걸 몰랐어. 나는 그의 시를 읽고 그에 대해 더 많이 배우고 싶어.

보라: 아주 좋아. 사실 나는 곧 윤동주 박물관을 방문할 계획이야. 너도 나와 함께 가길 원하니?

Andy: 응, 언제 갈 거니?

보라: 다음 주 토요일에. 그곳은 경복궁 근처에 있어. 오후 2시에 궁에서 만날 수 있니?

Andy: 물론이지. 거기서 만나자.

보라: 좋아. 나는 그 방문을 정말 기대하고 있어.

B: 내일 우리 한국 전통 의상인 한복을 입고 인사동에 가자.

G: 좋아, 그런데 나 내일 독일에 있는 내 친구들을 위한 선물을 사고 싶어.

B: 인사동에 선물 가게가 많아.

G: 잘됐네. 쇼핑하고 나서 점심으로 뭘 먹을까?

B: 흠. 너는 삼계탕에 대해 알고 있지, 그렇지 않니?

G: 아니. 그게 뭐야?

B: 전통적인 한국의 국물 음식이야. 그것은 맛이 좋고 너를 건강하게 만들어 줄 거야.

G: 멋지네. 나는 그것을 먹어보는 것을 기대하고 있어.

대화문 Test

※ 다음 우리말에 맞도록 대화를 영어로 쓰시오.

Listen & Speak 1 A

1. B: _____
   G: _____
   B: _____
   G: _____
   B: _____
   _____
   G: _____

2. G: _____
   B: _____
   G: _____
   B: _____
   G: _____
   B: _____
   G: _____

Listen & Speak 2 A

1. G: _____
   B: _____
   G: _____
   B: _____
   G: _____
   _____
   B: _____
   G: _____

2. B: _____
   G: _____
   B: _____

1. B: 수원 화성을 봐, 그것은 거대해.
   G: 그것은 또한 튼튼해 보여.
   B: 왜냐하면 그것은 전쟁 중에 사람들을 보호하기 위해 지어졌기 때문이야.
   G: 우와. 너는 누가 그것을 지었는지 아니?
   B: 응. 정조가 정약용에게 건설 과정을 감독할 것을 지시했어. 너는 정약용에 대해 알고 있지, 그렇지 않니?
   G: 응, 그에 대해 들어봤어. 그는 조선의 훌륭한 과학자였어.

2. G: Brian, 너 태극기를 알고 있지, 그렇지 않니?
   B: 물론이지. 그것은 한국의 국기잖아, 그렇지 않니?
   G: 맞아. 너는 태극기에 있는 상징들이 무엇을 의미하는지 알고 있니?
   B: 아니, 몰라. 그것에 대해 말해 줘.
   G: 가운데 원은 조화와 평화를 의미해.
   B: 네 모서리의 검은 선들은 무엇을 의미하니?
   G: 그것은 하늘, 불, 물 그리고 땅을 의미해.

1. G: 나는 간송 미술관에 갈 예정이야.
   B: 간송 미술관이 뭐야?
   G: 간송 전형필에 의해 지어진 미술관이야.
   B: 나는 그가 나라를 위해 훌륭한 일들을 했다고 들었어.
   G: 응. 그는 몇몇 일본 사람들이 일본으로 가져갔던 한국의 많은 문화재들을 샀어.
   B: 우와. 그 미술관은 틀림없이 흥미로울 거야.
   G: 응. 나는 그곳을 기대하고 있어!

2. B: 소연아, 지난 주말에 무엇을 했니?
   G: 나는 봉사 활동을 하러 현충원에 갔어.
   B: 그곳에서 어떤 종류의 봉사 활동을 했어?

대화문 Test **07**

G: _____

_____

B: _____

G: _____

B: _____

G: 나는 묘 주변을 청소했어. 나는 나라를 위해 돌아가신 분들에게 깊은 경의를 느꼈어.
B: 대단하게 들린다. 나도 그것을 할 수 있을까?
G: 물론이지. 나는 다음 주 수요일에 그곳에 다시 갈 계획이야. 너도 나와 함께 갈래?
B: 물론이지. 나는 그것을 기대하고 있어.

Real Life Task

Andy: _____

Bora: _____

_____

Andy: _____

Bora: _____

_____

Andy: _____

_____

Bora: _____

_____

Andy: _____

Bora: _____

Andy: _____

Bora: _____

Andy: 보라, 너 무엇을 읽고 있니?
보라: 윤동주 시인의 「하늘과 바람과 별과 시」를 읽고 있어. 너는 윤동주에 대해 알고 있지, 그렇지 않니?
Andy: 나는 그의 이름을 들어 본 적 있지만 그에 대해 잘 알지는 못해.
보라: 그는 한국이 일본의 통치하에 있을 때 아름다운 시를 많이 썼어. 나라에 대한 그의 사랑과 독립에 대한 염원이 그의 시에서 느껴질 수 있어.
Andy: 정말? 나는 그걸 몰랐어. 나는 그의 시를 읽고 그에 대해 더 많이 배우고 싶어.
보라: 아주 좋아. 사실 나는 곧 윤동주 박물관을 방문할 계획이야. 너도 나와 함께 가길 원하니?
Andy: 응, 언제 갈 거니?
보라: 다음 주 토요일에. 그곳은 경복궁 근처에 있어. 오후 2시에 궁에서 만날 수 있니?
Andy: 물론이지. 거기서 만나자.
보라: 좋아. 나는 그 방문을 정말 기대하고 있어.

Wrap Up

B: _____

G: _____

B: _____

G: _____

B: _____

G: _____

B: _____

G: _____

B: 내일 우리 한국 전통 의상인 한복을 입고 인사동에 가자.
G: 좋아, 그런데 나 내일 독일에 있는 내 친구들을 위한 선물을 사고 싶어.
B: 인사동에 선물 가게가 많아.
G: 잘됐네. 쇼핑하고 나서 점심으로 뭘 먹을까?
B: 흠. 너는 삼계탕에 대해 알고 있지, 그렇지 않니?
G: 아니. 그게 뭐야?
B: 전통적인 한국의 국물 음식이야. 그것은 맛이 좋고 너를 건강하게 만들어 줄 거야.
G: 멋지네. 나는 그것을 먹어보는 것을 기대하고 있어.

※ 다음 우리말과 일치하도록 빈칸에 알맞은 것을 골라 쓰시오.

My Wish

1 _____ _____ my history club _____ _____ Hyochang Park.

   A. went   B. last   C. to   D. week

2 We _____ the Kim Koo Museum _____ the _____.

   A. inside   B. visited   C. park

3 At the _____ of the _____, we _____ a white _____ of Kim Koo.

   A. statue   B. entrance   C. saw   D. museum

4 Kim Koo is a great _____ _____ who spent most of his life _____ for the _____ of Korea from Japanese rule.

   A. fighting   B. hero   C. national   D. independence

5 In the 1900s, he _____ _____ young people _____ _____ schools.

   A. educate   B. building   C. helped   D. by

6 In 1919, when the independence _____ had _____ _____ the country, he _____ to Shanghai, China.

   A. throughout   B. movement   C. moved   D. spread

7 There he _____ the Government of the Republic of Korea and _____ _____ its _____.

   A. later   B. joined   C. president   D. became

8 The _____ hall in the museum _____ a _____ of things about Kim Koo's _____.

   A. life   B. exhibition   C. lot   D. shows

9 _____ _____ _____ the hall, we _____ at a photo of the Korean Patriotic Organization's members.

   A. stopped   B. looking   C. while   D. around

10 Kim Koo _____ the _____ organization in 1931 to _____ _____ Japan.

   A. against   B. secret   C. fight   D. formed

11 Lee Bongchang and Yun Bonggil _____ _____ the _____.

   A. to   B. group   C. belonged

12 At one _____ in the _____, we saw two _____ _____ a photo of Kim Koo and Yun Bonggil.

   A. under   B. place   C. watches   D. hall

나의 소원

1 지난주에 우리 역사 동아리는 효창 공원에 갔다.

2 우리는 공원 안에 있는 김구 기념관을 방문했다.

3 기념관 입구에서 우리는 하얀색의 김구 조각상을 보았다.

4 김구는 일본 통치로부터 대한의 독립을 위해 싸우는 데 그의 삶 대부분을 보낸 위대한 국민 영웅이다.

5 1900년대에 그는 학교를 설립함으로써 젊은이들을 교육시키는 것을 도왔다.

6 1919년에 3.1 운동이 나라 전체에 걸쳐 퍼져나갔을 때, 그는 중국 상하이로 이동했다.

7 그곳에서 그는 대한민국 임시정부에 합류했고 나중에는 그것의 대표자가 되었다.

8 기념관 안에 있는 전시관은 김구의 삶에 관한 많은 것들을 보여준다.

9 우리는 전시관을 둘러보면서 한인 애국단의 단원들 사진 앞에 섰다.

10 김구는 일본에 맞서 싸우기 위해 1931년에 비밀 조직을 형성했다.

11 이봉창과 윤봉길이 그 집단에 속해 있었다.

12 전시관의 한 곳에서, 우리는 김구와 윤봉길의 사진 아래에 있는 시계 두 개를 보았다.

13 In 1932, Kim Koo _____ a _____ to _____ Japanese _____ in a park in Shanghai.

    A. kill   B. generals   C. made   D. plan

14 As the leader of the Korean Patriotic Organization, he _____ Yun to _____ _____ the _____.

    A. carry   B. directed   C. mission   D. out

15 When Yun _____ for the mission, he told Kim, "Sir, you are wearing a very old watch. Mine is new, but I won't _____ it _____. Please take my watch, and _____ me have yours."

    A. anymore   B. left   C. let   D. need

16 Kim Koo always _____ Yun's watch in his jacket _____ that he would not _____ Yun's _____.

    A. forget   B. carried   C. so   D. sacrifice

17 After _____ the _____ of the museum, we moved to the _____ of the three _____, Lee Bongchang, Yun Bonggil, and Baek Jeonggi.

    A. tombs   B. completing   C. heroes   D. tour

18 Their _____ had _____ in Japan, but after Korea's _____ Kim Koo _____ them to Hyochang Park.

    A. independence   B. been   C. brought   D. bodies

19 _____ doing so, he showed his _____ love and _____ for the _____ of the three heroes.

    A. respect   B. deep   C. by   D. sacrifice

20 _____ I left Hyochang Park, I _____ about Kim Koo's _____ in My Wish that I had read in the _____ hall.

    A. exhibition   B. thought   C. as   D. words

21 It _____ _____ _____ *Baekbeomilji*.

    A. written   B. was   C. in

22 If God asks me _____ my _____ is, I would _____ _____, "It is Korea's Independence."

    A. clearly   B. what   C. say   D. wish

23 If he asks me what my _____ wish is, I _____ say, "It is the _____ of my _____."

    A. independence   B. second   C. would   D. country

24 If he asks me _____ my third wish is, I would say _____, "It is the _____ _____ of my country." That is my answer.

    A. complete   B. what   C. loudly   D. independence

13 1932년에 김구는 상해에 있는 한 공원에서 일본 장군들을 암살하기 위한 계획을 세웠다.

14 한인 애국단의 지도자로서 그는 윤봉길이 임무를 수행하도록 지시했다.

15 윤봉길이 임무를 위해 떠날 때, 그는 김구에게 말했다. "선생님. 당신은 매우 낡은 시계를 차고 계시는군요. 제 것은 새것이나, 저는 그것이 더 이상 필요하지 않을 것입니다. 부디 제 시계를 가져가시고, 제가 선생님 것을 가지도록 해주십시오."

16 김구는 윤봉길의 희생을 잊지 않기 위해서 윤봉길의 시계를 항상 상의에 넣고 다녔다.

17 기념관 관람을 마치고, 우리는 이봉창. 윤봉길, 그리고 백정기 의사들이 묻힌 삼의사의 묘로 이동했다.

18 그들의 시신은 일본에 있다가 독립이 되고 나서 김구가 그들의 시신을 효창 공원으로 가져왔다.

19 그는 그렇게 함으로써 삼의사들의 희생에 대한 그의 깊은 사랑과 경의를 보여 주었다.

20 내가 효창 공원을 떠날 때, 나는 전시관에서 읽었던 「나의 소원」에 있는 김구의 말을 생각했다.

21 그것은 『백범일지』에 쓰여 있었다.

22 만약 신이 나의 소원이 무엇이냐고 묻는다면, "그것은 대한 독립이오."라고 명확하게 말할 것이다.

23 만약에 그가 나의 두 번째 소원이 무엇이냐고 묻는다면, 나는 "그것은 내 나라의 독립이오."라고 말할 것이다.

24 만약 그가 나의 세 번째 소원이 무엇이냐고 묻는다면, "그것은 내 나라의 완전한 독립이오."라고 큰 소리로 말할 것이다. 그것이 니의 대답이다.

※ 다음 우리말과 일치하도록 빈칸에 알맞은 말을 쓰시오.

My Wish

1 Last week _____ _____ _____ went to Hyochang Park.

2 We _____ the Kim Koo Museum _____ _____ _____.

3 _____ the _____ of the museum, we saw a _____ _____ of Kim Koo.

4 Kim Koo is _____ _____ _____ _____ who _____ most of his life _____ for the _____ of Korea _____ _____ _____.

5 In the 1900s, he _____ _____ young people _____ _____ schools.

6 _____ 1919, _____ _____ _____ had spread _____ the country, he _____ _____ Shanghai, China.

7 There he _____ the Government of the Republic of Korea and _____ _____ _____ _____.

8 _____ _____ _____ in the museum _____ a lot of things about Kim Koo's life.

9 _____ _____ _____ the hall, we _____ _____ a photo of the Korean _____ _____ members.

10 Kim Koo _____ the _____ _____ in 1931 _____ _____ _____ Japan.

11 Lee Bongchang and Yun Bonggil _____ _____ the group.

12 _____ one place in the hall, we _____ _____ _____ _____ a photo of Kim Koo and Yun Bonggil.

나의 소원

1 지난주에 우리 역사 동아리는 효창 공원에 갔다.

2 우리는 공원 안에 있는 김구 기념관을 방문했다.

3 기념관 입구에서 우리는 하얀색의 김구 조각상을 보았다.

4 김구는 일본 통치로부터 대한의 독립을 위해 싸우는 데 그의 삶 대부분을 보낸 위대한 국민 영웅이다.

5 1900년대에 그는 학교를 설립함으로써 젊은이들을 교육시키는 것을 도왔다.

6 1919년에 3.1 운동이 나라 전체에 걸쳐 퍼져나갔을 때, 그는 중국 상하이로 이동했다.

7 그곳에서 그는 대한민국 임시정부에 합류했고 나중에는 그것의 대표자가 되었다.

8 기념관 안에 있는 전시관은 김구의 삶에 관한 많은 것들을 보여준다.

9 우리는 전시관을 둘러보면서 한인 애국단의 단원들 사진 앞에 섰다.

10 김구는 일본에 맞서 싸우기 위해 1931년에 비밀 조직을 형성했다.

11 이봉창과 윤봉길이 그 집단에 속해 있었다.

12 전시관의 한 곳에서, 우리는 김구와 윤봉길의 사진 아래에 있는 시계 두 개를 보았다.

13 _____ 1932, Kim Koo _____ _____ _____ _____ kill _____ _____ in a park in Shanghai.

14 As the leader of the Korean _____ _____, he _____ Yun _____ _____ _____ the mission.

15 When Yun _____ _____ the mission, he told Kim, "Sir, you are _____ _____ _____ _____ _____. _____ is new, but I _____ need _____ _____. Please _____ my watch, and _____ me _____ yours."

16 Kim Koo _____ _____ Yun's watch in his jacket _____ _____ he _____ _____ _____ Yun's _____.

17 After _____ the tour of the museum, we _____ _____ the _____ of the _____ _____, Lee Bongchang, Yun Bonggil, and Baek Jeonggi.

18 Their bodies _____ _____ in Japan, but _____ Korea's _____ Kim Koo brought _____ to Hyochang Park.

19 _____ _____ _____, he showed his _____ _____ and respect _____ _____ _____ of the three heroes.

20 _____ I _____ Hyochang Park, I _____ about Kim Koo's _____ in My Wish _____ I _____ _____ in the _____ _____.

21 _____ was _____ _____ *Baekbeomilji*.

22 If God asks me _____ _____ _____ _____, I would say _____, "It is _____ _____."

23 If he asks me _____ _____ _____ _____ _____ is, I would say, "It is the _____ of my country."

24 If he _____ _____ _____ _____ _____ _____ _____, I would say _____, "It is the _____ _____ of my country." That is my answer.

13 1932년에 김구는 상해에 있는 한 공원에서 일본 장군들을 암살하기 위한 계획을 세웠다.

14 한인 애국단의 지도자로서 그는 윤봉길이 임무를 수행하도록 지시했다.

15 윤봉길이 임무를 위해 떠날 때, 그는 김구에게 말했다. "선생님, 당신은 매우 낡은 시계를 차고 계시는군요. 제 것은 새것이나, 저는 그것이 더 이상 필요하지 않을 것입니다. 부디 제 시계를 가져가시고, 제가 선생님 것을 가지도록 해주십시오."

16 김구는 윤봉길의 희생을 잊지 않기 위해서 윤봉길의 시계를 항상 상의에 넣고 다녔다.

17 기념관 관람을 마치고, 우리는 이봉창, 윤봉길, 그리고 백정기 의사들이 묻힌 삼의사의 묘로 이동했다.

18 그들의 시신은 일본에 있다가 독립이 되고 나서 김구가 그들의 시신을 효창 공원으로 가져왔다.

19 그는 그렇게 함으로써 삼의사들의 희생에 대한 그의 깊은 사랑과 경의를 보여 주었다.

20 내가 효창 공원을 떠날 때, 나는 전시관에서 읽었던 「나의 소원」에 있는 김구의 말을 생각했다.

21 그것은 「백범일지」에 쓰여 있었다.

22 만약 신이 나의 소원이 무엇이냐고 묻는다면, "그것은 대한 독립이오."라고 명확하게 말할 것이다.

23 만약에 그가 나의 두 번째 소원이 무엇이냐고 묻는다면, 나는 "그것은 내 나라의 독립이오."라고 말할 것이다.

24 만약 그가 나의 세 번째 소원이 무엇이냐고 묻는다면, "그것은 내 나라의 완전한 독립이오."라고 큰 소리로 말할 것이다. 그것이 나의 대답이다.

※ 다음 문장을 우리말로 쓰시오.

1 Last week my history club went to Hyochang Park.

➡ _____

2 We visited the Kim Koo Museum inside the park.

➡ _____

3 At the entrance of the museum, we saw a white statue of Kim Koo.

➡ _____

4 Kim Koo is a great national hero who spent most of his life fighting for the independence of Korea from Japanese rule.

➡ _____

5 In the 1900s, he helped educate young people by building schools.

➡ _____

6 In 1919, when the independence movement had spread throughout the country, he moved to Shanghai, China.

➡ _____

7 There he joined the Government of the Republic of Korea and later became its president.

➡ _____

8 The exhibition hall in the museum shows a lot of things about Kim Koo's life.

➡ _____

9 While looking around the hall, we stopped at a photo of the Korean Patriotic Organization's members.

➡ _____

10 Kim Koo formed the secret organization in 1931 to fight against Japan.

➡ _____

11 Lee Bongchang and Yun Bonggil belonged to the group.

➡ _____

12 At one place in the hall, we saw two watches under a photo of Kim Koo and Yun Bonggil.

➡ _____

13 In 1932, Kim Koo made a plan to kill Japanese generals in a park in Shanghai.

➡ _____

14 As the leader of the Korean Patriotic Organization, he directed Yun to carry out the mission.

➡ _____

15 When Yun left for the mission, he told Kim, "Sir, you are wearing a very old watch. Mine is new, but I won't need it anymore. Please take my watch, and let me have yours."

➡ _____

_____

_____

16 Kim Koo always carried Yun's watch in his jacket so that he would not forget Yun's sacrifice.

➡ _____

17 After completing the tour of the museum, we moved to the tombs of the three heroes, Lee Bongchang, Yun Bonggil, and Baek Jeonggi.

➡ _____

18 Their bodies had been in Japan, but after Korea's independence Kim Koo brought them to Hyochang Park.

➡ _____

19 By doing so, he showed his deep love and respect for the sacrifice of the three heroes.

➡ _____

20 As I left Hyochang Park, I thought about Kim Koo's words in My Wish that I had read in the exhibition hall.

➡ _____

21 It was written in *Baekbeomilji*.

➡ _____

22 If God asks me what my wish is, I would say clearly, "It is Korea's independence."

➡ _____

23 If he asks me what my second wish is, I would say, "It is the independence of my country."

➡ _____

24 If he asks me what my third wish is, I would say loudly, "It is the complete independence of my country." That is my answer.

➡ _____

_____

본문 Test

※ 다음 괄호 안의 단어들을 우리말에 맞도록 바르게 배열하시오.

My wish

1 (week / last / history / my / went / club / Hyochang / to / Park.)
➡ _____

2 (visited / we / Kim / the / Koo / inside / Museum / park. / the)
➡ _____

3 (the / at / of / entrance / museum, / the / saw / we / white / a / statue / Kim / of / Koo.)
➡ _____

4 (Koo / Kim / a / is / national / great / who / hero / most / spent / his / of / fighting / life / the / for / of / independence / from / Korea / rule. / Japanese)
➡ _____

5 (the / in / 1900s, / helped / he / young / educate / people / by / schools. / building)
➡ _____

6 (1919, / in / the / when / movement / independence / spread / had / the / throughout / contry, / he / to / moved / China. / Shanghai,)
➡ _____

7 (he / there / the / joined / Government / the / of / Republic / Korea / of / and / became / later / president. / its)
➡ _____

8 (exhibition / the / in / hall / museum / the / shows / lot / a / of / things / about / Koo's / life. / Kim)
➡ _____

9 (looking / while / the / around / hall, / the / stopped / we / a / at / photo / of / Korean / the / Patriotic / members. / Organization)
➡ _____

10 (Koo / Kim / the / formed / secret / in / organization / 1931 / fight / to / Japan. / against)
➡ _____

11 (Bongchang / Lee / and / Bonggil / Yun / to / belonged / group. / the)
➡ _____

12 (one / at / in / place / hall, / the / saw / we / watches / two / a / under / photo / Kim / of / Koo / and / Bonggil. / Yun)
➡ _____

나의 소원

1 지난주에 우리 역사 동아리는 효창 공원에 갔다.

2 우리는 공원 안에 있는 김구 기념관을 방문했다.

3 기념관 입구에서 우리는 하얀색의 김구 조각상을 보았다.

4 김구는 일본 통치로부터 대한의 독립을 위해 싸우는 데 그의 삶 대부분을 보낸 위대한 국민 영웅이다.

5 1900년대에 그는 학교를 설립함으로써 젊은이들을 교육시키는 것을 도왔다.

6 1919년에 3.1 운동이 나라 전체에 걸쳐 퍼져나갔을 때, 그는 중국 상하이로 이동했다.

7 그곳에서 그는 대한민국 임시정부에 합류했고 나중에는 그것의 대표자가 되었다.

8 기념관 안에 있는 전시관은 김구의 삶에 관한 많은 것들을 보여준다.

9 우리는 전시관을 둘러보면서 한인 애국단의 단원들 사진 앞에 섰다.

10 김구는 일본에 맞서 싸우기 위해 1931년에 비밀 조직을 형성했다.

11 이봉창과 윤봉길이 그 집단에 속해 있었다.

12 전시관의 한 곳에서, 우리는 김구와 윤봉길의 사진 아래에 있는 시계 두 개를 보았다.

13 (1932, / in / Koo / Kim / a / made / plan / kill / to / generals / Japanese / in / park / a / Shanghai. / in)

➡ _____

14 (the / as / of / leader / Korean / the / Organization, / Patriotic / directed / he / to / Yun / out / carry / mission. / the)

➡ _____

15 (Yun / when / for / left / mission, / the / told / he / you / Kim, / "Sir, / wearing / are / very / a / watch. / old // is / mine / new, / I / but / need / it / won't / anymore. // take / please / watch, / my / and / me / let / yours." / have)

➡ _____
_____

16 (Koo / Kim / carried / always / watch / Yun's / in / jacket / his / that / so / would / he / forget / not / sacrifice. / Yun's)

➡ _____

17 (completing / after / tour / the / the / of / museum, / moved / we / the / to / tombs / the / of / heroes, / three / Bongchang, / Lee / Bonggil, / Yun / and / Jeonggi. / Baek)

➡ _____

18 (bodies / their / been / had / Japan, / in / after / but / independence / Korea's / Koo / Kim / them / brought / Hyochang / to / Park.)

➡ _____

19 (doing / by / so, / showed / he / deep / his / and / love / for / respect / sacrifice / the / the / of / heroes. / three)

➡ _____

20 (I / as / left / Park, / Hyochang / thought / I / Kim / about / words / Koo's / in / Wish / My / that / had / I / read / the / in / hall. / exhibition)

➡ _____

21 (was / it / written / *Baekbeomilji.* / in)

➡ _____

22 (God / if / me / asks / my / what / is, / wish / would / I / clearly, / say / is / "it / Independence." / Korea's)

➡ _____

23 (he / if / asks / what / me / my / wish / second / is, / would / I / say, / is / "it / independence / the / of / country." / my)

➡ _____

24 (he / if / me / asks / my / what / wish / third / is, / would / I / loudly, / say / is / "it / complete / the / of / independence / country." / my // is / that / answer. / my)

➡ _____
_____

13 1932년에 김구는 상해에 있는 한 공원에서 일본 장군들을 암살하기 위한 계획을 세웠다.

14 한인 애국단의 지도자로서 그는 윤봉길이 임무를 수행하도록 지시했다.

15 윤봉길이 임무를 위해 떠날 때, 그는 김구에게 말했다. "선생님, 당신은 매우 낡은 시계를 차고 계시는군요. 제 것은 새것이나, 저는 그것이 더 이상 필요하지 않을 것입니다. 부디 제 시계를 가져가시고, 제가 선생님 것을 가지도록 해주십시오."

16 김구는 윤봉길의 희생을 잊지 않기 위해서 윤봉길의 시계를 항상 상의에 넣고 다녔다.

17 기념관 관람을 마치고, 우리는 이봉창, 윤봉길, 그리고 백정기 의사들이 묻힌 삼의사의 묘로 이동했다.

18 그들의 시신은 일본에 있다가 독립이 되고 나서 김구가 그들의 시신을 효창 공원으로 가져왔다.

19 그는 그렇게 함으로써 삼의사들의 희생에 대한 그의 깊은 사랑과 경의를 보여 주었다.

20 내가 효창 공원을 떠날 때, 나는 전시관에서 읽었던 「나의 소원」에 있는 김구의 말을 생각했다.

21 그것은 「백범일지」에 쓰여 있었다.

22 만약 신이 나의 소원이 무엇이냐고 묻는다면, "그것은 대한 독립이오."라고 명확하게 말할 것이다.

23 만약에 그가 나의 두 번째 소원이 무엇이냐고 묻는다면, 나는 "그것은 내 나라의 독립이오."라고 말할 것이다.

24 만약 그가 나의 세 번째 소원이 무엇이냐고 묻는다면, "그것은 내 나라의 완전한 독립이오."라고 큰 소리로 말할 것이다. 그것이 나의 대답이다.

※ 다음 우리말을 영어로 쓰시오.

1 지난주에 우리 역사 동아리는 효창 공원에 갔다.

➡ _____

2 우리는 공원 안에 있는 김구 기념관을 방문했다.

➡ _____

3 기념관 입구에서 우리는 하얀색의 김구 조각상을 보았다.

➡ _____

4 김구는 일본 통치로부터 대한의 독립을 위해 싸우는 데 그의 삶 대부분을 보낸 위대한 국민 영웅이다.

➡ _____

_____

5 1900년대에 그는 학교를 설립함으로써 젊은이들을 교육시키는 것을 도왔다.

➡ _____

6 1919년에 3.1 운동이 나라 전체에 걸쳐 퍼져나갔을 때, 그는 중국 상하이로 이동했다.

➡ _____

_____

7 그곳에서 그는 대한민국 임시정부에 합류했고 나중에는 그것의 대표자가 되었다.

➡ _____

8 기념관 안에 있는 전시관은 김구의 삶에 관한 많은 것들을 보여 준다.

➡ _____

9 우리는 전시관을 둘러보면서 한인 애국단의 단원들 사진 앞에 섰다.

➡ _____

10 김구는 일본에 맞서 싸우기 위해 1931년에 비밀 조직을 형성했다.

➡ _____

11 이봉창과 윤봉길이 그 집단에 속해 있었다.

➡ _____

12 전시관의 한 곳에서, 우리는 김구와 윤봉길의 사진 아래에 있는 시계 두 개를 보았다.

➡ _____

13 1932년에 김구는 상해에 있는 한 공원에서 일본 장군들을 암살하기 위한 계획을 세웠다.

➡ _____

14 한인 애국단의 지도자로서 그는 윤봉길이 임무를 수행하도록 지시했다.

➡ _____

15 윤봉길이 임무를 위해 떠날 때, 그는 김구에게 말했다. "선생님, 당신은 매우 낡은 시계를 차고 계시는군요. 제 것은 새것이나, 저는 그것이 더 이상 필요하지 않을 것입니다. 부디 제 시계를 가져가시고, 제가 선생님 것을 가지도록 해주십시오."

➡ _____

_____

16 김구는 윤봉길의 희생을 잊지 않기 위해서 윤봉길의 시계를 항상 상의에 넣고 다녔다.

➡ _____

17 기념관 관람을 마치고, 우리는 이봉창, 윤봉길, 그리고 백정기 의사들이 묻힌 삼의사의 묘로 이동했다.

➡ _____

18 그들의 시신은 일본에 있다가 독립이 되고 나서 김구가 그들의 시신을 효창 공원으로 가져왔다.

➡ _____

_____

19 그는 그렇게 함으로써 삼의사들의 희생에 대한 그의 깊은 사랑과 경의를 보여 주었다.

➡ _____

20 내가 효창 공원을 떠날 때, 나는 전시관에서 읽었던 「나의 소원」에 있는 김구의 말을 생각했다.

➡ _____

_____

21 그것은 『백범일지』에 쓰여 있었다.

➡ _____

22 만약 신이 나의 소원이 무엇이냐고 묻는다면, "그것은 대한 독립이오."라고 명확하게 말할 것이다.

➡ _____

23 만약에 그가 나의 두 번째 소원이 무엇이냐고 묻는다면, 나는 "그것은 내 나라의 독립이오."라고 말할 것이다.

➡ _____

24 만약 그가 나의 세 번째 소원이 무엇이냐고 묻는다면, "그것은 내 나라의 완전한 독립이오."라고 큰 소리로 말할 것이다. 그것이 나의 대답이다.

➡ _____

_____

※ 다음 우리말과 일치하도록 빈칸에 알맞은 말을 쓰시오.

Real Life Talk Step 3

1. My group members _____ An Junggeun _____ we _____
   _____ _____ his _____ _____ the country.

2. You _____ _____ _____ _____ him _____ _____
   the An Junggeun Museum or An Junggeun Park.

1. 우리 그룹은 안중근을 선택했는데, 우리 나라를 위한 희생에 깊은 인상을 받았기 때문입니다.
2. 여러분은 안중근 기념관이나 안중근 공원을 방문함으로써 그에 관하여 더 많은 것을 알 수 있습니다.

Enjoy Writing

Dosan An Changho

1. An Changho _____ _____ _____ 1878.

2. _____ he was _____ _____ _____, he _____ _____
   Seoul and _____ _____ school _____.

3. In 1902, he _____ _____ America _____ _____ he could
   _____ _____ _____ _____.

4. In America, An _____ _____ _____ _____ _____ of the Korean
   people there and _____ _____ _____ _____ _____.

5. After he _____ _____ _____ Korea, he _____ the New Korean
   Society in 1907 _____ _____ _____ _____ _____.

6. He also joined the _____ _____ _____ _____ _____
   _____ in Shanghai in 1919.

7. After that, he _____ _____ _____ _____ schools _____
   _____ people _____ he _____ _____ 1938.

도산 안창호
1. 안창호는 1878년에 태어났다.
2. 그가 십 대였을 때, 그는 서울로 이사를 하고 그곳에서 학교를 다녔다.
3. 1902년에 그는 더 나은 교육을 받기 위해서 미국으로 떠났다.
4. 안창호는 미국에서 한국인들의 삶을 개선하는 것을 도왔고, 존경받는 지도자가 되었다.
5. 그가 한국으로 돌아오고 나서, 그는 대한의 독립을 위해 싸우고자 1907년에 신민회를 설립했다.
6. 그는 또한 1919년에 상해의 대한민국 임시정부에 합류했다.
7. 그 후에, 그는 1938년에 죽을 때까지 사람들을 교육하기 위해 많은 학교들을 세웠다.

Project Step 1

1. A: I want _____ _____ Bulguksa _____ _____. You
   know Bulguksa, _____ _____?

2. B: Yes, I do. It's _____ _____ _____ Gyeongju.

3. C: Yes. It's _____ _____ _____ _____ _____
   in Korea.

4. D: It also _____ _____ _____ _____ _____ the Dabotop.

1. A: 나는 외국인에게 불국사를 소개하고 싶어. 너는 불국사를 알고 있지, 그렇지 않니?
2. B: 응, 알고 있어. 그것은 경주에 있는 절이야.
3. C: 응. 그것은 한국에서 가장 아름다운 절 중 하나야.
4. D: 그것은 또한 다보탑과 같은 많은 문화재들을 보유하고 있어.

※ 다음 우리말을 영어로 쓰시오.

Real Life Talk Step 3

1. 우리 그룹은 안중근을 선택했는데, 우리 나라를 위한 희생에 깊은 인상을 받았기 때문입니다.

   ➡ _____

   _____

2. 여러분은 안중근 기념관이나 안중근 공원을 방문함으로써 그에 관하여 더 많은 것을 알 수 있습니다.

   ➡ _____

Enjoy Writing

Dosan An Changho

1. 안창호는 1878년에 태어났다.

   ➡ _____

2. 그가 십 대였을 때, 그는 서울로 이사를 하고 그곳에서 학교를 다녔다.

   ➡ _____

3. 1902년에 그는 더 나은 교육을 받기 위해서 미국으로 떠났다.

   ➡ _____

4. 안창호는 미국에서 한국인들의 삶을 개선하는 것을 도왔고, 존경받는 지도자가 되었다.

   ➡ _____

5. 그가 한국으로 돌아오고 나서, 그는 대한의 독립을 위해 싸우고자 1907년에 신민회를 설립했다.

   ➡ _____

   _____

6. 그는 또한 1919년에 상해의 대한민국 임시정부에 합류했다.

   ➡ _____

7. 그 후에, 그는 1938년에 죽을 때까지 사람들을 교육하기 위해 많은 학교들을 세웠다.

   ➡ _____

Project Step 1

1. A: 나는 외국인에게 불국사를 소개하고 싶어. 너는 불국사를 알고 있지, 그렇지 않니?

   ➡ _____

2. B: 응, 알고 있어. 그것은 경주에 있는 절이야.

   ➡ _____

3. C: 응. 그것은 한국에서 가장 아름다운 절 중 하나야.

   ➡ _____

4. D: 그것은 또한 다보탑과 같은 많은 문화재들을 보유하고 있어.

   ➡ _____

※ 다음 영어를 우리말로 쓰시오.

01 success _____

02 match _____

03 abroad _____

04 achieve _____

05 symbol _____

06 experience _____

07 regularly _____

08 appreciate _____

09 clearly _____

10 trail _____

11 amaze _____

12 hot spring _____

13 landscape _____

14 throughout _____

15 main _____

16 confused _____

17 natural _____

18 plaid _____

19 culture _____

20 recommend _____

21 wildly _____

22 view _____

23 surely _____

24 rival _____

25 several _____

26 society _____

27 wedding _____

28 suggest _____

29 traditional _____

30 someday _____

31 village _____

32 waterfall _____

33 native _____

34 nickname _____

35 long before _____

36 be covered with _____

37 filled with _____

38 with the help of _____

39 be famous for _____

40 all year round _____

41 be known as _____

42 prepare for _____

43 come to one's mind _____

※ 다음 우리말을 영어로 쓰시오.

01 경쟁자 _____

02 추천하다 _____

03 (특정한 곳의) 토박이의 _____

04 해외에(서), 해외로 _____

05 언젠가, 언제든 _____

06 달성하다, 성취하다 _____

07 풍경 _____

08 도처에 _____

09 몇몇의 _____

10 폭포 _____

11 성공, 성과 _____

12 경관, 전망 _____

13 확실히, 분명히 _____

14 가지고 가다 _____

15 진가를 알아보다 _____

16 격자무늬, 격자무늬 천 _____

17 흔한 _____

18 명확하게 _____

19 경기, 시합 _____

20 결혼(식) _____

21 자취, 오솔길 _____

22 (대단히) 놀라게 하다 _____

23 쌍둥이의; 쌍둥이 _____

24 마을, 부락, 촌락 _____

25 자연의, 천연의 _____

26 겪다, 경험하다 _____

27 별명 _____

28 제안하다 _____

29 상징, 상징물 _____

30 온천 _____

31 주요한, 주된 _____

32 (사람이) 혼란스러워 하는 _____

33 전통적인 _____

34 정보 _____

35 (옷을) 입어보다 _____

36 ~로 가득 찬 _____

37 ~로 유명하다 _____

38 ~을 준비하다 _____

39 일 년 내내 _____

40 ~로 알려져 있다 _____

41 ~으로 덮이다 _____

42 ~의 도움을 받아서 _____

43 생각이 나다, 생각이 떠오르다 _____

※ 다음 영영풀이에 알맞은 단어를 <보기>에서 골라 쓴 후, 우리말 뜻을 쓰시오.

1 _____ : a New Zealand bird that cannot fly: _____

2 _____ : in or to a foreign country: _____

3 _____ : a place where hot water flows out of the ground: _____

4 _____ : a pattern of crossed lines and squares: _____

5 _____ : a contest between two or more players or teams: _____

6 _____ : a rough path across countryside or through a forest: _____

7 _____ : a ceremony at which two people are married to each other: _____

8 _____ : to successfully complete something or get a good result: _____

9 _____ : happening often and to many people or in many places: _____

10 _____ : someone who belongs to the race of people that first lived in New Zealand: _____

11 _____ : a person, company or thing that competes with another in sport, business, etc.: _____

12 _____ : a meal in which everyone who is invited brings something to eat: _____

13 _____ : an outdoor game played by two teams with an oval(= egg-shaped) ball: _____

14 _____ : everything you can see when you look across a large area of land, especially in the country: _____

15 _____ : an area of land that is higher than the land around it, but not as high as a mountain: _____

16 _____ : a picture or shape that has a particular meaning or represents a particular organization or idea: _____

보기			
rugby	abroad	common	wedding
Maori	match	landscape	plaid
hill	hot spring	rival	achieve
symbol	trail	potluck	kiwi

※ 다음 우리말과 일치하도록 빈칸에 알맞은 말을 쓰시오.

Listen & Speak 1 A

1. **B:** _____ _____ about _____ _____ from _____ countries.

   G: Hmm... Do you know _____ _____ _____ _____?

   B: No, I don't. What is it?

   G: It is _____ _____ from Scotland. It _____ _____ a _____ skirt and has a _____ _____.

   B: A skirt of knee length _____ a _____ _____?

   G: Yes. It is _____ _____ it is a skirt for men.

   B: That sounds _____. I want _____ _____ one _____.

2. **G:** Brian, _____ _____ _____ we will _____ for the World Food Festival.

   B: I will make a meat pie. It is _____ in Australia. _____ _____ you, Sera?

   G: I want to make a _____ English _____, fish and chips.

   B: Fish and chips? _____ does it _____ _____?

   G: It's _____ fish _____ hot _____ _____.

   B: That sounds _____. _____ _____ _____ them.

1. **B:** 다른 나라의 전통 의상에 대해 이야기해 보자.
   G: 흠… 너는 킬트가 뭔지 아니?
   B: 아니, 몰라. 그게 뭐야?
   G: 킬트는 스코틀랜드의 전통 의상이야. 그건 무릎길이의 치마같이 생겼고, 체크무늬가 있어.
   B: 무릎길이의 체크무늬 치마라고?
   G: 응. 킬트는 남자를 위한 치마이기 때문에 특이해.
   B: 흥미롭게 들린다. 나는 킬트를 입어보고 싶어.

2. **G:** Brian, 우리 세계 음식 축제에 무엇을 준비할 것인지 이야기해 보자.
   B: 나는 미트 파이를 만들 거야. 그건 호주에서 유명해. 너는 어때, 세라야?
   G: 나는 영국의 유명한 요리인 피시 앤 칩스를 만들고 싶어.
   B: 피시앤칩스? 그건 어떻게 생겼어?
   G: 그건 뜨거운 감자튀김이 곁들여진 튀긴 생선이야.
   B: 그거 흥미롭다. 우리 함께 그것들을 준비하자.

Listen & Speak 2 A

1. **B:** Wow, we _____ _____ _____ Hong Kong, Mom.

   W: I'm _____ _____ _____ our visit. What _____ we _____ today, Mike?

   B: I _____ we _____ Victoria Peak.

   W: Victoria Peak?

   B: It is _____ _____ _____ in Hong Kong and is _____ _____ _____ movies. We can enjoy the _____ _____.

   W: That _____ good. _____ go.

1. **B:** 와, 엄마, 우리가 마침내 홍콩에 도착했어요.
   W: 우리가 방문할 곳들이 기대된다. 오늘 우리는 무엇을 해야 하니, Mike?
   B: 저는 우리가 빅토리아 피크에 가는 것을 제안해요.
   W: 빅토리아 피크?
   B: 빅토리아 피크는 홍콩에서 가장 높은 산이고, 영화에도 많이 나왔어요. 우리는 환상적인 경관을 즐길 수 있어요.
   W: 그거 좋겠구나. 가 보자.

2. **G:** My American friend _____ me to a _____ dinner next Friday.

   B: You _____, you should take _____ _____ _____ at the dinner.

   G: What would you _____ _____ I take?

   B: I _____ you _____ some Korean food. _____ _____ Gimbap, Suji?

   G: Yes. It's not _____ and it's _____ _____ _____.

   B: I think it'll be good _____ dinner.

Real Life Talk

Seho: Good morning.

Jessie, Andy: Hi, Seho.

Seho: I will visit my uncle in Philadelphia this winter. _____ _____ _____ _____ _____ the city?

Jessie: Sure. I was there _____ _____ _____ _____. _____, _____ _____ about food.

Seho: Okay. _____ _____ is Philadelphia _____ _____?

Jessie: _____ _____ _____ food in Philadelphia is the cheese steak sandwich. It is a big sandwich _____ _____ beef and _____ cheese.

Seho: Good _____. I _____ _____ _____ it. _____ _____ any places _____ _____ _____ _____ tourists?

Andy: I _____ you visit _____ Hall. It is very important in American _____.

Seho: Wonderful. Thank you for the _____.

Andy: My _____.

Wrap Up

M: _____ to Australia. The _____ of Australia is Canberra. People speak English. Meat pie is a _____ _____ in Australia. _____ _____, _____ _____ _____ visit the Sydney Opera House and the _____ _____ in Melbourne.

---

2. G: 나의 미국인 친구가 다음 주 금요일에 있을 포틀럭 저녁 식사에 나를 초대했어.
B: 네가 알다시피, 너는 저녁 식사에 함께 나눠 먹을 음식을 가지고 가야 해.
G: 무엇을 가져갈지 추천해 줄래?
B: 나는 네가 한국 음식을 가져가는 것을 추천해. 수지야, 김밥 어때?
G: 그래. 김밥은 맵지도 않고, 들고 가기도 쉽겠다.
B: 내 생각에는 김밥이 저녁 식사에 좋을 것 같아.

세호: 안녕.
Jessie, Andy: 안녕, 세호야.
세호: 나 이번 겨울에 필라델피아에 계신 삼촌을 뵈러 가. 너희들 나한테 그 도시에 대해 알려줄 수 있니?
Jessie: 물론이지. 난 몇 년 전에 거기에 갔었어. 먼저 음식에 대해 이야기해 보자.
세호: 좋아. 필라델피아는 어떤 음식이 유명해?
Jessie: 필라델피아에서 가장 유명한 음식은 치즈 스테이크 샌드위치야. 소고기와 녹인 치즈로 채워진 큰 샌드위치지.
세호: 멋진 제안이다. 먹어 볼게. 여행자들에게 인기 있는 장소가 있니?
Andy: 나는 네가 독립 기념관에 방문하는 것을 제안해. 그곳은 미국 역사에서 아주 중요해.
세호: 멋지겠다. 정보 고마워.
Andy: 천만에.

M: 호주에 온 것을 환영한다. 호주의 수도는 캔버라다. 사람들은 영어로 말한다. 고기 파이는 호주에서 인기 있는 음식이다. 매년 많은 관광객이 시드니 오페라 하우스와 멜버른의 아름다운 해변을 방문한다.

※ 다음 우리말에 맞도록 대화를 영어로 쓰시오.

해석

Listen & Speak 1 A

1. B: _____
   G: _____
   B: _____
   G: _____
   _____
   B: _____
   G: _____
   B: _____

2. G: _____
   B: _____
   G: _____
   B: _____
   G: _____
   B: _____

1. B: 다른 나라의 전통 의상에 대해 이야기해 보자.
   G: 흠… 너는 킬트가 뭔지 아니?
   B: 아니, 몰라. 그게 뭐야?
   G: 킬트는 스코틀랜드의 전통 의상이야. 그건 무릎길이의 치마같이 생겼고, 체크무늬가 있어.
   B: 무릎길이의 체크무늬 치마라고?
   G: 응. 킬트는 남자를 위한 치마이기 때문에 특이해.
   B: 흥미롭게 들린다. 나는 킬트를 입어보고 싶어.

2. G: Brian, 우리 세계 음식 축제에 무엇을 준비할 것인지 이야기해 보자.
   B: 나는 미트 파이를 만들 거야. 그건 호주에서 유명해. 너는 어때, 세라야?
   G: 나는 영국의 유명한 요리인 피시 앤 칩스를 만들고 싶어.
   B: 피시앤칩스? 그건 어떻게 생겼어?
   G: 그건 뜨거운 감자튀김이 곁들여진 튀긴 생선이야.
   B: 그거 흥미롭다. 우리 함께 그것들을 준비하자.

Listen & Speak 2 A

1. B: _____
   W: _____
   B: _____
   W: _____
   B: _____
   W: _____

1. B: 와, 엄마, 우리가 마침내 홍콩에 도착했어요.
   W: 우리가 방문할 곳들이 기대된다. 오늘 우리는 무엇을 해야 하니, Mike?
   B: 저는 우리가 빅토리아 피크에 가는 것을 제안해요.
   W: 빅토리아 피크?
   B: 빅토리아 피크는 홍콩에서 가장 높은 산이고, 영화에도 많이 나왔어요. 우리는 환상적인 경관을 즐길 수 있어요.
   W: 그거 좋겠구나. 가 보자.

2. G: _____
   B: _____
   G: _____
   B: _____
   G: _____
   B: _____

2. G: 나의 미국인 친구가 다음 주 금요일에 있을 포틀럭 저녁 식사에 나를 초대했어.
   B: 네가 알다시피, 너는 저녁 식사에 함께 나눠 먹을 음식을 가지고 가야 해.
   G: 무엇을 가져갈지 추천해 줄래?
   B: 나는 네가 한국 음식을 가져가는 것을 추천해. 수지야, 김밥 어때?
   G: 그래. 김밥은 맵지도 않고, 들고 가기도 쉽겠다.
   B: 내 생각에는 김밥이 저녁 식사에 좋을 것 같아.

Real Life Talk

Seho: _____

Jessie, Andy: _____

Seho: _____
_____

Jessie: _____

Seho: _____

Jessie: _____
_____

Seho: _____
_____

Andy: _____
_____

Seho: _____

Andy: _____

세호: 안녕.
Jessie, Andy: 안녕, 세호야.
세호: 나 이번 겨울에 필라델피아에 계신 삼촌을 뵈러 가. 너희들 나한테 그 도시에 대해 알려줄 수 있니?
Jessie: 물론이지. 난 몇 년 전에 거기에 갔었어. 먼저 음식에 대해 이야기해 보자.
세호: 좋아. 필라델피아는 어떤 음식이 유명해?
Jessie: 필라델피아에서 가장 유명한 음식은 치즈 스테이크 샌드위치야. 소고기와 녹인 치즈로 채워진 큰 샌드위치지.
세호: 멋진 제안이다. 먹어 볼게. 여행자들에게 인기 있는 장소가 있니?
Andy: 나는 네가 독립 기념관에 방문하는 것을 제안해. 그곳은 미국 역사에서 아주 중요해.
세호: 멋지겠다. 정보 고마워.
Andy: 천만에.

Wrap Up

M: _____
_____
_____

M: 호주에 온 것을 환영한다. 호주의 수도는 캔버라다. 사람들은 영어로 말한다. 고기 파이는 호주에서 인기 있는 음식이다. 매년 많은 관광객들이 시드니 오페라 하우스와 멜버른의 아름다운 해변을 방문한다.

※ 다음 우리말과 일치하도록 빈칸에 알맞은 것을 골라 쓰시오.

Hello! New Zealand

1 New Zealand is a _____ of _____ _____. It has many beautiful lakes and _____.
A. waterfalls   B. natural   C. place   D. beauty

2 New Zealand _____ _____ _____ _____, the South Island and the North Island.
A. main   B. two   C. islands   D. has

3 In the South Island, there are mountains that are _____ _____ snow _____ year _____.
A. covered   B. round   C. all   D. with

4 You will _____ _____ _____ the fantastic _____.
A. by   B. be   C. views   D. amazed

5 In the North Island, there are many _____ _____, lakes, and _____ _____ green grass.
A. with   B. hot   C. areas   D. springs

6 _____ _____ its natural beauty, many famous movies have _____ _____ in New Zealand.
A. been   B. of   C. made   D. because

7 If you visit New Zealand, you _____ _____ _____ its _____.
A. nature   B. surely   C. will   D. appreciate

8 When you _____ the word kiwi, what _____ _____ your _____?
A. mind   B. comes   C. hear   D. to

9 _____ a fruit, _____, in New Zealand the word kiwi has a _____ of _____.
A. couple   B. maybe   C. meanings   D. but

10 First, kiwi is the _____ of a _____, green _____.
A. delicious   B. name   C. fruit

11 A lot of kiwi fruit is _____ there, _____ New Zealand is _____ _____ the land of kiwi fruit.
A. known   B. grown   C. as   D. so

12 Kiwi is _____ the name of _____ of New Zealand's _____ _____.
A. native   B. one   C. also   D. birds

13 The kiwi is _____ to New Zealanders _____ it is the _____ of the _____.
A. because   B. special   C. nation   D. symbol

14 _____, kiwi is a _____ _____ people _____ New Zealand.
A. from   B. nickname   C. also   D. for

15 Today, New Zealanders _____ _____ _____ Kiwis _____ the world.
A. called   B. throughout   C. sometimes   D. are

16 Now, you know _____ kiwi is the _____ of a _____, a bird, and _____ a people.
A. fruit   B. that   C. also   D. name

안녕! 뉴질랜드

1 뉴질랜드는 자연의 아름다움이 가득한 곳이다. 뉴질랜드는 아름다운 호수와 폭포들이 많다.

2 뉴질랜드에는 남섬과 북섬, 두 개의 본섬이 있다.

3 남섬에는 일 년 내내 눈으로 덮인 산들이 있다.

4 당신은 굉장히 멋진 경관에 놀랄 것이다.

5 북섬에는 많은 온천과 호수, 초원 지역이 있다.

6 뉴질랜드 자연의 아름다움 때문에 많은 유명한 영화들이 뉴질랜드에서 촬영되었다.

7 뉴질랜드를 방문하면, 분명히 그 자연의 진가를 인정할 것이다.

8 키위라는 단어를 들을 때, 무엇이 떠오르는가?

9 아마도 과일이 떠오르겠지만, 뉴질랜드에서 키위는 몇 가지 뜻이 있다.

10 먼저, 키위는 맛있는 초록색 과일의 이름이다.

11 많은 키위가 그곳에서 자라기 때문에 뉴질랜드는 키위의 나라로 알려져 있다.

12 키위는 뉴질랜드 토종 새의 이름이기도 하다.

13 키위 새는 국가의 상징이기 때문에, 뉴질랜드 사람들에게 특별하다.

14 또한, 키위는 뉴질랜드 출신의 사람들을 부르는 별명이기도 하다.

15 오늘날 뉴질랜드인들은 전 세계적으로 키위라고 불리기도 한다.

16 이제, 당신은 키위가 과일과 새, 그리고 국민의 명칭이라는 것을 알았다.

17 Next time, don't become _____ when someone _____ the word kiwi, _____ has several _____.

    A. uses   B. which   C. confused   D. meanings

18 Now, _____ _____ about the Maori. They are the _____ _____ of New Zealand.

    A. native   B. talk   C. people   D. let's

19 They went to live _____ the islands _____ _____ Europeans _____.

    A. arrived   B. long   C. on   D. before

20 The Maori culture is an _____ _____ _____ of _____ New Zealand _____.

    A. part   B. society   C. today's   D. important

21 The Maori language _____ _____ at some schools and _____ _____ Maori language radio and TV stations.

    A. are   B. taught   C. there   D. is

22 There are Maori _____ in _____ _____ of the _____.

    A. country   B. many   C. villages   D. parts

23 You can _____ Maori _____ and _____ Maori _____.

    A. experience   B. visit   C. culture   D. villages

24 If you _____ "kia ora" to the villagers, they will be _____ to _____ it. It _____ "hi" in English.

    A. means   B. say   C. hear   D. glad

25 _____ you _____ _____ the haka?

    A. ever   B. have   C. watched

26 The haka may look _____ because haka dancers _____ and _____ their bodies _____.

    A. wildly   B. move   C. shout   D. scary

27 The Maori people, _____ you've already _____ about, started _____ the haka _____ a war dance.

    A. as   B. who   C. doing   D. heard

28 Today, _____, New Zealanders do the haka at sport _____, weddings, or _____ important _____.

    A. matches   B. other   C. however   D. events

29 For _____, New Zealand's _____ rugby team members do the haka _____ every _____.

    A. before   B. example   C. national   D. match

30 It is _____ _____ _____ the world.

    A. all   B. famous   C. over

31 If you see the haka, you will probably _____ _____ the rival team _____ be _____.

    A. scared   B. agree   C. that   D. must

32 _____ the kiwi bird, the haka is a _____ _____.

    A. symbol   B. like   C. national

---

17 다음에는 누군가가 키위라는 단어를 사용할 때 혼동하지 마라. 그 단어는 여러 뜻을 가지고 있기 때문이다.

18 이제, 마오리족에 대해 이야기해 보자. 마오리족은 뉴질랜드의 원주민이다.

19 그들은 유럽인들이 도착하기 오래 전에 이 섬에 와서 살았다.

20 마오리족의 문화는 오늘날 뉴질랜드 사회의 중요한 부분이다.

21 몇몇 학교에서 마오리어를 가르치고 있으며, 마오리어의 라디오와 TV 방송국이 있다.

22 나라의 여러 곳에 마오리 마을이 있다.

23 당신은 마오리 마을을 방문해 마오리 문화를 경험할 수 있다.

24 당신이 마을 사람들에게 "kia ora"라고 말한다면 그들은 그것을 듣고 좋아할 것이다. 그것은 영어로 "안녕"이라는 뜻이다.

25 하카를 본 적이 있는가?

26 하카 춤을 추는 사람들이 소리 지르고, 그들의 몸을 사납게 움직이기 때문에 하카는 무서워 보일 수도 있다.

27 당신이 이미 그들에 대해 들은 적이 있겠지만, 마오리인들은 전쟁 춤으로 하카를 추기 시작했다.

28 하지만, 오늘날 뉴질랜드 사람들은 하카를 운동 경기, 결혼식 또는 다른 중요한 행사가 있을 때 한다.

29 예를 들어, 뉴질랜드의 럭비 국가 대표 팀 선수들은 모든 경기 전에 하카를 춘다.

30 그것은 전 세계적으로 유명하다.

31 당신이 하카를 본다면, 상대 팀이 틀림없이 겁을 먹을 것이라는 것에 아마 동의할 것이다.

32 키위와 마찬가지로 하카는 나라의 상징이다.

※ 다음 우리말과 일치하도록 빈칸에 알맞은 것을 골라 쓰시오.

Hello! New Zealand

1　New Zealand is _____ _____ _____ _____ _____ .
　　It has many beautiful _____ and _____ .

2　New Zealand has _____ _____ _____ , the South Island
　　and the North Island.

3　In the South Island, there _____ _____ that _____
　　_____ _____ snow _____ _____ _____ .

4　You will _____ _____ _____ the _____ _____ .

5　In the North Island, there are _____ _____ _____ , lakes,
　　and areas _____ green grass.

6　_____ _____ its _____ _____ , many famous movies
　　_____ _____ _____ in New Zealand.

7　If you visit New Zealand, you _____ _____ _____ its
　　nature.

8　When you _____ the word kiwi, what _____ _____
　　_____ _____ ?

9　Maybe a fruit, but, in New Zealand the word kiwi has _____
　　_____ _____ _____ .

10　First, kiwi is _____ _____ of a _____ , green fruit.

11　A lot of kiwi fruit _____ _____ there, _____ New
　　Zealand _____ _____ _____ the land of kiwi fruit.

12　Kiwi is also the name of _____ of _____ _____
　　_____ .

13　The kiwi is _____ _____ New Zealanders _____ it is
　　the _____ of the nation.

14　Also, kiwi is _____ _____ _____ people _____ New
　　Zealand.

15　Today, New Zealanders _____ _____ _____ Kiwis
　　_____ _____ _____ .

16　Now, you know _____ kiwi is _____ _____ _____ a
　　fruit, a bird, and also a people.

1　뉴질랜드는 자연의 아름다움이 가득한 곳이다. 뉴질랜드는 아름다운 호수와 폭포들이 많다.

2　뉴질랜드에는 남섬과 북섬, 두 개의 본섬이 있다.

3　남섬에는 일 년 내내 눈으로 덮인 산들이 있다.

4　당신은 굉장히 멋진 경관에 놀랄 것이다.

5　북섬에는 많은 온천과 호수, 초원 지역이 있다.

6　뉴질랜드 자연의 아름다움 때문에 많은 유명한 영화들이 뉴질랜드에서 촬영되었다.

7　뉴질랜드를 방문하면, 분명히 그 자연의 진가를 인정할 것이다.

8　키위라는 단어를 들을 때, 무엇이 떠오르는가?

9　아마도 과일이 떠오르겠지만, 뉴질랜드에서 키위는 몇 가지 뜻이 있다.

10　먼저, 키위는 맛있는 초록색 과일의 이름이다.

11　많은 키위가 그곳에서 자라기 때문에 뉴질랜드는 키위의 나라로 알려져 있다.

12　키위는 뉴질랜드 토종 새의 이름이기도 하다.

13　키위 새는 국가의 상징이기 때문에, 뉴질랜드 사람들에게 특별하다.

14　또한, 키위는 뉴질랜드 출신의 사람들을 부르는 별명이기도 하다.

15　오늘날 뉴질랜드인들은 전 세계적으로 키위라고 불리기도 한다.

16　이제, 당신은 키위가 과일과 새, 그리고 국민의 명칭이라는 것을 알았다.

17 Next time, don't become _____ when someone _____ the word kiwi, _____ _____ _____ _____ .

18 Now, _____ _____ about the Maori. _____ are _____ _____ _____ of New Zealand.

19 They went to _____ _____ the islands _____ _____ _____ _____ .

20 The Maori culture is _____ _____ _____ of _____ New Zealand _____ .

21 The Maori language _____ _____ at some schools and _____ _____ Maori language radio and TV stations.

22 _____ _____ Maori villages _____ _____ _____ the country.

23 You can _____ Maori _____ and _____ Maori _____ .

24 If you _____ "kia ora" _____ the villagers, they _____ _____ _____ _____ _____ it. It _____ "hi" in English.

25 _____ you _____ _____ the haka?

26 The haka may _____ _____ _____ haka dancers _____ and _____ their bodies _____ .

27 The Maori people, _____ you've already _____ _____ , started _____ the haka _____ a war dance.

28 Today, _____ , New Zealanders _____ the haka _____ _____ , weddings, or _____ _____ _____ .

29 _____ _____ , New Zealand's _____ _____ _____ _____ do the haka _____ _____ _____ .

30 It is _____ _____ _____ the world.

31 If you see the haka, you _____ probably _____ the rival team _____ _____ _____ .

32 _____ the kiwi bird, the haka is _____ _____ _____ .

17 다음에는 누군가가 키위라는 단어를 사용할 때 혼동하지 마라. 그 단어는 여러 뜻을 가지고 있기 때문이다.

18 이제, 마오리족에 대해 이야기해 보자. 마오리족은 뉴질랜드의 원주민이다.

19 그들은 유럽인들이 도착하기 오래 전에 이 섬에 와서 살았다.

20 마오리족의 문화는 오늘날 뉴질랜드 사회의 중요한 부분이다.

21 몇몇 학교에서 마오리어를 가르치고 있으며, 마오리어의 라디오와 TV 방송국이 있다.

22 나라의 여러 곳에 마오리 마을이 있다.

23 당신은 마오리 마을을 방문해 마오리 문화를 경험할 수 있다.

24 당신이 마을 사람들에게 "kia ora"라고 말한다면 그들은 그것을 듣고 좋아할 것이다. 그것은 영어로 "안녕"이라는 뜻이다.

25 하카를 본 적이 있는가?

26 하카 춤을 추는 사람들이 소리 지르고, 그들의 몸을 사납게 움직이기 때문에 하카는 무서워 보일 수도 있다.

27 당신이 이미 그들에 대해 들은 적이 있겠지만, 마오리인들은 전쟁 춤으로 하카를 추기 시작했다.

28 하지만, 오늘날 뉴질랜드 사람들은 하카를 운동 경기, 결혼식 또는 다른 중요한 행사가 있을 때 한다.

29 예를 들어, 뉴질랜드의 럭비 국가 대표 팀 선수들은 모든 경기 전에 하카를 춘다.

30 그것은 전 세계적으로 유명하다.

31 당신이 하카를 본다면, 상대 팀이 틀림없이 겁을 먹을 것이라는 것에 아마 동의할 것이다.

32 키위와 마찬가지로 하카는 나라의 상징이다.

※ 다음 문장을 우리말로 쓰시오.

1 New Zealand is a place of natural beauty. It has many beautiful lakes and waterfalls.
➡ _____

2 New Zealand has two main islands, the South Island and the North Island.
➡ _____

3 In the South Island, there are mountains that are covered with snow all year round.
➡ _____

4 You will be amazed by the fantastic views.
➡ _____

5 In the North Island, there are many hot springs, lakes, and areas with green grass.
➡ _____

6 Because of its natural beauty, many famous movies have been made in New Zealand.
➡ _____

7 If you visit New Zealand, you will surely appreciate its nature.
➡ _____

8 When you hear the word kiwi, what comes to your mind?
➡ _____

9 Maybe a fruit, but, in New Zealand the word kiwi has a couple of meanings.
➡ _____

10 First, kiwi is the name of a delicious, green fruit.
➡ _____

11 A lot of kiwi fruit is grown there, so New Zealand is known as the land of kiwi fruit.
➡ _____

12 Kiwi is also the name of one of New Zealand's native birds.
➡ _____

13 The kiwi is special to New Zealanders because it is the symbol of the nation.
➡ _____

14 Also, kiwi is a nickname for people from New Zealand.
➡ _____

15 Today, New Zealanders are sometimes called Kiwis throughout the world.
➡ _____

16 Now, you know that kiwi is the name of a fruit, a bird, and also a people.
➡ _____

17 Next time, don't become confused when someone uses the word kiwi, which has several meanings.

➡ _____

18 Now, let's talk about the Maori. They are the native people of New Zealand.

➡ _____

19 They went to live on the islands long before Europeans arrived.

➡ _____

20 The Maori culture is an important part of today's New Zealand society.

➡ _____

21 The Maori language is taught at some schools and there are Maori language radio and TV stations.

➡ _____

22 There are Maori villages in many parts of the country.

➡ _____

23 You can visit Maori villages and experience Maori culture.

➡ _____

24 If you say "kia ora" to the villagers, they will be glad to hear it. It means "hi" in English.

➡ _____

25 Have you ever watched the haka?

➡ _____

26 The haka may look scary because haka dancers shout and move their bodies wildly.

➡ _____

27 The Maori people, who you've already heard about, started doing the haka as a war dance.

➡ _____

28 Today, however, New Zealanders do the haka at sport matches, weddings, or other important events.

➡ _____

29 For example, New Zealand's national rugby team members do the haka before every match.

➡ _____

30 It is famous all over the world.

➡ _____

31 If you see the haka, you will probably agree that the rival team must be scared.

➡ _____

32 Like the kiwi bird, the haka is a national symbol.

➡ _____

※ 다음 괄호 안의 단어들을 우리말에 맞도록 바르게 배열하시오.

Hello! New Zealand

1 (Zealand / New / a / is / place / natural / of / beauty. // has / it / beautiful / many / and / waterfalls. / lakes)
➡ _____

2 (Zealand / New / two / has / islands, / main / South / the / and / Island / North / the / Island.)
➡ _____

3 (the / in / Island, / South / are / there / that / mountains / are / with / covered / all / snow / round. / year)
➡ _____

4 (will / you / amazed / be / the / by / views. / fantastic)
➡ _____

5 (the / in / Island, / North / are / there / hot / many / lakes, / springs, / areas / and / with / grass. / green)
➡ _____

6 (of / because / its / beauty, / natural / famous / many / have / movies / been / in / made / Zealand. / New)
➡ _____

7 (you / if / New / visit / Zealand, / will / you / appreciate / surely / nature. / its)
➡ _____

8 (you / when / hear / word / the / kiwi, / comes / what / your / to / mind?)
➡ _____

9 (a / maybe / fruit, / in / but, / Zealand / New / word / the / has / kiwi / a / of / couple / meanings.)
➡ _____

10 (kiwi / first, / the / is / of / name / delicious, / a / fruit. / green)
➡ _____

11 (lot / a / kiwi / of / is / fruit / there, / grown / New / so / Zealand / known / is / as / land / the / kiwi / of / fruit.)
➡ _____

12 (is / kiwi / the / also / of / name / of / one / Zealand's / New / birds. / native)
➡ _____

13 (kiwi / the / special / is / New / to / because / Zealanders / is / it / the / symbol / the / of / nation.)
➡ _____

14 (kiwi / also, / is / a / nickname / people / for / New / from / Zealand.)
➡ _____

15 (New / today, / Zealanders / sometimes / are / called / throughout / Kiwis / world. / the)
➡ _____

16 (you / now, / that / know / is / kiwi / the / of / name / fruit, / a / bird, / a / also / and / people. / a)
➡ _____

안녕! 뉴질랜드

1 뉴질랜드는 자연의 아름다움이 가득한 곳이다. 뉴질랜드는 아름다운 호수와 폭포들이 많다.

2 뉴질랜드에는 남섬과 북섬, 두 개의 본섬이 있다.

3 남섬에는 일 년 내내 눈으로 덮인 산들이 있다.

4 당신은 굉장히 멋진 경관에 놀랄 것이다.

5 북섬에는 많은 온천과 호수, 초원 지역이 있다.

6 뉴질랜드 자연의 아름다움 때문에 많은 유명한 영화들이 뉴질랜드에서 촬영되었다.

7 뉴질랜드를 방문하면, 분명히 그 자연의 진가를 인정할 것이다.

8 키위라는 단어를 들을 때, 무엇이 떠오르는가?

9 아마도 과일이 떠오르겠지만, 뉴질랜드에서 키위는 몇 가지 뜻이 있다.

10 먼저, 키위는 맛있는 초록색 과일의 이름이다.

11 많은 키위가 그곳에서 자라기 때문에 뉴질랜드는 키위의 나라로 알려져 있다.

12 키위는 뉴질랜드 토종 새의 이름이기도 하다.

13 키위 새는 국가의 상징이기 때문에, 뉴질랜드 사람들에게 특별하다.

14 또한, 키위는 뉴질랜드 출신의 사람들을 부르는 별명이기도 하다.

15 오늘날 뉴질랜드인들은 전 세계적으로 키위라고 불리기도 한다.

16 이제, 당신은 키위가 과일과 새, 그리고 국민의 명칭이라는 것을 알았다.

17 (time, / next / become / don't / when / confused / uses / someone / word / the / kiwi, / has / which / meanings. / several)
➡ _____
_____

18 (let's / now, / about / talk / Maori. / the // are / they / native / the / people / New / of / Zealand.)
➡ _____

19 (went / they / live / to / the / on / long / islands / before / arrived. / Europeans)
➡ _____

20 (Maori / the / culture / an / is / part / important / an / of / New / today's / society. / Zealand)
➡ _____

21 (Maori / the / language / taught / is / some / at / schools / there / and / Maori / are / radio / lauguage / TV / and / stations.)
➡ _____

22 (are / there / villages / Maori / many / in / of / parts / country. / the)
➡ _____

23 (can / you / Maori / visit / villages / and / Maori / experience / culture.)
➡ _____

24 (you / if / say / ora" / "kia / the / to / villagers, / will / they / glad / be / hear / to / it. // means / it / in / "hi" / English.)
➡ _____

25 (you / have / watched / ever / haka? / the)
➡ _____

26 (haka / the / look / may / because / scary / dancers / haka / and / shout / their / move / widely. / bodies)
➡ _____
_____

27 (Maori / the / people, / you've / who / heard / already / about, / doing / started / haka / the / a / as / dance. / war)
➡ _____
_____

28 (however, / today, / Zealanders / New / the / do / haka / sport / at / matches, / or / weddings, / important / other / events.)
➡ _____
_____

29 (example, / for / Zealand's / New / rugby / national / memebers / team / the / do / before / haka / match. / every)
➡ _____
_____

30 (is / it / all / famous / the / over / world.)
➡ _____

31 (you / if / the / see / haka, / will / you / agree / probably / the / that / team / rival / be / must / scared.)
➡ _____
_____

32 (the / like / bird, / kiwi / haka / the / a / is / symbol. / national)
➡ _____

17 다음에는 누군가가 키위라는 단어를 사용할 때 혼동하지 마라. 그 단어는 여러 뜻을 가지고 있기 때문이다.

18 이제, 마오리족에 대해 이야기해 보자. 마오리족은 뉴질랜드의 원주민이다.

19 그들은 유럽인들이 도착하기 오래 전에 이 섬에 와서 살았다.

20 마오리족의 문화는 오늘날 뉴질랜드 사회의 중요한 부분이다.

21 몇몇 학교에서 마오리어를 가르치고 있으며, 마오리어의 라디오와 TV 방송국이 있다.

22 나라의 여러 곳에 마오리 마을이 있다.

23 당신은 마오리 마을을 방문해 마오리 문화를 경험할 수 있다.

24 당신이 마을 사람들에게 "kia ora"라고 말한다면 그들은 그것을 듣고 좋아할 것이다. 그것은 영어로 "안녕"이라는 뜻이다.

25 하카를 본 적이 있는가?

26 하카 춤을 추는 사람들이 소리지르고, 그들의 몸을 사납게 움직이기 때문에 하카는 무서워보일 수도 있다.

27 당신이 이미 그들에 대해 들은 적이 있겠지만, 마오리인들은 전쟁 춤으로 하카를 추기 시작했다.

28 하지만, 오늘날 뉴질랜드 사람들은 하카를 운동 경기, 결혼식 또는 다른 중요한 행사가 있을 때 한다.

29 예를 들어, 뉴질랜드의 럭비 국가 대표 팀 선수들은 모든 경기 전에 하카를 춘다.

30 그것은 전 세계적으로 유명하다.

31 당신이 하카를 본다면, 상대 팀이 틀림없이 겁을 먹을 것이라는 것에 아마 동의할 것이다.

32 키위와 마찬가지로 하카는 나라의 상징이다.

※ 다음 우리말을 영어로 쓰시오.

1 뉴질랜드는 자연의 아름다움이 가득한 곳이다. 뉴질랜드는 아름다운 호수와 폭포들이 많다.

➡ _____

2 뉴질랜드에는 남섬과 북섬, 두 개의 본섬이 있다.

➡ _____

3 남섬에는 일 년 내내 눈으로 덮인 산들이 있다.

➡ _____

4 당신은 굉장히 멋진 경관에 놀랄 것이다.

➡ _____

5 북섬에는 많은 온천과 호수, 초원 지역이 있다.

➡ _____

6 뉴질랜드 자연의 아름다움 때문에 많은 유명한 영화들이 뉴질랜드에서 촬영되었다.

➡ _____

7 뉴질랜드를 방문하면, 분명히 그 자연의 진가를 인정할 것이다.

➡ _____

8 키위라는 단어를 들을 때, 무엇이 떠오르는가?

➡ _____

9 아마도 과일이 떠오르겠지만, 뉴질랜드에서 키위는 몇 가지 뜻이 있다.

➡ _____

10 먼저, 키위는 맛있는 초록색 과일의 이름이다.

➡ _____

11 많은 키위가 그곳에서 자라기 때문에 뉴질랜드는 키위의 나라로 알려져 있다.

➡ _____

12 키위는 뉴질랜드 토종 새의 이름이기도 하다.

➡ _____

13 키위 새는 국가의 상징이기 때문에, 뉴질랜드 사람들에게 특별하다.

➡ _____

14 또한, 키위는 뉴질랜드 출신의 사람들을 부르는 별명이기도 하다.

➡ _____

15 오늘날 뉴질랜드인들은 전 세계적으로 키위라고 불리기도 한다.

➡ _____

16 이제, 당신은 키위가 과일과 새, 그리고 국민의 명칭이라는 것을 알았다.

➡ _____

17 다음에는 누군가가 키위라는 단어를 사용할 때 혼동하지 마라. 그 단어는 여러 뜻을 가지고 있기 때문이다.
➡ _____

18 이제, 마오리족에 대해 이야기해 보자. 마오리족은 뉴질랜드의 원주민이다.
➡ _____

19 그들은 유럽인들이 도착하기 오래 전에 이 섬에 와서 살았다.
➡ _____

20 마오리족의 문화는 오늘날 뉴질랜드 사회의 중요한 부분이다.
➡ _____

21 몇몇 학교에서 마오리어를 가르치고 있으며, 마오리어의 라디오와 TV 방송국이 있다.
➡ _____

22 나라의 여러 곳에 마오리 마을이 있다.
➡ _____

23 당신은 마오리 마을을 방문해 마오리 문화를 경험할 수 있다.
➡ _____

24 당신이 마을 사람들에게 "kia ora"라고 말한다면 그들은 그것을 듣고 좋아할 것이다. 그것은 영어로 "안녕"이라는 뜻이다.
➡ _____

25 하카를 본 적이 있는가?
➡ _____

26 하카 춤을 추는 사람들이 소리 지르고, 그들의 몸을 사납게 움직이기 때문에 하카는 무서워 보일 수도 있다.
➡ _____

27 당신이 이미 그들에 대해 들은 적이 있겠지만, 마오리인들은 전쟁 춤으로 하카를 추기 시작했다.
➡ _____

28 하지만, 오늘날 뉴질랜드 사람들은 하카를 운동 경기, 결혼식 또는 다른 중요한 행사가 있을 때 한다.
➡ _____

29 예를 들어, 뉴질랜드의 럭비 국가 대표 팀 선수들은 모든 경기 전에 하카를 춘다.
➡ _____

30 그것은 전 세계적으로 유명하다.
➡ _____

31 당신이 하카를 본다면, 상대 팀이 틀림없이 겁을 먹을 것이라는 것에 아마 동의할 것이다.
➡ _____

32 키위와 마찬가지로 하카는 나라의 상징이다.
➡ _____

※ 다음 우리말과 일치하도록 빈칸에 알맞은 말을 쓰시오.

Before You Read

1. Rugby is _____ _____ _____ in New Zealand.

2. New Zealand is _____ _____ _____ _____ _____ the world.

3. The Maori people are _____ _____ _____ of New Zealand and _____ _____ _____ .

Enjoy Writing

1. We _____ You

2. _____ you _____ _____ New Zealand?

3. It has _____ _____ _____ and 600 _____ _____ .

4. _____ _____ is Wellington.

5. The kiwi, _____ is _____ _____ _____ to New Zealand, is _____ _____ _____ _____ of the country.

6. _____ you _____ _____ New Zealand, you _____ _____ a _____ _____ , _____ shows _____ _____ _____ of New Zealand.

7. We _____ you _____ a _____ _____ of the Maori people.

8. They _____ _____ and _____ in the ground _____ _____ _____ . It is great.

9. Many people visit New Zealand _____ _____ _____ _____ _____ .

10. We are _____ _____ _____ you to this _____ _____ .

Project Step 1

1. A: _____ _____ about which country we _____ _____ _____ _____ _____ .

2. B: _____ _____ do you _____ , Australia _____ the UK?

3. C: I _____ we _____ _____ information _____ the UK.

4. There is _____ _____ _____ information _____ _____ .

5. D: _____ .

1. 럭비는 뉴질랜드에서 인기 있는 운동이다.
2. 뉴질랜드는 남반구에 있다.
3. 마오리족은 뉴질랜드의 원주민들이고, 그들의 문화가 있다.

1. 우리는 당신을 초대합니다
2. 당신은 뉴질랜드에 대해 아는가?
3. 그곳은 두 개의 본섬과 600개의 작은 섬들로 되어 있다.
4. 그곳의 수도는 웰링턴이다.
5. 키위는 뉴질랜드 태생의 새인데, 그 나라의 상징 중 하나이다.
6. 뉴질랜드에 온다면 마오리 마을을 반드시 방문해야 하는데, 왜냐하면 그 마을이 뉴질랜드 원주민들의 문화를 보여 주기 때문이다.
7. 우리는 당신이 마오리족의 전통 요리를 먹어 보는 것을 제안한다.
8. 그들은 열을 가한 돌로 땅 속에서 고기와 채소를 요리한다. 그것은 훌륭하다.
9. 많은 사람들은 아름다운 자연을 즐기기 위해 뉴질랜드를 방문한다.
10. 우리는 당신을 이 아름다운 나라에 초대하게 되어 기쁘다.

1. A: 어느 나라를 조사할 것인지 이야기해 보자.
2. B: 호주와 영국 중에서 어느 나라를 선호하니?
3. C: 나는 영국에 관한 정보를 찾아볼 것을 제안해.
4. 우리가 작업해야 할 많은 정보들이 있잖아.
5. D: 그래

※ 다음 우리말을 영어로 쓰시오.

Before You Read

1. 럭비는 뉴질랜드에서 인기 있는 운동이다.
➡ _____

2. 뉴질랜드는 남반구에 있다.
➡ _____

3. 마오리족은 뉴질랜드의 원주민들이고, 그들의 문화가 있다.
➡ _____

Enjoy Writing

1. 우리는 당신을 초대합니다
➡ _____

2. 당신은 뉴질랜드에 대해 아는가?
➡ _____

3. 그곳은 두 개의 본섬과 600개의 작은 섬들로 되어 있다.
➡ _____

4. 그곳의 수도는 웰링턴이다.
➡ _____

5. 키위는 뉴질랜드 태생의 새인데, 그 나라의 상징 중 하나이다.
➡ _____

6. 뉴질랜드에 온다면 마오리 마을을 반드시 방문해야 하는데, 왜냐하면 그 마을이 뉴질랜드 원주민들의 문화를 보여 주기 때문이다.
➡ _____
_____

7. 우리는 당신이 마오리족의 전통 요리를 먹어 보는 것을 제안한다.
➡ _____

8. 그들은 열을 가한 돌로 땅 속에서 고기와 채소를 요리한다. 그것은 훌륭하다.
➡ _____

9. 많은 사람들은 아름다운 자연을 즐기기 위해 뉴질랜드를 방문한다.
➡ _____

10. 우리는 당신을 이 아름다운 나라에 초대하게 되어 기쁘다.
➡ _____

Project Step 1

1. A: 어느 나라를 조사할 것인지 이야기해 보자.
➡ _____

2. B: 호주와 영국 중에서 어느 나라를 선호하니?
➡ _____

3. C: 나는 영국에 관한 정보를 찾아볼 것을 제안해.
➡ _____

4. 우리가 작업해야 할 많은 정보들이 있잖아.
➡ _____

5. D: 그래.
➡ _____

※ 다음 영어를 우리말로 쓰시오.

01	sincerely	22	apology
02	accidentally	23	relaxed
03	relationship	24	sincere
04	delete	25	wound
05	emotional	26	apologize
06	prepare	27	brave
07	especially	28	ignore
08	responsibility	29	appreciate
09	proper	30	borrow
10	generous	31	nervous
11	humorous	32	loud
12	include	33	intend
13	break	34	tray
14	case	35	trip over
15	serious	36	care about
16	casual	37	bump into
17	suggestion	38	at once
18	thoughtful	39	with all one's heart
19	necessary	40	turn down
20	mind	41	laugh off
21	regret	42	take responsibility for
		43	think nothing of

※ 다음 우리말을 영어로 쓰시오.

01 삭제하다

02 의견, 제안

03 사려 깊은, 생각에 잠긴

04 우연히, 뜻하지 않게

05 꺼리다, 싫어하다

06 고마워하다, 감사하다

07 대충하는, 건성의

08 특히, 유난히

09 너그러운

10 사례, 경우

11 책임

12 ~을 준비하다

13 (관계를) 끝내다, 끊다

14 의도하다

15 심각한, 진지한

16 진정한, 진심 어린

17 적절한, 제대로 된

18 후회하다

19 무시하다

20 포함하다

21 느긋한, 여유 있는

22 사과하다

23 감정적인

24 재미있는, 유머러스한

25 용감한

26 실수, 잘못

27 사과

28 관계

29 진심으로

30 상처, 부상

31 소리가 큰, 시끄러운

32 처리하다, 대우하다

33 빌리다

34 필요한

35 ~에 부딪히다

36 ~을 웃어넘기려 하다

37 지나가다

38 ~에 걸려 넘어지다

39 (소리를) 줄이다

40 ~에 책임을 지다

41 선택하다, 고르다

42 진심으로

43 ~와 잘 지내다

※ 다음 영영풀이에 알맞은 단어를 <보기>에서 골라 쓴 후, 우리말 뜻을 쓰시오.

1 _____ : to be grateful for something: _____

2 _____ : a wrong action, statement, or judgment: _____

3 _____ : to intentionally not listen or give attention to: _____

4 _____ : the way in which two things are connected: _____

5 _____ : something that it is your job or duty to deal with: _____

6 _____ : in a way that was not planned or intended: _____

7 _____ : showing no fear of dangerous or difficult things: _____

8 _____ : done without much thought, effort, or concern: _____

9 _____ : to remove part or all of a written or electronic text: _____

10 _____ : an act of saying that you are sorry for something wrong you have done: _____

11 _____ : honest and true, and based on what you really feel and believe: _____

12 _____ : an idea, plan, or action that is suggested or the act of suggesting it: _____

13 _____ : always thinking of the things you can do to make people happy or comfortable: _____

14 _____ : to make or get something or someone ready for something that will happen in the future: _____

15 _____ : to feel sorry about something you have done or about something that you have not been able to do: _____

16 _____ : willing to give money, help, kindness, etc., especially more than is usual or expected: _____

보기			
sincere	accidentally	generous	brave
thoughtful	ignore	suggestion	mistake
apology	responsibility	prepare	relationship
regret	casual	delete	appreciate

※ 다음 우리말과 일치하도록 빈칸에 알맞은 말을 쓰시오.

Listen & Speak 1 A-1

B: Judy, do you _____ _____ _____ the volume?

G: _____, _____ _____ . Is it too _____?

B: Yes, it is. I can _____ it in my room.

G: I'm sorry. I'll _____ _____ _____ .

B: _____ a _____ .

B: Judy, 볼륨을 좀 낮춰 줄래?
G: 그래. 소리가 너무 크니?
B: 응, 소리가 커. 내 방에서도 들려
G: 미안해. 내가 볼륨을 낮출게.
B: 정말 고마워.

Listen & Speak 1 A-2

G: I _____ _____ my mom's _____ _____ .

B: _____ _____ , Mina.

G: _____ _____ _____ _____ m e _____ _____ _____ _____ _____ her?

B: No, _____ _____ _____ . You should _____ _____ .

G: I see. I'll talk to her _____ _____ _____ _____ .

G: 내가 실수로 엄마가 제일 좋아하는 접시를 깼어.
B: 그것 참 안됐구나, 미나야.
G: 엄마한테 미안하다고 어떻게 말해야 하는지 말해 줄래?
B: 응, 물론이지. 너는 진심으로 사과해야 해.
G: 알겠어. 엄마에게 진심으로 이야기해야겠어.

Listen & Speak 1 A-3

B: Karen, do you _____ _____ to my house tomorrow at 7 a.m.?

G: That's very _____ .

B: I know, but I need the book _____ you _____ _____ _____ .

G: I see. Then _____ meet at seven.

B: See you _____ .

B: Karen, 내일 오전 7시에 우리 집에 와 줄래?
G 그건 너무 이른데.
B: 그건 알지만, 수업 시작하기 전에 네가 빌려 갔던 책이 필요하거든.
G: 알겠어. 그럼 7시에 보자.
B: 그때 보자

Listen & Speak 1 B

A: Hellen, do you _____ _____ _____ ?

B: No, I don't. / Sorry _____ I _____ .

A: Hellen, do you _____ _____ _____ _____ ?

B: No, I don't. / Sorry but I _____ .

A: Hellen, 조용히 좀 해 줄래?
B: 알았어. / 미안하지만 그럴 수 없어.

A: Hellen, 쓰레기 좀 주워 줄래?
B: 알았어. / 미안하지만 그럴 수 없어.

G: You _____ _____ _____ _____, Minsu. Can I come in?

B: Sure. I'm _____ _____ the dance _____, but it's not easy.

G: I can help you. I was in the _____ _____ _____.

B: Really? That would be _____, Amy.

G: You _____ _____ _____ _____ into the _____. But one thing you _____ _____ do is to be more _____. You are too _____.

B: Your _____ is very _____. I really _____ your _____.

G: It's my _____.

Listen & Speak 2 A-2

B: Irene, what are you doing?

G: Well, I've _____ my favorite cap. I can't find it.

B: _____ _____ _____ you. _____ does it look _____?

G: It's red. My name _____ _____ in black on the side.

B: Oh, is this _____? It was _____ the table.

G: Yes, it is. Thank you, Jim. I _____ your _____.

B: _____ _____.

Listen & Speak 2 B

A: _____ me _____ you the way.

B: I _____ your time.

A: _____ _____ _____ your _____.

B: I _____ _____.

Real Life Talk

Jessie: Hi, Andy. _____ _____?

Andy: Hi, Jessie. I'm going to buy a _____ for Amy. You'_____ _____ friends with her _____ a long time, _____ you?

Jessie: Yes, _____ first grade in _____ school.

Andy: Well, I know you're really _____ _____, but _____ _____ _____ me? I am sure you could _____ _____ _____ _____ _____.

G: 민수야, 너 바빠 보인다. 나 들어가도 되니?

B: 물론. 나 춤 경연대회를 준비하고 있는데 쉽지 않아.

G: 내가 도와줄게. 나 작년에 대회에 참가했었거든.

B: 정말? Amy, 그거 정말 좋을 거 같아.

G: 너는 리듬을 타는 건 잘하는 편이야. 하지만 네가 해야 할 한 가지는 긴장을 더 푸는 것이야. 너는 너무 긴장을 해.

B: 네 조언이 정말 도움이 된다. 너의 조언 정말 고마워.

G: 도움이 됐다니 기뻐.

B: Irene, 너 뭐 하고 있어?

G: 음, 내가 제일 좋아하는 모자를 잃어버렸어. 그 모자를 못 찾겠어.

B: 내가 도와줄게. 그것은 어떻게 생겼어?

G: 그건 빨간색이야. 모자 옆 부분에 내 이름이 검은색으로 쓰여 있어.

B: 오, 이거 네 것이니? 이거 탁자 아래에 있었어.

G: 응, 맞아. 고마워, Jim. 도와줘서 고마워.

B: 천만에.

A: 제가 길을 알려 줄게요.

B: 시간 내 줘서 감사합니다.

A: 내가 너의 가방을 들어 줄게.

B: 도와 줘서 고마워.

Jessie: 안녕, Andy. 무슨 일이니?

Andy: 안녕, Jessie. 나는 Amy한테 줄 선물을 사려고 해. 너는 그 애와 오랫동안 친구로 지냈지, 그렇지 않니?

Jessie: 응, 초등학교 1학년 때부터.

Andy: 음, 네가 공부하느라 바쁘다는 것을 알지만, 나를 좀 도와줄 수 있니? 괜찮은 것을 고르도록 네가 도와줄 수 있을 것이라고 확신해.

Jessie: No _____. What's the _____ _____? It's not her birthday.

Andy: Well, two months ago, when my leg _____ _____, she _____ my backpack to school.

Jessie: That was nice _____ _____.

Andy: Yes, it was. What should I get for her?

Jessie: Well, _____ _____ a case for her smartphone? She _____ her case _____.

Andy: Really? _____ _____ for your _____.

Jessie: 좋아. 무엇을 위한 선물이니? 그 애의 생일은 아닌데.

Andy: 음, 두 달 전에 내 다리가 부러 졌을 때, 그 애가 학교까지 내 가 방을 들어줬어.

Jessie: 그 애는 정말 친절했구나.

Andy: 응, 그랬어. 그 애를 위해 무엇을 사야 할까?

Jessie: 음, 스마트폰 케이스는 어떠 니? 그 애는 최근에 케이스를 깨뜨렸어.

Andy: 정말? 제안해 줘서 고마워.

Wrap Up 1

G: I _____ _____ _____ _____ to Jejudo.

B: That's _____, Suhee. I _____ _____ _____ there.

G: _____ _____ _____ me _____ _____ _____ in Jejudo?

B: _____ _____ _____. Jejudo has many beautiful _____. You _____ _____ them.

G: Good. I will go _____. What _____ can I do?

B: Why _____ _____ hike Halla Mountain? You can see the mountain from _____ on the island.

G: Great. _____ _____ food?

B: If you like fish, on Jejudo _____ _____ is _____ and _____.

G: I'll try everything. I _____ your _____.

G: 나는 제주도에 갈 계획이야.

B: 그거 멋지다, 수희야. 나 예전에 제주 도에 살았어.

G: 내가 제주에서 뭘 해야 하는지 말 해 줄래?

B: 물론. 제주도에는 아름다운 해변들이 많아. 그 해변들을 꼭 가봐야 해.

G: 좋아. 나는 수영하러 갈 거야. 그 밖 에 내가 할 수 있는 것은 무엇이니?

B: 한라산을 등반해 보는 건 어때? 섬의 모든 곳에서 그 산을 볼 수 있어.

G: 좋아. 음식은 어때?

B: 네가 생선을 좋아한다면, 제주도에 서는 회가 신선하고 맛있어.

G: 나는 모든 걸 다 해 볼 거야. 조언해 줘서 고마워.

Wrap Up 2

W: Mike does not feel very _____. He _____ _____ _____ a cold. He _____ _____ see a doctor, but he has a meeting with Jane _____ _____. He wants _____ _____ her tomorrow _____. What _____ he _____ to her?

W: Mike는 몸이 좋지 않아. 그는 감기 에 걸렸을지도 몰라. 그는 병원에 가 야 하지만, 한 시간 후에 Jane과 회 의가 있어. 그는 대신 내일 그녀를 만 나기를 원해. 그는 그녀에게 뭐라고 말해야 할까?

※ 다음 우리말에 맞도록 대화를 영어로 쓰시오.

Listen & Speak 1 A-1

B: _____

G: _____

B: _____

G: _____

B: _____

B: Judy, 볼륨을 좀 낮춰 줄래?
G: 그래. 소리가 너무 크니?
B: 응, 소리가 커. 내 방에서도 들려
G: 미안해. 내가 볼륨을 낮출게.
B: 정말 고마워.

Listen & Speak 1 A-2

G: _____

B: _____

G: _____

B: _____

G: _____

G: 내가 실수로 엄마가 제일 좋아하는 접시를 깼어.
B: 그것 참 안됐구나, 미나야.
G: 엄마한테 미안하다고 어떻게 말해야 하는지 말해 줄래?
B: 응, 물론이지. 너는 진심으로 사과해야 해.
G: 알겠어. 엄마에게 진심으로 이야기해야겠어.

Listen & Speak 1 A-3

B: _____

G: _____

B: _____

G: _____

B: _____

B: Karen, 내일 오전 7시에 우리 집에 와 줄래?
G 그건 너무 이른데.
B: 그건 알지만, 수업 시작하기 전에 네가 빌려 갔던 책이 필요하거든.
G: 알겠어. 그럼 7시에 보자.
B: 그때 보자

Listen & Speak 1 B

A: _____

B: _____

A: _____

B: _____

A: Hellen, 조용히 좀 해 줄래?
B: 알았어. / 미안하지만 그럴 수 없어.

A: Hellen, 쓰레기 좀 주워 줄래?
B: 알았어. / 미안하지만 그럴 수 없어.

Listen & Speak 2 A-1

G: _____
B: _____
G: _____
B: _____
G: _____
   _____
B: _____
G: _____

G: 민수야, 너 바빠 보인다. 나 들어가도 되니?
B: 물론. 나 춤 경연대회를 준비하고 있는데 쉽지 않아.
G: 내가 도와줄게. 나 작년에 대회에 참가했었거든.
B: 정말? Amy, 그거 정말 좋을 거 같아.
G: 너는 리듬을 타는 건 잘하는 편이야. 하지만 네가 해야 할 한 가지는 긴장을 더 푸는 것이야. 너는 너무 긴장을 해.
B: 네 조언이 정말 도움이 된다. 너의 조언 정말 고마워.
G: 도움이 됐다니 기뻐.

Listen & Speak 2 A-2

B: _____
G: _____
B: _____
G: _____
B: _____
G: _____
B: _____

B: Irene, 너 뭐 하고 있어?
G: 음, 내가 제일 좋아하는 모자를 잃어버렸어. 그 모자를 못 찾겠어.
B: 내가 도와줄게. 그것은 어떻게 생겼어?
G: 그건 빨간색이야. 모자 옆 부분에 내 이름이 검은색으로 쓰여 있어.
B: 오, 이거 네 것이니? 이거 탁자 아래에 있었어.
G: 응, 맞아. 고마워, Jim. 도와줘서 고마워.
B: 천만에.

Listen & Speak 2 B

A: _____
B: _____
A: _____
B: _____

A: 제가 길을 알려 줄게요.
B: 시간 내 줘서 감사합니다.

A: 내가 너의 가방을 들어 줄게.
B: 도와 줘서 고마워.

Real Life Talk

Jessie: _____
Andy: _____
       _____
Jessie: _____
Andy: _____
       _____

Jessie: 안녕, Andy. 무슨 일이니?
Andy: 안녕, Jessie. 나는 Amy한테 줄 선물을 사려고 해. 너는 그 애와 오랫동안 친구로 지냈지, 그렇지 않니?
Jessie: 응, 초등학교 1학년 때부터.
Andy: 음, 네가 공부하느라 바쁘다는 것을 알지만, 나를 좀 도와줄 수 있니? 괜찮은 것을 고르도록 네가 도와줄 수 있을 것이라고 확신해.

Jessie: _____

Andy: _____

_____

Jessie: _____

Andy: _____

Jessie: _____

Andy: _____

Jessie: 좋아. 무엇을 위한 선물이니? 그 애의 생일은 아닌데.
Andy: 음, 두 달 전에 내 다리가 부러졌을 때, 그 애가 학교까지 내 가방을 들어줬어.
Jessie: 그 애는 정말 친절했구나.
Andy: 응, 그랬어. 그 애를 위해 무엇을 사야 할까?
Jessie: 음, 스마트폰 케이스는 어떠니? 그 애는 최근에 케이스를 깨뜨렸어.
Andy: 정말? 제안해 줘서 고마워.

Wrap Up 1

G: _____

B: _____

G: _____

B: _____

G: _____

B: _____

_____

G: _____

B: _____

G: _____

G: 나는 제주도에 갈 계획이야.
B: 그거 멋지다, 수희야. 나 예전에 제주도에 살았어.
G: 내가 제주도에서 뭘 해야 하는지 말해 줄래?
B: 물론. 제주도에는 아름다운 해변들이 많아. 그 해변들을 꼭 가봐야 해.
G: 좋아. 나는 수영하러 갈 거야. 그 밖에 내가 할 수 있는 것은 무엇이니?
B: 한라산을 등반해 보는 건 어때? 섬의 모든 곳에서 그 산을 볼 수 있어.
G: 좋아. 음식은 어때?
B: 네가 생선을 좋아한다면, 제주도에서는 회가 신선하고 맛있어.
G: 나는 모든 걸 다 해 볼 거야. 조언해 줘서 고마워.

Wrap Up 2

W: _____

_____

_____

W: Mike는 몸이 좋지 않아. 그는 감기에 걸렸을지도 몰라. 그는 병원에 가야 하지만, 한 시간 후에 Jane과 회의가 있어. 그는 대신 내일 그녀를 만나기를 원해. 그는 그녀에게 뭐라고 말해야 할까?

※ 다음 우리말과 일치하도록 빈칸에 알맞은 것을 골라 쓰시오.

1 _____ we are _____, we all make _____. It is not easy to get _____ with everyone all the time.

  A. mistakes   B. along   C. human   D. because

2 Sometimes we hurt people's feelings _____ _____ to. Sometimes, we do something _____ and _____ it later.

  A. wrong   B. without   C. regret   D. intending

3 When _____ _____, what should we do? We _____ _____.

  A. happens   B. apologize   C. that   D. should

4 Read the _____ _____ studies and learn three things about a _____ _____.

  A. proper   B. case   C. apology   D. following

5 When June _____ _____ a backpack and fell, Mike found it funny and _____. He took a picture and _____ it on an SNS.

  A. uploaded   B. tripped   C. laughed   D. over

6 June saw the picture and _____ _____. Mike said, _____ a laugh, "Sorry, June!" and _____ it.

  A. angry   B. deleted   C. became   D. with

7 After that, June felt _____ more _____ of Mike's _____ apology.

  A. because   B. even   C. casual   D. hurt

8 June didn't like how Mike had _____. Mike _____ to think it was _____ _____.

  A. seemed   B. nothing   C. acted   D. serious

9 What did you learn from this _____? Yes. You _____ right. You should be _____ when you _____.

  A. guessed   B. apologize   C. case   D. sincere

10 _____ is necessary to _____ good friendships. _____ you're sorry is more than just _____.

  A. saying   B. build   C. apologizing   D. words

11 You need to show that you _____ the other person and _____ _____ his or her _____.

  A. about   B. feelings   C. care   D. respect

12 If you truly want to _____ _____ _____, be _____ in your apology.

  A. sincere   B. things   C. make   D. right

13 The _____ sincere your _____ is, the _____ it will be _____.

  A. better   B. more   C. received   D. apology

14 Here is _____ case. While Kate was hurrying across the cafeteria, she _____ _____ _____ Hojun.

  A. bumped   B. another   C. into   D. accidently

15 Some food on Hojun's _____ _____ on his jacket. Kate didn't _____. Hojun felt _____.

  A. fell   B. apologize   C. bad   D. tray

---

1 우리는 인간이기 때문에 모두가 실수한다. 모든 사람과 항상 잘 지내기는 쉽지 않다.

2 때때로 우리는 의도하지 않게 다른 사람의 감정을 상하게 한다. 때때로 우리는 나쁜 일을 하고 나중에 그것을 후회한다.

3 이런 일이 생기면, 우리는 무엇을 해야 할까? 우리는 사과해야 한다.

4 다음 사례 연구들을 읽고 올바른 사과를 위한 세 가지를 알아보자.

5 June이 가방에 걸려 넘어졌을 때, Mike는 그것이 재미있다고 생각하고 웃었다. 그는 사진을 찍어서 SNS에 올렸다.

6 June은 그 사진을 보고 화가 났다. Mike는 웃으면서 "미안해, June!"이라고 말하고 사진을 삭제했다.

7 그 후, June은 Mike의 가벼운 사과에 한층 더 화가 났다.

8 June은 Mike의 행동 방식이 마음에 들지 않았다. Mike는 이 일이 심각한 일이 아니라고 생각하는 것처럼 보였다.

9 이 사례로부터 무엇을 배웠는가? 맞다. 당신은 바르게 추측했다. 당신은 사과할 때에 진실해야 한다.

10 사과하는 것은 좋은 교우 관계를 만들기 위해 필요하다. 미안하다고 말하는 것은 단지 말 이상이다.

11 당신이 타인을 존중하고, 타인의 감정에 관심을 갖고 있음을 보여주어야 한다.

12 당신이 진실로 일을 바로잡기를 원한다면, 당신의 사과는 진실해야 한다.

13 당신의 사과가 진실할수록, 그것은 더 잘 받아들여질 것이다.

14 또 다른 사례가 있다. Kate가 급식실을 가로질러 급하게 뛰어갈 때, 호준이와 실수로 부딪쳤다.

15 호준이의 급식판에 있던 음식이 그의 재킷에 떨어졌다. Kate는 사과하지 않았다. 호준이는 기분이 나빴다.

16 He thought, 'Why _____ she _____ something? It would be nothing _____ she apologized _____ now.'
　　A. right　　　　B. say　　　　C. doesn't　　　D. if

17 This case shows _____ when an apology is _____, you should _____ at _____.
　　A. necessary　　B. once　　　　C. that　　　　D. apologize

18 A quick apology _____ that you are _____ and take _____ for your _____.
　　A. action　　　　B. shows　　　C. responsibility　D. thoughtful

19 All you need to do is to say, "I'm sorry." Then, the hurt friend will _____ _____ of it and _____ it _____.
　　A. laugh　　　　B. nothing　　C. off　　　　D. think

20 _____, apologies are necessary _____ family members and _____ ones, _____.
　　A. among　　　　B. finally　　C. loved　　　D. too

21 One day, Sunmin _____ her sister's _____ book. _____, she _____ it.
　　A. favorite　　　B. borrowed　　C. lost　　　D. later

22 Sunmin didn't _____ because she _____ it was not _____. She thought, 'We're sisters, _____ all.'
　　A. important　　　B. apologize　　C. after　　　D. thought

23 Sunmin's sister _____ Sunmin had _____ her. How could her own sister _____ her feelings?
　　A. treated　　　B. disliked　　C. ignore　　　D. how

24 This was not the first time Sunmin _____ _____ to her _____ _____.
　　A. sister　　　　B. little　　　C. hadn't　　　D. apologized

25 People need to _____ when they do _____ _____. This includes family members and the people who are _____ to you.
　　A. close　　　　B. apologize　　C. wrong　　　D. something

26 People _____ more _____ when the hurt _____ from a family member or a friend.
　　A. comes　　　　B. hurt　　　C. easily　　　D. get

27 We may think that they will _____ it _____ _____ they are _____ to us.
　　A. close　　　　B. let　　　　C. because　　　D. go

28 Remember, however, that small _____ and no apology _____ _____ to big _____ wounds.
　　A. add　　　　B. mistakes　　C. up　　　　D. emotional

29 This is _____ true _____ family members and _____ _____.
　　A. among　　　　B. especially　　C. ones　　　D. loved

30 Have you ever _____ of the _____, "No _____ apologies, no more _____"?
　　A. chances　　　B. heard　　　C. more　　　D. saying

31 People make _____, but don't _____ one mistake _____ a beautiful _____.
　　A. break　　　　B. mistakes　　C. relationship　D. let

32 Do you want to _____ to someone? _____ to do it now. A quick and _____ "I'm sorry" can _____ many problems.
　　A. try　　　　B. sincere　　C. apologize　　D. solve

16 그는 '왜 그녀는 아무 말도 하지 않지? 그녀가 즉시 사과한다면 아무 일도 아닐 텐데.' 라고 생각했다.

17 이 사례는 사과가 필요할 때는 사과를 즉시 해야 한다는 것을 보여준다.

18 신속한 사과는 당신이 사려 깊고, 당신의 행동에 책임을 진다는 것을 보여준다.

19 당신이 해야 할 행동은 "미안해."라고 말하는 것뿐이다. 그러면 상처받은 친구는 당신의 잘못을 아무렇지 않게 생각하고, 웃어넘길 것이다.

20 마지막으로 사과는 가족이나 사랑하는 사람들 사이에서도 필요하다.

21 어느 날, 선민이는 여동생이 가장 좋아하는 책을 빌렸다. 나중에 그녀는 그것을 잃어버렸다.

22 선민이는 그것이 중요하지 않다고 생각하여 사과하지 않았다. 그녀는 '우리는 어쨌든 자매니까.'라고 생각했다.

23 선민이의 여동생은 언니가 본인을 대했던 방식이 마음에 들지 않았다. 어떻게 자신의 언니가 그녀의 기분을 무시할 수 있는가?

24 선민이가 여동생에게 사과하지 않았던 것은 이번이 처음이 아니었다.

25 사람들은 잘못했을 때, 사과해야 한다. 이것은 가족이나 당신에게 가까운 사람도 포함한다.

26 사람들은 마음의 상처가 가족이나 친구에게서 올 때 더 쉽게 상처 받는다.

27 우리는 아마 그들이 가깝기 때문에 그냥 넘어갈 것이라고 생각할지 모른다.

28 하지만 작은 실수를 하고 사과하지 않는 것은 큰 감정적인 상처가 된다는 것을 기억하라.

29 이것은 가족과 사랑하는 사람들에게 특히 더 그러하다.

30 당신은 "더 이상 사과하지 않는다면 더 이상 기회가 없다."는 말을 들어본 적이 있는가?

31 사람들은 실수하지만, 그 실수가 아름다운 관계를 깨뜨리게 해서는 안 된다.

32 누군가에게 사과하고 싶은가? 지금 하려고 노력하라. 빠르고 진정한 "미안해."라는 말이 많은 문제를 해결해 줄 것이다.

※ 다음 우리말과 일치하도록 빈칸에 알맞은 것을 골라 쓰시오.

1 _____ we are human, we all make mistakes. _____ _____ not easy _____ _____ _____ _____ everyone _____ _____ _____.

2 Sometimes we _____ people's feelings _____ _____. Sometimes, we do _____ _____ and _____ it later.

3 When _____ happens, what should we do? We _____ _____.

4 Read the _____ _____ studies and learn three things about _____ _____ _____.

5 When June _____ _____ a backpack and fell, Mike found _____ _____ and _____. He _____ a picture and _____ it _____ an SNS.

6 June _____ the picture and _____ _____. Mike said, _____ a _____, "Sorry, June!" and _____ _____.

7 After that, June felt _____ more hurt _____ _____ Mike's _____ _____.

8 June didn't like _____ _____ _____ _____. Mike _____ _____ _____ it was _____ _____.

9 What did you learn from this case? Yes. You guessed right. You _____ _____ _____ when you _____.

10 _____ is necessary _____ build good _____. _____ you're sorry is _____ _____ just words.

11 You need to show _____ you _____ the _____ person and _____ _____ his or her _____.

12 If you truly want to _____ _____ _____, be _____ in your apology.

13 _____ _____ _____ your apology is, _____ _____ it will be _____.

14 Here is _____ case. While Kate was _____ _____ the cafeteria, she _____ _____ _____ Hojun.

15 Some food _____ Hojun's tray _____ _____ his jacket. Kate didn't _____. Hojun _____ _____.

16 He thought, '_____ _____ she _____ something? It would be nothing _____ she _____ _____ _____.'

17 This case shows _____ when an apology _____ _____, you should _____ _____ _____.

18 A quick apology _____ _____ you are _____ and _____ _____ _____ your action.

19 _____ you need _____ _____ is to say, "I'm sorry." Then, the hurt friend will _____ _____ of it and _____ _____ _____.

20 Finally, apologies _____ necessary _____ family _____ and _____ _____, too.

21 One day, Sunmin _____ her sister's _____ book. _____, she _____ it.

22 Sunmin didn't _____ because she thought it was _____ _____. She thought, 'We're sisters, _____ _____.'

23 Sunmin's sister disliked how Sunmin _____ _____ her. How could her own sister _____ her feelings?

24 This was not the first time Sunmin _____ _____ her _____ _____.

25 People need _____ _____ when they do _____ _____. This _____ family members and the people _____ _____ to you.

26 People _____ _____ _____ _____ when the hurt _____ _____ a family member or a friend.

27 We may think that they will _____ _____ _____ because they _____ _____ to us.

28 Remember, however, that _____ _____ and _____ _____ _____ _____ _____ big _____ _____.

29 This is especially true _____ family members and _____ _____.

30 Have you ever _____ _____ the saying, "_____ _____ apologies, _____ _____ _____ _____"?

31 People _____ mistakes, but don't _____ one mistake _____ a _____ _____.

32 Do you want to _____ _____ someone? _____ _____ it now. A _____ and _____ "I'm sorry" _____ _____ many problems.

---

16 그는 '왜 그녀는 아무 말도 하지 않지? 그녀가 즉시 사과한다면 아무 일도 아닐 텐데.' 라고 생각했다.

17 이 사례는 사과가 필요할 때는 사과를 즉시 해야 한다는 것을 보여준다.

18 신속한 사과는 당신이 사려 깊고, 당신의 행동에 책임을 진다는 것을 보여준다.

19 당신이 해야 할 행동은 "미안해."라고 말하는 것뿐이다. 그러면 상처받은 친구는 당신의 잘못을 아무렇지 않게 생각하고, 웃어넘길 것이다.

20 마지막으로 사과는 가족이나 사랑하는 사람들 사이에서도 필요하다.

21 어느 날, 선민이는 여동생이 가장 좋아하는 책을 빌렸다. 나중에 그녀는 그것을 잃어버렸다.

22 선민이는 그것이 중요하지 않다고 생각하여 사과하지 않았다. 그녀는 '우리는 어쨌든 자매니까.'라고 생각했다.

23 선민이의 여동생은 언니가 본인을 대했던 방식이 마음에 들지 않았다. 어떻게 자신의 언니가 그녀의 기분을 무시할 수 있는가?

24 선민이가 여동생에게 사과하지 않았던 것은 이번이 처음이 아니었다.

25 사람들은 잘못했을 때, 사과해야 한다. 이것은 가족이나 당신에게 가까운 사람도 포함한다.

26 사람들은 마음의 상처가 가족이나 친구에게서 올 때 더 쉽게 상처 받는다.

27 우리는 아마 그들이 가깝기 때문에 그냥 넘어갈 것이라고 생각할지 모른다.

28 하지만 작은 실수를 하고 사과하지 않는 것은 큰 감정적인 상처가 된다는 것을 기억하라.

29 이것은 가족과 사랑하는 사람들에게 특히 더 그러하다.

30 당신은 "더 이상 사과하지 않는다면 더 이상 기회가 없다."는 말을 들어본 적이 있는가?

31 사람들은 실수하지만, 그 실수가 아름다운 관계를 깨뜨리게 해서는 안 된다.

32 누군가에게 사과하고 싶은가? 지금 하려고 노력해라. 빠르고 진정한 "미안해."라는 말이 많은 문제를 해결해 줄 것이다.

※ 다음 문장을 우리말로 쓰시오.

1 ▶ Because we are human, we all make mistakes. It is not easy to get along with everyone all the time.

➡ _____

2 ▶ Sometimes we hurt people's feelings without intending to. Sometimes, we do something wrong and regret it later.

➡ _____

3 ▶ When that happens, what should we do? We should apologize.

➡ _____

4 ▶ Read the following case studies and learn three things about a proper apology.

➡ _____

5 ▶ When June tripped over a backpack and fell, Mike found it funny and laughed. He took a picture and uploaded it on an SNS.

➡ _____

6 ▶ June saw the picture and became angry. Mike said, with a laugh, "Sorry, June!" and deleted it.

➡ _____

7 ▶ After that, June felt even more hurt because of Mike's casual apology.

➡ _____

8 ▶ June didn't like how Mike had acted. Mike seemed to think it was nothing serious.

➡ _____

9 ▶ What did you learn from this case? Yes. You guessed right. You should be sincere when you apologize.

➡ _____

10 ▶ Apologizing is necessary to build good friendships. Saying you're sorry is more than just words.

➡ _____

11 ▶ You need to show that you respect the other person and care about his or her feelings.

➡ _____

12 ▶ If you truly want to make things right, be sincere in your apology.

➡ _____

13 ▶ The more sincere your apology is, the better it will be received.

➡ _____

14 ▶ Here is another case. While Kate was hurrying across the cafeteria, she accidentally bumped into Hojun.

➡ _____

15 ▶ Some food on Hojun's tray fell on his jacket. Kate didn't apologize. Hojun felt bad.

➡ _____

16 He thought, 'Why doesn't she say something? It would be nothing if she apologized right now.'

➡ _____

17 This case shows that when an apology is necessary, you should apologize at once.

➡ _____

18 A quick apology shows that you are thoughtful and take responsibility for your action.

➡ _____

19 All you need to do is to say, "I'm sorry." Then, the hurt friend will think nothing of it and laugh it off.

➡ _____

20 Finally, apologies are necessary among family members and loved ones, too.

➡ _____

21 One day, Sunmin borrowed her sister's favorite book. Later, she lost it.

➡ _____

22 Sunmin didn't apologize because she thought it was not important. She thought, 'We're sisters, after all.'

➡ _____

23 Sunmin's sister disliked how Sunmin had treated her. How could her own sister ignore her feelings?

➡ _____

24 This was not the first time Sunmin hadn't apologized to her little sister.

➡ _____

25 People need to apologize when they do something wrong. This includes family members and the people who are close to you.

➡ _____

26 People get hurt more easily when the hurt comes from a family member or a friend.

➡ _____

27 We may think that they will let it go because they are close to us.

➡ _____

28 Remember, however, that small mistakes and no apology add up to big emotional wounds.

➡ _____

29 This is especially true among family members and loved ones.

➡ _____

30 Have you ever heard of the saying, "No more apologies, no more chances"?

➡ _____

31 People make mistakes, but don't let one mistake break a beautiful relationship.

➡ _____

32 Do you want to apologize to someone? Try to do it now. A quick and sincere "I'm sorry" can solve many problems.

➡ _____

Step4

※ 다음 괄호 안의 단어들을 우리말에 맞도록 바르게 배열하시오.

1 (we / because / human, / are / all / we / mistakes. / make // is / it / easy / not / get / to / along / everyone / with / the / all / time.)
➡ _____

2 (we / sometimes / people's / hurt / without / feelings / to. / intending // we / sometimes, / something / do / and / wrong / it / regret / later.)
➡ _____

3 (that / when / happens, / should / what / do? / we // should / we / apologize.)
➡ _____

4 (the / read / case / following / studies / learn / and / things / three / about / proper / a / apology.)
➡ _____

5 (June / when / over / tripped / backpack / a / fell, / and / found / Mike / funny / it / laughed. / and // took / he / picture / a / and / it / uploaded / on / SNS. / an)
➡ _____

6 (saw / June / picture / the / and / angry. / became // said, / Mike / a / with / laugh, / June!" / "sorry, / and / it. / deleted)
➡ _____

7 (that, / after / felt / June / more / even / hurt / of / because / Mike's / apology. / causal)
➡ _____

8 (didn't / June / how / like / had / Mike / acted. // seemed / Mike / think / to / was / it / serious. / nothing)
➡ _____

9 (did / what / learn / you / this / from / case? // yes. // guessed / you / right. // should / you / sincere / be / you / when / apologize.)
➡ _____

10 (is / apologizing / to / necessary / good / build / friendships. // you're / saying / is / sorry / than / more / words. / just)
➡ _____

11 (need / you / show / to / you / that / the / respect / other / and / person / about / care / her / or / feelings. / her)
➡ _____

12 (you / if / want / truly / to / things / make / right, / sincere / be / your / in / apology.)
➡ _____

13 (more / the / your / sincere / is, / apology / better / the / will / it / received. / be)
➡ _____

14 (is / here / case. / another // Kate / while / hurrying / was / the / across / cafeteria, / accidentally / she / into / bumped / Hojun.)
➡ _____

15 (food / some / Hojun's / on / fell / tray / his / on / jacket. // didn't / Kate / apologize. // felt / bad. / Hojun)
➡ _____

1 우리는 인간이기 때문에 모두가 실수한다. 모든 사람과 항상 잘 지내기는 쉽지 않다.

2 때때로 우리는 의도하지 않게 다른 사람의 감정을 상하게 한다. 때때로 우리는 나쁜 일을 하고 나중에 그것을 후회한다.

3 이런 일이 생기면, 우리는 무엇을 해야 할까? 우리는 사과해야 한다.

4 다음 사례 연구들을 읽고 올바른 사과를 위한 세 가지를 알아보자.

5 June이 가방에 걸려 넘어졌을 때, Mike는 그것이 재미있다고 생각하고 웃었다. 그는 사진을 찍어서 SNS에 올렸다.

6 June은 그 사진을 보고 화가 났다. Mike는 웃으면서 "미안해, June!"이라고 말하고 사진을 삭제했다.

7 그 후, June은 Mike의 가벼운 사과에 한층 더 화가 났다.

8 June은 Mike의 행동 방식이 마음에 들지 않았다. Mike는 이 일이 심각한 일이 아니라고 생각하는 것처럼 보였다.

9 이 사례로부터 무엇을 배웠는가? 맞다. 당신은 바르게 추측했다. 당신은 사과할 때에 진실해야 한다.

10 사과하는 것은 좋은 교우 관계를 만들기 위해 필요하다. 미안하다고 말하는 것은 단지 말 이상이다.

11 당신이 타인을 존중하고, 타인의 감정에 관심을 갖고 있음을 보여주어야 한다.

12 당신이 진실로 일을 바로잡기를 원한다면, 당신의 사과는 진실해야 한다.

13 당신의 사과가 진실할수록, 그것은 더 잘 받아들여질 것이다.

14 또 다른 사례가 있다. Kate가 급식실을 가로질러 급하게 뛰어갈 때, 호준이와 실수로 부딪쳤다.

15 호준이의 급식판에 있던 음식이 그의 재킷에 떨어졌다. Kate는 사과하지 않았다. 호준이는 기분이 나빴다.

16 (thought, / he / doesn't / 'why / she / something? / say // would / it / nothing / be / she / if / right / apologized / now.')
➡ _____

17 (case / this / that / shows / an / when / is / apology / necessary, / should / you / at / apologize / once.)
➡ _____

18 (quick / a / shows / apology / you / that / thoughtful / are / responsibility / and / take / your / for / action.)
➡ _____

19 (you / all / to / need / is / do / say, / to / sorry." / "I'm // the / then, / friend / hurt / think / will / of / nothing / it / laugh / and / off. / it)
➡ _____

20 (apologies / finally, / necessary / are / family / among / and / members / ones, / loved / too.)
➡ _____

21 (day, / one / borrowed / Sunmin / sister's / her / book. / favorite // she / later, / it. / lost)
➡ _____

22 (didn't / Sunmin / because / apologize / she / it / thought / not / was / important. // thought, / she / sisters, / 'we're / all.' / after)
➡ _____

23 (sister / Sunmin's / how / disliked / had / Sunmin / her. / treated // could / how / own / her / ignore / sister / feelings? / her)
➡ _____

24 (was / this / the / not / time / first / hadn't / Sunmin / to / apologized / her / sister. / little)
➡ _____

25 (need / people / apologize / to / they / when / something / do / wrong. // includes / this / members / family / the / and / who / people / close / are / you. / to)
➡ _____

26 (get / people / more / hurt / when / easily / hurt / the / from / comes / family / a / or / member / friend. / a)
➡ _____

27 (may / think / we / that / will / they / it / let / because / go / are / they / to / close / us.)
➡ _____

28 (however, / remember, / small / that / and / mistakes / no / add / apology / up / big / to / wounds. / emotional)
➡ _____

29 (is / this / true / especially / family / among / and / members / ones. / loved)
➡ _____

30 (you / have / heard / ever / the / of / saying, / more / "no / apologies, / more / no / chances?")
➡ _____

31 (make / people / mistakes, / don't / but / one / let / break / mistake / beautiful / a / relationship.)
➡ _____

32 (you / do / to / want / to / apologize / someone? // to / try / it / do / now. // quick / a / sincere / and / sorry" / "I'm / solve / can / problems. / many)
➡ _____
➡ _____

16 그는 '왜 그녀는 아무 말도 하지 않지? 그녀가 즉시 사과한다면 아무 일도 아닐 텐데.' 라고 생각했다.

17 이 사례는 사과가 필요할 때는 사과를 즉시 해야 한다는 것을 보여준다.

18 신속한 사과는 당신이 사려 깊고, 당신의 행동에 책임을 진다는 것을 보여준다.

19 당신이 해야 할 행동은 "미안해."라고 말하는 것뿐이다. 그러면 상처받은 친구는 당신의 잘못을 아무렇지 않게 생각하고, 웃어넘길 것이다.

20 마지막으로 사과는 가족이나 사랑하는 사람들 사이에서도 필요하다.

21 어느 날, 선민이는 여동생이 가장 좋아하는 책을 빌렸다. 나중에 그녀는 그것을 잃어버렸다.

22 선민이는 그것이 중요하지 않다고 생각하여 사과하지 않았다. 그녀는 '우리는 어쨌든 자매니까.'라고 생각했다.

23 선민이의 여동생은 언니가 본인을 대했던 방식이 마음에 들지 않았다. 어떻게 자신의 언니가 그녀의 기분을 무시할 수 있는가?

24 선민이가 여동생에게 사과하지 않았던 것은 이번이 처음이 아니었다.

25 사람들은 잘못했을 때, 사과해야 한다. 이것은 가족이나 당신에게 가까운 사람도 포함한다.

26 사람들은 마음의 상처가 가족이나 친구에게서 올 때 더 쉽게 상처 받는다.

27 우리는 아마 그들이 가깝기 때문에 그냥 넘어갈 것이라고 생각할지 모른다.

28 하지만 작은 실수를 하고 사과하지 않는 것은 큰 감정적인 상처가 된다는 것을 기억하라.

29 이것은 가족과 사랑하는 사람들에게 특히 더 그러하다.

30 당신은 "더 이상 사과하지 않는다면 더 이상 기회가 없다."는 말을 들어본 적이 있는가?

31 사람들은 실수하지만, 그 실수가 아름다운 관계를 깨뜨리게 해서는 안 된다.

32 누군가에게 사과하고 싶은가? 지금 하려고 노력해라. 빠르고 진정한 "미안해."라는 말이 많은 문제를 해결해 줄 것이다.

※ 다음 우리말을 영어로 쓰시오.

1 우리는 인간이기 때문에 모두가 실수한다. 모든 사람과 항상 잘 지내기는 쉽지 않다.

➡ _____

2 때때로 우리는 의도하지 않게 다른 사람의 감정을 상하게 한다. 때때로 우리는 나쁜 일을 하고 나중에 그것을 후회한다.

➡ _____

_____

3 이런 일이 생기면, 우리는 무엇을 해야 할까? 우리는 사과해야 한다.

➡ _____

4 다음 사례 연구들을 읽고 올바른 사과를 위한 세 가지를 알아보자.

➡ _____

5 June이 가방에 걸려 넘어졌을 때, Mike는 그것이 재미있다고 생각하고 웃었다. 그는 사진을 찍어서 SNS에 올렸다.

➡ _____

_____

6 June은 그 사진을 보고 화가 났다. Mike는 웃으면서 "미안해, June!"이라고 말하고 사진을 삭제했다.

➡ _____

7 그 후, June은 Mike의 가벼운 사과에 한층 더 화가 났다.

➡ _____

8 June은 Mike의 행동 방식이 마음에 들지 않았다. Mike는 이 일이 심각한 일이 아니라고 생각하는 것처럼 보였다.

➡ _____

9 이 사례로부터 무엇을 배웠는가? 맞다. 당신은 바르게 추측했다. 당신은 사과할 때에 진실해야 한다.

➡ _____

10 사과하는 것은 좋은 교우 관계를 만들기 위해 필요하다. 미안하다고 말하는 것은 단지 말 이상이다.

➡ _____

11 당신이 타인을 존중하고, 타인의 감정에 관심을 갖고 있음을 보여 주어야 한다.

➡ _____

12 당신이 진실로 일을 바로잡기를 원한다면, 당신의 사과는 진실해야 한다.

➡ _____

13 당신의 사과가 진실할수록, 그것은 더 잘 받아들여질 것이다.

➡ _____

14 또 다른 사례가 있다. Kate가 급식실을 가로질러 급하게 뛰어갈 때, 호준이와 실수로 부딪쳤다.

➡ _____

_____

15 호준이의 급식판에 있던 음식이 그의 재킷에 떨어졌다. Kate는 사과하지 않았다. 호준이는 기분이 나빴다.

➡ _____

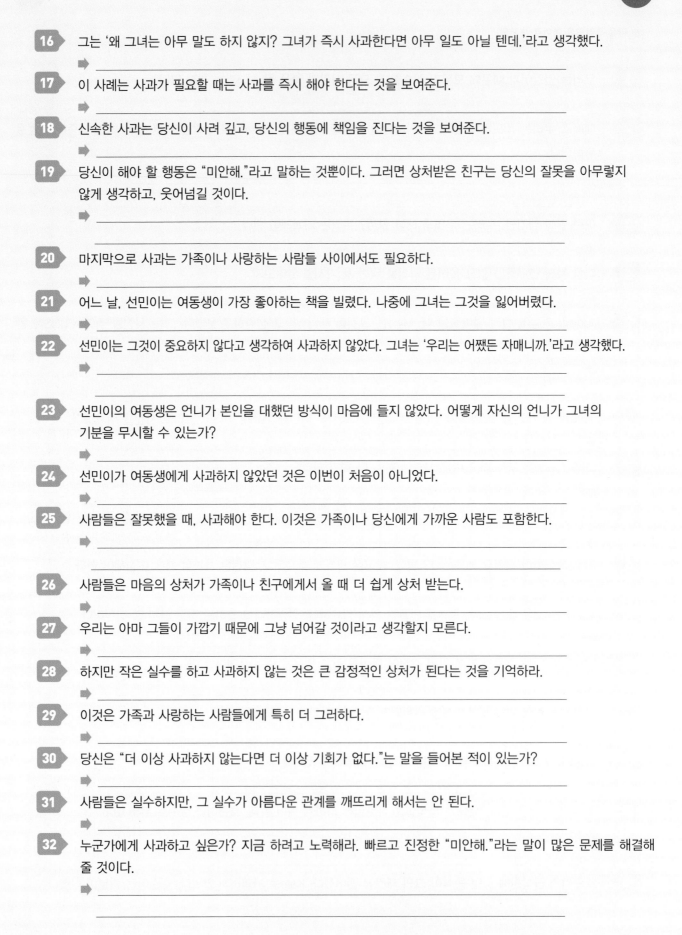

16 그는 '왜 그녀는 아무 말도 하지 않지? 그녀가 즉시 사과한다면 아무 일도 아닐 텐데.'라고 생각했다.
➡ _____

17 이 사례는 사과가 필요할 때는 사과를 즉시 해야 한다는 것을 보여준다.
➡ _____

18 신속한 사과는 당신이 사려 깊고, 당신의 행동에 책임을 진다는 것을 보여준다.
➡ _____

19 당신이 해야 할 행동은 "미안해."라고 말하는 것뿐이다. 그러면 상처받은 친구는 당신의 잘못을 아무렇지 않게 생각하고, 웃어넘길 것이다.
➡ _____

20 마지막으로 사과는 가족이나 사랑하는 사람들 사이에서도 필요하다.
➡ _____

21 어느 날, 선민이는 여동생이 가장 좋아하는 책을 빌렸다. 나중에 그녀는 그것을 잃어버렸다.
➡ _____

22 선민이는 그것이 중요하지 않다고 생각하여 사과하지 않았다. 그녀는 '우리는 어쨌든 자매니까.'라고 생각했다.
➡ _____

23 선민이의 여동생은 언니가 본인을 대했던 방식이 마음에 들지 않았다. 어떻게 자신의 언니가 그녀의 기분을 무시할 수 있는가?
➡ _____

24 선민이가 여동생에게 사과하지 않았던 것은 이번이 처음이 아니었다.
➡ _____

25 사람들은 잘못했을 때, 사과해야 한다. 이것은 가족이나 당신에게 가까운 사람도 포함한다.
➡ _____
_____

26 사람들은 마음의 상처가 가족이나 친구에게서 올 때 더 쉽게 상처 받는다.
➡ _____

27 우리는 아마 그들이 가깝기 때문에 그냥 넘어갈 것이라고 생각할지 모른다.
➡ _____

28 하지만 작은 실수를 하고 사과하지 않는 것은 큰 감정적인 상처가 된다는 것을 기억하라.
➡ _____

29 이것은 가족과 사랑하는 사람들에게 특히 더 그러하다.
➡ _____

30 당신은 "더 이상 사과하지 않는다면 더 이상 기회가 없다."는 말을 들어본 적이 있는가?
➡ _____

31 사람들은 실수하지만, 그 실수가 아름다운 관계를 깨뜨리게 해서는 안 된다.
➡ _____

32 누군가에게 사과하고 싶은가? 지금 하려고 노력해라. 빠르고 진정한 "미안해."라는 말이 많은 문제를 해결해 줄 것이다.
➡ _____
_____

Step1

※ 다음 우리말과 일치하도록 빈칸에 알맞은 말을 쓰시오.

After You Read C

1. Inho went to a _____ _____ _____ _____.

2. He _____ _____ _____ a woman's bag accidentally _____ _____ _____ _____.

3. The woman said, "Sorry," and she _____ _____ _____.

4. Inho was angry _____ the woman did not make a _____ and _____ _____.

5. He thought _____ the woman should _____ _____ _____ _____.

1. 인호는 신발을 사려고 가게에 갔다.
2. 어떤 여자가 지나갈 때 그는 우연히 그 여자의 가방에 부딪혔다.
3. 그 여자는 "미안해."라고 말하고는 빠르게 걸어갔다.
4. 인호는 그녀가 진실되고 올바른 사과를 하지 않았다고 생각했기 때문에 화가 났다.
5. 그는 그 여자가 그의 감정에 신경 써야 한다고 생각했다.

Enjoy Writing C

1. My _____ _____, Jinsu

2. I'd _____ _____ _____ my friend, Jinsu.

3. I _____ _____ him _____ elementary school.

4. He is always _____, _____, and _____.

5. This is _____ _____ _____ me.

6. Last Friday I was _____ and _____ _____ _____ _____.

7. Jinsu _____ _____ _____ _____ _____ _____.

8. I am _____ _____ _____ him _____ my friend.

9. _____ _____ I know him, _____ _____ our friendship becomes.

1. 나의 훌륭한 친구, 진수
2. 나는 나의 친구 진수를 소개하고 싶어.
3. 나는 그를 초등학교 때부터 알았어.
4. 그는 항상 재미있고, 용감하고, 발랄해.
5. 이게 그가 나를 도와주었던 방법이야.
6. 지난 금요일 나는 아파서 수학 수업을 못 들었어.
7. 진수가 내게 자신의 수업 노트를 보여줬어.
8. 나는 그를 친구로 두어서 행운이야.
9. 내가 그를 많이 알수록 우리의 우정은 더 깊어져.

Project Step 1

1. A: Do you know _____ _____ _____ _____ _____ _____ _____?

2. B: Yes. First, write about _____ _____ _____.

3. C: Then write _____ _____ _____ _____ _____ _____ it.

4. D: _____ _____ _____ _____ _____ for our actions.

5. A: Thank you _____ _____ _____. I _____ _____ it.

1. A: 너는 우리가 어떻게 사과 편지를 쓰는지 아니?
2. B: 응. 먼저, 우리가 뭘 했는지 써야 해.
3. C: 그리고 나서 그것에 대해 미안하다고 써야 해.
4. D: 우리 행동에 대해 변명은 하면 안돼.
5. A: 조언해 줘서 고마워. 정말 고마워.

※ 다음 우리말을 영어로 쓰시오.

After You Read C

1. 인호는 신발을 사려고 가게에 갔다.
   ➡ _____

2. 어떤 여자가 지나갈 때 그는 우연히 그 여자의 가방에 부딪혔다.
   ➡ _____

3. 그 여자는 "미안해."라고 말하고는 빠르게 걸어갔다.
   ➡ _____

4. 인호는 그녀가 진실되고 올바른 사과를 하지 않았다고 생각했기 때문에 화가 났다.
   ➡ _____

5. 그는 그 여자가 그의 감정에 신경 써야 한다고 생각했다.
   ➡ _____

Enjoy Writing C

1. 나의 훌륭한 친구, 진수
   ➡ _____

2. 나는 나의 친구 진수를 소개하고 싶어.
   ➡ _____

3. 나는 그를 초등학교 때부터 알았어.
   ➡ _____

4. 그는 항상 재미있고, 용감하고, 발랄해.
   ➡ _____

5. 이게 그가 나를 도와주었던 방법이야.
   ➡ _____

6. 지난 금요일 나는 아파서 수학 수업을 못 들었어.
   ➡ _____

7. 진수가 내게 자신의 수업 노트를 보여 줬어.
   ➡ _____

8. 나는 그를 친구로 두어서 행운이야.
   ➡ _____

9. 내가 그를 많이 알수록 우리의 우정은 더 깊어져.
   ➡ _____

Project Step 1

1. A: 너는 우리가 어떻게 사과 편지를 쓰는지 아니?
   ➡ _____

2. B: 응. 먼저, 우리가 뭘 했는지 써야 해.
   ➡ _____

3. C: 그러고 나서 그것에 대해 미안하다고 써야 해.
   ➡ _____

4. D: 우리 행동에 대해 변명은 하면 안 돼.
   ➡ _____

5. A: 조언해 줘서 고마워. 정말 고마워.
   ➡ _____

영어 기출 문제집

적중100

2학기

정답 및 해설

시사 | 박준언

중 3

적중100

영어 기출 문제집

정답 및 해설

2학기

시사 | 박준언

중 3

Love for My Country

시험대비 실력평가 　　　　　　　　　　p.08

01 ③　　　　　02 independence

03 look forward to　　　　04 ②　　　　05 ⑤

06 ③　　　　　07 specialist　　08 ④

01 처칠의 동상이 의회 건물 밖에 서 있다.

02 다른 나라에 의해 지배되거나 통치되는 것으로부터의 해방[벗어남]: independence(독립)

03 look forward to+동명사: ~하기를 기대하다

04 예술 작품, 그림 또는 기타 흥미로운 것들의 공개적인 전시

05 누군가, 특히 중요한 사람이 묻혀 있는 큰 석조 구조물이나 지하 공간

06 (A) 건물 전체로 불이 빠르게 퍼졌다. (B) 투표는 당신의 애국적인 의무 중 일부다.

07 유의어 관계이다. 바람, 소원 : 전문가

08 나는 독도가 한국에 속한다는 것을 많은 사람들에게 알리고 싶다. '~에 속하다'라는 의미로 'belong to'를 사용한다.

서술형 시험대비 　　　　　　　　　　p.09

01 (1) harmony　(2) movement　(3) kill　(4) poem

02 republic

03 (1) entrance　(2) president　(3) government
　　(4) Japanese

04 (1) amusement park, 놀이공원
　　(2) organization, 조직　(3) poem, 시
　　(4) sacrifice, 희생

05 complete

01 (1) 많은 종교 지도자들은 세상에 평화와 화합을 가져오기 위해 열심히 노력하고 있습니다. (2) 그녀는 저명한 과학자이며 세계 환경 운동의 선구자이다. (3) 가뭄은 작물을 죽일 수도 있다. (4) 그녀의 시는 우리에게 강하고 용감하게 살라고 말합니다.

02 공화국은 국민이나 그들이 선출하는 대표자들에 의해 권력이 유지되는 나라이다.

03 (1) entrance: 입구 (2) president: 대통령 (3) government: 정부 (4) Japanese: 일본의

04 (1) 박람회장 놀이기구, 쇼, 그리고 다른 오락거리가 있는 넓은 야외 공간 (2) 조직화될 목적으로 함께 일하는 사람들의 집단

(3) 깊은 의미를 암시하고 읽을 때 리드미컬하게 들리는 아름다운 단어를 사용하는 한 편의 글 (4) 특정한 목적을 위해 귀중한 어떤 것을 포기하는 것

05 • 몇몇 사람들은 예체능 수업이 완전한 시간 낭비라고 생각한다.
　　• 때때로, 그는 단지 하나의 작품을 끝내기 위해 20 시간을 보내기도 한다.

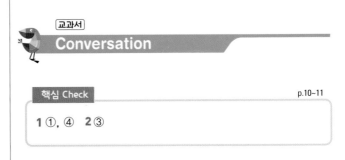

교과서 Conversation

핵심 Check 　　　　　　　　　　p.10~11

1 ①, ④　2 ③

교과서 대화문 익히기

Check(√) True or False 　　　　　　　　　　p.12

1 T　2 F　3 T　4 F

교과서 확인학습 　　　　　　　　　　p.14~15

Listen & Speak 1 A

1. at, huge / looks strong / Because, was built, protect, during / who built / ordered, to direct, process, don't you / heard of, scientist

2. don't you / national flag, isn't / what, symbols, mean / circle, harmony, peace / lines, corners / mean, earth

Listen & Speak 2 A

1. planning to go / built / heard, great / treasures that, had taken / must be interesting / looking forward to

2. what did you do / volunteer work / What kind / cleaned, tombs, respect, who / Sounds / planning to go, join / I'm looking forward to

Real Life Talk

reading / Poetry, know, don't you / heard / poems when, under, rule, desire, independence, be felt, poems / to read, poems, learn / In fact, to visit / when / near, Palace, palace / Let's / looking forward to, visit

시험대비 기본평가   p.16

01 looking forward to   02 ⑤   03 ③
04 ②

01 앞으로 하고 싶은 일에 대한 기대를 표현할 때 'I'm looking forward to ~.'나 'I look forward to ~.'의 표현을 사용한다.

02 빈칸 뒤의 부가의문문 형태가 'don't you?'인 것으로 보아 앞의 평서문은 일반동사 긍정문 형태가 오는 것이 적절하고, B가 대답으로 '그것에 관해 들었어.'라고 말하므로 그것에 관해 아는지 확인하는 말이 적절하다.

03 앞으로 하고 싶은 일에 대한 기대를 표현할 때 'be dying to+동사원형'을 사용한다.

04 'You know ~, don't you?'는 알고 있는지 물어보는 표현이다.

시험대비 실력평가   p.17~18

01 ⑤   02 ④   03 ④   04 ③
05 I'm looking forward to making it.   06 ④
07 King Jeongjo ordered Jeong Yakyong to direct the building process.   08 ②, ⑤   09 ③
10 ④

01 'look forward to'에서 to는 전치사이므로 명사나 동명사가 온다. trying이 적절하다.

02 Judy와 Seho는 점심으로 삼계탕을 먹을 것이다.

03 봉사 활동하러 현충원에 갔다는 말에 → (D) 거기(현충원)서 어떤 종류의 봉사 활동을 했는지 묻고 → (B) 묘 주변을 청소했다는 대답을 하고 → (A) 자기도 할 수 있는지 묻는 말에 → 마지막으로 (C) '물론이지.'라고 승낙의 답을 한다.

04 '너는 안중근에 대해 알지, 그렇지 않니?'라는 물음에 '너는 안중근 박물관에 가서 그에 대해 더 많은 정보를 얻을 수 있어.'라고 답하는 것은 어색하다.

05 '~하는 것을 기대하고 있다'라는 의미로 'be dying to+동사원형'은 'look forward to+동명사'로 쓸 수 있다.

06 ④번은 '나는 간송 박물관에 갈 예정이야.'라는 말에 '그러고 싶지만, 그곳을 방문하는 것이 기대가 돼.'라고 말하는 것은 어색하다.

07 '~에게 …하라고 명령[지시]하다'는 'order+목적어+to부정사'

구문을 사용한다. direct를 to direct로 바꾸어 쓴다.

09 'know'의 목적어로 '의문사+주어+동사' 어순의 간접의문문으로 사용해야 한다. 'what the symbols in Taegeukgi mean'이 되어야 한다.

10 각각의 모서리에 4개의 선이 있는 것이 아니라 네 모서리에 검은 선들이 있다.

서술형 시험대비   p.19

01 His love for the country and his desire for independence can be felt in his poems.
02 I'm (really) looking forward to the visit.
03 (A) you know Taegeukgi, don't you?
     (B) Do you know what the symbols in Taegeukgi mean?
     (C) They mean four things: sky, fire, water, and earth.
04 You know about Jeong Yakyong, don't you?

01 질문: 윤동주의 시를 통해 무엇이 느껴질 수 있나?

02 기대나 희망을 나타낼 때 'look forward to+명사/동명사'를 사용한다.

교과서
Grammar

핵심 Check   p.20~21

1 (1) had   (2) visited
2 (1) that   (2) so that

시험대비 기본평가   p.22

01 ⑤   02 ③   03 ②
04 (1) that, could[might]   (2) so hot that
     (3) that, he can[may]   (4) so hard that, can't

01 본동사의 시제가 과거이고, 그 이전에 일어난 약속이므로 과거완료시제를 쓴다.

02 'so as to V' 또는 'so that ~ 주어 can'은 '~하기 위해서'라는 뜻이며, 'so 형용사 that 주어 V'는 '너무 ~해서 …하다'라는 의미이다.

03 ① came(과거) 이전에 일어난 일이므로 had gone으로 써야 한다. ③ had found → found, ④ had lived → have lived, ⑤ when은 '시점'을 묻는 의문사이므로 완료시제와 함

3

께 쓸 수 없다.

04 '목적'을 나타내는 'so that'과 '결과'를 나타내는 'so+수식어+that+can[can't]'를 이해하고, 적용하는 문제이다. that을 기준으로 앞, 뒤 문장에 나타난 동사의 시제를 일치시키는데 유의하여, so that을 활용하도록 한다.

시험대비 실력평가   p.23~25

01 ③	02 ④	03 ⑤	04 ③
05 ⑤	06 ⑤	07 ①	
08 has → had	09 ④	10 ⑤	11 ④
12 ①			

13 (1) Father Lee Taeseok returned to Sudan in order that he could help poor people there.

(2) Amy practices every day so that she can join our sports club.

(3) Clara left for Paris in order that she could study fashion.

(4) Thames ran fast so that he would not be late for the meeting.

14 (1) squeezed out the pimples so that they would disappear

(2) in order that he could get a full college scholarship

01 과거 시점 이전에 발생한 일이다. has broken → had broken

03 'so that+주어+조동사'가 적절히 사용된 것을 찾는다.

04 ① had not eaten → has not eaten ② 까마귀가 도시로 이주하기 전 정글에 살았다는 문장이므로 The crow had lived in the jungle before it moved to the city.가 옳은 문장이다. ④ 설거지를 끝내야 한다고 요구한 것이므로 had finished → (should) finish ⑤ had read → have read

05 ① in order for → in order that ② not being → would not be ③ so joy that → so joyful that ④ so to → so as to 또는 in order to

06 다른 문장들은 모두 '목적'을 나타내는 표현인데, ⑤의 두 번째 문장은 '결과'를 나타낸다. 보통, '결과'의 so (that)는 앞 문장의 끝에 컴마(쉼표)를 쓴다.

07 <보기>의 had solved는 과거완료시제 중 '완료' 용법으로 쓰였다. ②, ③, ⑤는 '계속' 용법이다. ④는 '경험' 용법이다.

08 과거의 특정 시점 이전에 계속된 일이므로 과거완료시제이다.

09 '일본을 물리치기 위해 군인들은 열심히 훈련했다'라는 문장들로서 모두 '목적'을 나타내는데, ④만 '군인들은 열심히 훈련해서 일본을 물리쳤다'라는 뜻의 '결과'를 나타낸다.

10 ⑤ 'Irene이 진보다 더 열심히 공부했기 위해서 시험에 떨어졌

다'는 이상한 문장이다. (al)though와 같은 '양보'의 접속사로 바꾸는 것이 적절하다.

11 ① has → had ② had picked → has picked 또는 picked ③ have → had ⑤ had been given → had given

12 ② be stay → be 또는 stay로 동사를 하나만 쓴다. ③ in order to that → in order that ④ so that 생략 또는 in order to → I can ⑤ she can → she could *subtitles: 자막

13 '목적'을 나타내는 to부정사 또는 'in order to', 'so as to' 등의 표현은 'so[in order]+that+주어+조동사'로 바꿔 쓸 수 있다.

14 '목적'을 나타내는 부사절 'so that', 'in order that' 뒤의 문장 구조에 유의하여, 그림에 맞게 적절히 영작한다. *squeeze out: 짜내다 *pimple: 여드름

서술형 시험대비   p.26~27

01 (1) bought many Korean treasures that some Japanese had taken to Japan

(2) made the Turtle Ship so that he could protect the people

(3) walked slowly so that no one could hear him

02 had searched, had made

03 (1) Could you remind me of the time so that I won't be late for the party? 또는 Could you remind me of the time in order that I won't be late for the party?

(2) Whenever Jane was ill, her mom used to make her a bowl of porridge in order for her to get well.

(3) They are saving money so that they can buy a big house.

(4) Remember my number in order that you can contact me. 또는 Remember my number in order for you to contact me.

(5) The foreigners from Italy went to Gyeongju so that they could see Bulguksa.

(6) Many people joined the New Korean Society in order to support the Independence movement.

04 (1) We need ice and sugar so that we can make patbingsu.

(2) We went to the river so that she could catch some fish.

(3) A firefighter ran into the woods so that she could rescue the koalas.

(4) My grandma exercises every day in order that she can keep healthy.

05 had lived alone in the house for thirty-three years until the official visited him last year

06 (1) ⓐ, 내가 그 곳에 도착했을 때, Peter는 이미 뉴욕으로 떠나 버렸다.

(2) ⓓ, 작년까지 William은 14년간 부산에서 살았다.

(3) ⓓ, 콘서트가 시작되기 전까지 그들은 그 가수를 거의 하루 동안 기다렸다.

(4) ⓑ, Maria는 이번 겨울에 한국에 올 때까지 눈을 본 적이 없었다.

(5) ⓐ, 내가 공항에 도착했을 무렵 탑승 수속이 이미 끝났다.

(6) ⓒ, 우리가 집에 왔을 때, 누군가가 창문을 깬 것을 알게 되었다.

(7) ⓑ, 나는 전에 그 사람을 만난 적이 없어서 그 사람을 알아보지 못했다.

(8) ⓐ, 그 부부가 깨었을 때, 누군가가 구두 만들기를 끝내놓았다.

01 (1) 과거의 특정 시점 이전에 일어난 일은 '과거완료시제'로 사용하는 것에 유의한다. (2), (3) '목적'을 나타내는 부사절에 'so that 주어 could'를 사용한다.

02 과거의 어느 특정 시점을 기준으로 먼저 일어난 일을 과거완료시제로 표현한다. Before, After가 있을 때, 시간의 전후관계가 명확하므로 과거시제도 쓸 수 있으나, 문제에서 완료시제로 쓸 것을 요구했음에 유의한다.

03 (1) so order that → so that 또는 in order that (2) of her → for her (3) so which → so that (4) in order for you can → in order for you to 또는 in order that you can (5) can → could (6) so order to → in order to

04 주어진 단어들 중 동사의 수와 시제에 유의하여, 'so that' 또는 'in order that'으로 적절한 문장을 영작한다. (3) 소방대원은, 괄호에 주어진 단어가 she이므로 여성임에 유의한다.

05 과거의 어느 특정 시점을 기준으로 그 전부터 시작된 동작이나 상태는 과거완료시제로 표현한다. 작년에 공무원이 방문한 과거의 시점을 기준으로 노인이 혼자 산 것이므로 'had lived alone'을 쓰는 것이 적절하다.

06 과거완료시제는 완료, 경험, 결과, 계속 등의 용법으로 구분할 수 있으며, 해석을 정확하게 하는 것이 중요하다.

[교과서]
Reading

🔖 확인문제   p.28

1 F   2 F   3 T   4 T

🔖 확인문제   p.29

1 F   2 T   3 F   4 F   5 T

교과서 확인학습 A   p.30~31

01 my history club

02 visited, inside the park

03 At, entrance

04 a great national hero, spent, from

05 helped educate, by building

06 In, when the independence movement, moved to

07 joined, became its president

08 The exhibition hall, shows

09 looking around, stopped at, Patriotic Organization's

10 formed, organization, to fight against

11 belonged to

12 At, saw two watches

13 In, made a plan to

14 Patriotic Organization, directed, to carry

15 left for, wearing a very old watch, Mine, it, take, let, have

16 always carried, so that, forget, sacrifice

17 completing, moved to, tombs

18 had been, independence, them

19 By doing so, for the sacrifice

20 As, left, words, that, had read

21 It, written in

22 what my wish is, Korea's Independence

23 what my second wish, independence

24 asks me what my third wish is, complete independence

교과서 확인학습 B   p.32~33

1 Last week my history club went to Hyochang Park.

2 We visited the Kim Koo Museum inside the park.

3 At the entrance of the museum, we saw a white statue of Kim Koo.

4 Kim Koo is a great national hero who spent most of his life fighting for the independence of Korea from Japanese rule.

5 In the 1900s, he helped educate young people by building schools.

6 In 1919, when the independence movement had spread throughout the country, he moved to Shanghai, China.

7 There he joined the Government of the Republic of Korea and later became its president.

8 The exhibition hall in the museum shows a lot of things about Kim Koo's life.

9 While looking around the hall, we stopped at a photo of the Korean Patriotic Organization's members.

10 Kim Koo formed the secret organization in 1931 to fight against Japan.

11 Lee Bongchang and Yun Bonggil belonged to the group.

12 At one place in the hall, we saw two watches under a photo of Kim Koo and Yun Bonggil.

13 In 1932, Kim Koo made a plan to kill Japanese generals in a park in Shanghai.

14 As the leader of the Korean Patriotic Organization, he directed Yun to carry out the mission.

15 When Yun left for the mission, he told Kim, "Sir, you are wearing a very old watch. Mine is new, but I won't need it anymore. Please take my watch, and let me have yours."

16 Kim Koo always carried Yun's watch in his jacket so that he would not forget Yun's sacrifice.

17 After completing the tour of the museum, we moved to the tombs of the three heroes, Lee Bongchang, Yun Bonggil, and Baek Jeonggi.

18 Their bodies had been in Japan, but after Korea's independence Kim Koo brought them to Hyochang Park.

19 By doing so, he showed his deep love and respect for the sacrifice of the three heroes.

20 As I left Hyochang Park, I thought about Kim Koo's words in My Wish that I had read in the exhibition hall.

21 It was written in *Baekbeomilji*.

22 If God asks me what my wish is, I would say clearly, "It is Korea's Independence."

23 If he asks me what my second wish is, I would say, "It is the independence of my country."

24 If he asks me what my third wish is, I would say loudly, "It is the complete independence of my country." That is my answer.

01 ②   02 ④

03 It is at the entrance of the museum.

04 He moved to Shanghai in 1919.

05 ②, ④

06 He planned to kill the Japanese generals in a park in Shanghai.

07 ④   08 ⑤   09 ①, ③   10 ⑤

11 Kim Koo's firm wish for the complete independence of Korea was written in *Baekbeomilji*.

12 visit the Kim Koo Museum inside the park

13 ④

14 He fought for the independence of Korea from Japanese rule.

15 ④   16 exhibition   17 ②

18 There were two watches.

19 ③   20 ⑤   21 my watch 22 ④

23 ③   24 ⑤

25 They are written in *Baekbeomilji*.

01 동명사와 함께 쓰이면서 '~함으로써'라는 의미를 완성하는 전치사 by가 적절하다.

02 김구 선생은 학교를 설립함으로써 젊은이들을 교육시키는 것을 도왔다. ③ 그는 생의 대부분을 일본을 위해 싸우느라 보낸 것이 아니라 일본에 대항해서 싸우느라 보냈다.

03 기념관 입구에 김구 선생의 동상이 있다고 하였다.

04 김구가 중국 상해로 이동한 때는 1919년이라고 하였다.

05 기념관 안에 있는 전시관에는 한인 애국단 멤버의 사진, 김구와 윤봉길의 사진 아래에 있는 두 개의 시계가 있다고 하였다.

06 김구는 상해에 있는 한 공원에서 일본 장군들을 죽일 계획을 하였다.

07 김구가 일본에 맞서 싸우기 위해 1931년에 만든 것은 비밀 조직이었다.

08 윤봉길의 희생을 잊지 않기 위해서 김구는 그의 시계를 항상 가지고 다녔다.

09 선행사가 Kim Koo's words in My Wish이므로 which나 that을 쓰는 것이 적절하다.

10 (B)의 대명사 Their가 가리키는 것은 (C)의 이봉창, 윤봉길, 백정기이며, 독립 이후 이들의 시신을 일본에서 효창공원으로 모셔왔다. (A)에서 말하는 By doing so는 김구의 이러한 행동을 의미하는 말이다.

11 백범일지에는 한국의 독립에 대한 김구의 단호한 소망이 적혀있다고 하였다.

12 역사 동아리는 효창 공원 안에 있는 김구 기념관을 방문하기 위하여 그 공원으로 갔다.

13 효창공원 입구에는 하얀색의 김구 조각상이 있다고 하였다.

14 김구는 일본 통치로부터 한국의 독립을 위해 싸웠다고 하였다.

15 역사 동아리가 어떻게 효창 공원으로 갔는지는 위 글을 읽고 답할 수 없다.

16 사진, 조각 혹은 다른 흥미로운 물건들이 전시되는 공개 행사는 '전시회(exhibition)'이다.

17 '전시관을 둘러보던 중'이라는 말이므로 around라고 쓰는 것이 적절하다.

18 김구와 윤봉길 사진 아래에는 두 개의 시계가 있었다고 하였다.

19 모두 김구를 가리키는 말이지만 ③번은 윤봉길을 가리키는 말이다.

20 (A)는 '~로서'라고 해석되는 전치사로 자격을 나타낼 때 쓰인다.
① 전치사(~처럼) ② 부사(~만큼 …한) ③ 접속사(~이기 때문에) ④ 접속사(~이듯이) ⑤ 전치사(~로서)

21 자신의 시계를 가리키는 말이다.

22 글의 흐름상 나라의 완전한 독립을 의미하는 것이므로 'complete'라고 쓰는 것이 적절하다. *complement: 보충[보족]물

23 나의 소원'에 따르면 김구가 가장 바란 것은 한국의 독립이었다.

24 세 영웅의 시신을 일본에서 한국으로 모셔온 사람은 김구이다.

25 김구의 말이 쓰여 있는 책은 '백범일지'이다.

서술형 시험대비   p.38~39

01 Shanghai, China

02 They went to Hyochang Park last week.

03 A white statue of Kim Koo was (at the entrance of the museum).

04 It was in Shanghai, China.

05 national hero, the independence of Korea

06 The writer saw a photo of the Korean Patriotic Organization's members.

07 It was because he tried to fight against Japan.

08 belonged to the secret group

09 His plan was to kill Japanese generals in a park in Shanghai.

10 exchanged watches

11 It was because he would not forget Yun's sacrifice.

12 They moved to the tombs of the three heroes, Lee Bongchang, Yun Bonggil, and Baek Jeonggi.

13 일본에 있던 삼의사의 시신을 독립 이후에 효창 공원으로 모셔온 것

14 The writer read it in the exhibition hall.

15 It(=His third wish) was the complete independence of his country.

01 중국 상해를 가리키는 말이다.

02 글쓴이의 역사 동아리가 지난주에 간 곳은 효창공원이다.

03 기념관 입구에는 하얀색의 김구의 조각상이 있다고 하였다.

04 위 글의 내용에 따르면 대한민국 임시 정부는 중국 상하이에 있었다.

05 김구는 일본 통치로부터 한국의 독립을 위해 싸우는 데 그의 삶 대부분을 보낸 위대한 국민 영웅이다.

06 글쓴이는 한인 애국단 단원들의 사진을 보았다고 하였다.

07 김구가 비밀 조직을 만든 이유는 일본에 맞서 싸우기 위해서라고 하였다.

08 대답으로 미루어 보아 김구가 만든 비밀 조직에 누가 속해 있었는지를 묻는 말을 쓰는 것이 적절하다.

09 김구의 계획은 상해에 있는 한 공원에서 일본 장군들을 암살하는 것이었다.

10 윤봉길은 김구가 지시한 임무를 수행하기 위해 떠나기 전 그와 함께 시계를 교환하였다. exchange: 교환하다

11 윤봉길의 희생을 잊지 않기 위하여 그의 시계를 항상 가지고 다녔다.

12 기념관 관람을 마치고 이봉창, 윤봉길, 백정기 의사들이 묻힌 삼의사의 묘로 이동했다.

13 세 사람의 시신은 일본에 있었지만, 독립 이후에 김구가 그들을 효창 공원으로 모셔온 것을 의미한다.

14 글쓴이는 전시관에서 '나의 소원'을 읽었다고 하였다.

15 김구의 세 번째 소원은 나라의 완전한 독립이라고 하였다.

영역별 핵심문제   p.41~45

01 entrance   02 ⑤   03 ③   04 ①

05 (e)xhibition 06 ④

07 He bought many Korean treasures that some Japanese had taken to Japan.

08 You know, don't   09 ②

10 They are planning to visit the Yun Dongju Museum.

11 ③   12 ⑤   13 ④   14 ③

15 (1) so that they can show
   (2) so that they could see the *Mona Lisa*

16 (1) had killed   (2) had been   (3) made
   (4) had gone   (5) had pulled

17 (1) The rabbit regretted that she had slept in the middle of the race.
   (2) The ant reminded the grasshopper that he had played in the summer.

18 ①

19 He built schools in order to help educate young people.

01 반의어 관계이다. 독립-의존 : 출구-입구

02 (A) 나는 UN과 같은 국제 조직에서 일하고 싶다. (B) 희생 없
　는 사랑은 없다.

03 보통 기둥 끝에 붙어 있고 국가나 협회를 대표하는 천 조각:
　flag(깃발)

04 특정한 결과를 위해 차례로 일어나는 일련의 일들: process(과
　정)

05 박물관은 피카소 작품을 전시하고 있다.

06 'desire'는 '바람, 갈망'의 뜻이다.

07 대화의 내용상 전형필이 한 훌륭한 일에 대한 글로, 주격인 he를
　주어로 시작하여 동사는 bought를 사용하고 목적어로는 many
　Korean treasures가 오는 것이 적절하다. 그 다음 many
　Korean treasures를 수식하는 목적격 관계대명사절로 '주어+
　동사' 어순으로 영작한다.

08 상대방이 알고 있는지 확인하는 표현으로 'You know ~, don't
　you?'를 사용한다.

09 주어진 문장이 '정말? 난 그걸 몰랐어.'라고 말하고 있으므로
　'that'은 앞 문장에 언급된 윤동주의 나라에 대한 사랑과 독립에
　대한 염원이 시에서 느껴진다는 것을 가리킨다.

10 질문: 그들은 다음 주 토요일에 무엇을 할 예정인가?

11 보라가 Andy에게 윤동주의 시를 많이 읽어 보라고 제안하는 내
　용은 대화에서 언급되어 있지 않다.

12 so that 뒤에는 절을 써야 한다. for her to get을 she could
　get으로 고치는 것이 적절하다. 아니면, so that for her를 삭제
　해도 무방하다.

13 과거완료시제가 사용된 문장들이다. begin의 과거분사형은
　began이 아니라 begun이다.

14 not은 to부정사 앞에 위치해야 한다. in order not for him →
　in order for him not to

15 (1) 학생들이 좋은 공연을 보여줄 수 있도록 열심히 연습 중이
　다. (2) 많은 관광객들이 모나리자를 보려고 루브르 박물관에 모
　여들었다.

16 (1), (2), (4), (5) 과거의 어느 특정시점을 기준으로 그 이전에
　시작된 일은 과거완료시제로 표현한다. (3) 역사적 사실은 주절
　의 동사 시제와 상관없이 과거시제를 쓴다.

17 우리말에 맞게 과거완료시제와 주어진 단어들을 적절히 사용하
　여 배열한다.

18 주어진 문장의 the park는 효창공원을 의미한다. 공원 안에 있는
　김구 기념관을 방문했다는 말이 나온 후 기념관 입구에서 김구 선
　생의 동상을 보았다고 말하는 것이 자연스럽다.

19 젊은이들을 교육시키는 데 도우려고 학교를 설립했다고 하였다.

20 김구는 중국 상해에서 대한민국 임시 정부에 가입하였다.

21 '존경받는 지도자'라는 의미가 자연스럽다. 따라서 과거분사
　respected를 쓰는 것이 적절하다.

22 안창호는 1907년 신민회(the New Korean Society)를 설
　립하였다. find-found-found(발견하다), found-founded-
　founded(설립하다).

23 안창호가 몇 개의 학교를 설립했는지는 위 글을 읽고 답할 수 없
　다.

24 모두 '많은(= many)'이라는 의미로 쓰일 수 있지만 'the
　number of'는 '~의 수'라는 의미이다.

25 김구가 한인 애국단을 조직한 때는 1931년이다.

26 김구는 한인 애국단의 지도자로서 윤봉길에게 일본 장군들을 암
　살하도록 지시하였다.

단원별 예상문제　　　　　　　　　p.46~49

01 반의어 관계이다. 완전한 - 불완전한 : 깊은 - 얕은

02 왕이나 여왕이 쓰는 금으로 만들어지고 보석으로 장식된 원형
　장식물: crown(왕관)

03 '주어(I)+동사(felt)+목적어(respect)'를 먼저 쓰고, 우리말 해
　석의 '나라를 위해 돌아가신'이 'the people'을 수식하는 구조로

'for the people who died for the country'의 어순을 사용하여 문장을 완성한다.

04 Soyeon이가 봉사활동을 한 곳은 박물관이 아니라 현충원이다.

05 대화의 내용상 태극기의 상징이 무엇을 의미하는지 묻는 말이 적절하다.

06 사람들이 평화롭고 서로 동의하거나 일이 옳거나 적절해 보이는 상황.

07 'You know ~, don't you?'는 알고 있는지 물어보는 표현이다.

08 주어인 '나라에 대한 그의 사랑과 독립에 대한 염원'이 느껴질 수 있는 것이므로 수동태인 'can be felt'가 적절하다.

09 'It is ~'로 문장의 주어, 동사가 있기 때문에 동사 'was built'를 사용할 수 없다. museum을 수식하는 과거분사 built만 남겨두고 was는 생략해야 한다. 또는 관계대명사를 첨가하여 'which[that] was built'로 고칠 수 있다.

10 모든 빈칸에 들어갈 단어는 so이다. ⑤는 '너무 ~해서 …하다'라는 '결과'를 나타내는 상관접속사 'so ~ that'이다. 나머지는 모두 '목적'을 뜻하는 'so that'이다.

11 목적을 나타내는 'so that'과 같은 의미의 표현들로 'in order that', 'so as to', 'in order to' 등을 활용하도록 한다.

12 과거 이전에 발생한 일은 과거완료시제로 표현한다. ② has overworked → had overworked ③ has been → had been ④번 문장은 내용의 인과관계상 사건의 발생 순서를 바로잡아야 한다. '내가 경기장에 도착했을 때, 1피어어드가 시작되었다.'는 내용이므로 The first period had begun when I arrived at the court.로 하는 것이 적절하다.

13 (a)+(C): Vicky는 그의 아들이 위대한 음악가가 될 수 있게 매일 그에게 클래식 음악을 들려준다. (b)+(D): Kate는 금메달을 따기 위해 지난 4년간 하루 500개씩 슛 연습을 해왔다. (c)+(A): Taylor는 벌금을 물지 않기 위해 연체된 모든 책들을 도서관에 반납했다. (d)+(B): Clara는 건강해지기 위해 정크푸드 섭취를 중단했다.

14 spend+시간+Ving: V하느라 시간을 쓰다

15 1900년대에 김구는 젊은 사람들을 교육하는 데 도움이 되기 위하여 학교를 설립하였다.

16 효창 공원 안에는 김구 기념관이 있다고 하였다.

17 ②번 앞 문장에서는 안창호가 10대 때 서울로 갔다고 하였고, ②번 뒤 문장에서는 안창호의 미국 활동에 대해 이야기하고 있으므로, 안창호가 미국으로 이주했다는 내용은 ②번에 들어가는 것이 적절하다.

18 안창호는 1938년 그가 죽을 때까지 사람들을 교육시키기 위하여 많은 학교를 설립하였다.

19 안창호는 한국으로 돌아와 1907년에 신민회를 설립하였다.

20 (A)는 a plan을 수식하는 형용사로 쓰인 to부정사이다. ①, ④ 부사적 용법 중 목적(~하기 위해서) ② any chance를 수식하는 형용사 ③ 명사적 용법으로 쓰인 진주어 ⑤ 부사적 용법 중 판단의 이유

21 'to kill Japanese generals in a park in Shanghai'를 의미한다.

서술형 실전문제　p.50~51

01 was built to protect, directed, building process
02 ⓐ allowed, ⓑ to use, ⓒ completed, ⓓ had burnt,
　ⓔ disappointed, (A) so that, ⓕ like
03 ④ I found out that she had lost her bag.
04 (1) so that it could warm my body
　(2) which my uncle had bought
　(3) in order to show
05 in order to / to
06 He founded it to fight for Korea's independence.
07 **미국에 있는 한국인들의 삶을 향상시키는 것을 도왔다.**
08 My Wish
09 They are in Hyochang Park.
10 desire, love

01 수원 화성은 전쟁 동안 사람들을 보호하기 위해 지어졌다. 정약용이 건설 과정을 감독했다.

02 ⓐ when이 이끄는 부사절이 과거시제이므로 과거동사 allowed, ⓑ 'allow+목적어+목적격보어(to부정사)', ⓒ 30분 전이 과거 시점이므로 과거동사 completed, ⓓ 과거 이전의 시점이므로 had burnt, ⓔ 실망하게 된 것이므로 disappointed ⓕ 조동사 뒤에 동사원형이 나와야 하므로 like, (A)에는 '그가 나를 좋아하도록'의 뜻이 되어야 하므로 2 단어는 'so that'이 적절하다.

03 내가 알아낸 것과 그녀가 가방을 잃어버린 것의 전후 관계를 정리하면, '나는 그녀가 가방을 잃어버린 것을 알아냈다'가 된다. 그에 적절하게 과거완료시제를 사용한다.

04 (1), (3) <보기>의 단어들을 사용하고, 중복 없이 문맥에 맞게 영작해야 하므로, '목적'의 의미를 표현할 때, 'so that 부사절'과 'in order to 부사구'를 어디에 쓰는 것이 좋을지 결정하는 것에 유의한다. (2) 과거완료시제를 적절히 사용한다.

05 so that은 목적을 이끄는 부사절 접속사이다. 따라서 '~하기 위해서'라고 해석되는 in order to 혹은 to부정사 구문으로 대체할 수 있으며, in order to를 대신하여 so as to를 써도 무방하다.

06 안창호가 신민회를 설립한 이유는 한국의 독립을 위해 싸우기 위함이었다.

07 미국으로 간 안창호는 미국에 거주하는 한국인들의 삶을 향상시키는 것을 도왔다고 하였다.

07 미국으로 간 안창호는 미국에 거주하는 한국인들의 삶을 향상시키는 것을 도왔다고 하였다.

08 백범일지에 쓰여 있는 '나의 소원'을 가리키는 말이다.

09 이봉창, 윤봉길, 백정기 삼의사의 묘는 효창 공원에 있음을 알 수 있다.

10 '나의 소원'에 있는 김구의 말은 한국의 독립에 대한 그의 열망과 조국에 대한 그의 사랑을 느끼게 한다.

창의사고력 서술형 문제   p.52

|모범답안|

01 (1) A: You know Dokdo is windy and foggy, don't you?
      B: Yes, I heard about it.
 (2) A: You know that there is a rock on Dokdo that looks like Korea, don't you?
      B: Yes, I heard about it.

02 (1) He shouted so that a passing ship could rescue him.
 (2) He used a telescope so that he could better look at the birds.

03 in 1889, who fought against Japanese rule. gathered and trained soldiers, where his soldiers earned one of their greatest victories against Japan

02 어법과 그림에 어울리는 내용으로 적절하게 영작한다.

단원별 모의고사   p.53~57

01 ⑤   02 rule[govern]   03 ①
04 ④   05 ②, ④
06 I'm dying to try it.
07 ⑤   08 ④   09 ①
10 (A) the symbols in Taegeukgi
   (B) the black lines
11 (1) was built   (2) built   (3) built
12 (a) You know about   (b) I'm looking forward
13 ②   14 ④   15 ④
16 (1) The goddess said that Pinocchio had lied.
   (2) Pooh was stung by bees after he had touched the hive.   17 ④   18 ⑤
19 ④   20 ②   21 ③
22 It shows a lot of things about Kim Koo's life.
23 ⓔ—ⓒ—ⓕ—ⓐ—ⓓ—ⓑ
24 He founded the New Korean Society in 1907 (to fight for Korea's independence).

01 ⑤번은 'statue(조각상)'에 관한 설명이다. 'state(상태)'에 대한 영어 설명은 'a condition or way of being that exists at a particular time'이다.

02 유의어 관계이다. 교육하다 : 통치하다

03 사체를 땅에 묻거나 어떤 것을 땅에 묻고 그것을 덮다

04 안중근에 대해 들어본 적이 있는지 묻는 말에 '아니, 없어. 그는 독립 운동가였어.'라고 답하는 것은 자연스럽지 못하다.

05 대화의 흐름상 '삼계탕을 요리하는 법을 아니?'라고 묻는 말은 어색하다.

06 'be dying to+동사원형'을 이용하여 '몹시 ~하고 싶다'는 기대를 나타낼 수 있다.

07 ⑤번의 'to'는 전치사로 명사나 동명사가 와야 한다.

08 보라가 얼마나 많은 시를 읽기를 원하는지는 대화에서 언급되어 있지 않다.

09 (A)는 'heard'의 목적어를 이끄는 명사절 접속사 'that'이 들어가고, (B)는 선행사 'treasures'를 수식하는 관계대명사절을 이끄는 'that'이 적절하다.

11 (1) 수원 화성이 지어졌다는 수동의 의미를 나타내므로 'be+과거분사'가 적절하다. (2) '누가 그것을 지었니?'라는 능동형 과거동사 'built'가 적절하고, (3)은 'a museum'을 수식하는 과거분사 'built'가 적절하다.

12 (a) You know ~, don't you?는 알고 있는지 물어보는 표현이고, (b) 앞으로 하고 싶은 일에 대한 기대를 표현할 때 'be looking forward to ~.'를 사용한다.

13 ② '~하기 위해서'라는 목적의 부사절을 만들 때, so that 또는 in order that 절 뒤에 can[may] 또는 could[might] 등의 조동사를 쓴다. became을 could[might] become으로 고치는 것이 적절하다.

14 자동차가 짙은 모래먼지로 뒤덮인 것은 하루 종일 황사가 온 탓이고, 과거보다 더 앞선 시점의 일이다. 과거완료시제로 쓰는 것이 적절하다.

15 모두 '목적'을 나타내는 부사절 접속사 'so that'인데, ④번만 '결과'의 의미로 쓰였다.

16 (1) 여신은 피노키오가 거짓말을 했다고 말했다. (2) 푸우는 벌집을 건드린 후에 벌들에게 쏘였다. hive: 벌집

17 김구는 1919년에 중국 상하이로 이동했다고 하였으므로 평생을 한국에서 살았다는 것은 위 글의 내용과 맞지 않다.

18 훗날 임시 정부의 주석이 되었다고 하였으므로 임시 정부를 떠난 것(left)이 아니라 가입한 것(joined)이라고 말하는 것이 적절하다.

19 한인 애국단은 김구가 일본에 맞서 싸우기 위해 1931년에 만든 비밀 조직으로, 이봉창과 윤봉길은 이 조직 소속이었다.

20 carry out은 '수행하다'라는 의미이므로 ②번이 적절하다.

21 밑줄 친 (B)는 목숨을 걸고 임무를 수행하려는 윤봉길의 의지를 나타낸다.

22 전시관은 김구의 삶에 관한 많은 것들을 보여 준다고 하였다.

23 안창호는 10대 때 서울에서 공부하였고(ⓔ) 더 나은 교육을 받기 위하여 미국으로 건너갔다(ⓒ). 미국에 거주하는 한국인들의 삶을 향상시켰고 그는 존경받는 지도자가 되었다(ⓕ). 다시 한국으로 돌아온 안창호는(ⓐ), 신민회를 설립하고(ⓓ) 임시 정부에도 가입하였다(ⓑ).

24 안창호는 한국의 독립을 위해 신민회를 설립하였다.

Meet the World

시험대비 실력평가 p.62

01 ③　　　02 knee　　　03 ④　　　04 ②

05 be covered with　　　06 ①

07 suggest　　08 ⑤

01 • 이 옷감은 천연(natural) 섬유로 만들어졌다. • 북악산은 방문객들에게 경탄할 만한 자연의(natural) 아름다움과 문화적 자산으로 깊은 인상을 남긴다.

02 헬멧과 무릎 보호대를 포함한 안전 장비를 착용하는 것 또한 권고된다. <영영풀이> '다리가 구부러지는 관절'의 의미로 'knee(무릎)'가 적절하다.

03 '외국에 있거나 외국으로 가는'의 의미로 'abroad(해외에, 해외로)'가 적절하다. 'aboard'는 '(배·항공기·열차·버스 등을) 타고'의 의미이다.

04 '자주 그리고 많은 사람에게 또는 많은 장소에서 일어나는'의 의미로 'common(흔한)'이 적절하다.

05 be covered with: ~로 덮여 있다

06 (A) 그녀는 네 명의 심사위원들을 놀라게 했고, 그들 모두로부터 '합격'을 얻었습니다. (B) 그들은 요한 바흐, 게오르크 헨델, 그리고 안토니오 비발디가 작곡한 음악을 추천합니다.

07 유의어 관계다. 풍경 : 제안하다

08 너한테서 멋진 생일 선물 받기를 기대하고 있을게! / '~을 기대하다'는 'look forward to+동명사'를 쓴다.

서술형 시험대비 p.63

01 (1) filled　(2) suggests　(3) appreciate

　　(4) landscape

02 waterfall(s)

03 (1) throughout　(2) confused　(3) wildly

　　(4) hot spring

04 (1) length, 길이　(2) north, 북쪽　(3) rival, 경쟁자

　　(4) wedding, 결혼식

05 tradition(s), traditional

01 (1) 그는 세상을 건강한 사람들로 가득 찬 더 나은 곳으로 만들길 희망합니다. (2) 아처 교수는 여러분의 삶에서 좋고 긍정적인 것을 보라고 제안합니다. (3) 이 행사는 어린이들로 하여금 모든 형태의 예술의 진가를 알아보는 것을 가르칩니다. (4) 뉴질랜드는 숨이 멎을 듯한 아름나운 경치와 풍부한 야생동물로 유명한 니리

이다.

02 나이아가라 폭포는 북아메리카에서 가장 인기 있는 폭포입니다.

03 (1) throughout: 도처에 (2) confused: 혼란스러워 하는 (3) wildly: 거칠게 (4) hot spring: 온천

04 (1) 한쪽 끝에서 반대편 끝까지 어떤 것을 측정하는 것 (2) 일출을 바라볼 때 당신의 왼쪽에 있는 방향 (3) 다른 사람과 같은 목적이나 목표를 위해 경쟁하는 사람 (4) 결혼식과 그에 따르는 식사나 파티와 같은 축하 행사

05 • 한국은 훌륭한 문화와 독특한 전통(tradition)을 가진 아름다운 나라입니다. • 그것은 "이열치열"이라는 전통적인(traditional) 방법이야. 명사 'way'를 수식하는 형용사가 적절하다.

교과서 Conversation

핵심 Check p.64~65

1 let's talk about what we will prepare for the World Food Festival

2 visit

교과서 대화문 익히기

Check(√) True or False p.66

1 T　　2 F　　3 T　　4 T

교과서 확인학습 p.68~69

Listen & Speak 1 A

1. Let's talk, other / what a kilt is / traditional clothing, looks like, knee-length, plaid pattern / with / unique because / interesting, to try, on

2. about, prepare / famous / popular, dish / What, look like / fried, with / interesting. Let's prepare

Listen & Speak 2 A

1. arrived in / looking forward to / suggest, visit / the highest, in a lot of / fantastic view / sounds

2. invited, potluck / know, share / recommend that /

suggest, take, How / spicy, to carry / for

Can you tell me about / a few years ago. First, let's / What food, famous for / The most famous, filled with, melted / suggestion, that are popular / suggest, Independence, history / information / pleasure

Welcome, capital, popular dish, lots of, beaches

시험대비 기본평가   p.70

01 suggest, visit   02 ④   03 ②
04 ⑤

01 상대방에게 무언가를 제안하거나 권유할 때 쓰는 표현으로 'I suggest (that)+주어+(should)+동사원형'을 사용한다.

02 B의 대답으로 보아 여행에 관한 주제로 이야기를 한다는 것을 알 수 있다. 'Let's talk about ~.(~에 대하여 이야기해 봅시다.)'라는 주제를 소개하는 표현이 적절하다.

03 '인도를 방문하면 무엇을 할 수 있을까?'라는 물음에 '나는 우리가 그곳을 방문할 것을 제안해.'라고 말하는 것은 어색하다.

04 'Let's talk about ~.(~에 대하여 이야기해 봅시다.)'는 주제를 소개하는 표현이다.

시험대비 실력평가   p.71~72

01 ⑤   02 ④   03 ③   04 ②
05 it is a skirt for men   06 ②
07 the highest mountain in Hong Kong and is in a lot of movies
08 visit Victoria Peak, enjoy the fantastic view   09 ④

01 Jessie가 몇 년 전에 거기에 갔었다는 말을 한 다음 '먼저 음식에 대해 이야기해 보자.'라고 말하는 것으로 보아 빈칸에는 그 도시에 관한 정보를 알려달라는 표현이 적절하다.

02 독립 기념관이 Andy가 가장 좋아하는 장소라는 내용은 대화에 언급되어 있지 않다.

03 포틀럭 저녁 모임에 나를 초대했다는 말에 이어서 → (C) 'the dinner'가 'a potluck dinner'를 받는 명사로 이어지고→ (B) 가져갈 음식을 추천해 달라고 부탁하고 → (A) 김밥을 추천한다. 마지막으로 (D) 긍정의 대답이 오는 것이 자연스럽다.

04 학생들은 다섯 살에 학교에 간다는 B의 대답으로 보아 영국의 학교생활에 관해 이야기해 보자는 ②가 자연스럽다.

05 남자를 위한 치마이기 때문에 킬트가 독특하다.

---

06 단수 주어인 It 다음에 looks와 병렬 관계인 단수 동사 has가 되어야 한다.

07 'the 최상급+단수 명사' 형태로 정관사 'the'를 추가하고, 'high'는 'highest'로 변형시킨다.

08 Mike와 그의 어머니는 빅토리아 피크를 방문하고 홍콩의 환상적인 경관을 즐길 것이다.

09 ④번은 '어느 나라를 조사할 것인지 이야기해 보자.'라는 말에 '그러고 싶지만, 그곳을 방문하는 것이 기대 돼.'라고 말하는 것은 어색하다.

서술형 시험대비   p.73

01 It is Independence Hall.
02 I suggest you visit Independence Hall, which is very important in American history.
03 I suggest you take some Korean food.
04 'Let's talk about traditional clothing from other countries.'

01 질문: 필라델피아에서 관광객들에게 인기 있는 장소는 어디인가?

02 '명사, who/which ~'에서 'who/which ~'는 앞에 오는 명사의 추가적인 설명을 하고 '접속사+대명사'로 바꾸어 쓸 수 있다.

03 동사 'suggest(제안하다)' 다음에는 명사절을 이끄는 접속사 'that'이 생략되고 'that'절에서는 조동사 'should'를 쓰는데, 이를 생략하고 동사원형을 사용하여 'I suggest (that)+주어+(should)+동사원형 ~.'의 구문으로 나타낸다.

04 'Let's talk about ~(~에 대하여 이야기해 보자.)'를 이용하여 영작한다.

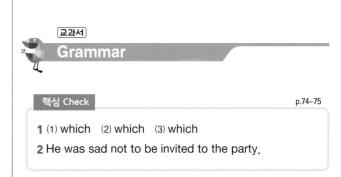

교과서
Grammar

핵심 Check   p.74~75

1 (1) which   (2) which   (3) which
2 He was sad not to be invited to the party.

시험대비 기본평가   p.76

01 ③   02 ⑤   03 ④   04 ⑤

01 '접속사+대명사'는 관계대명사로 바꿀 수 있고, 앞에 콤마가 있으면 '계속적 용법'의 관계대명사가 된다. 선행사가 사물이므로

계속적 용법의 관계대명사 which가 적절하다.

02 ① 부사적 용법(목적) ② 부사적 용법(목적) ③ 부사적 용법(감정의 원인) ④ 부사적 용법(판단의 근거) 조동사 must는 '~임에 틀림없다'는 의미로 판단에 쓰인다. ⑤ 명사적 용법(목적어)

03 who는 계속적 용법의 관계대명사로서, 선행사는 사람인 the boy이다. 콤마 뒤에 접속사 and와 주어로 대명사 he로 바꿔 쓸 수 있다.

04 <보기>는 부사적 용법(감정의 원인)이다. ①, ② 부사적 용법(목적) ③ 명사적 용법(목적어) ④ 부사적 용법(판단의 근거) 조동사 can't는 '~일 리 없다'라는 의미로 '판단'에 쓰인다. ⑤ 부사적 용법(감정의 원인)

01 ⓑ that → which, ⓒ which → who, ⓓ speak → speaks 또는 spoke, ⓔ which → that 또는 생략 또는 in which, ⓕ where → which 또는 lived in → lived

02 ③   03 who you have already heard about
04 ⑤   05 ④   06 ⑤   07 ④
08 ①   09 ④
10 She goes there to feed the cats.   11 ④
12 ④   13 ④   14 ①   15 ②

01 ⓑ 선행사는 the lecture of the professor Potter인데 계속적 용법이므로 that은 쓸 수 없다. ⓒ 선행사가 사람이므로 who ⓓ 선행사 a parrot이 단수이므로 관계대명사 뒤의 동사도 일치시킨다. ⓔ the way+that[in which] ⓕ 전치사 in이 있으므로, where를 which로 고치거나 in을 생략한다.

02 ③은 to부정사의 명사적 용법으로 사용되었다. 나머지는 모두 부사적 용법이다.

03 관계대명사의 계속적 용법으로 선행사 The Maori people을 받아 who로 시작하여 about으로 마무리하는 것이 적절하다.

04 빈칸은 모두 계속적 용법의 관계대명사가 들어가는 자리이다. 문장의 선행사는 각각 (A) 앞 문장 전체, (B) Wellington, (C) someone이다.

05 ①, ②, ③번은 계속적 용법의 관계대명사 which가 적절하다. ⑤번은 동사의 수의 일치가 부적절, ① that → which, ② who → which, ③ of which → which, ⑤ come → comes

06 to부정사의 부정은 to부정사 바로 앞에 not을 쓴다. not to see는 in order not to see 또는 so as not to see로도 표현 가능하다.

07 be동사 뒤에 감정을 나타내는 형용사와 to부정사가 결합하면, '감정의 원인이나 이유'가 되는데, be동사 앞에 조동사 will이 오면, '~한다면'의 뜻이 되어, '조건'의 용법으로 쓰인다. ②의 경우, 'be heard to say' 형태는 '마을 사람들이 말하는 것이 들리다'는 내용

이 되므로 옳지 않다.

08 ① 내가 삼촌에게 수리를 맡겼고, '삼촌이 차를 수리한 것'이 선행사이므로, 관계대명사 which가 적절하다.

09 ④ 내용상 '코로나 전염병이 발발한' 2019년을 선행사로 받는 관계대명사이므로, 관계대명사 앞에 in이 있어야 한다. basketball court와는 무관하다. which를 in which 또는 관계부사 when으로 바꾸는 것이 적절하다.

10 엄마가 미주에게 미나가 공원에 매일 가는 이유를 물었고, 고양이들에게 '먹이를 주기 위해' 가는 것이므로, to부정사의 부사적 용법을 활용한다. 3인칭 단수 현재시제이므로 go를 goes로 하는 것에 유의한다.

11 주어진 문장의 to threaten과 ④번은 to부정사의 부사적 용법의 '목적'으로 쓰였다. ① 명사적 용법 ② 부사적 용법의 '결과' ③ 부사적 용법의 '감정의 원인' ⑤ 가주어 It과 함께 쓰인 진주어로 명사적 용법 *threaten: 위협하다

12 주어진 문장의 to watch와 ④번은 부사적 용법의 '판단의 근거'로 쓰였다. '적은 마오리 전사들의 하카 동작들을 보고 두려웠음에 틀림없다' ① 부사적 용법의 '목적' ② 부사적 용법의 '결과' ③ 부사적 용법의 '감정의 이유, 원인' ⑤ 형용사적 용법의 '명사 수식'(아기 고양이들을 덮어 줄 어떤 것)

13 주어진 문장의 to learn은 to부정사의 부사적 용법의 '목적'으로 쓰였다. ④만 부사적 용법 중 '감정의 원인, 이유'이다.

14 주어진 문장의 to scare는 to부정사의 부사적 용법의 '목적'으로 쓰였다. ①만 형용사적 용법(명사 수식)으로 사용되었다.

15 옳은 문장은 ⓐ, ⓔ 2개이다. ⓑ who → which, ⓒ and who → who, 또는 and who → and she ⓓ who → which

01 (1) The Maori people dance to scare the enemy.
(2) Dolphins come up to the surface to breathe.
(3) She must be unwise to believe the word.
(4) The native people of New Zealand will be glad to hear the word.
(5) Jiho's room is not easy to clean.
(6) Simcheong was pleased to see her father again.

02 (1) George Washington is widely known for the episode of his honesty, which was not true.
(2) Sumin fell in love with Brian, who met her only twice.
(3) The Maori people were so good at haka dancing, which made the visitors also dance with excitement.
(4) I added some more hot sauce into the food, which made my mom upset.

03 (1) Jack walked to school to save some money.

(2) Caroline exercises hard every day to lose weight.

(3) Potter was surprised to watch the news.

(4) Angela woke up to find herself alone in the dark.

(5) Sam must be happy to meet her old friend.

04 Jisoo's parents volunteered to serve the meal during lunchtime, which made her feel proud.

05 (1) My grandma exercises every day to keep healthy.

(2) She was pleased to receive thank-you notes from her neighbors.

(3) Sandra went to the river to catch some fish.

(4) The stone was too heavy for me to lift.

(5) You need ice and sugar to make Bingsu.

(6) The problem was impossible for Peter to solve in an hour.

(7) A lot of firefighters ran into the woods to rescue the koalas.

06 (1) that → which

(2) who → which

(3) who → which

07 we learned the word kiwi, which has several meanings

---

01 (1) to부정사의 부사적 용법 중 '목적'이다. (2) to부정사의 부사적 용법 중 '목적'이다. '~로 올라오다'는 come up to로 표현한다. (3) to부정사의 부사적 용법 중 '판단의 근거'이다. 조동사 must는 '~임에 틀림없다'로 사용한다. (4) to부정사의 부사적 용법 중 '조건'이다. (5) to부정사의 부사적 용법 중 '형용사 수식'이다. '형용사+to부정사'는 '~하기에 …한'으로 해석한다. (6) to부정사의 부사적 용법 중 '감정의 원인'이다.

02 각 문장의 관계대명사의 선행사는 (1)은 the episode, (2)는 Brian, (3), (4)는 앞 문장 전체이다.

03 각 문장의 to부정사는 부사 용법 중 (1) 목적, (2) 목적, (3) 감정의 원인 (4) 결과 (5) 판단의 근거 등으로 사용되었다. (5)에 조동사 must를 반드시 사용해야 하기 때문에 Sam must be happy로 문장을 만드는 것에 유의한다.

04 앞 문장 전체 내용을 선행사로, '계속적' 용법의 관계대명사 which를 사용한다. volunteer가 동사로 사용되는 것에 유의한다.

05 to부정사의 부사적 용법을 사용하는 것이므로, 해석과 어법에 맞게 고친다. (1) 내 할머니는 건강을 유지하기 위해 매일 운동하신다. (2) 그녀는 이웃들로부터 감사 쪽지들을 받아서 기뻤다. (3) Sandra는 물고기를 잡으러 강에 갔다. (4) 그 돌은 내가 들기에는 너무 무거웠다. (5) 네가 빙수를 만들기 위해서는 얼음과

설탕이 필요하다. (6) 그 문제는 Peter가 한 시간 안에 풀기에 불가능했다. (7) 수많은 소방관들이 코알라들을 구출하기 위해서 숲으로 뛰어들었다.

06 모든 문장이 앞 문장 전체가 선행사이므로, 계속적 용법의 which가 적절하다.

07 우리말을 영작하면 Yesterday, we learned the word kiwi, and it has several meanings.가 된다. 이 문장에서 and it을 계속적 용법의 관계대명사 which로 바꿔 영작하는 것이 적절하다.

교과서
Reading

확인문제   p.82

1 T 2 F 3 F 4 T

확인문제   p.83

1 T 2 F 3 T 4 T 5 T 6 F

교과서 확인학습 A   p.84~85

01 a place of natural beauty, lakes, waterfalls

02 two main islands

03 are mountains, are covered with

04 be amazed by

05 many hot springs, with

06 Because of, have been made

07 will surely appreciate

08 hear, comes to

09 a couple of meanings

10 the name, delicious

11 is grown, is known as

12 one, New Zealand's native birds

13 special to, because, symbol

14 a nickname for, from

15 are sometimes called

16 that, the name of

17 confused, uses, which has

18 let's talk, They, the native people

19 live on, long before, arrived

20 an important part, today's

21 is taught, there are

22 in many parts of

23 visit, villages, experience, culture

24 say, to, will be glad to hear, means

25 Have, watched

26 look scary because, shout, move, wildly

27 who, heard about, doing, as

28 however, do, at sport matches

29 For example, national rugby team members, before

30 famous all over

31 will, agree that, must be scared

32 Like, a national symbol

교과서 확인학습 B
p.86~87

1 New Zealand is a place of natural beauty. It has many beautiful lakes and waterfalls.

2 New Zealand has two main islands, the South Island and the North Island.

3 In the South Island, there are mountains that are covered with snow all year round.

4 You will be amazed by the fantastic views.

5 In the North Island, there are many hot springs, lakes, and areas with green grass.

6 Because of its natural beauty, many famous movies have been made in New Zealand.

7 If you visit New Zealand, you will surely appreciate its nature.

8 When you hear the word kiwi, what comes to your mind?

9 Maybe a fruit, but, in New Zealand the word kiwi has a couple of meanings.

10 First, kiwi is the name of a delicious, green fruit.

11 A lot of kiwi fruit is grown there, so New Zealand is known as the land of kiwi fruit.

12 Kiwi is also the name of one of New Zealand's native birds.

13 The kiwi is special to New Zealanders because it is the symbol of the nation.

14 Also, kiwi is a nickname for people from New Zealand.

15 Today, New Zealanders are sometimes called Kiwis throughout the world.

16 Now, you know that kiwi is the name of a fruit, a bird, and also a people.

17 Next time, don't become confused when someone uses the word kiwi, which has several meanings.

18 Now, let's talk about the Maori. They are the native people of New Zealand.

19 They went to live on the islands long before Europeans arrived.

20 The Maori culture is an important part of today's New Zealand society.

21 The Maori language is taught at some schools and there are Maori language radio and TV stations.

22 There are Maori villages in many parts of the country.

23 You can visit Maori villages and experience Maori culture.

24 If you say "kia ora" to the villagers, they will be glad to hear it. It means "hi" in English.

25 Have you ever watched the haka?

26 The haka may look scary because haka dancers shout and move their bodies wildly.

27 The Maori people, who you've already heard about, started doing the haka as a war dance.

28 Today, however, New Zealanders do the haka at sport matches, weddings, or other important events.

29 For example, New Zealand's national rugby team members do the haka before every match.

30 It is famous all over the world.

31 If you see the haka, you will probably agree that the rival team must be scared.

32 Like the kiwi bird, the haka is a national symbol.

시험대비 실력평가
p.88~91

01 ④   02 ③

03 New Zealand is made up with two main islands, the South Island and the North Island.

04 It's because it is the symbol of the nation.

05 ④   06 ②   07 ④   08 ③

09 ⑤

10 They do the haka before every match.

11 the rival team must be scared

12 ③   13 ⑤

14 They do the haka at sport matches, weddings, or other important events.

15 ④   16 ②   17 ④

18 It's because a lot of kiwi fruit is grown there.

19 ⑤   20 We can experience Maori culture.

21 ④   22 appreciate 23 ③   24 ③

01 이어지는 내용은 뉴질랜드 자연의 아름다움에 관하여 이야기하고 있으므로 ④번이 가장 적절하다.

02 ⓑ는 '일 년 내내'라는 의미이다. ①, ④ 가끔, ② 갑자기, ③ 일 년 내내, ⑤ 여기저기에

03 뉴질랜드는 두 개의 주요한 섬인 남섬과 북섬으로 이루어져 있다.

04 키위새가 뉴질랜드 사람들에게 특별한 이유는 그 새가 국가의 상징이기 때문이다.

05 키위는 뉴질랜드 출신 사람에 대한 별명이라고 하였다.

06 위 글은 뉴질랜드에서 키위라는 단어가 갖는 여러 가지 의미에 관한 글이다. 따라서 ②번이 가장 적절하다.

07 마오리어를 몇몇 학교에서 가르친다고 하였다.

08 마오리족은 전쟁 춤으로 하카를 추었지만 오늘날 뉴질랜드 사람들은 하카를 운동 경기, 결혼식, 또는 다른 중요한 행사가 있을 때 한다는 연결이 자연스럽다. 따라서 however가 적절하다.

09 마오리족은 하카 춤을 줄 때 소리 지르고 몸을 사납게 움직인다고 하였다.

10 뉴질랜드의 럭비 국가 대표 팀 선수들은 모든 경기 전에 하카를 춘다고 하였다.

11 must는 강한 추측을 나타내는 의미로 쓰일 수 있다.

12 하카는 무섭게 보이고 전쟁 춤으로 추었다고 하였으므로 문맥상 ③번이 가장 적절하다.

13 당신이 하카를 본다면, 상대 팀이 겁을 먹을 것이라는 것에 동의할 것이라고 하였으므로 ⑤번이 글의 내용과 일치한다.

14 오늘날 사람들은 운동 경기나 결혼식, 다른 중요한 행사에서 하카를 춘다고 하였다.

15 every 뒤에는 단수 명사가 온다. 따라서 match라고 써야 한다.

16 키위는 여러 뜻을 가지고 있기 때문에 그 단어를 사용할 때 혼동하지 말라는 말이 문맥상 가장 적절하다.

17 키위가 뉴질랜드 출신의 사람들을 부르는 별명이라고 말하고 난 후 오늘날 뉴질랜드인들이 전 세계적으로 키위라고 불린다는 설명이 이어지는 것이 적절하다.

18 뉴질랜드가 키위의 나라로 알려진 이유는 많은 키위가 그곳에서 자라기 때문이다.

19 마오리족에 대해 이야기해 보자고 말하며 (C) 마오리족이 누구인지 설명, 그들이 오늘날 뉴질랜드 사회의 중요한 부분이라고 말함. - (B) 그것에 대한 뒷받침 문장을 진술. - (A) (B)에서 언급한 마오리 마을에 방문하여 그들의 문화를 경험할 수 있다고 말함.

20 마오리 마을을 방문하면 마오리 문화를 경험할 수 있다.

21 밑줄 친 ⓐ는 감정의 원인을 나타내는 to부정사의 부사적 용법으로 쓰였다. ① 부사적 용법 중 판단의 이유 ② 진주어 ③ 형용사

적 용법(paper 수식) ④ 부사적 용법 중 감정의 원인 ⑤ 부사적 용법 중 목적(~하기 위해서)

22 무언가의 좋은 질을 알아봤기 때문에 그것을 좋아하게 되는 것은 '진가를 알아보다, 인정하다(appreciate)'이다.

23 사물을 선행사로 취하는 관계대명사이므로 which가 적절하다.

24 굉장히 멋진 경관에 놀랄 것이라고 하였으므로 ③번이 글의 내용과 일치한다.

서술형 시험대비
p.92~93

01 In the South Island, there are mountains that are covered with snow all year around.

02 We should go to the North Island.

03 If you visit New Zealand, you will surely appreciate its nature.

04 It is famous for its natural beauty.

05 a fruit, a bird, and also a people

06 which

07 A lot of kiwi fruit is grown in New Zealand.

08 several meanings of kiwi

09 The Maori went to live on New Zealand long before Europeans arrived.

10 We can find Maori villages in many parts of the country.

11 We should say "kia ora."

12 Canada → New Zealand
their food → their culture

13 Have you ever watched the haka?

14 It's because haka dancers shout and move their bodies wildly.

15 We are likely to see them do the haka before their match.

16 The haka, the kiwi bird

01 뉴질랜드의 남섬에는 일 년 내내 눈으로 덮인 산들이 있다고 하였다.

02 북섬에는 많은 온천이 있다고 하였으므로, 온천을 즐기고 싶다면 북섬으로 가야한다.

03 시간이나 조건의 부사절에서 현재시제로 미래를 표현한다. 따라서 will visit이 아닌 visit이라고 쓰는 것이 적절하다.

04 뉴질랜드는 자연의 아름다움으로 유명한 곳임을 알 수 있다.

05 위 글에 언급된 키위의 다양한 의미로는 과일, 새, 그리고 국민의 명칭이 있다.

06 불완전한 절을 이끌며 콤마 뒤에서 쓰이는 것은 관계대명사 which이다.

07 많은 키위들이 뉴질랜드에서 자란다고 하였다.

08 해석: 키위의 몇 가지 의미를 이해하지 않으면, 당신은 혼란을 느낄 것이다.

09 마오리족은 유럽인들이 도착하기 오래 전에 뉴질랜드에 와서 살았다고 하였다.

10 나라의 여러 곳에 마오리 마을이 있다고 하였다.

11 "kia ora"는 영어로 "안녕"이라는 의미의 마오리어라고 하였다.

12 마오리족은 뉴질랜드의 원주민이며 그들의 문화는 오늘날 뉴질랜드 사회의 중요한 부분이라고 하였다.

13 하카를 본 적이 있는지 경험을 묻고 있으므로 현재완료 시제를 사용하여 답하는 것이 적절하다.

14 하카 춤을 추는 사람들이 소리 지르고, 그들의 몸을 사납게 움직이기 때문에 하카는 무서워 보일 수도 있다고 하였다.

15 위 글의 내용에 따르면, 우리는 뉴질랜드 럭비 선수들이 경기 전에 하카를 추는 것을 볼 수 있다.

16 키위뿐만 아니라 하카는 나라의 상징이다.

영역별 핵심문제
p.95~99

01 (a)chieve　02 ④　03 ⑤　04 ①
05 With the help of　06 ③　07 ④
08 I suggest we watch a soccer game.　09 ④
10 It is a big sandwich filled with beef and melted cheese.
11 ③　12 ③, ⑤　13 ④　14 ④
15 ⑤
16 The public library introduced a new system, which would help the people to easily borrow the audio books that had always been difficult to borrow.　17 ②
18 ①
19 do the haka to scare their opponents
20 There are many hot springs, lakes, and areas with green grass in the North Island of New Zealand.　21 ②　22 ⑤　23 ③
24 scare　25 ⑤　26 (C)–(B)–(A)
27 We should visit a Maori village.
28 Many people visit New Zealand to enjoy the beautiful nature.　29 ④

01 유의어 관계다. 해외에 – 성취하다, 달성하다

02 (A) 중국인들은 판다를 용기의 상징으로 여깁니다. (B) 마오리족 사람들은 뉴질랜드의 원주민입니다.

03 십자 모양의 선과 사각형으로 된 무늬

04 '초대받은 사람들이 먹을 것을 가지고 오는 식사'의 의미로 'potluck(각자 준비한 음식을 나눠먹는 식사)'이 적절하다.

05 with the help of: ~의 도움을 받아서

06 ③ recommend: 추천하다

07 '그룹 1의 사진이 매우 좋다고 생각한다.'라는 B의 답으로 보아 그룹 1의 사진에 대한 주제로 이야기를 하고 있다는 것을 알 수 있다.

08 제안하는 표현은 'I suggest (that)+주어+(should)+동사원형'을 이용한다.

09 주어진 문장이 '멋진 제안이야. 먹어볼게.'라는 뜻이므로 샌드위치에 관한 이야기 다음인 ④가 적절하다.

10 cheese steak sandwich는 '소고기와 녹인 치즈로 채워진 큰 샌드위치'라고 하고 있다.

11 '미국의 독립 기념관은 무엇을 위한 것인가?'에 대한 답은 대화에 언급되어 있지 않다.

12 ① 선행사가 lecture이고, 계속적 용법이다. that → which ② 계속적 용법의 관계대명사 which는 맞게 쓰였으나 선행사가 a traditional market이므로, 동사는 단수 형태를 써야 한다. sell → sells ④ 내용상 선행사가 사람이 아닌 the works이다. 관계대명사 뒤의 be동사도 are이다. who → which

13 '모든 문장이 '회사에 늦지 않기 위해서'라는 목적을 나타내는데, ④만 '일찍 일어나지만 늦지 않는다'라는 이상한 내용이 되고 있다.

14 주어진 문장의 to find는 부사적 용법의 '목적'으로 사용되었으며, ④를 제외한 모든 문장은 쓰임이 같다. ④의 to make는 동사 like의 '목적어'로서, 명사적 용법으로 사용되었다.

15 주어진 문장의 to film은 부사적 용법의 '목적'으로 사용되었다. ⑤의 to smoke는 동사 promised의 '목적어'로서, 명사적 용법으로 사용되었다. 나머지는 각각 ①, ④ 부사적 용법의 '목적' ② 부사적 용법의 '원인' ③ 부사적 용법의 '결과'이다.

16 본문에 나온 표현만으로 계속적 관계대명사와 제한적 관계대명사를 모두 사용해야 하기 때문에, 보충 설명이 필요한 두 번째 문장을 계속적 용법의 'which'로 연결하는 것이 적절하다.

17 관계대명사 뒤의 동사는 선행사의 수에 일치시켜야 한다. 선행사가 class이므로, which are → which is로 하는 것이 적절하다.

18 '접속사와 대명사 and it은 관계대명사 which로 쓸 수 있고, 'the one that(선행사+관계대명사)'는 what과 같다. ①은 선행사 뒤에 what이 있어 부적절하다.

19 to부정사의 부사적 용법을 활용하여 알맞게 영작한다.

20 뉴질랜드의 북섬에는 많은 온천과 호수, 초원 지역이 있다고 하였다.

21 빈칸 (A)에는 전치사 with가 들어간다. ① be anxious about: 조바심을 내다 ② be crowded with: ~으로 붐비다 ③ devote oneself to: ~에 전념하다, 몰두하다 ④ apply for: ~에 지원하다 ⑤ be accustomed to: ~에 익숙하다

22 Because는 접속사이므로 주어와 동사가 포함된 절을 이끌어야

한다. 따라서 Because of라고 쓰는 것이 적절하다.

23 마오리인들이 전쟁 춤으로 하카를 추기 시작했다는 문장에 이어지는 예시문은 뉴질랜드 럭비 국가 대표 팀이 경기 전에 하카를 하는 것에 관한 내용이므로, 오늘날 뉴질랜드 사람이 운동 경기에서 하카를 한다는 말이 ③번에 들어가는 것이 적절하다.

24 '당신이 하카를 본다면, 상대 팀이 겁을 먹을 것이라는 것에 아마 동의할 것이다'라고 하였으므로 뉴질랜드 럭비 국가 대표 팀 선수들이 경기 전에 하카를 추는 이유는 상대 팀 선수들을 겁주기 위해서임을 알 수 있다.

25 하카 춤을 추는 사람들이 소리 지르고, 그들의 몸을 사납게 움직이기 때문에 하카는 무서워 보일 수 있다고 하였다.

26 (C) 뉴질랜드에 대해 아는지 물으며 간단한 소개 (B) 뉴질랜드에 온다면 마오리 마을을 방문하여 마오리족의 전통 요리를 먹어 보는 것을 제안함 (A) 그들의 요리 방법에 관한 이야기로 이어지는 것이 가장 자연스럽다.

27 뉴질랜드 원주민 문화를 보고 싶다면 마오리 마을을 방문해야 한다.

28 많은 사람들은 아름다운 자연을 즐기기 위해 뉴질랜드를 방문한다고 하였다.

29 뉴질랜드는 두 개의 본섬과 600개의 작은 섬들로 되어 있다고 하였다.

단원별 예상문제
p.100~103

01 natural 02 ③
03 I'm looking forward to our visit. 04 ③
05 ④ 06 traditional 07 ③
08 ⑤
09 are spoken → speak, visits → visit
10 ①
11 (1) ⓐ (2) ⓒ (3) ⓕ (4) ⓓ (5) ⓓ (6) ⓔ (7) ⓖ (8) ⓑ
   (9) ⓕ (10) ⓒ (11) ⓔ (12) ⓖ (13) ⓐ
12 ③ 13 ② 14 ④ 15 ⑤
16 ③ 17 Because of its natural beauty.
18 hills → mountains / tall trees → green grass
19 ③ 20 ③

01 반의어 관계다. 혼란스러워 하는-침착한 : 인위적인-자연의, 천연의

02 시골을 가로지르거나 숲을 지나가는 거친 길

03 '~을 기대하다'라는 표현으로 'I'm looking forward to+명사/동명사'를 사용한다.

04 Victoria Peak은 홍콩에서 가장 높은 산이다.

05 남자를 위한 치마라고 했기 때문에 'common'을 'unique'로 바꾸어야 한다.

06 '오랜 시간 동안 한 무리의 사람들에게 계속되어 온 관습이나 행

동 방식을 따르는'의 의미로 'traditional(전통적인)'이 적절하다.

07 빈칸 다음에 '그건 뜨거운 감자튀김이 곁들여진 튀긴 생선이야.'라고 G가 말하는 것으로 보아 'fish and chips'가 어떻게 생겼는지 묻는 말이 적절하다.

08 미트 파이가 어떻게 생겼는지는 대화에서 언급되어 있지 않다.

09 사람들이 영어를 사용하는 능동의 의미이므로 수동태 'are spoken'을 'speak'로 고치고, 복수 주어 'lots of tourists' 뒤에 복수 동사 'visit'이 적절하다.

10 관계대명사 '계속적' 용법의 문장들이다. ①번의 that을 which로 고쳐야 한다.

11 (3) only to V는 '~했으나 결국 ~하다'라는 뜻이다. (6) must have p.p.는 '~했음에 틀림없다'는 뜻이므로 '판단'을 표현한다. (13) '진주어'로 쓰인 '명사적' 용법

12 ③번은 선행사가 sea water가 아니라 '앞 문장 전체'이다.

13 ⓐ, ⓒ, ⓓ, ⓔ는 to부정사의 부사적 용법 중 '목적'이다. 나머지는 각각 명사적 용법으로 ⓑ, ⓕ는 목적어로, ⓖ는 진주어로 쓰였다.

14 주어진 문장의 to부정사는 부사적 용법 중 '감정의 원인'으로 쓰였다. 일반적으로 '감정의 형용사+to부정사'의 결합에서 앞에 조동사 will이 오면, 부사적 용법 중 '조건'이 되는데, 지금 주어진 문장의 경우에는 조건의 If절이 있으므로, '감정의 원인'으로 보는 것이 적절하다. ④만 부사적 용법 중 '감정의 원인, 이유'이다. ① 부사 용법 중 '결과' ② 명사적 용법(진주어) ③ 부사적 용법 중 '목적' ⑤ 명사적 용법(목적어)

15 이어지는 내용으로 보아 마오리족의 문화는 오늘날 뉴질랜드 사회의 중요한 부분이라고 말하는 것이 가장 적절하다.

16 나라의 여러 곳에 마오리 마을이 있다고 하였으므로 한 장소에 집중되어 있다는 ③번은 글의 내용과 일치하지 않는다.

17 뉴질랜드 자연의 아름다움 때문에 많은 유명한 영화들이 뉴질랜드에서 촬영되었다.

18 남섬에는 일 년 내내 눈으로 덮인 산들이 있으며, 북섬에는 높은 나무가 아닌 초원 지역이 있다고 하였다.

19 주격 관계대명사 which의 선행사는 a Maori village이므로 단수 취급하는 것이 적절하다.

20 뉴질랜드의 상징이 몇 개 있는지는 위 글을 읽고 알 수 없다.

서술형 실전문제
p.104~105

01 She will prepare fish and chips for the festival.
02 Why don't we visit Victoria Peak?
03 (1) New Zealand is known as the land of kiwi fruit, where a lot of kiwi fruit is grown.
   (2) I won't get confused when somebody uses the word kiwi, which has several meanings.

(3) Janet received a letter of invitation from her friend, which she didn't read.

(4) All the employees in the company stop working at noon, when they go out for lunch.

(5) The boss praised Sean, who didn't mean to do well this time.

04 to take pictures of the beautiful night scenery

05 you will probably agree that the rival team must be scared

06 sing → shout / happy → scary

07 The Maori people started doing the haka as a war dance.

08 which is a bird native to New Zealand

09 600 smaller islands

01 세라는 음식 축제를 위해 무엇을 준비할 것인가?

02 제안이나 권유를 나타내는 표현으로 'Why don't we ~?(~하는 것이 어때?)'를 사용할 수 있다.

03 선행사에 따라 who, which, when, where 등에 유의하여 영작한다.

04 to부정사의 부사적 용법 중 '목적'을 이용한다.

05 상대팀이 겁을 먹는 것은 감정을 느끼는 것이므로 과거분사 scared를 쓰는 것에 유의한다.

06 하카 춤을 추는 사람들은 소리 지르고 그들의 몸을 사납게 움직이기 때문에 하카는 무서워 보일 수도 있다고 하였다.

07 마오리인들은 전쟁 춤으로 하카를 추기 시작했다고 하였다. 는 뉴질랜드 태생의 새라는 부연 설명을 제시하는 절이다.

09 뉴질랜드는 두 개의 본섬과 600개의 작은 섬들로 되어 있다고 하였다.

창의사고력 서술형 문제 p.106

|모범답안|

01 (1) A: Let's talk about school life in Canada.
   B: Students start a new school year in September.

(2) A: Let's talk about school life in the UK.
   B: Students go to school at the age of five.

(3) A: Let's talk about school life in New Zealand.
   B: Students learn the Maori language.

02 (1) which means she likes foreign cultures (2) which can offer her opportunities to study foreign cultures more (3) where she can study foreign languages deeply 등 어법과 내용에 맞으면 정답

03 the third largest island in Europe, Dublin, which stands for the green land, the Cliffs of Moher,

which show the beautiful nature of Ireland, traditional dish, bread boiled in milk with some sugar, get refreshed

단원별 모의고사 p.107~111

01 ⑤   02 activity   03 ③   04 ④
05 ⑤   06 ③   07 ⑤
08 What would you recommend that I take?
09 I suggest we look right before
10 ③
11 (1) People are afraid of the corona virus, which causes the critical disease.
   (2) People hope the cure will come out soon not to worry any longer.
12 ③   13 ③
14 (1) Ladders are linked with a strange belief, and it is that passing under them brings bad luck.
   (2) Ladders are linked with a strange belief, which is that passing under them brings bad luck.
15 ②   16 ③
17 which would bring me good luck   18 ③
19 (B) a fruit   (C) a bird   (D) a people
20 We can call them kiwi.   21 ③
22 ①   23 ④
24 It means "hi" in English. 25 ②

01 ⑤번은 'collaborator(협력자)'에 관한 설명이다. 'rival(경쟁자)'에 대한 영어 설명은 'a person who is competing for the same object or goal as another'이다.

02 '동사-명사'의 관계이다. 성취하다-업적 : 행동하다-활동

03 '갑자기 어떤 생각을 하다'라는 의미로 'come to one's mind(생각이 떠오르다)'가 적절하다.

04 '키위라는 단어를 들으면 무엇이 떠오르니?'라는 A의 물음에 '사과보다 키위를 더 좋아해.'라고 말하는 것은 어색하다.

05 ⑤번은 요청을 하는 표현이다.

06 ③번의 'filled'는 명사 'sandwich'를 수식하는 과거분사로 올바르게 사용되었다.

07 미국 역사에서 중요하기 때문에 독립 기념관을 방문해 보라고 제안한다.

09 'look right'를 이용하여 '길을 건너기 전에 오른쪽을 보는 것을 제안해'라고 말하는 것이 적절하다.

10 나머지는 제안이나 권유를 나타내는 표현이고, ③은 이야기하고 싶은 주제를 소개할 때 사용하는 표현이다.

11 내용을 정확히 이해하고, 조건에 맞게 질문에 답하도록 한다. (1) 관계대명사 which를 활용한다. (2) to부정사의 '부사적' 용법을 사용해야 하므로 to worry를 쓰되, not은 to 앞에 쓰는 것에 유의한다.

12 ③의 to call은 동사 like의 목적어로 쓰인 명사적 용법이고, 다른 문장들은 모두 부사적 용법으로 쓰였다. 내용상으로도, Kiwi라고 부르는 것이 아니라, 다른 나라 사람들에 의해 불리는 것이므로 to be called라고 하는 것이 적절하다.

13 ③의 to learn은 부사적 용법 중 '감정의 원인'으로 쓰였다. ①, ④, ⑤는 명사적 용법, ②는 형용사적 용법이다.

14 선행사는 a strange belief이고, 'and it is that'은 'which is that'으로 명사절 접속사 that을 쓰는 것에 유의한다.

15 밑줄 친 which는 '계속적' 용법의 관계대명사이다. ①, ④는 의문대명사, ③, ⑤번은 전치사의 목적어 역할로 쓰인 관계대명사의 제한적 용법이다.

16 to be는 '늦지 않기 위해서'라는 부사적 용법 중 '목적'으로 쓰였다. ③만 부사적 용법 중 '목적'이다. ① likes의 목적어로 쓰인 명사적 용법 ② 진주어로 쓰인 명사적 용법 ④ forget의 목적어로 쓰인 명사적 용법 ⑤ 주어로 쓰인 명사적 용법이다.

17 글자 수를 맞추려면 계속적 용법의 관계대명사 which를 사용해야 한다. 7 단어로 영작한다면 which 대신 and it을 쓰는 것이 적절하다.

18 (A) be known as ~: ~로 알려지다 ① introduce A to B: A를 B에게 소개하다 ② be worried about: ~에 대해 걱정하다 ③ think of A as B: A를 B로 여기다 ④ look into: ~을 조사하다 ⑤ deal with: ~를 상대하다, 다루다

19 키위는 과일, 새, 그리고 국민의 명칭이라고 하였다.

20 뉴질랜드 출신 사람들을 부르는 별명이 키위라고 하였다. 따라서 우리는 그들을 키위라고 부를 수 있다.

21 뉴질랜드에서 많은 키위가 자란다고 했을 뿐, 키위가 뉴질랜드 사람들이 가장 좋아하는 과일이라는 말은 나와 있지 않다.

22 뉴질랜드에는 두 개의 본섬이 있다는 문장이 제시된 후 남섬과 북섬에 대한 소개가 이어지는 것이 적절하다.

23 뉴질랜드에서 몇 편의 영화가 촬영되었는지는 위 글을 읽고 답할 수 없다.

24 "kia ora"는 영어로 "안녕하세요."를 의미한다.

25 밑줄 친 (A)에 이어지는 문장에서 제시된 바와 같이, 몇몇 학교에서 마오리어를 가르치고 있고, 마오리어의 라디오와 TV 방송국이 있고, 그 나라의 여러 곳에 마오리 마을이 있으므로 ②번이 가장 적절하다.

Lesson 7

How to Get Along with People

시험대비 실력평가 — p.116

01 ③　　　02 thoughtful　　　03 ⑤
04 ②　　　05 get along, with　　　06 ④
07 ⑤

01 • 저것들은 인터뷰를 위한 적절한 옷이 아니다. • 그들의 목표는 한국인들 사이에서 적절한 한국어 사용을 촉진하는 것이다.

02 그 고등학교 교장은 그러한 사려 깊은 표현에 감동을 받았다. <영영풀이> '사람들을 행복하게 하거나 편안하게 하기 위해 할 수 있는 일들을 항상 생각하는'의 의미로 'thoughtful(사려 깊은)'이 적절하다.

03 '정직하고 진실하며, 당신이 정말로 느끼고 믿는 것에 근거하는'이라는 의미로 'sincere(진심어린)'가 적절하다.

04 '어떤 일이나 사람이 미래에 일어날 일에 준비가 되도록 하다'의 의미로 'prepare(준비하다)'가 적절하다.

05 get along with: ~와 어울리다, 잘 지내다

06 (A) 당신이 인터넷에 게시하는 정보는 삭제할지라도 영원히 인터넷에 남아 있다는 것을 기억하라. (B) 여러분이 이 프로그램에 관심이 있다면, 단지 100명의 운이 좋은 학생들만이 이 학교에 다닐 수 있기 때문에 서둘러야 합니다.

07 나머지는 '형용사-명사'의 관계이지만, ⑤는 '동사-명사'의 관계이다.

서술형 시험대비 — p.117

01 (1) suggestions　(2) emotional　(3) relaxed
　　(4) appreciate
02 (n)ervous
03 (1) ignore　(2) regret　(3) accidentally　(4) mind
04 (1) responsibility, 책임　(2) apology, 사과
　　(3) relationship, 관계　(4) generous, 너그러운

01 (1) 교육과 여러분의 학교를 나아지게 하기 위한 제안이나 의견이 있으세요? (2) 어떤 사람들은 애완동물들이 감정적인 지원으로 환자들이 더 빨리 회복되도록 도울 수도 있다고 믿습니다. (3) 스트레칭은 건강하고 느긋한 마음을 갖기 위한 좋은 방법이다. (4) 누군가 우리말을 경청해 주면 그건 그 사람의 관심을 나타내는 것이므로 그것을 고마워한다.

02 • 만약 당신이 긴장한다면, 당신의 어깨를 뒤로 한 채 똑바로 서려

고 노력하라. • 비록 초조하다 할지라도 자신 있게 행동하려고 해라. • 차분하게 있을 거라고 생각했지만 TV 카메라와 마주했을 때 나는 매우 긴장했다.

03 (1) ignore: 무시하다 (2) regret: 후회하다 (3) accidentally: 우연히 (4) mind: 꺼리다

04 (1) 당신이 처리해야 할 일이나 의무인 것 (2) 당신이 저지른 잘못된 일에 미안하다고 말하는 행위 (3) 두 가지가 연결되는 방식 (4) 평소 또는 예상 했던 것 보다 더 많이 돈, 도움, 친절을 기꺼이 주는

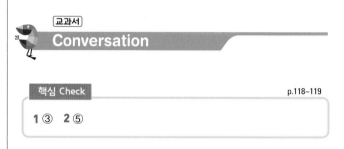

교과서
Conversation

핵심 Check — p.118~119

1 ③　2 ⑤

교과서 대화문 익히기

Check(√) True or False — p.120

1 F　2 T　3 F　4 T

Check(√) True or False — p.121

5 F　6 T　7 F　8 T

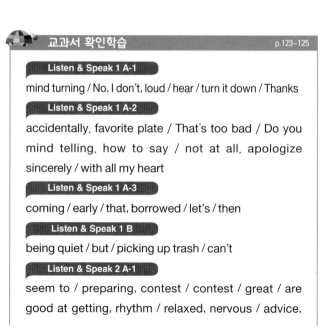

교과서 확인학습 — p.123~125

Listen & Speak 1 A-1
mind turning / No, I don't, loud / hear / turn it down / Thanks

Listen & Speak 1 A-2
accidentally, favorite plate / That's too bad / Do you mind telling, how to say / not at all, apologize sincerely / with all my heart

Listen & Speak 1 A-3
coming / early / that, borrowed / let's / then

Listen & Speak 1 B
being quiet / but / picking up trash / can't

Listen & Speak 2 A-1
seem to / preparing, contest / contest / great / are good at getting, rhythm / relaxed, nervous / advice,

helpful, appreciate / pleasure

lost / Let me help, What, like / is written / yours /
appreciate / No problem

Listen & Speak 2 B

Let, show / appreciate / Let me carry / appreciate your
help

Real Life Talk

What's up / (You')ve, been, haven't / since, elementary /
busy studying, do you mind helping, help me pick
out / problem. for / was broken / of her / how about,
recently / suggestion

Wrap Up 1

am planning to go / cool, used to live / Do you mind
telling, what to do / Not at all, beaches / swimming, else
/ don't you, everywhere / How about / raw fish, fresh,
delicious / appreciate, tips

Wrap Up 2

well, might have caught, needs to, to meet, instead

시험대비 기본평가   p.126

01 mind helping   02 ①, ④, ⑤   03 ②
04 ⑤

01 'Do you mind ~ing?'는 '당신은 ~하는 것이 괜찮으신가요?'
라는 뜻으로 상대방에게 무엇인가를 조심스럽고 정중하게 요청
할 때 사용하는 표현이다.

02 상대방의 도움에 대해 감사하는 표현이 적절하다.

03 빈칸 다음의 대답으로 보아, 상대방의 요청에 승낙한다는 것을
알 수 있다. 요청을 승낙할 때 mind는 '꺼리다'라는 뜻이므로 부
정어(not)를 써서 승낙을 표현한다. Of course not. / Not at
all. / Surely not. / Certainly not. / No, I don't (mind).
등으로 표현한다.

04 'I appreciate ~.'는 감사하는 표현이다.

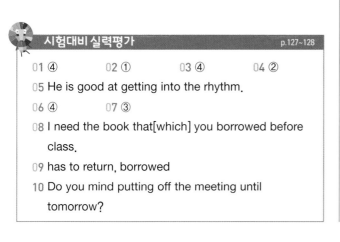

시험대비 실력평가   p.127~128

01 ④   02 ①   03 ④   04 ②
05 He is good at getting into the rhythm.
06 ④   07 ③
08 I need the book that[which] you borrowed before
   class.
09 has to return, borrowed
10 Do you mind putting off the meeting until
   tomorrow?

01 빈칸 다음의 Andy가 한 말로 보아 도움을 요청하는 표현이 적
절하다.

02 Amy와 Jessie가 초등학교 1학년 때부터 친구로 지내고 있다.

03 무엇을 하고 있는지 묻는 말에 → (C) 모자를 잃어버려서 찾을
수 없다는 내용이 오고 → (D) 도와준다는 말과 함께 모자가 어
떻게 생겼는지 묻고 → (A) 모자의 색깔과 모자에 이름이 적혔
다는 것을 말해주고 → (B) 식탁 아래에 모자가 있었다고 모자
를 찾아주는 내용이 자연스럽다.

04 B의 대답이 'Of course not.'인 것으로 보아 요청하는 말은
'Do you mind ~?'로 표현하는 것이 적절하다.

05 질문: Amy의 말에 의하면 민수는 무엇을 잘하는가?

06 단수 주어인 'one thing' 다음에 단수 동사 is가 와야 한다.

07 ③ 'Do you mind ~?'로 요청하는 말에 'Of course.'로 답하는
것은 거절을 할 때 사용하는 표현으로 'Go ahead.(그렇게 하세
요.)'와 어울리지 않는다.

08 선행사 'the book'을 수식하는 목적격 관계대명사절을 이용하고
목적격 관계대명사 'that' 또는 'which'를 추가한다.

09 '~해야 한다'라는 의미로 'have to'는 3인칭 단수 주어 뒤에서
'has to'로 바꾸어 쓰고, 수식받는 명사 'book'이 '빌려진' 수동의
의미로 주어진 동사 'borrow'를 과거분사로 변형하여 쓴다

10 'Do you mind+동명사 ~?' 형태로 상대방에게 요청하는 표현을
사용한다.

서술형 시험대비   p.129

01 Because his leg was broken.
02 You've been friends with her for a long time,
   haven't you?
03 Do you mind telling me what to do in Jejudo?
04 What does it look like?

01 질문: 두 달 전에 왜 Amy는 Andy의 가방을 들어 주었는가?

02 (a)의 'since first grade in elementary school'로 보아 과
거부터 현재까지 친구로 지내고 있음을 알 수 있다. 현재완료를
사용하고, 부가의문문도 조동사 have의 부정문인 haven't로 바
꾸어 주어야 한다.

03 'Do you mind+-ing?' 형태를 사용하고, '무엇을 ~할지'는
'what to do'를 사용한다.

04 대화의 흐름상 모자의 모습을 묻는 표현이 적절하다. 'What ~
look like?'를 사용한다.

핵심 Check   p.130~131

1 (1) how (2) why
2 The more homework they have, the more tired the students feel.

시험대비 기본평가   p.132

01 ③
02 (1) in which / how (2) in which / where
03 ②
04 (1) The hotter, more (2) higher, to climb
　　　(3) older, less flexible

01 often의 비교급은 more 또는 less를 앞에 쓰는 것이 좋고 (oftener를 쓸 수도 있음), 의미상 less often이 적절하다.

02 '전치사+관계대명사'는 관계부사로 표현한다. 선행사가 the way일 때, 관계부사는 how이지만, 둘을 동시에 쓰지 않는다. 선행사가 장소일 때 where를 쓴다.

03 관계부사가 오면 뒤의 문장은 완전한 절의 형태여야 한다. 선행사 the way와 관계부사 how는 함께 쓸 수 없다.

04 'The+비교급 ~, the+비교급 …' 구문이다. 형용사 또는 부사의 비교급에 대해 꼼꼼하게 공부해야 하며, hot, high 등은 er을 뒤에 쓰지만, flexible은 more 또는 less를 쓰고, much나 many는 more처럼 다른 단어가 비교급이 된다. (2)번 문장은 내용상 가주어-진주어 구문이므로 동사 climb을 to부정사로 변형하는 것이 적절하다.

시험대비 실력평가   p.133~135

01 ④	**02** ④	**03** ③	**04** ④
05 ⑤	**06** ④	**07** ②	**08** ④
09 ③	**10** ⑤	**11** ③	**12** how

13 when
14 The more you watch the news, the better you know
15 The more expensive some products are, the more people want to buy them.
16 ③ **17** ④

01 ④ 선행사 the way와 관계부사 how는 함께 쓸 수 없다. 둘 중 하나를 삭제하면 옳은 문장이 된다.

02 'The+비교급 ~, the+비교급 …' 구문이다. '당신이 더 많이 일

할수록 더 많은 돈을 벌 수 있다.'

03 'The+비교급 ~, the+비교급 …' 구문이다. '한국의 역사에 대해 방문객들이 더 알게 될수록, 그들은 아마도 더 많이 흥미를 느끼게 될 것이다.'

04 선행사가 the reason일 때, '전치사+관계대명사'는 for which를, '관계부사'는 why를 쓰는 것이 적절하며, the reason과 why 둘 중 하나만 쓰는 것도 가능하다. ① 선행사 the reason 필요 ② which 앞에 for 필요 ③ 마지막에 for 불필요 ⑤ on → for

05 선행사가 the place이므로 '관계부사' where 또는 '전치사+관계대명사'로 at which 또는 in which 등으로 연결해서 표현 가능하며, 일반적 장소인 the place를 생략해도 괜찮다. ① where 뒤의 어순은 '주어+동사'가 되어야 한다. ② know 동사가 있을 때 의문사를 문두로 보낼 수 없다. ③ 관계부사 where 앞에 전치사 불필요 ④ 마지막에 in이 있으므로 on 불필요

06 '친한 친구가 자신의 실수에 대해 진심으로 사과하지 않을수록, 사람들은 더 쉽게 상처 받는다.'라는 내용이다.

07 '당신의 사과가 더욱 진실할수록, 그것들은 더 잘 받아들여진다'는 내용이다. ① 더 많이 필요해진다 ③ 더 가볍게 여겨진다 ④ 더욱 건성으로 받아들여진다 ⑤ 더 많이 무시된다

08 선행사가 the way일 때, 관계부사 how는 같이 쓰지 않으며, 관계부사 앞에 전치사 in을 쓰지도 않는다.

09 선행사가 the time일 때, 관계부사는 when을 쓰며, that으로도 바꿔 쓸 수 있다. 일반적으로 관계대명사 which를 쓸 때는 전치사 at, on, in 등이 쓰이지만, 선행사가 the first time일 경우 in과 함께 for which도 가능하다. of는 시간을 나타내는 선행사 뒤에 쓰지 않는다.

10 선행사가 the reason일 때, 관계부사는 why를 쓰며, that으로도 바꿔 쓸 수 있다. the reason 또는 why 둘 중 하나를 생략해도 무방하며, 관계대명사를 쓸 때는 for가 함께 온다. ⑤는 관계부사 뒤의 어순이 잘못되었다.

11 <보기>는 '더 빠른 사과가 당신이 더 사려 깊고 책임감 있음을 보여줄 것이다'라는 뜻이다. 'The+비교급 ~, the+비교급 …' 구문을 사용해서 정확하게 표현한 문장은 ③이다. '당신의 사과가 더 빠를수록, 당신은 더 사려 깊고 책임감 있게 보인다.' 나머지는 모두 어법상 옳지 않은 문장들이다.

12 두 문장을 연결해 주는 빈칸 뒤에 완전한 문장이 오고, 선행사가 the way일 때는 관계부사 how를 쓰는데, 둘 중 하나만 써야 한다. 두 단어를 쓰는 것이 조건이라면 the way를 쓴다.

13 두 문장을 연결해 주는 빈칸 뒤에 완전한 문장이 오고, 선행사가 시간일 때는 관계부사 when을 쓰는 것이 적절하다. 두 단어를 쓰는 것이 조건이라면 선행사 the day가 있으므로 on which가 좋다.

14 'The+비교급 ~, the+비교급 ⋯' 구문을 사용한 문장이다. '뉴스를 많이 보는 것'을 'the more'로, '더 잘 알게 되는 것'을 'the better'로 쓰는 것에 유의한다.

15 'The+비교급 ~, the+비교급 ⋯' 구문을 사용한 문장이다. '더 많은 사람들'을 'the more people'로 쓰는 것에 유의한다.

16 (A) the way가 있으므로 how는 불가능하고, that 또는 in which를 써야 한다. (B) 관계대명사 주격이 필요하므로 which[that]가 적절하다. (C) 선행사가 the day이며 뒤에 완전한 문장이므로 when 또는 on which가 적절하다.

17 (A)는 관계부사 why, how, when 모두 가능하다. (B) the reason 뒤에 관계부사 why 또는 for which가 적절하다. (C) 장소의 선행사 cafe 뒤에 where 또는 at[in] which가 적절하다.

서술형 시험대비   p.136~137

01 (1) The sooner you apologize for the mistake, the less hurt people get.

(2) The more we have, the more we want.

(3) The more options you have, the more difficult it is to decide.

(4) The more I know the friend, the stronger my trust in her becomes.

(5) The more we give, the more we will get in return.

(6) The harder he works, the brighter his future will be.

02 (1) like the way her son made excuses

(2) how the turtle has managed his health

(3) where people line up every morning to eat Bulgogi

03 (1) The older, the more

(2) The more, the more intelligent

(3) The louder, the better

(4) The farther, the healthier

04 (1) the way how → the way 또는 how 삭제

(2) the more happier → more 삭제

05 (1) The researchers found the special planet where life can live.

(2) The director taught us how he made his films.

(3) Her favorite season is winter when she can enjoy white snow and skiing.

(4) Please let me know the reason why my professor was mad at me.

(5) This is the hotel where the President of Brazil stayed.

(6) I would never forget the day when my daughter walked for herself.

---

01 'The+비교급 ~, the+비교급 ⋯' 구문을 사용한 문장이다. *trust in A: A에 대한 신뢰

02 (1) 'Ms. Kim은 그녀의 아들이 그 문제에 대해 변명하는 방식이 마음에 들지 않았다.' (2) '동물들은 거북이가 어떻게 그의 건강을 유지해왔는지 궁금하다.' (3) 저기가 사람들이 불고기를 먹으러 매일 아침 줄을 서는 그 유명한 식당이다.

03 (1) 그 학생이 나이를 먹을수록, 그의 할아버지를 더 닮아 보인다. (2) 당신의 자녀들이 더 많은 책들을 읽을수록, 그들은 더욱 똑똑해질 것이다. (3) 당신이 더 큰 소리로 연습할수록, 당신은 외국어를 더 잘 말할 수 있다. (4) 그 환자가 매일 더 멀리 걸을수록, 그녀는 더욱 건강해질 것이다.

04 (1) 선행사가 the way일 때, 관계부사 how는 함께 쓸 수 없다. 둘 중 하나만 써도 어법상 문제 없다. (2) happy의 비교급은 happier이다. more는 불필요하다.

05 (1) 그 연구자들이 생명체가 살 수 있는 특별한 행성을 발견했다. (2) 그 감독이 우리에게 자신이 영화를 만드는 방법을 가르쳐 줬다. (3) 그녀가 가장 좋아하는 계절은 흰 눈과 스키를 즐길 수 있는 겨울이다. (4) 제발 교수님이 나에게 화가 난 이유를 나에게 알려주세요. (5) 이곳이 브라질의 대통령이 머물렀던 호텔이다. (6) 나는 나의 딸이 스스로 걸었던 날을 결코 잊을 수 없다.

교과서 Reading

확인문제   p.138

1 T   2 F   3 T

확인문제   p.139

1 T   2 F   3 T

교과서 확인학습 A   p.140~141

01 Because, It is, to get along with

02 hurt, without intending to, something wrong

03 that, should apologize

04 following case, a proper apology

05 tripped over, it funny, laughed, took, uploaded

06 saw, became angry, with, deleted it

07 even, because of

08 how Mike had acted, seemed to think, nothing

serious

09 should be sincere

10 Apologizin, to, Saying, more than

11 that, respect, care about, feelings

12 make things right, sincere

13 The more, the better, received

14 another, accidentally bumped into

15 on, fell on, apologize, felt bad

16 Why doesn't, say, if, right now

17 that, is necessary, apologize at once

18 shows that, thoughtful, responsibility

19 All, to do, think nothing, laugh it off

20 are, among, members, loved ones

21 borrowed, favorite, lost

22 apologize, not important

23 ignore

24 hadn't apologized to

25 to apologize, something wrong, includes, who are close

26 get hurt more easily, comes from

27 let it go, are close

28 small mistakes, no apology add up to

29 among, loved ones

30 heard of, No more, no more chances

31 make, let, break

32 apologize to, Try to do, can solve

교과서 확인학습 B　　　　　　p.142~143

1 Because we are human, we all make mistakes. It is not easy to get along with everyone all the time.

2 Sometimes we hurt people's feelings without intending to. Sometimes, we do something wrong and regret it later.

3 When that happens, what should we do? We should apologize.

4 Read the following case studies and learn three things about a proper apology.

5 When June tripped over a backpack and fell, Mike found it funny and laughed. He took a picture and uploaded it on an SNS.

6 June saw the picture and became angry. Mike said, with a laugh, "Sorry, June!" and deleted it.

7 After that, June felt even more hurt because of Mike's casual apology.

8 June didn't like how Mike had acted. Mike seemed to think it was nothing serious.

9 What did you learn from this case? Yes. You guessed right. You should be sincere when you apologize.

10 Apologizing is necessary to build good friendships. Saying you're sorry is more than just words.

11 You need to show that you respect the other person and care about his or her feelings.

12 If you truly want to make things right, be sincere in your apology.

13 The more sincere your apology is, the better it will be received.

14 Here is another case. While Kate was hurrying across the cafeteria, she accidentally bumped into Hojun.

15 Some food on Hojun's tray fell on his jacket. Kate didn't apologize. Hojun felt bad.

16 He thought, 'Why doesn't she say something? It would be nothing if she apologized right now.'

17 This case shows that when an apology is necessary, you should apologize at once.

18 A quick apology shows that you are thoughtful and take responsibility for your action.

19 All you need to do is to say, "I'm sorry." Then, the hurt friend will think nothing of it and laugh it off.

20 Finally, apologies are necessary among family members and loved ones, too.

21 One day, Sunmin borrowed her sister's favorite book. Later, she lost it.

22 Sunmin didn't apologize because she thought it was not important. She thought, 'We're sisters, after all.'

23 Sunmin's sister disliked how Sunmin had treated her. How could her own sister ignore her feelings?

24 This was not the first time Sunmin hadn't apologized to her little sister.

25 People need to apologize when they do something wrong. This includes family members and the people who are close to you.

26 People get hurt more easily when the hurt comes from a family member or a friend.

27 We may think that they will let it go because they are close to us.

28 Remember, however, that small mistakes and no apology add up to big emotional wounds.

29 This is especially true among family members and loved ones.

30 Have you ever heard of the saying, "No more

apologies, no more chances"?

31 People make mistakes, but don't let one mistake break a beautiful relationship.

32 Do you want to apologize to someone? Try to do it now. A quick and sincere "I'm sorry" can solve many problems..

시험대비 실력평가
p.144~147

01 ⑤   02 proper   03 ②   04 ③
05 ④   06 ④
07 We should be sincere.   08 ③
09 some food on his tray   10 ⑤   11 ②
12 ④   13 ②
14 People need to apologize when they do something wrong.
15 (C)—(A)—(D)—(B)   16 ②   17 ④
18 ②   19 ⑤
20 We should apologize at once when an apology is necessary
21 She lost it later.   22 ③
23 when they do something wrong   24 ④
25 ⑤번 → now

01 나쁜 일을 하고 그것을 후회하는 일이 생기면 무엇을 해야 하는지를 묻고 이에 대한 답으로 주어진 문장이 제시되는 것이 가장 자연스럽다.

02 '옳거나 가장 적합한'이라는 의미는 '적절한, 제대로 된 (proper)'이다.

03 사례 연구들을 읽고 올바른 사과를 위한 세 가지를 알아보자고 하였으므로 '적절히 사과하는 법'이 가장 적절하다.

04 빈칸 (A)에는 비교급을 강조하는 부사가 들어가야 한다. very는 원급의 형용사나 부사를 강조하는 말이다.

05 이어지는 조언에서 사과는 진실해야 함을 강조하고 있다. 따라서 Mike의 사과가 가벼웠기 때문에 June이 더 화가 난 것이다.

06 June은 Mike의 행동 방식이 마음에 들지 않았다.

07 사과할 때는 진실해야 한다고 하였다.

08 '즉시'라는 의미의 ③번이 가장 적절하다. for once: 이번 한 번만, from time to time: 이따금씩

09 Kate가 호준이와 부딪쳤을 때, 그는 급식판에 음식을 들고 있었다. 그 부딪힘은 음식이 그의 재킷에 떨어지게 했다.

10 호준이는 Kate가 사과하지 않아서 기분이 나빴다고 하였으므로 ⑤번이 글의 내용과 일치한다.

11 여동생이 가장 좋아하는 책을 빌리고 이것을 잃어버린 것을 가

12 모두 선민이를 가리키지만 ④번은 선민이의 여동생을 가리키는 말이다.

13 가깝기 때문에 사과하지 않고 그냥 넘어갈 수도 있지만 이것이 쌓이면 큰 감정적 상처가 된다는 연결이 자연스럽다.

14 잘못했을 때 사과해야 한다고 하였다.

15 (C) June이 가방에 걸려 넘어짐 (A) Mike는 사진을 찍어서 SNS에 올리고 June은 사진을 보고 화가 남 (D) Mike가 가볍게 사과함 (B) June은 그의 행동 방식에 더 화가 남

16 receive는 '받다'라는 의미이다. 사과가 더 잘 받아들여질 것이라는 의미이므로 ②번이 적절하다.

17 사과하는 것은 좋은 교우 관계를 만들기 위해 필요하다고 하였다. be related to: ~와 관계가 있다

18 이어지는 조언은 사과를 즉시 해야 한다는 것이므로 ②번이 적절하다.

19 빈칸 (B)에는 off가 들어간다. ① work out: 운동하다 ② come across: 우연히 만나다 ③ consist of: ~으로 구성되다 ④ keep ~ from Ving: ~가 V하지 못하게 막다 ⑤ give off: 발산하다

20 사과가 필요할 때는 즉시 해야 한다.

21 선민이는 여동생이 가장 좋아하는 책을 빌렸다가 나중에 그것을 잃어버렸다.

22 글의 내용으로 미루어보아 선민이의 여동생은 선민이가 그녀의 기분을 무시하고 사과하지 않는 방식이 마음에 들지 않는 것임을 알 수 있다

23 -thing으로 끝나는 대명사는 형용사의 수식을 뒤에서 받는 것에 유의한다.

24 위 글은 사과하는 것의 중요성에 관한 글이다.

25 이어지는 문장에서 빠르고 진정한 사과가 많은 문제를 해결해 줄 것이라고 하였으므로 '지금 하려고 노력해라'고 말하는 것이 적절하다.

서술형 시험대비
p.148~149

01 to hurt people's feelings
02 It is not easy to get along with everyone all the time.
03 apology
04 The more sincere your apology is, the better it will be received.
05 He uploaded it on an SNS.
06 It's because Mike apologized to him casually.
07 you respect the other person and care about his or her feelings
08 Because Kate bumped into him.

01 다른 사람의 감정을 상하게 할 의도 없이 그들의 감정을 상하게 한다는 의미이다.

02 모든 사람과 항상 잘 지내기는 쉽지 않다고 하였다.

03 누군가에게 상처주거나 그들에게 물의를 일으켜 미안하다고 말하기 위해 말하거나 쓰는 어떤 것은 '사과(apology)'이다.

04 사과가 받아들여지는 것이므로 receive를 과거분사 형태로 써서 수동태를 만드는 것에 유의한다.

05 Mike는 June의 사진을 찍어서 SNS에 올렸다.

06 Mike가 June에게 가볍게 사과했기 때문에 June은 더 화가 났다.

07 당신의 사과를 진실하게 만드는 것은 당신이 타인을 존중하고 타인의 감정에 관심을 갖고 있음을 보여주는 것이다.

08 음식이 호준이의 재킷에 떨어진 이유는 Kate가 그와 부딪쳤기 때문이다.

09 호준이는 Kate로부터 어떠한 사과도 받지 못했고, 그래서 그는 기분이 나빴다.

10 해석: 당신의 행동에 책임을 진다는 것을 보여주고 싶다면, 가능한 빨리 사과해라.

11 선민이의 여동생은 언니가 그녀의 기분을 무시한다고 생각해서 화가 난 것이다.

12 앞 문장을 가리키는 말이다.

13 사람들은 마음의 상처가 가족이나 친구에게서 올 때 더 쉽게 상처 받는다고 하였다.

14 아무리 당신과 가까운 사람이라 할지라도, 당신이 무언가를 잘못한다면 그들에게 사과해야 한다.

영역별 핵심문제

01 '동사-명사'의 관계이다. 포함하다-포함 : 해결하다-해결

02 (A) 너는 친구들과 부딪힌다. 그러면 너와 친구들은 다치게 될 거야. (B) 학생들은 아침에 그들의 옷을 고르기 위한 충분한 시간이 없다.

03 계획되거나 의도되지 않은 방식으로

04 서면이나 전자 텍스트의 일부 또는 전부를 제거하다

05 with all my heart: 진심으로

06 요청하는 표현으로 'Do you mind+-ing?'를 사용한다.

07 도움을 요청하는 표현으로 'Do you mind+-ing?' 형태를 사용한다.

08 주어진 문장이 '괜찮은 것을 고르도록 네가 도와줄 수 있을 것이라고 확신해.'라는 뜻이므로 요청하는 말 다음에 오는 것이 적절하다.

09 질문: Jessie는 Andy가 Amy를 위해 무엇을 사라고 제안하는가? / 동사 'suggest'의 목적절인 'that'절의 해석이 '~해야 한다'는 '당위성'을 나타낼 때는 '주어+should+동사원형' 형태를 사용하고 이때 'should'는 생략 가능하다.

10 두 달 전에 Andy가 다리를 다친 이유는 대화에 언급되어 있지 않다.

11 '날씨가 더 추워질수록 사람들이 전보다 더 감기에 많이 걸리는 경향이 있다.'라는 문장은 '날씨가 더 추워질수록 더 많은 사람들이 감기에 걸린다.'와 가장 유사하며, 'The 비교급, the 비교급' 구문을 통해 표현하는 것이 적절하다.

12 선행사가 the way일 때는 관계부사 how를 쓰는데, 둘 중 하나만 써야 한다. the way 뒤에 how 대신 that을 쓸 수 있다. 관계대명사로 표현할 때는 the way in which를 쓴다.

13 ② '어항은 물고기나 수중 생물들을 집어넣는 유리 용기이다.'라는 문장에서 마지막에 전치사 in이 있으므로 선행사 container 뒤에는 관계대명사 which만 있으면 된다. in을 모두 지우고, 관계부사 where로 쓰는 것도 적절하다.

14 ① '더 높이 올라갈수록, 우리가 숨 쉬는 것이 더 어려워졌다.'는 문장이다. the more it was difficult가 아니라, the more difficult it was의 어순이 적절하다.

15 나는 Paul이 그 어려운 문제를 푼 방법을 알아내고 싶다.'라는

문장이다. 일반적으로 선행사 the way는 관계부사 how와 짝이고, 둘은 나란히 쓸 수 없어서 둘 중 하나만 쓰면 된다. 그러나, how 대신에 that을 썼을 경우 the way를 생략하면 that이 더 이상 관계부사가 아니라 접속사가 되어 의미가 달라지고, 어법상으로도 옳지 않게 된다.

16 ① in which → which ② which → to which 또는 where ④ where → which ⑤ where → which

17 ① do → are 또는 will be ② More → The more, more → the more ④ the more earlier → the earlier ⑤ the more you will be careful → the more careful you will be
   *destination: 목적지

18 ① 선행사 the way와 관계부사 how는 함께 쓸 수 없다. the way how → the way 또는 how ② why → which ③ when → which ④ at when → at which 또는 at 삭제

19 글의 내용으로 미루어 보아 Mike는 심각한 일이 아니라고 생각하는 것처럼 보였다고 말하는 것이 자연스럽다. 따라서 serious라고 쓰는 것이 적절하다.

20 (A)는 to부정사의 부사적 용법으로 쓰였다. ① 형용사적 용법 ② 진주어 ③ 부사적 용법 ④, ⑤ 동사의 목적어

21 글의 내용은 사과를 진실하게 해야 한다는 것이다.

22 Mike가 사진을 올리기 위해서 어떤 SNS를 사용했는지는 알 수 없다.

23 주어진 문장의 This가 가리키는 것은 사람들은 잘못했을 때 사과해야 한다는 문장이다. 따라서 ②번이 가장 적절하다.

24 result in을 대신하여 add up to를 써서 답해도 좋다.

25 선민이의 여동생은 선민이가 자신의 기분을 무시한다고 생각했다. 따라서 ③번이 글의 내용과 일치한다.

26 위 글은 글쓴이를 도와준 친구를 소개하는 글이다. 따라서 ②번이 가장 적절하다.

27 지난 금요일에 글쓴이는 아파서 수학 수업을 못 들었다고 하였다.

28 진수는 항상 재미있고, 용감하고, 발랄하다고 하였다.

단원별 예상문제
p.156~159

01 thoughtful　02 ⑤　　03 ①　　04 ④
05 one thing you need to do is to be more relaxed
06 appreciate　07 ①　　08 ⑤
09 might catch → might have caught
10 ①　　11 ④　　12 ⑤　　13 ⑤
14 ②　　15 ⑤　　16 ②　　17 ⑤
18 ②　　19 ⑤번 → how Mike had acted
20 ③
21 We need to show that we respect the other person and care about his or her feelings.

01 유의어 관계이다. 무시하다 : 사려 깊은

02 위험하거나 어려운 일에 대해 어떠한 두려움도 보이지 않는

03 '~하곤 했다'는 'used to+동사원형'을 사용한다.

04 Minjun이가 'Why don't you hike Halla Mountain?' (한라산을 등반해 보는 건 어때?)이라고 제안하고 있다.

05 우리말에서 '네가 해야 할'이 명사를 수식한다는 것을 알 수 있다. 주어부는 one thing 뒤에 관계대명사절인 'you need to do'를 쓰고, 동사 is를 쓴다. 마지막으로 부정사 to be를 사용하면 된다.

06 '무언가에 고마워하다'라는 의미로 'appreciate'가 적절하다.

07 빈칸 앞에서 Irene이 '도와줘서 고마워.'라고 말하고 있으므로 '천만에.'라고 답하는 말이 적절하다.

08 Irene이 왜 모자를 잃어버렸는지를 알 수 없다.

09 Mike가 몸이 좋지 않다는 말 다음에 그가 감기에 걸렸을지 모른다는 과거의 추측을 나타내는 말이 오는 것이 자연스럽다. 'might catch'는 'may catch'보다 가능성이 약한 현재의 추측으로, 과거의 추측은 'might have+과거분사'를 사용해야 한다.

10 평서문의 동사가 'have+과거분사'인 현재완료이므로, 부가의문문은 조동사 have를 부정해야 한다. 'weren't'를 'haven't'로 바꾸어야 한다.

11 방법을 나타내는 관계부사 how와 용법이 다른 것을 찾는 문제이다. ④는 의문사로 사용되었다. '나는 그 곰들이 성숙한 상태가 되면 얼마나 강해질지 궁금하다.'라는 문장이다.

12 관계부사가 아닌 것을 찾는 문제이다. ⑤는 접속사로서 부사절을 이끄는 역할을 한다. *the Mediterranean Sea: 지중해

13 'The+비교급 ~, the+비교급 …' 구문과 특수한 경우를 제외하고는 비교급 앞에 the를 쓰지 않는다. 접속사 when과 as가 있는 ①, ②번 문장과 ④번에서 the+비교급은 적절하지 않고, ③은 worse 앞에 more가 있어 부적절하다.

14 'The+비교급 ~, the+비교급 …' 구문이다. 형용사 hot은 ①과 ④처럼 more hotter 또는 more hot으로 비교급을 쓰지 않는다. ③은 시제가 부적절하며, ⑤는 내용상 better보다는 more를 쓰는 것이 적절하다.

15 (A)는 to부정사의 명사적 용법으로 진주어로 쓰였다. ① 형용사적 용법 ②, ③ 부사적 용법 중 목적 ④ 부사적 용법 중 결과 ⑤ 진주어

16 나쁜 일을 하고 그것을 후회한다는 의미이므로 ②번이 가장 적절하다.

17 잘못을 하면 가까운 사람에게도 반드시 사과해야 하며, 그들이 나와 가깝기 때문에 그냥 넘어갈 것이라고 생각해서는 안 된다는 내용이므로 ⑤번이 가장 적절하다.

18 실수에 대해 즉시 사과하지 않으면, 그것은 아름다운 관계를 깨뜨릴 수 있다.

19 간접의문문이므로 '의문사+주어+동사'의 어순이 옳다.

20 사과는 좋은 교우 관계를 만들기 위해 필요하다고 하였다.

21 사과할 때 타인을 존중하고 타인의 감정에 관심을 갖고 있음을 보여 주어야 한다.

서술형 실전문제
p.160~161

01 (A) studying   (B) helping   (C) (to) pick
   (D) was broken

02 I appreciate

03 You seem to be busy, Minsu.

04 (1) how   (2) where   (3) why

05 (1) harder, more   (2) clearer, longer
   (3) fewer, happier   (4) older, smarter
   (5) sooner, better

06 (1) Tell me how Mary persuaded her parents to
       give her the car.
   (2) No one knows the day when Minju will marry
       the handsome guy of the idol group.
   (3) Bucheon is the city where International
       Fantastic Film Festival will take place.

07 작은 실수를 하고 사과하지 않는 것이 큰 감정적인 상처가
   되는 것.

08 necessary, oved, hurt, close

09 It's because she thought it was not important.

01 (A) be busy –ing: ~하느라 바쁘다, (B) mind는 목적어로
   동명사를 취한다, (C) help는 목적보어 자리에 '동사원형' 또는
   'to부정사'를 취한다. (D) 다리가 부러졌다는 수동의 의미이므
   로 'was broken'이 적절하다.

02 감사하는 표현으로 'Thank you for ~'나 'I appreciate ~'를
   사용할 수 있다.

03 'It seems that+주어+동사 ~'는 '주어+seem to+부정사'로 바
   꾸어 쓸 수 있다.

04 각각의 선행사가 (1) 방법, (2) 장소, (3) 이유 등이다. 관계부사
   how는 선행사 the way와 함께 쓰지 않는다.

05 (1) 더 열심히 일할수록, 너는 더 많은 돈을 번다. (2) 동영상의
   화질이 더 선명할수록, 그것을 내려 받는 데 더 오랜 시간이 걸린
   다. (3) 더운 여름 날 수업이 더 적을수록, 학생들은 더 행복하게
   느낀다. (4) 그 소녀가 나이를 먹을수록, 그녀는 더 똑똑해졌다.
   (5) 당신이 그 프로젝트를 일찍 끝낼수록, 협상에서 더 유리한 위
   치를 차지할 수 있다.

06 각각의 선행사에 맞게 관계부사를 쓰되, the way는 how와 같이
   쓸 수 없으므로, (1)에서 선행사 없이 관계부사가 이끄는 절만 쓰
   는 것에 유의한다.

07 앞 문장의 내용을 가리키는 말이다.

08 사과는 가족이나 사랑하는 사람들 사이에서도 필요하며, 사람들
   은 마음의 상처가 가족이나 친구에게서 올 때 더 쉽게 상처받는다
   고 하였다.

09 선민이가 그녀의 여동생에게 사과하지 않은 이유는 책을 잃어버린
   것이 중요하지 않다고 생각했기 때문이다.

창의사고력 서술형 문제
p.162

|모범답안|

01 (1) I'll let you know how you can find the way.
   (2) This is how I help you walk freely.
   (3) I know how you set the table.
   (4) I wonder how you read the directions.

02 for ten years / funny, generous, and cheerful /
   she helped me / Two weeks ago / I forgot to
   take my lunch to school / shared her lunch with
   me

01 보기의 단어들을 적절히 조합하여 그림과 어법에 맞게 영작한 답
   이면 된다.

단원별 모의고사
p.163~167

01 ⑤   02 (s)tingy   03 ③   04 ④
05 ⑤   06 ②

07 I know you're really busy studying, but do you
   mind helping me?

08 Andy asks her[Jessie] to help him pick out something
   nice for Amy.

09 ④   10 ③   11 ①   12 ④
13 ④

14 (1) for which   (2) in which   (3) in which
   (4) on which

15 (1) The more it rained, the more depressed she
       felt.
   (2) The more sincere her apology is, the better he
       will accept it.

16 ②   17 ⑤   18 ④   19 ③

20 Mike seemed to think it was nothing serious.

21 ③   22 sincere

01 ⑤번은 'lend(빌려주다)'에 관한 설명이다. 'borrow(빌리
   다)'의 영어 설명은 'to get or receive something from
   someone with the intention of giving it back after a
   period of time(일정 기간 후에 돌려줄 의도를 가지고 어떤 사
   람에게서 무언거를 얻거나 받다)'이다.

02 반의어 관계다. 바른-틀린 : 후한-인색한

03 '걷거나 달리고 있을 때 무언가에 발을 부딪친 후 균형을 잃거나, 누군가에게 이렇게 하도록 하다'는 의미로 'trip over(~에 걸려 넘어지다)'가 적절하다.

04 ④번은 'Do you mind ~?'로 요청하는 표현이므로 직역을 하면 '당신은 ~을 싫어하나요?'가 된다. B의 대답 'Yes, I do.'는 '네, 싫어합니다.'라는 거절의 표현인데, '볼륨을 줄일게.'라고 말하는 것은 어색하다.

05 ⑤번은 'Do you mind ~?'로 묻는 요청의 말에 대한 거절의 표현이다.

06 ②번의 'mind'의 목적어 자리에는 동명사만 사용 가능하기 때문에 부정사 'to tell'로 바꾸어 쓸 수 없다.

07 'be busy+-ing' 구문을 이용하여 '~하느라 바쁘다'를 표현하고, 'do you mind+-ing' 구문을 이용하여 '~해 주겠니?'라는 요청의 표현을 쓴다.

08 Andy는 Jessie에게 Amy에게 줄 선물로 괜찮은 것을 고르는 것을 도와달라고 부탁하고 있다.

09 Minsu가 여유를 가지기 위해 무엇을 할지는 대화에서 언급되어 있지 않다.

10 Mina는 엄마에게 미안하다고 어떻게 말해야 할지 조언을 구하고 있고, 상대방이 진심으로 사과해야 한다고 충고하고 있으므로 ③번이 가장 적절하다.

11 '산 위로 더 높이 올라갈수록, 날씨가 더 추워진다.'라는 문장이다. as로 시작하는 부사절로 바꿀 수 있다. ① '당신이 산을 더 높이 올라감에 따라 날씨가 더 추워진다.'의 뜻이다.

12 '우리가 나이를 먹을수록, 우리의 근육과 뼈는 유연성이 덜해진다.'는 내용이다. 'The+비교급 ~, the+비교급 …' 구문이 정확하게 사용된 문장이 답이다.

13 선행사가 the way일 때 how는 같이 사용하지 않는다.

14 일반적으로 선행사가 the way일 때, '전치사+관계대명사'는 in which를, 선행사가 the reason일 때 for which를 쓰며, 장소나 시간의 명사가 선행사로 쓰일 경우, 각 단어에 알맞게 at/on/in 등과 관계대명사 which를 활용하는 것이 적절하다. (2)의 경우 in 외에도 at이 가능하다.

15 (1) 비가 내린다는 표현은 비인칭주어 it을 활용한다. 과거 시제임에 유의하여 영작한다. (2) well의 비교급이 better임에 유의한다.

16 빈칸 (A)에는 동사 take가 쓰인다. 모두 take가 사용되지만 ②번에는 동사 make가 쓰여 '결심하다'라는 의미의 make up one's mind라는 의미를 완성한다.

17 신속한 사과는 당신이 사려 깊고, 당신의 행동에 책임을 진다는 것을 보여준다는 의미가 자연스러우므로 thoughtful이라고 쓰는 것이 적절하다.

18 주어진 문장은 '누군가에게 사과하고 싶은가?'에 대한 답이며, it이 가리키는 것 역시 to apologize to someone이다. 따라서 ④번에 들어가는 것이 가장 적절하다.

19 가족과 사랑하는 사람들에게 작은 실수를 하고 사과하지 않는 것은 큰 감정적인 상처가 된다고 하였고, 가깝다는 이유로 사과하지 않고 그냥 넘어가는 것은 옳지 않으므로 ③번은 글의 내용과 일치하지 않는다.

20 Mike는 그 일이 심각한 일이 아니라고 생각하는 것처럼 보였다.

21 (A) Mike의 가벼운 사과에 더 상처를 받았다는 의미이고, (B) 사과할 때 타인을 존중하고 타인의 감정에 관심을 갖고 있음을 보여 주어야 하며, (C) 사과가 진실할수록 그것이 더 잘 받아들여진다는 의미가 자연스럽다. reject: 거절하다

22 Mike의 사과는 진실하지 않았고, 그 결과 June은 더 화가 난 것이다.

교과서 파헤치기

Lesson
5

01 매장, 장례식	02 존경, 경의	03 통치, 지배
04 희생; 희생하다	05 바람, 갈망	06 우편 번호
07 비밀, 비밀의	08 장군	09 정부
10 조화	11 교육시키다	12 전문가
13 퍼지다, 퍼뜨리다	14 먹이를 주다, 먹이다	
15 (정치적, 사회적) 운동		16 ~의 도처에, ~ 내내
17 입구	18 보호하다	19 지도자, 리더
20 주된, 주요한	21 임무	22 묘, 무덤
23 조직, 기구	24 궁전	25 보물
26 애국적인	27 안개 낀	28 대통령, 의장
29 독립	30 감독하다, 지휘[총괄]하다	
31 조각상	32 묻다, 매장하다	33 공화국
34 끝내다; 완전한	35 전시회	36 ~에 속하다
37 ~을 입다	38 ~에 관해 듣다	39 ~가 필요하다
40 ~을 수행하다	41 ~처럼 보이다	42 ~하기 위해서
43 ~을 기대하다		

01 bury	02 secret	03 desire
04 respect	05 government	06 rule
07 educate	08 burial	09 foggy
10 general	11 sacrifice	12 poem
13 independence	14 palace	15 main
16 tomb	17 direct	18 treasure
19 feed	20 patriotic	21 statue
22 protect	23 spread	24 zip code
25 entrance	26 complete	27 leader
28 organization	29 specialist	30 harmony
31 exhibition	32 mission	33 republic
34 throughout	35 movement	36 put on
37 belong to	38 carry out	39 look like+명사
40 be in need	41 hear of	
42 so that+주어+동사		
43 look forward to+명사/동명사		

1 treasure, 보물　2 republic, 공화국
3 exhibition, 전시회　4 mission, 임무　5 palace, 궁전
6 organization, 조직　7 bury, 묻다　8 process, 과정
9 sacrifice, 희생　10 statue, 조각상
11 burial, 매장, 장례식　12 tomb, 무덤
13 amusement park, 놀이공원　14 crown, 왕관
15 poem, 시　16 flag, 깃발

Listen & Speak 1 A

1. Look at, huge / looks strong / Because, was built to protect, during / who built / ordered, to direct, process, don't you / heard of, great scientist
2. don't you / national flag, isn't it / what, symbols, mean / Tell me, them / circle, means harmony, peace / lines, corners mean / mean, earth

Listen & Speak 2 A

1. planning to go / museum built by / heard, great things / bought, treasures that, had taken / must be interesting / looking forward to
2. what did you do / to do volunteer work / What kind of / cleaned around, tombs, respect, who died / Sounds, too / planning to go, join / I'm looking forward to

Real Life Talk

reading / Poetry, know, don't you / heard, much / poems when, under, rule, desire, independence, be felt, poems / to read, poems, learn more / In fact, planning to visit / when, going / near, Palace, palace at / Let's meet / looking forward to, visit

Wrap Up

let put on traditional / gifts for, Germany / there are, gift shops / shopping, for lunch / know, don't you / traditional, soup, delicious, make you healthy / looking forward to trying

Listen & Speak 1 A

1. B: Look at Suwon Hawseong. It's huge.
   G: It also looks strong.
   B: Because it was built to protect the people during wars.
   G: Wow. Do you know who built it?

B: Yes. King Jeongjo ordered Jeong Yakyong to direct the building process. You know about Jeong Yakyong, don't you?

G: Yes, I've heard of him. He was a great scientist in Joseon.

2. G: Brian, you know Taegeukgi, don't you?

B: Sure. It's the national flag of Korea, isn't it?

G: That's right. Do you know what the symbols in Taegeukgi mean?

B: No, I don't. Tell me about them.

G: The circle in the middle means harmony and peace.

B: What do the black lines on the four corners mean?

G: They mean four things: sky, fire, water, and earth.

Listen & Speak 2 A

1. G: I'm planning to go to the Gansong Museum.

B: What is the Gansong Museum?

G: It's a museum built by Gansong Jeon Hyeongpil.

B: I heard that he did great things for the country.

G: Yes. He bought many Korean treasures that some Japanese had taken to Japan.

B: Wow. The museum must be interesting.

G: Yes. I'm looking forward to it!

2. B: Soyeon, what did you do last weekend?

G: I went to Hyeonchungwon to do volunteer work.

B: What kind of volunteer work did you do there?

G: I cleaned around the tombs. I felt great respect for the people who diedfor the country.

B: Sounds great. Can I do it, too?

G: Sure. I'm planning to go there again next Wednesday. Will you join me?

B: Sure. I'm looking forward to it.

Real Life Talk

Andy: Bora, what are you reading?

Bora: I'm reading *Sky, Wind, Star, and Poetry* by Yun Dongju. You know about Yun Dongju, don't you?

Andy: I've heard his name, but I don't know much about him.

Bora: He wrote many beautiful poems when Korea was under Japanese rule. His love for the country and his desire for independence can be felt in his poems.

Andy: Really? I didn't know that. I want to read his poems and learn more about him.

Bora: Great. In fact, I'm planning to visit the Yun Dongju Museum soon. Do you want to come with me?

Andy: Yes, when are you going?

Bora: Next Saturday. It's near Gyeongbok Palace. Can you meet me at the palace at 2 p.m.?

Andy: Sure. Let's meet there.

Bora: Great. I'm really looking forward to the visit.

Wrap Up

B: Tomorrow let's put on traditional Korean clothes, hanbok, and go to Insadong.

G: Good, but I want to buy gifts for my friends in Germany tomorrow.

B: In Insadong, there are many gift shops.

G: Great. After shopping, what should we eat for lunch?

B: Hmm. You know Samgyetang, don't you?

G: No. What is it?

B: It's a traditional Korean soup. It's delicious and will make you healthy.

G: Sounds good. I'm looking forward to trying it.

본문 TEST Step 1 p.09~10

01 Last week, went to

02 visited, inside, park

03 entrance, museum, saw, statue

04 national hero, fighting, independence

05 helped educate, by building

06 movement, spread throughout, moved

07 joined, later became, president

08 exhibition, shows, lot, life

09 While looking around, stopped

10 formed, secret, fight against

11 belonged to, group

12 place, hall, watches under

13 made, plan, kill, generals

14 directed, carry out, mission

15 left, need, anymore, let

16 carried, so, forget, sacrifice

17 completing, tour, tombs, heroes

18 bodies, been, independence, brought

19 By, deep, respect, sacrifice

20 As, thought, words, exhibition

21 was written in

22 what, wish, say clearly

23 second, would, independence, country

24 what, loudly, complete independence

01 my history club

02 visited, inside the park

03 At, entrance, white statue

04 a great national hero, spent, fighting, independence, from Japanese rule

05 helped educate, by building

06 In, when the independence movement, throughout, moved to

07 joined, later became its president

08 The exhibition hall, shows

09 While looking around, stopped at, Patriotic Organization's

10 formed, secret organization, to fight against

11 belonged to

12 At, saw two watches under

13 In, made a plan to, Japanese generals

14 Patriotic Organization, directed, to carry out

15 left for, wearing a very old watch, Mine, won't, it anymore, take, let, have

16 always carried, so that, would not forget, sacrifice

17 completing, moved to, tombs, three heroes

18 had been, after, independence, them

19 By doing so, deep love, for the sacrifice

20 As, left, thought, words, that, had read, exhibition hall

21 It, written in

22 what my wish is, clearly, Korea's Independence

23 what my second wish, independence

24 asks me what my third wish is, loudly, complete independence

9 우리는 전시관을 둘러보면서 한인 애국단의 단원들 사진 앞에 섰다.

10 김구는 일본에 맞서 싸우기 위해 1931년에 비밀 조직을 형성했다.

11 이봉창과 윤봉길이 그 집단에 속해 있었다.

12 전시관의 한 곳에서, 우리는 김구와 윤봉길의 사진 아래에 있는 시계 두 개를 보았다.

13 1932년에 김구는 상해에 있는 한 공원에서 일본 장군들을 암살하기 위한 계획을 세웠다.

14 한인 애국단의 지도자로서 그는 윤봉길이 임무를 수행하도록 지시했다.

15 윤봉길이 임무를 위해 떠날 때, 그는 김구에게 말했다. "선생님, 당신은 매우 낡은 시계를 차고 계시는군요. 제 것은 새것이나, 저는 그것이 더 이상 필요하지 않을 것입니다. 부디 제 시계를 가져가시고, 제가 선생님 것을 가지도록 해 주십시오."

16 김구는 윤봉길의 희생을 잊지 않기 위해서 윤봉길의 시계를 항상 상의에 넣고 다녔다.

17 기념관 관람을 마치고, 우리는 이봉창, 윤봉길, 그리고 백정기 의사들이 묻힌 삼의사의 묘로 이동했다.

18 그들의 시신은 일본에 있다가 독립이 되고 나서 김구가 그들의 시신을 효창 공원으로 가져왔다.

19 그는 그렇게 함으로써 삼의사들의 희생에 대한 그의 깊은 사랑과 경의를 보여 주었다.

20 내가 효창 공원을 떠날 때, 나는 전시관에서 읽었던 「나의 소원」에 있는 김구의 말을 생각했다.

21 그것은 『백범일지』에 쓰여 있었다.

22 만약 신이 나의 소원이 무엇이냐고 묻는다면, "그것은 대한 독립이오."라고 명확하게 말할 것이다.

23 만약에 그가 나의 두 번째 소원이 무엇이냐고 묻는다면, 나는 "그것은 내 나라의 독립이오."라고 말할 것이다.

24 만약 그가 나의 세 번째 소원이 무엇이냐고 묻는다면, "그것은 내 나라의 완전한 독립이오."라고 큰 소리로 말할 것 이다. 그것이 나의 대답이다.

1 지난주에 우리 역사 동아리는 효창 공원에 갔다.

2 우리는 공원 안에 있는 김구 기념관을 방문했다.

3 기념관 입구에서 우리는 하얀색의 김구 조각상을 보았다.

4 김구는 일본 통치로부터 대한의 독립을 위해 싸우는 데 그의 삶 대부분을 보낸 위대한 국민 영웅이다.

5 1900년대에 그는 학교를 설립함으로써 젊은이들을 교육시키는 것을 도왔다.

6 1919년에 3.1 운동이 나라 전체에 걸쳐 퍼져나갔을 때, 그는 중국 상하이로 이동했다.

7 그곳에서 그는 대한민국 임시정부에 합류했고 나중에는 그것의 대표자가 되었다.

8 기념관 안에 있는 전시관은 김구의 삶에 관한 많은 것들을 보여 준다.

1 Last week my history club went to Hyochang Park.

2 We visited the Kim Koo Museum inside the park.

3 At the entrance of the museum, we saw a white statue of Kim Koo.

4 Kim Koo is a great national hero who spent most of his life fighting for the independence of Korea from Japanese rule.

5 In the 1900s, he helped educate young people by building schools.

6 In 1919, when the independence movement had spread throughout the country, he moved to Shanghai, China.

7 There he joined the Government of the Republic of Korea and later became its president.

8 The exhibition hall in the museum shows a lot of things about Kim Koo's life.

9 While looking around the hall, we stopped at a photo of the Korean Patriotic Organization's members.

10 Kim Koo formed the secret organization in 1931 to fight against Japan.

11 Lee Bongchang and Yun Bonggil belonged to the group.

12 At one place in the hall, we saw two watches under a photo of Kim Koo and Yun Bonggil.

13 In 1932, Kim Koo made a plan to kill Japanese generals in a park in Shanghai.

14 As the leader of the Korean Patriotic Organization, he directed Yun to carry out the mission.

15 When Yun left for the mission, he told Kim, "Sir, you are wearing a very old watch. Mine is new, but I won't need it anymore. Please take my watch, and let me have yours."

16 Kim Koo always carried Yun's watch in his jacket so that he would not forget Yun's sacrifice.

17 After completing the tour of the museum, we moved to the tombs of the three heroes, Lee Bongchang, Yun Bonggil, and Baek Jeonggi.

18 Their bodies had been in Japan, but after Korea's independence Kim Koo brought them to Hyochang Park.

19 By doing so, he showed his deep love and respect for the sacrifice of the three heroes.

20 As I left Hyochang Park, I thought about Kim Koo's words in My Wish that I had read in the exhibition hall.

21 It was written in *Baekbeomilji*.

22 If God asks me what my wish is, I would say clearly, "It is Korea's Independence."

23 YIf he asks me what my second wish is, I would say, "It is the independence of my country."

24 If he asks me what my third wish is, I would say loudly, "It is the complete independence of my country." That is my answer.

Real Life Talk Step 3

1. chose, because, were impressed by, sacrifice for

2. can learn more about, by visiting

Enjoy Writing

1. was born in

2. When, in his teens, moved to, went to, there

3. left for, so that, get a better education

4. helped improve the lives, became a respected leader

5. had returned to, founded, to fight for Korea's independence

6. Government of the Republic of Korea

7. built a lot of, to educate, until, died in

Project Step 1

1. to introduce, to foreigners, don't you

2. a temple in

3. one of the most beautiful temples

4. has many treasures like

Real Life Talk Step 3

1. My group members chose An Junggeun because we were impressed by his sacrifice for the country.

2. You can learn more about him by visiting the An Junggeun Museum or An Junggeun Park.

Enjoy Writing

1. An Changho was born in 1878.

2. When he was in his teens, he moved to Seoul and went to school there.

3. In 1902, he left for America so that he could get a better education.

4. In America, An helped improve the lives of the Korean people there and became a respected leader.

5. After he had returned to Korea, he founded the New Korean Society in 1907 to fight for Korea's independence.

6. He also joined the Government of the Republic of Korea in Shanghai in 1919.

7. After that, he built a lot of schools to educate people until he died in 1938.

Project Step 1

1. A: I want to introduce Bulguksa to foreigners. You know Bulguksa, don't you?

2. B: Yes, I do. It's a temple in Gyeongju.

3. C: Yes. It's one of the most beautiful temples in Korea.

4. D: It also has many treasures like the Dabotop.

Lesson 6

단어 TEST Step 1   p.21

01 성공, 성과   02 경기, 시합   03 해외에(서), 해외로
04 달성하다, 성취하다   05 상징, 상징물
06 흔한   07 겪다, 경험하다
08 진가를 알아보다, 인정하다   09 명확하게
10 자취, 오솔길   11 (대단히) 놀라게 하다
12 온천   13 풍경   14 도처에
15 주요한, 주된   16 (사람이) 혼란스러워 하는
17 자연의, 천연의 18 격자무늬, 격자무늬 천
19 문화   20 추천하다
21 걷잡을 수 없이, 극도로   22 경관, 전망
23 확실히, 분명히 24 경쟁자, 경쟁 상대
25 몇몇의   26 사회   27 결혼(식)
28 제안하다   29 전통적인
30 언젠가, 언제든, 훗날   31 마을, 부락, 촌락
32 폭포   33 (특정한 곳의) 토박이의
34 별명   35 훨씬 이전에   36 ~으로 덮이다
37 ~로 가득 찬   38 ~의 도움을 받아서
39 ~로 유명하다   40 일 년 내내   41 ~로 알려져 있다
42 ~을 준비하다   43 생각이 나다, 생각이 떠오르다

단어 TEST Step 2   p.22

01 rival   02 recommend   03 native
04 abroad   05 someday   06 achieve
07 landscape   08 throughout   09 several
10 waterfall   11 success   12 view
13 surely   14 carry   15 appreciate
16 plaid   17 common   18 clearly
19 match   20 wedding   21 trail
22 amaze   23 twin   24 village
25 natural   26 experience   27 nickname
28 suggest   29 symbol   30 hot spring
31 main   32 confused   33 traditional
34 information   35 try on   36 filled with
37 be famous for 38 prepare for   39 all year round
40 be known as   41 be covered with
42 with the help of 43 come to one's mind

단어 TEST Step 3   p.23

1 kiwi, 키위새   2 abroad, 해외에(서), 해외로
3 hot spring, 온천   4 plaid, 격자무늬   5 match, 경기, 시합

6 trail, 오솔길   7 wedding, 결혼식

8 achieve, 달성하다, 성취하다   9 common, 흔한

10 Maori, 마오리인   11 rival, 경쟁자, 경쟁 상대

12 potluck, 각자 준비한 음식을 나눠먹는 식사

13 rugby, 럭비   14 landscape, 풍경   15 hill, 언덕

16 symbol, 상징, 상징물

대화문 TEST Step 1 p.24~25

Listen & Speak 1 A

1. Let's talk, traditional clothing, other / what a kilt is / traditional clothing, looks like, knee-length, plaid pattern / with, plaid pattern / unique because / interesting, to try, on

2. let's talk about what, prepare / famous, How about / popular, dish / What, look like / fried, with, potato chips / interesting. Let's prepare

Listen & Speak 2 A

1. finally arrived in / looking forward to, should, do / suggest, visit / the highest mountain, in a lot of / fantastic view / sounds, Let's

2. invited, potluck / know, food to share / recommend that / suggest, take, How about / spicy, easy to carry / for

Real Life Talk

Can you tell me about / a few years ago. First, let's talk / What food, famous for / The most famous, filled with, melted / suggestion, will try, Are there, that are popular with / suggest, Independence, history / information / pleasure

Wrap Up

Welcome, capital, popular dish, Every year, lots of tourists, beautiful beaches

---

대화문 TEST Step 2 p.26~27

Listen & Speak 1 A

1. B: Let's talk about traditional clothing from other countries.

G: Hmm... Do you know what a kilt is?

B: No, I don't. What is it?

G: It is traditional clothing from Scotland. It looks like a knee-length skirt and has a plaid pattern.

B: A skirt of knee length with a plaid pattern?

G: Yes. It is unique because it is a skirt for men.

B: That sounds interesting. I want to try one on.

2. G: Brian, let's talk about what we will prepare for the World Food Festival.

B: I will make a meat pie. It is famous in Australia. How about you, Sera?

G: I want to make a popular English dish, fish and chips.

B: Fish and chips? What does it look like?

G: It's fried fish with hot potato chips.

B: That sounds interesting. Let's prepare them.

Listen & Speak 2 A

1. B: Wow, we finally arrived in Hong Kong, Mom.

W: I'm looking forward to our visit. What should we do today, Mike?

B: I suggest we visit Victoria Peak.

W: Victoria Peak?

B: It is the highest mountain in Hong Kong and is in a lot of movies. We can enjoy the fantastic view.

W: That sounds good. Let's go.

2. G: My American friend invited me to a potluck dinner next Friday.

B: You know, you should take food to share at the dinner.

G: What would you recommend that I take?

B: I suggest you take some Korean food. How about Gimbap, Suji?

G: Yes. It's not spicy and it's easy to carry.

B: I think it'll be good for dinner.

Real Life Talk

Seho: Good morning.

Jessie, Andy: Hi, Seho.

Seho: I will visit my uncle in Philadelphia this winter. Can you tell me about the city?

Jessie: Sure. I was there a few years ago. First, let's talk about food.

Seho: Okay. What food is Philadelphia famous for?

Jessie: The most famous food in Philadelphia is the cheese steak sandwich. It is a big sandwich filled with beef and melted cheese.

Seho: Good suggestion. I will try it. Are there any places that are popular with tourists?

Andy: I suggest you visit Independence Hall. It is bery important in American histoy.

Seho: Wonderful. Thank you for the information.

Andy: My pleasure.

Wrap Up

M: Welcome to Australia. The capital of Australia is Canberra. People speak English. Meat pie is a popular dish in Australia. Every year, lots of tourists visit the Sydney Opera House and the beautiful beaches in Melbourne.

본문 TEST Step 1   p.28~29

01 place, natural beauty, waterfalls
02 has two main islands
03 covered with, all, round
04 be amazed by, views
05 hot springs, areas with
06 Because of, been made
07 will surely appreciate, nature
08 hear, comes to, mind
09 Maybe, but, couple, meanings
10 name, delicious, fruit
11 grown, so, known as
12 also, one, native birds
13 special, because, symbol, nation
14 Also, nickname for, from
15 are sometimes called, throughout
16 that, name, fruit, also
17 confused, uses, which, meanings
18 let's talk, native people
19 on, long before, arrived
20 important part, today's, society
21 is taught, there are
22 villages, many parts, country
23 visit, villages, experience, culture
24 say, glad, hear, means
25 Have, ever watched
26 scary, shout, move, wildly
27 who, heard, doing, as
28 however, matches, other, events
29 example, national, before, match
30 famous all over
31 agree that, must, scared
32 Like, national symbol

본문 TEST Step 2   p.30~31

01 a place of natural beauty, lakes, waterfalls
02 two main islands
03 are mountains, are covered with, all year round
04 be amazed by, fantastic views
05 many hot springs, with

06 Because of, natural beauty, have been made
07 will surely appreciate
08 hear, comes to your mind
09 a couple of meanings
10 the name, delicious
11 is grown, so, is known as
12 one, New Zealand's native birds
13 special to, because, symbol
14 a nickname for, from
15 are sometimes called, throughout the world
16 that, the name of
17 confused, uses, which has several meanings
18 let's talk, They, the native people
19 live on, long before Europeans arrived
20 an important part, today's, society
21 is taught, there are
22 There are, in many parts of
23 visit, villages, experience, culture
24 say, to, will be glad to hear, means
25 Have, ever watched
26 look scary because, shout, move, wildly
27 who, heard about, doing, as
28 however, do, at sport matches, other important events
29 For example, national rugby team members, before every match
30 famous all over
31 will, agree that, must be scared
32 Like, a national symbol

본문 TEST Step 3   p.32~33

1 뉴질랜드는 자연의 아름다움이 가득한 곳이다. 뉴질랜드는 아름다운 호수와 폭포들이 많다.
2 뉴질랜드에는 남섬과 북섬, 두 개의 본섬이 있다.
3 남섬에는 일 년 내내 눈으로 덮인 산들이 있다.
4 당신은 굉장히 멋진 경관에 놀랄 것이다.
5 북섬에는 많은 온천과 호수, 초원 지역이 있다.
6 뉴질랜드 자연의 아름다움 때문에 많은 유명한 영화들이 뉴질랜드에서 촬영되었다.
7 뉴질랜드를 방문하면, 분명히 그 자연의 진가를 인정할 것이다.
8 키위라는 단어를 들을 때, 무엇이 떠오르는가?
9 아마도 과일이 떠오르겠지만, 뉴질랜드에서 키위는 몇 가지 뜻이 있다.
10 먼저, 키위는 맛있는 초록색 과일의 이름이다.
11 많은 키위가 그곳에서 자라기 때문에 뉴질랜드는 키위의 나라로 알려져 있다.

12 키위는 뉴질랜드 토종 새의 이름이기도 하다.

13 키위 새는 국가의 상징이기 때문에, 뉴질랜드 사람들에게 특별하다.

14 또한, 키위는 뉴질랜드 출신의 사람들을 부르는 별명이기도 하다.

15 오늘날 뉴질랜드인들은 전 세계적으로 키위라고 불리기도 한다.

16 이제, 당신은 키위가 과일과 새, 그리고 국민의 명칭이라는 것을 알았다.

17 다음에는 누군가가 키위라는 단어를 사용할 때 혼동하지 마라. 그 단어는 여러 뜻을 가지고 있기 때문이다.

18 이제, 마오리족에 대해 이야기해 보자. 마오리족은 뉴질랜드의 원주민이다.

19 그들은 유럽인들이 도착하기 오래 전에 이 섬에 와서 살았다.

20 마오리족의 문화는 오늘날 뉴질랜드 사회의 중요한 부분이다.

21 몇몇 학교에서 마오리어를 가르치고 있으며, 마오리어의 라디오와 TV 방송국이 있다.

22 나라의 여러 곳에 마오리 마을이 있다.

23 당신은 마오리 마을을 방문해 마오리 문화를 경험할 수 있다.

24 당신이 마을 사람들에게 "kia ora"라고 말한다면 그들은 그것을 듣고 좋아할 것이다. 그것은 영어로 "안녕"이라는 뜻이다.

25 하카를 본 적이 있는가?

26 하카 춤을 추는 사람들이 소리 지르고, 그들의 몸을 사납게 움직이기 때문에 하카는 무서워 보일 수도 있다.

27 당신이 이미 그들에 대해 들은 적이 있겠지만, 마오리인들은 전쟁 춤으로 하카를 추기 시작했다.

28 하지만, 오늘날 뉴질랜드 사람들은 하카를 운동 경기, 결혼식 또는 다른 중요한 행사가 있을 때 한다.

29 예를 들어, 뉴질랜드의 럭비 국가 대표 팀 선수들은 모든 경기 전에 하카를 춘다.

30 그것은 전 세계적으로 유명하다.

31 당신이 하카를 본다면, 상대 팀이 틀림없이 겁을 먹을 것이라는 것에 아마 동의할 것이다.

32 키위와 마찬가지로 하카는 나라의 상징이다.

본문 TEST Step 4 - Step 5   p.34~37

1 New Zealand is a place of natural beauty. It has many beautiful lakes and waterfalls.

2 New Zealand has two main islands, the South Island and the North Island.

3 In the South Island, there are mountains that are covered with snow all year round.

4 You will be amazed by the fantastic views.

5 In the North Island, there are many hot springs, lakes, and areas with green grass.

6 Because of its natural beauty, many famous movies have been made in New Zealand.

7 If you visit New Zealand, you will surely appreciate its nature.

8 When you hear the word kiwi, what comes to your mind?

9 Maybe a fruit, but, in New Zealand the word kiwi has a couple of meanings.

10 First, kiwi is the name of a delicious, green fruit.

11 A lot of kiwi fruit is grown there, so New Zealand is known as the land of kiwi fruit.

12 Kiwi is also the name of one of New Zealand's native birds.

13 The kiwi is special to New Zealanders because it is the symbol of the nation.

14 Also, kiwi is a nickname for people from New Zealand.

15 Today, New Zealanders are sometimes called Kiwis throughout the world.

16 Now, you know that kiwi is the name of a fruit, a bird, and also a people.

17 Next time, don't become confused when someone uses the word kiwi, which has several meanings.

18 Now, let's talk about the Maori. They are the native people of New Zealand.

19 They went to live on the islands long before Europeans arrived.

20 The Maori culture is an important part of today's New Zealand society.

21 The Maori language is taught at some schools and there are Maori language radio and TV stations.

22 There are Maori villages in many parts of the country.

23 You can visit Maori villages and experience Maori culture.

24 If you say "kia ora" to the villagers, they will be glad to hear it. It means "hi" in English.

25 Have you ever watched the haka?

26 The haka may look scary because haka dancers shout and move their bodies wildly.

27 The Maori people, who you've already heard about, started doing the haka as a war dance.

28 Today, however, New Zealanders do the haka at sport matches, weddings, or other important events.

29 For example, New Zealand's national rugby team

members do the haka before every match.

30 It is famous all over the world.

31 If you see the haka, you will probably agree that the rival team must be scared.

32 Like the kiwi bird, the haka is a national symbol.

Before You Read

1. a popular sport

2. in the southern part of

3. the native people, have their culture

Enjoy Writing

1. Invite

2. Do, know about

3. two main islands, smaller islands

4. Its capital

5. which, a bird native, one of the symbols

6. If, come to, should visit, Maori village, which, the native culture

7. suggest, try, traditional dish

8. cook meat, vegetables, with heated rocks

9. to enjoy the beautiful nature

10. happy to invite, beautiful country

Project Step 1

1. Let's talk, are going to look into

2. Which country, prefer, or

3. suggest, search for, on

4. a lot of, to work with

5. Okay

Before You Read

1. Rugby is a popular sport in New Zealand.

2. New Zealand is in the southern part of the world.

3. The Maori people are the native people of New Zealand and have their culture.

Enjoy Writing

1. We Invite You

2. Do you know about New Zealand?

3. It has two main islands and 600 smaller islands.

4. Its capital is Wellington.

5. The kiwi, which is a bird native to New Zealand, is one of the symbols of the country.

6. If you come to New Zealand, you should visit a Maori village, which shows the native culture of

New Zealand.

7. We suggest you try a traditional dish of the Maori people.

8. They cook meat and vegetables in the ground with heated rocks. It is great.

9. Many people visit New Zealand to enjoy the beautiful nature.

10. We are happy to invite you to this beautiful country.

Project Step 1

1. A: Let's talk about which country we are going to look into.

2. B: Which country do you prefer, Australia or the UK?

3. C: I suggest we search for information on the UK.

4. There is a lot of information to work with.

5. D: Okay.

단어 TEST Step 1 p.40

01 진심으로　　02 우연히, 뜻하지 않게
03 관계　　04 삭제하다　　05 감정적인
06 ~을 준비하다　　07 특히, 유난히　　08 책임
09 적절한, 제대로 된　　10 너그러운
11 재미있는, 유머러스한　　12 포함하다
13 (관계를) 끝내다, 끊다　　14 사례, 경우
15 심각한, 진지한　　16 대충하는, 건성의　　17 의견, 제안
18 사려 깊은, 생각에 잠긴　　19 필요한
20 꺼리다, 싫어하다　　21 후회하다　　22 사과
23 느긋한, 여유 있는　　24 진정한, 진심 어린　　25 상처, 부상
26 사과하다　　27 용감한　　28 무시하다
29 고마워하다, 감사하다　　30 빌리다
31 긴장하는, 초조해 하는
32 소리가 큰, 시끄러운　　33 의도하다
34 식판, 쟁반　　35 ~에 걸려 넘어지다
36 ~에 마음을 쓰다, ~에 관심을 가지다　　37 ~에 부딪히다
38 즉시　　39 진심으로　　40 (소리를) 줄이다
41 ~을 웃어넘기려 하다　　42 ~에 책임을 지다
43 ~를 아무렇지 않게 여기다

단어 TEST Step 2 p.41

01 delete　　02 suggestion　　03 thoughtful
04 accidentally　　05 mind　　06 appreciate
07 casual　　08 especially　　09 generous
10 case　　11 responsibility　　12 prepare
13 break　　14 intend　　15 serious
16 sincere　　17 proper　　18 regret
19 ignore　　20 include　　21 relaxed
22 apologize　　23 emotional　　24 humorous
25 brave　　26 mistake　　27 apology
28 relationship　　29 sincerely　　30 wound
31 loud　　32 treat　　33 borrow
34 necessary　　35 bump into　　36 laugh off
37 pass by　　38 trip over　　39 turn down
40 take responsibility for　　41 pick out
42 with all one's heart　　43 get along with

단어 TEST Step 3 p.42

1 appreciate, 감사하다　　2 mistake, 실수
3 ignore, 무시하다　　4 relationship, 관계
5 responsibility, 책임　　6 accidentally, 우연히
7 brave, 용감한　　8 casual, 대충하는, 건성의
9 delete, 삭제하다　　10 apology, 사과
11 sincere, 진정한, 진심어린　　12 suggestion, 제안
13 thoughtful, 사려 깊은　　14 prepare, 준비하다
15 regret, 후회하다　　16 generous, 관대한, 너그러운

대화문 TEST Step 1 p.43~45

Listen & Speak 1 A-1
mind turning down / No, I don't, loud / hear / turn it down / Thanks, lot

Listen & Speak 1 A-2
accidentally broke, favorite plate / That's too bad / Do you mind telling, how to say sorry to / not at all, apologize sincerely / with all my heart

Listen & Speak 1 A-3
mind coming / early / that, borrowed before class / let's / then

Listen & Speak 1 B
mind being quiet / but, can't / mind picking up trash / can't

Listen & Speak 2 A-1
seem to be busy / preparing for, contest / contest last year / great / are good at getting, rhythm / need to, relaxed, nervous / advice, helpful, appreciate, advice / pleasure

Listen & Speak 2 A-2
lost / Let me help, What, like / is written / yours, under / appreciate, help / No problem

Listen & Speak 2 B
Let, show / appreciate / Let me carry, backpack / appreciate your help

Real Life Talk
What's up / present, (You')ve, been, for, haven't / since, elementary / busy studying, do you mind helping, help me pick out something nice / problem, present for / was broken, carried / of her / how about, broke, recently / Thank you, suggestion

Wrap Up 1
am planning to go / cool, used to live / Do you mind telling, what to do / Not at all, beaches, should visit / swimming, else / don't you, everywhere / How about / raw fish, fresh, delicious / appreciate, tips

Wrap Up 2
well, might have caught, needs to, in an hour, to meet, instead, should, say

Listen & Speak 1 A-1

B: Judy, do you mind turning down the volume?

G: No, I don't. Is it too loud?

B: Yes, it is. I can hear it in my room.

G: I'm sorry. I'll turn it down.

B: Thanks a lot.

Listen & Speak 1 A-2

G: I accidentally broke my mom's favorite plate.

B: That's too bad, Mina.

G: Do you mind telling me how to say sorry to her?

B: No, not at all. You should apologize sincerely.

G: I see. I'll talk to her with all my heart.

Listen & Speak 1 A-3

B: Karen, do you mind coming to my house tomorrow at 7 a.m.?

G: That's very early.

B: I know, but I need the book that you borrowed before class.

G: I see. Then let's meet at seven.

B: See you then.

Listen & Speak 1 B

A: Hellen, do you mind being quiet?

B: No, I don't. / Sorry but I can't.

A: Hellen, do you mind picking up trash?

B: No, I don't. / Sorry but I can't.

Listen & Speak 2 A-1

G: You seem to be busy, Minsu. Can I come in?

B: Sure. I'm preparing for the dance contest, but it's not easy.

G: I can help you. I was in the contest last year.

B: Really? That would be great, Amy.

G: You are good at getting into the rhythm. But one thing you need to do is to be more relaxed. You are too nervous.

B: Your advice is very helpful. I really appreciate your advice.

G: It's my pleasure.

Listen & Speak 2 A-2

B: Irene, what are you doing?

G: Well, I've lost my favorite cap. I can't find it.

B: Let me help you. What does it look like?

G: It's red. My name is written in black on the side.

B: Oh, is this yours? It was under the table.

G: Yes, it is. Thank you, Jim. I appreciate your help.

B: No problem.

Listen & Speak 2 B

A: Let me show you the way.

B: I appreciate your time.

A: Let me carry your backpack.

B: I appreciate your help.

Real Life Talk

Jessie: Hi, Andy. What's up?

Andy: Hi, Jessie. I'm going to buy a present for Amy. You've been friends with her for a long time, haven't you?

Jessie: Yes, since first grade in elementary school.

Andy: Well, I know you're really busy studying, but do you mind helping me? I am sure you could help me pick out something nice.

Jessie: No problem. What's the present for? It's not her birthday.

Andy: Well, two months ago, when my leg was broken, she carried my backpack to school.

Jessie: That was nice of her.

Andy: Yes, it was. What should I get for her?

Jessie: Well, how about a case for her smartphone? She broke her case recently.

Andy: Really? Thank you for your suggestion.

Wrap Up 1

G: I am planning to go to Jejudo.

B: That's cool, Suhee. I used to live there.

G: Do you mind telling me what to do in Jejudo?

B: Not at all. Jejudo has many beautiful beaches. You should visit them.

G: Good. I will go swimming. What else can I do?

B: Why don't you hike Halla Mountain? You can see the mountain from everywhere on the island.

G: Great.

B: If you like fish, on Jejudo raw fish is fresh and delicious.

G: I'll try everything. I appreciate your tips.

Wrap Up 2

W: Mike does not feel very well. He might have caught a cold. He needs to see a doctor, but he has a meeting with Jane in an hour. He wants to meet her tomorrow instead. What should he say to her?

01 Because, human, mistakes, along

02 without intending, wrong, regret

03 that happens, should apologize

04 following case, proper apology

05 tripped over, laughed, uploaded
06 became angry, with, deleted
07 even, hurt because, casual
08 acted, seemed, nothing serious
09 case, guessed, sincere, apologize
10 Apologizing, build, Saying, words
11 respect, care about, feelings
12 make things right, sincere
13 more, apology, better, received
14 another, accidentally bumped into
15 tray fell, apologize, bad
16 doesn't, say, if, right
17 that, necessary, apologize, once
18 shows, thoughtful, responsibility, action
19 think nothing, laugh, off
20 Finally, among, loved, too
21 borrowed, favorite, Later, lost
22 apologize, thought, important, after
23 disliked how, treated, ignore
24 hadn't apologized, little sister
25 apologize, something wrong, close
26 get hurt, easily, comes
27 let, go because, close
28 mistakes, add up, emotional
29 especially, among, loved ones
30 heard, saying, more, chances
31 mistakes, let, break, relationship
32 apologize, Try, sincere, solve

14 another, hurrying across, accidentally bumped into
15 on, fell on, apologize, felt bad
16 Why doesn't, say, if, apologized right now
17 that, is necessary, apologize at once
18 shows that, thoughtful, take responsibility for
19 All, to do, think nothing, laugh it off
20 are, among, members, loved ones
21 borrowed, favorite, Later, lost
22 apologize, not important, after all
23 had treated, ignore
24 hadn't apologized to, little sister
25 to apologize, something wrong, includes, who are close
26 get hurt more easily, comes from
27 let it go, are close
28 small mistakes, no apology add up to, emotional wounds
29 among, loved ones
30 heard of, No more, no more chances
31 make, let, break, beautiful relationship
32 apologize to, Try to do, quick, sincere, can solve

01 Because, It is, to get along with, all the time
02 hurt, without intending to, something wrong, regret
03 that, should apologize
04 following case, a proper apology
05 tripped over, it funny, laughed, took, uploaded, on
06 saw, became angry, with, laugh, deleted it
07 even, because of, casual apology
08 how Mike had acted, seemed to think, nothing serious
09 should be sincere, apologize
10 Apologizing, to, friendships, Saying, more than
11 that, respect, other, care about, feelings
12 make things right, sincere
13 The more sincere, the better, received

1 우리는 인간이기 때문에 모두가 실수한다. 모든 사람과 항상 잘 지내기는 쉽지 않다.
2 때때로 우리는 의도하지 않게 다른 사람의 감정을 상하게 한다. 때때로 우리는 나쁜 일을 하고 나중에 그것을 후회한다.
3 이런 일이 생기면, 우리는 무엇을 해야 할까? 우리는 사과해야 한다.
4 다음 사례 연구들을 읽고 올바른 사과를 위한 세 가지를 알아보자.
5 June이 가방에 걸려 넘어졌을 때, Mike는 그것이 재미있다고 생각하고 웃었다. 그는 사진을 찍어서 SNS에 올렸다.
6 June은 그 사진을 보고 화가 났다. Mike는 웃으면서 "미안해, June!"이라고 말하고 사진을 삭제했다.
7 그 후, June은 Mike의 가벼운 사과에 한층 더 화가 났다.
8 June은 Mike의 행동 방식이 마음에 들지 않았다. Mike는 이 일이 심각한 일이 아니라고 생각하는 것처럼 보였다.
9 이 사례로부터 무엇을 배웠는가? 맞다. 당신은 바르게 추측했다. 당신은 사과할 때에 진실해야 한다.
10 사과하는 것은 좋은 교우 관계를 만들기 위해 필요하다. 미안하다고 말하는 것은 단지 말 이상이다.
11 당신이 타인을 존중하고, 타인의 감정에 관심을 갖고 있음을 보여 주어야 한다.
12 당신이 진실로 일을 바로잡기를 원한다면, 당신의 사과는

13 당신의 사과가 진실할수록, 그것은 더 잘 받아들여질 것이다.

14 또 다른 사례가 있다. Kate가 급식실을 가로질러 급하게 뛰어갈 때, 호준이와 실수로 부딪쳤다.

15 호준이의 급식판에 있던 음식이 그의 재킷에 떨어졌다. Kate는 사과하지 않았다. 호준이는 기분이 나빴다.

16 그는 '왜 그녀는 아무 말도 하지 않지? 그녀가 즉시 사과한다면 아무 일도 아닐 텐데.'라고 생각했다.

17 이 사례는 사과가 필요할 때는 사과를 즉시 해야 한다는 것을 보여준다.

18 신속한 사과는 당신이 사려 깊고, 당신의 행동에 책임을 진다는 것을 보여준다.

19 당신이 해야 할 행동은 "미안해."라고 말하는 것뿐이다. 그러면 상처받은 친구는 당신의 잘못을 아무렇지 않게 생각하고, 웃어넘길 것이다.

20 마지막으로 사과는 가족이나 사랑하는 사람들 사이에서도 필요하다.

21 어느 날, 선민이는 여동생이 가장 좋아하는 책을 빌렸다. 나중에 그녀는 그것을 잃어버렸다.

22 선민이는 그것이 중요하지 않다고 생각하여 사과하지 않았다. 그녀는 '우리는 어쨌든 자매니까.'라고 생각했다.

23 선민이의 여동생은 언니가 본인을 대했던 방식이 마음에 들지 않았다. 어떻게 자신의 언니가 그녀의 기분을 무시할 수 있는가?

24 선민이가 여동생에게 사과하지 않았던 것은 이번이 처음이 아니었다.

25 사람들은 잘못을 때, 사과해야 한다. 이것은 가족이나 당신에게 가까운 사람도 포함한다.

26 사람들은 마음의 상처가 가족이나 친구에게서 올 때 더 쉽게 상처 받는다.

27 우리는 아마 그들이 가깝기 때문에 그냥 넘어갈 것이라고 생각할지 모른다.

28 하지만 작은 실수를 하고 사과하지 않는 것은 큰 감정적인 상처가 된다는 것을 기억하라.

29 이것은 가족과 사랑하는 사람들에게 특히 더 그러하다.

30 당신은 "더 이상 사과하지 않는다면 더 이상 기회가 없다."는 말을 들어본 적이 있는가?

31 사람들은 실수하지만, 그 실수가 아름다운 관계를 깨뜨리게 해서는 안 된다.

32 누군가에게 사과하고 싶은가? 지금 하려고 노력해라. 빠르고 진정한 "미안해."라는 말이 많은 문제를 해결해 줄 것이다.

1 Because we are human, we all make mistakes. It is not easy to get along with everyone all the time.

2 Sometimes we hurt people's feelings without intending to. Sometimes, we do something wrong and regret it later.

3 When that happens, what should we do? We should apologize.

4 Read the following case studies and learn three things about a proper apology.

5 When June tripped over a backpack and fell, Mike found it funny and laughed. He took a picture and uploaded it on an SNS.

6 June saw the picture and became angry. Mike said, with a laugh, "Sorry, June!" and deleted it.

7 After that, June felt even more hurt because of Mike's casual apology.

8 June didn't like how Mike had acted. Mike seemed to think it was nothing serious.

9 What did you learn from this case? Yes. You guessed right. You should be sincere when you apologize.

10 Apologizing is necessary to build good friendships. Saying you're sorry is more than just words.

11 You need to show that you respect the other person and care about his or her feelings.

12 If you truly want to make things right, be sincere in your apology.

13 The more sincere your apology is, the better it will be received.

14 Here is another case. While Kate was hurrying across the cafeteria, she accidentally bumped into Hojun.

15 Some food on Hojun's tray fell on his jacket. Kate didn't apologize. Hojun felt bad.

16 He thought, 'Why doesn't she say something? It would be nothing if she apologized right now.'

17 This case shows that when an apology is necessary, you should apologize at once.

18 A quick apology shows that you are thoughtful and take responsibility for your action.

19 All you need to do is to say, "I'm sorry." Then, the hurt friend will think nothing of it and laugh it off.

20 Finally, apologies are necessary among family members and loved ones, too.

21 One day, Sunmin borrowed her sister's favorite book. Later, she lost it.

22 Sunmin didn't apologize because she thought it was not important. She thought, 'We're sisters, after all.'

23 Sunmin's sister disliked how Sunmin had treated her. How could her own sister ignore her feelings?

24 This was not the first time Sunmin hadn't apologized to her little sister.

25 People need to apologize when they do something wrong. This includes family members and the people who are close to you.

26 People get hurt more easily when the hurt comes from a family member or a friend.

27 We may think that they will let it go because they are close to us.

28 Remember, however, that small mistakes and no apology add up to big emotional wounds.

29 This is especially true among family members and loved ones.

30 Have you ever heard of the saying, "No more apologies, no more chances"?

31 People make mistakes, but don't let one mistake break a beautiful relationship.

32 Do you want to apologize to someone? Try to do it now. A quick and sincere "I'm sorry" can solve many problems..

3. that we are sorry for

4. Do not make excuses

5. for the tips, really appreciate

구석구석지문 TEST Step 2 — p.60

After You Read C

1. Inho went to a a store buy shoes.

2. He was hit by a woman's bag accidentally as she passed by.

3. The woman said, "Sorry," and she walked away quickly.

4. Inho was angry because the woman did not make a sincere and proper apology.

5. He thought that the woman should care about his feelings.

Enjoy Writing C

1. My Wonderful Friend, Jinsu

2. I'd like to introduce my friend, Jinsu.

3. I have known him since elementary school.

4. He is always humorous, brave, and cheerful.

5. This is how he helped me.

6. Last Friday I was sick and missed a math class.

7. Jinsu showed me his class notes.

8. I am lucky to have him as my friend.

9. The more I know him, the deeper our friendship becomes.

Project Step 1

1. A: Do you know how we write a note of apology?

2. B: Yes. First, write about what we did.

3. C: Then write that we are sorry for it.

4. D: Do not make excuses for our actions.

5. A: Thank you for the tips. I really appreciate it.

구석구석지문 TEST Step 1 — p.59

After You Read C

1. a store buy shoes

2. was hit by, as she passed by

3. walked away quickly

4. because, sincere, proper apology

5. that, care about his feelings

Enjoy Writing C

1. Wonderful Friend

2. like to introduce

3. have known, since

4. humorous, brave, cheerful

5. how he helped

6. sick, missed a math class

7. showed me his class notes

8. lucky to have, as

9. The more, the deeper

Project Step 1

1. how we write a note of apology

2. what we did

MEMO

MEMO

MEMO